Communications
in Computer and Information Science 1023

Commenced Publication in 2007
Founding and Former Series Editors:
Phoebe Chen, Alfredo Cuzzocrea, Xiaoyong Du, Orhun Kara, Ting Liu,
Krishna M. Sivalingam, Dominik Ślęzak, Takashi Washio, and Xiaokang Yang

More information about this series at http://www.springer.com/series/7899

Ernesto Damiani · George Spanoudakis ·
Leszek A. Maciaszek (Eds.)

Evaluation of Novel Approaches to Software Engineering

13th International Conference, ENASE 2018
Funchal, Madeira, Portugal, March 23–24, 2018
Revised Selected Papers

 Springer

Editors
Ernesto Damiani
Khalifa University
Abu Dhabi, United Arab Emirates

George Spanoudakis
City University London
London, UK

Leszek A. Maciaszek
Wrocław University of Economics
Wrocław, Poland

Macquarie University
Sydney, Australia

ISSN 1865-0929   ISSN 1865-0937 (electronic)
Communications in Computer and Information Science
ISBN 978-3-030-22558-2   ISBN 978-3-030-22559-9 (eBook)
https://doi.org/10.1007/978-3-030-22559-9

This Springer imprint is published by the registered company Springer Nature Switzerland AG
The registered company address is: Gewerbestrasse 11, 6330 Cham, Switzerland

Preface

The present book includes extended and revised versions of a set of selected papers from the 13th International Conference on Evaluation of Novel Approaches to Software Engineering (ENASE 2018), held in Funchal-Madeira, Portugal, during March 23–24, 2018.

ENASE 2018 received 95 paper submissions from 26 countries, of which 18% are included in this book. The papers were selected by the event chairs and their selection is based on a number of criteria that include the classifications and comments provided by the Program Committee members, the session chairs' assessment, and also the program chairs' global view of all papers included in the technical program. The authors of selected papers were then invited to submit a revised and extended version of their papers having at least 30% innovative material.

The mission of ENASE (Evaluation of Novel Approaches to Software Engineering) is to be a prime international forum to discuss and publish research findings and IT industry experiences with relation to novel approaches to software engineering. The conference acknowledges the evolution in systems and software thinking due to contemporary shifts of computing paradigm to e-services, cloud computing, mobile connectivity, business processes, and societal participation. By publishing the latest research on novel approaches to software engineering and by evaluating them against systems and software quality criteria, ENASE conferences advance knowledge and research in software engineering, including and emphasizing service-oriented, business-process driven, and ubiquitous mobile computing. ENASE aims at identifying the most hopeful trends and proposing new directions for consideration by researchers and practitioners involved in large-scale systems and software development, integration, deployment, delivery, maintenance and evolution.

The papers included in this book contribute to the understanding of relevant trends of current research on novel approaches to software engineering for the development and maintenance of systems and applications, specifically with relation to: requirements engineering (p.22, p.112, p.226), model-driven engineering (p.67, p.91, p.202, p.271), software patterns and refactoring (p.130, p.176, p.314), reverse software engineering (p.130, p.202), software architecture (p.42, p.156, p.295), formal methods (p.130, p.246, p.330), service-oriented and cloud computing (p.3, p.42), software change and adaptation (p.271, p.295, p.351), and information systems development (p.22, p.112, p.226).

We would like to thank all the authors for their contributions and the reviewers for ensuring the quality of this publication.

March 2018

Ernesto Damiani
George Spanoudakis
Leszek A. Maciaszek

Organization

Conference Chair

Leszek Maciaszek   Wrocław University of Economics, Poland
and Macquarie University, Australia

Program Co-chairs

Ernesto Damiani   EBTIC-KUSTAR, UAE
George Spanoudakis   City University London, UK

Program Committee

Marco Aiello	University of Stuttgart, Germany
Mehmet Aksit	University of Twente, The Netherlands
Claudio Ardagna	Università degli Studi di Milano, Italy
Mourad Badri	University of Quebec at Trois-Rivières, Canada
Richard Banach	University of Manchester, UK
Jan Blech	RMIT University, Australia
Kelly Blincoe	University of Auckland, New Zealand
Danilo Caivano	University of Bari, Italy
Jessie Carbonnel	LIRMM, CNRS and University of Montpellier, France
Glauco Carneiro	Universidade Salvador (UNIFACS), Brazil
Tomas Cerny	Baylor University, USA
Rem Collier	University College Dublin, Ireland
Rebeca Cortazar	University of Deusto, Spain
Bernard Coulette	Université Toulouse Jean Jaurès, France
Mads Dam	KTH, Royal Institute of Technology, Sweden
Guglielmo De Angelis	CNR, IASI, Italy
Mariangiola Dezani	Università di Torino, Italy
Fatma Dhaou	Faculty of Sciences of Tunis, Tunisia
Mahmoud EL Hamlaoui	IMS-ADMIR Team, ENSIAS, Rabat IT Center, University of Mohammed V in Rabat, Morocco
Angelina Espinoza	Universidad Autónoma Metropolitana, Iztapalapa (UAM-I), Spain
Vladimir Estivill-Castro	Griffith University, Australia
Anna Fasolino	Università degli Studi di Napoli Federico II, Italy
João Ferreira	University of São Paulo, Brazil
Maria Ferreira	Universidade Portucalense, Portugal
Stéphane Galland	Université de Technologie de Belfort Montbéliard, France
Frédéric Gervais	Université Paris-Est, LACL, France

Claude Godart	Henri Poincare University, Nancy 1, France
John Grundy	Deakin University, Australia
José-María Gutiérrez-Martínez	Universidad de Alcalá, Spain
Hatim Hafiddi	INPT, Morocco
Peter Herrmann	NTNU, Norway
Rene Hexel	Griffith University, Australia
Lom Hillah	Laboratoire d'Informatique de Paris 6 (CNRS, Sorbonne Université), France
Ow Hock	University of Malaya, Malaysia
Mirjana Ivanovic	University of Novi Sad, Serbia
Stefan Jablonski	University of Bayreuth, Germany
Stanislaw Jarzabek	Białystok University of Technology, Poland
Georgia Kapitsaki	University of Cyprus, Cyprus
Osama Khaled	The American University in Cairo, Egypt
Siau-cheng Khoo	National University of Singapore, Singapore
Diana Kirk	EDENZ Colleges, New Zealand
Piotr Kosiuczenko	WAT, Poland
Rosa Lanzilotti	University of Bari, Italy
Bixin Li	Southeast University, China
Jorge López	SAMOVAR, CNRS, Télécom SudParis, Université Paris-Saclay, France
Ivan Lukovic	University of Novi Sad, Serbia
Lech Madeyski	Wroclaw University of Science and Technology, Poland
Nazim Madhavji	University of Western Ontario, Canada
Johnny Marques	Instituto Tecnológico de Aeronáutica, Brazil
Arthur-Jozsef Molnar	University of Babes-Bolyai, Romania
Sascha Mueller-Feuerstein	Ansbach University of Applied Sciences, Germany
Malcolm Munro	Durham University, UK
Andrzej Niesler	Wroclaw University of Economics, Poland
Janis Osis	Riga Technical University, Latvia
Naveen Prakash	IIITD, India
Adam Przybylek	Gdansk University of Technology, Poland
Elke Pulvermueller	University of Osnabrück, Germany
Lukasz Radlinski	West Pomeranian University of Technology, Poland
José Redondo López	University of Oviedo, Spain
Philippe Roose	LIUPPA/IUT de Bayonne/UPPA, France
Stefano Russo	Università di Napoli Federico II, Italy
Krzysztof Sacha	Warsaw University of Technology, Poland
Antonella Santone	University of Molise, Italy
Markus Schatten	University of Zagreb, Croatia
Stefan Schönig	University of Bayreuth, Germany
Richa Sharma	BML Munjal University, India
Keng Siau	Missouri University of Science and Technology, USA
Josep Silva	Universitat Politècnica de València, Spain

Michal Smialek	Warsaw University of Technology, Poland
Ouali Sonya	University of Sfax-Tunisia, Tunisia
Ioana Sora	Politehnica University of Timisoara, Romania
Andreas Speck	Christian Albrechts University Kiel, Germany
Maria Spichkova	RMIT University, Australia
Miroslaw Staron	University of Gothenburg, Sweden
Chang-ai Sun	University of Science and Technology Beijing, China
Jakub Swacha	University of Szczecin, Poland
Stephanie Teufel	University of Fribourg, Switzerland
Olegas Vasilecas	Vilnius Gediminas Technical University, Lithuania
Bernhard Westfechtel	University of Bayreuth, Germany
Martin Wirsing	Ludwig-Maximilians-Universität München, Germany
Igor Wojnicki	AGH University of Science and Technology, Poland
Alfred Zimmermann	Reutlingen University, Germany

Additional Reviewers

Önder Babur	Eindhoven University of Technology, The Netherlands
Milan Celikovic	University of Novi Sad, Serbia
Marta Cimitile	Unitelma Sapienza, Italy
Zineb El Akkaoui	The National Institute of Posts and Telecommunications, Morocco
Tarik Fissaa	ENSIAS Mohammed V University rabat, Morocco
Dusan Gajic	University of Novi Sad, Serbia
Roberto Pietrantuono	Università degli Studi di Napoli Federico II, Italy
Vincenzo Riccio	Università degli Studi di Napoli Federico II, Italy
Brian Setz	University of Groningen, The Netherlands

Invited Speakers

Bashar Nuseibeh	The Open University, UK
Plamen Angelov	Lancaster University, UK
Salvatore Distefano	Università degli Studi di Messina, Italy

Contents

Service Science and Business Information Systems

Lessons Learned from an Action Research Study on the Use of Cloud
Computing in Undergraduate Computer Science Courses . . . .　3
    Heleno Cardoso da Silva Filho and Glauco de Figueiredo Carneiro

Involvement of Business Roles in Auditing with Process Mining . . . .　24
    Ella Roubtsova and Niels Wiersma

Architecting Service-Dominant Digital Products . . . .　45
    Alfred Zimmermann, Rainer Schmidt, Kurt Sandkuhl, Dierk Jugel,
    Justus Bogner, and Michael Möhring

Software Engineering

Risk-Based Elicitation of Security Requirements According
to the ISO 27005 Standard. . . . .　71
    Roman Wirtz, Maritta Heisel, Angela Borchert, Rene Meis,
    Aida Omerovic, and Ketil Stølen

Incremental Bidirectional Transformations: Comparing Declarative
and Procedural Approaches Using the Families to Persons Benchmark. . . . . .　98
    Bernhard Westfechtel and Thomas Buchmann

Adopting Collaborative Games into Agile Software Development . . . .　119
    Mateusz Zakrzewski, Dagmara Kotecka, Yen Ying Ng,
    and Adam Przybyłek

Detecting Behavioral Design Patterns from Software Execution Data. . . . . . .　137
    Cong Liu, Boudewijn F. van Dongen, Nour Assy,
    and Wil M. P. van der Aalst

Portable Synthesis of Multi-core Real-Time Systems
with Reconfiguration Constraints. . . . .　165
    Wafa Lakhdhar, Rania Mzid, Mohamed Khalgui, and Georg Frey

From Object-Oriented to Workflow: Refactoring of OO Applications
into Workflows for an Efficient Resources Management in the Cloud . . . . . .　186
    Anfel Selmadji, Abdelhak-Djamel Seriai, Hinde Lilia Bouziane,
    and Christophe Dony

Crowdsourced Reverse Engineering: Experiences in Applying
Crowdsourcing to Concept Assignment 215
   Sebastian Heil, Valentin Siegert, and Martin Gaedke

A Detailed Analysis of the Influence of Saudi Arabia Culture
on the Requirement Engineering Process 240
   Tawfeeq Alsanoosy, Maria Spichkova, and James Harland

Formal Verification of Cyber-physical Feature Coordination
with Minimalist Qualitative Models............................ 261
   *Hermann Kaindl, Ralph Hoch, Michael Rathmair,
   and Christoph Luckeneder*

AHM: Handling Heterogeneous Models Matching and Consistency
via MDE 288
   *Mahmoud El Hamlaoui, Saloua Bennani, Sophie Ebersold,
   Mahmoud Nassar, and Bernard Coulette*

GenesLove.Me 2.0: Improving the Prioritization of Genetic Variations...... 314
   *José Fabián Reyes Román, Alberto García, Urko Rueda,
   and Óscar Pastor*

Automated Multi-objective Refactoring Based on Quality
and Code Element Recentness 334
   Michael Mohan and Des Greer

The Formal Reference Model for Software Requirements............... 352
   Erika Nazaruka and Jānis Osis

Effective Decision Making in Self-adaptive Systems Using Cost-Benefit
Analysis at Runtime and Online Learning of Adaptation Spaces 373
   *Jeroen Van Der Donckt, Danny Weyns, M. Usman Iftikhar,
   and Sarpreet Singh Buttar*

Author Index 405

Service Science and Business
Information Systems

Lessons Learned from an Action Research Study on the Use of Cloud Computing in Undergraduate Computer Science Courses

Heleno Cardoso da Silva Filho(ID) and Glauco de Figueiredo Carneiro(✉)(ID)

Universidade Salvador (UNIFACS), Salvador, BA, Brazil
heleno.filho@area1.edu.br, glauco.carneiro@unifacs.br
http://www.unifacs.br

Abstract. Companies have made efforts to migrate their assets to the cloud aiming to use in a more effective way computing resources to provide services to their market share. However, this is not a trivial task due to the lack of information on how to accomplish the migration, which services should be selected and which providers offer the best cost benefit ratio. This paper presents a study from the point of view of undergraduate students enrolled in System Analysis and Operating Systems courses from the University of Salvador (UNIFACS). The goal is to investigate the learning process in these courses using cloud computing scenarios. The results of this study provided initial evidence that the cloud computing capabilities integrated into the content of the above mentioned courses can contribute to motivate and engage students in the proposed activities.

Keywords: Cloud computing · Active learning · Action research

1 Introduction

Cloud computing refers to both the applications delivered as services over the Internet and the hardware and systems software in the data centers that provide those service [1]. Cloud computing, according to [1], has the potential to transform a large part of the IT industry, making software even more attractive as a service and shaping the way IT hardware is designed and purchased [29]. Many factors may influence the adoption of cloud computing as discussed in [18]. They argue that the relative advantage, complexity, technological readiness, top management support, and firm size have a direct effect on the adoption of cloud computing. Moreover, the use of cloud computing has a direct impact on the cost-benefit ratio in the use of resources.

Researchers have identified key advantages and challenges faced by practitioners regarding the use of cloud computing. As advantages, several studies

© Springer Nature Switzerland AG 2019
E. Damiani et al. (Eds.): ENASE 2018, CCIS 1023, pp. 3–23, 2019.
https://doi.org/10.1007/978-3-030-22559-9_1

have highlighted *elasticity* [1], *scalability* [14], *storage capacity* [5], *cost reduction* [14], and *mobility* [7]. As challenges that are bound to concerns faced during Cloud Computing adoption, they have argued the following [19,26]: *security*[1], *reliability* [26], *privacy and confidentiality* [21], *portability* [12], and *interoperability* [20]. Considering that universities are active adopters of cloud computing in their STEM curricula [11], companies have increasingly looked for proficient professionals to manage, optimize, and configure cloud computing capabilities. This is an opportunity to qualify students to operate in the market on cloud computing tasks.

Considering this scenario, undergraduate students should be prepared to operate in the cloud computing segment. For this purpose, one effective way to maintain them motivated and engaged is through the use of active learning techniques [13,25]. Active learning improves the cognitive performance of activities. For this reason, undergraduate courses need to stimulate students with hands-on activities that deal with cloud computing scenarios [13]. For example, feasibility analysis related to the migration of potential assets of the company to use the computational resources exploited by cloud providers. The challenges faced by new students during the execution of cloud activities may include identifying which cloud providers to hire and the resources to allocate to a new cloud service [18,22]. It is possible to use empirical instruments to analyze the effectiveness of the aforementioned activities. In fact, studies have reported the use of these instruments in Computer Science undergraduate courses to provide an environment in which students can experience real-life problems while increasing their motivation and the quality of learning outcomes [25,26,28]. Following the Goal-Question-Metric (GQM) approach [3], the goal of our study is stated as follows (Table 1):

Table 1. The GQM approach.

Analyze	the use of cloud computing scenarios
for the purpose of	understanding its effectiveness
with respect to	the adoption of these scenarios in "Software Analysis and Design" and "Operating Systems" courses
from the viewpoint of	students
in the context of	Computer Science undergraduate courses at Salvador University (UNIFACS)

Our challenge in this study was the analysis of the use of cloud computing scenarios on students' qualifications to meet the challenges and opportunities in the cloud computing job market.

The rest of this paper is organized as follows. Next section presents the context of this work. Section 3 describes the strategy we applied to identify the tools. Section 4 presents the tools and respective challenges and advantages of their use by SMEs. Section 5 presents the conclusion, threats to validity and scope for future research.

---

[1] www.cloudsecurityalliance.org.

2 Context of This Work

Many researchers have argued that the traditional classroom setting has key shortcomings. And that alternatives, such as the flipped classroom, have been used with interesting results [4,30]. The main concept behind the flipped classroom approach is to flip the lecture-based classroom instruction and utilize interactive activities and reading assignments in advance of class [27]. Class time is then used to engage learners in problem-based, collaborative learning and advancing concepts. After class, students can check understanding and extend learning to more complex tasks. Most importantly, the learner has control of the pace and time it takes to learn the material [8]. Figure 1, adapted from the Faculty Innovation Center[2], illustrates this scenario.

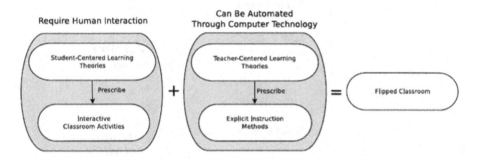

Fig. 1. Flipped classroom [4].

Flipping a class can be a worthwhile approach, especially in courses where the concepts and underlying theory are traditionally difficult for students to grasp [30]. And this can be the case of Computer Science Undergraduate courses. Moreover, student-centered, technology-based, and active learning approaches such as flipped classroom relies on students taking control of their learning. This approach enables students to set goals, monitor their progress, supporting the development of critical thinking and problem solving skills [17].

In recent years, the advent of DevOps and Cloud Computing require solid knowledge in operating systems [5]. On the other hand, the quality of the software product depends directly on the quality of the artifacts produced during the software development life cycle. For this reason, the course of System Analysis and Design plays an important role to consolidate the knowledge regarding the development of artifacts that comprise the software. Students usually have reported the challenge to understand and register the problem accordingly in artifacts such as use cases or user stories and to derive this information in other artifacts throughout the software life cycle such as class and sequence diagrams [2].

---

[2] https://facultyinnovate.utexas.edu/flipped-classroom.

3   The Study

In the action research term, *action* refers to improving practice and *research* refers to creating knowledge from the practice experience [15]. When conducting an action research study, the researcher is immersed in the target situation under investigation. The work unfolds in response to the situation and not only to the researcher's requirements. Descriptions and theories are built up as a result of the iteration within the context in close collaboration between researchers and participants [10]. The action research steps are iterative and incremental [9]. Figure 2 shows these steps integrated to the flipped classroom approach.

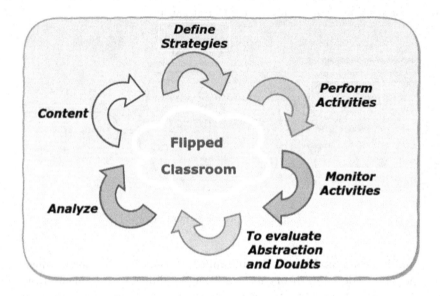

Fig. 2. Action research iterative steps. Adapted from [15].

We used the Goal Question Metric (GQM) approach to plan the action research study. From the research question (**RQ**) presented before, we defined the goals of this study. The goal was then refined into questions that break down the issue into its major components. Each question was in the sequence refined into metrics. The same metric can be used to answer different questions under the same goal. In Fig. 3 we show diagrammatically the relationship among goals, questions and metrics of this study. The action research was conducted during the first semester of the academic year of 2017.

3.1   Action-Research Planning Phase

The planning phase has two key moments as described below. In the first moment, the course syllabus is the input for the identification of the course characteristics. In the sequence, the set of key cloud resources are indicated as requirements to decide which cloud computing scenarios should be included in the activities. In the second moment, we plan the activities based on the topics/components of the syllabus and contextualized in the selected scenario. We then configure the environment for the execution of the activities in the context of the selected scenarios. An important issue in this phase is the diagnosis of the characteristics of each course, especially the components of the syllabus to promote an effective alignment of the proposed activities with the course goals. It is important to mention that, following the characteristics of an action-research study, the activities created to each course can be adjusted based on feedback provided by the students, researcher or teacher. In these cases, we should return to the Phase 2 of the planning to promote the activities adjustments.

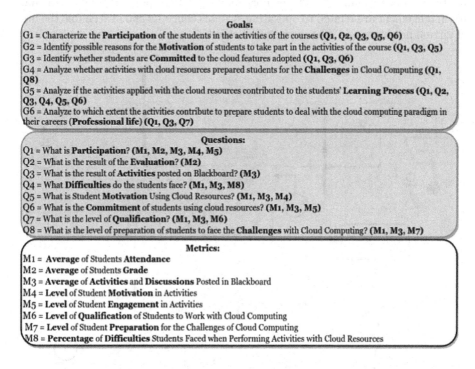

Fig. 3. Action research goals, questions and metrics [24].

Figure 4 shows the spiral meta-model of the the action-research approach we envisioned to be instantiated in each course. This meta-model is composed of the following phases: planning (green rectangles), execution (yellow rectangle), monitoring, analysis and feedback phases (blue, gray and white rectangles). When conducting the action research study, we repeatedly passe through these phases in iterations (called Spirals). This was needed particularly for the execution of all topics of the course syllabus until the end.

3.2 The Targeted Courses

We decided to conduct the action research study focusing on two courses: *Operating Systems (OS)* and *System Analysis and Design (SAD)* for the following two reasons. The first is the potential to explore the use of cloud resources [16] in both courses. The second is the opportunity to illustrate how to perform real activities in the context of topics from the syllabus of the two courses. An operating system is a program that manages a computer's hardware. It also provides a basis for application programs and acts as an intermediary between the computer user and the computer hardware [23]. The Ubuntu Linux distribution was adopted as the operating system to perform the planned activities. This distribution is available in several cloud providers such as Google Cloud[3] and Amazon AWS[4]. Moreover, this distribution is well-known and popular in the open source community[5]. The topics related to process management, memory management, input/output system, and file management are related to operating systems concepts and also enable the use of virtual machines and containers in the cloud.

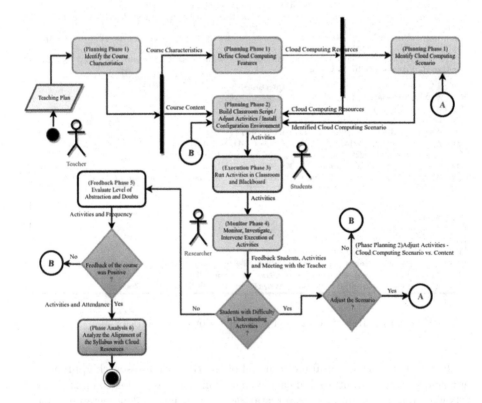

Fig. 4. Action research meta-model [24]. (Color figure online)

---

[3] https://cloud.google.com/compute/docs/images.
[4] https://aws.amazon.com/marketplace/pp/B01JBL2I8U.
[5] https://distrowatch.com/dwres.php?resource=popularity.

System Analysis and Design (SAD) deals with planning the development of software systems based on the understanding and specification in detail of what a system should do and how the components of the system should be implemented and work together. The discipline also focuses on identifying characteristics of the software architecture and its components and addresses the concepts of deploy and orchestration of applications in the IaaS layer (infrastructure as a service). Both courses deal with contents that for some extent can require the use of cloud computing capabilities. Therefore, the two courses can be integrated with activities related to cloud computing activities, such as those required for the migration of legacy systems to the cloud.

3.3   Selecting Projects from Github

We used the following criteria to select software projects from Github: Stars, Forks, Contributors, Recent Updates, and Open Source Version. These criteria are the same as adopted by [6]. These projects are used as scenarios for the activities in each course. The selection also considered that they have an installation script and can be accessed/installed in Ubuntu. Table 2 lists the selected projects (Web applications) based on the highest scores in each domain.

3.4   Cloud Scenarios and Activities

We used the virtualization and containers features in the cloud computing scenarios. The virtualization aimed at simulating a remote server that provided cloud services according to the Infrastructure as a Service (IaaS) model.

Table 2. Projects selected from Github [24].

Domain	Stars	Forks	Contributors	Updates	Version
Health-OpenEmr	352	490	85	Yes	GNU GPL
Conference Talk-OpenCFP	313	130	50	Sim	MIT
Wine-Nodecellar	14	44	26	Yes	APACHE 2.0
Taxi-App	2	8	5	No	No
Network Monitoring - Zabbix	141	66	1	Yes	GPL-2.0

Scenario 1: Nodecellar Wine Store (virtual machine and container versions). For the execution of this cloud computing scenario, we used the Cloudify Gigaspaces platform to simulate an application running in the cloud through virtualization (Virtual Box[6]), according to an Infrastucture as a Service (IaaS) model. The Nodecellar[7] is based on Node.js, a JavaScript runtime, to manage (retrieve, create, update, delete) the wines in a wine cellar database[8]. This application has been used by the open source community to demonstrate the steps required to migrate, deploy and orchestrate a legacy application to the cloud.

---

[6] https://www.virtualbox.org/.

[7] http://nodecellar.coenraets.org/.

[8] https://github.com/cloudify-cosmo/cloudify-nodecellar-example.

Scenario 2: OpenEMR (virtual machine and container versions). OpenEMR[9] is an open source electronic health record and medical practice management solution. It can run on Windows, Linux, Mac OS X and several other platforms. Its source code has PHP5+ as programming language, MySQL or MariaDB as database, as well as Apache or other PHP related webserver.

Scenario 3: OpenCFP (virtual machine and container versions). OpenCFP[10] is a PHP-based conference talk submission system that enables the discussion of concepts related to the analysis (problem) and project (solution) in a software system. It also enables the discussion of process management, memory management and input/output management in the context of the operating system course.

Scenario 4: Zabbix (virtual machine and container versions). It is an open source enterprise-level software designed for real-time monitoring of metrics collected from remote servers, virtual machines and network devices. This scenario was analyzed in the Amazon Web Services Cloud Service (AWS) through the use of containers (Docker) and Virtual Machines (VM).

Scenario 5: Mobile Taxi Application (virtual machine and container versions). For use of this cloud computing scenario, the artifacts of the mobile taxi-app application are available in the GitHub[11] to discuss the concepts of reverse engineering and UML diagrams.

Scenario 6: Portal Amazon. It is a worldwide online shopping of books, magazines, music, DVDs, videos and many other items.

As presented in Fig. 2, the activities to be performed by the students were posted and available in the Blackboard portal of the university. It is a virtual learning environment adopted at Salvador University (UNIFACS) for both face-to-face and distance learning courses. The activities can be reached at the url indicated in this footnote[12].

3.5   Data Sources for the Analysis

We considered data provided by the following sources in this study: (a) Activities registered in Blackboard; (b) Questionnaire on Student profile; (c) Questionnaire for feedback about the adherence of cloud computing scenarios; (d) Midterm and Final Assignment; (e) Student Attendance; (f) Feedback from students during classes and activities; (g) Research and teacher perceptions.

The questionnaires used the Likert scale of 5. No identification was required to answer the questionnaires. Prior to the questionnaires application, we highlighted the importance of the answers to the study and the benefits that the

---

[9] http://www.open-emr.org/.
[10] https://github.com/opencfp/opencfp.
[11] https://github.com/mistryrn/taxi-app.
[12] https://cloudeduc.github.io/cloudeduc/.

results and findings from these study would bring to better prepare students to the cloud computing market. A total of 13 students in the discipline of Operating systems and 11 students in the discipline of System Analysis and Design completed the questionnaires. The questionnaire for the System Analysis and Design (SAD) students had 35 questions (33 closed and 2 open). The questionnaire for the Operating Systems students had 34 issues (32 closed and 2 open). The closed questions aimed at obtaining the degree of knowledge in the Computer Science field. The open questions aimed at obtaining the perceptions of the students regarding the engagement and what was learned while performing cloud computing related activities.

3.6   Profile of the Students

Both classes have 16 students enrolled in the first semester of 2017. We used questionnaires in May of 2017 to obtain data related to the profile of the students that took part in the action research study. The questionnaire was composed of 15 closed questions. The questions focused on issues related to academic background and knowledge related to cloud computing. The questionnaire can be reached at the same url indicated in the previous footnote.

3.7   The Role of the Authors of the Study

Among the two authors of the study, the second one took the role as the instructor of the two disciplines. He developed lesson plans, conducted face-to-face and online learning activities and participated in all of the action research process. The first author was one of the members of the Monitoring and Support Team (MST). The purpose of MST was to guide the instructor, conduct macro level analysis with the researcher, assess the process, increase the validity and reliability of data collection and analysis procedures, develop functional actions based on findings of the macro level analysis, and to help make the research process as much objective as possible. The MST consisted of 2 experts (the authors) from curriculum, instruction and educational technologies.

4   Analyzing the Data

In this section, we present the analysis of data obtained during the action research study to answer the **Research Question (RQ)**: "Analyze *the use of cloud computing scenarios* for the purpose of *understanding its effectiveness* with respect to *the adoption of these scenarios in "Software Analysis and Design" and "Operating Systems" courses* from the viewpoint of *students* in the context of *Computer Science undergraduate courses at Salvador University (UNIFACS)"*. With this analysis we intend to draw conclusions on how to engage students to face the challenges and opportunities of cloud computing in the market. In Fig. 5, we show diagrammatically the relationship among goals, questions and metrics. Based on this relationship, we explain first how the metrics were calculated, then we show how they were combined to answer the questions. Finally, we explain the goals. Within one-semester learning process of the proposed inclusion of cloud computing scenarios in the two disciplines, the way students reacted and performed the activities was monitored, as well as the ways students interacted with their peers and with the researchers. Moreover, the "ways of interaction" emerged during the activity process were carefully analyzed via content analysis.

Table 3. Goals, questions and metrics for OS discipline [24].

Research issues								Results
Q1 Participation	Q2 Evaluation	Q3 Activities	Q4 Difficulties	Q5 Motivated	Q6 Committed	Q7 Qualification	Q8 Challenges	
G1 Participation (63.98%)	(62.50%)	(46.35%) Low productivity	–	Motivated (61.91%)	Compromised (61.91%)	–	–	(59.33%)
G2 Participation (63.98%)	–	(46.35%) Low productivity	–	Motivated (61.91%)	–	–	–	(57.41%)
G3 Participation (63.98%)	–	(46.35%) Low productivity	–	–	Compromised (61.91%)	–	–	(57.41%)
G4 Participation (63.98%)	–	–	–	–	–	–	Little prepared (56.36%)	(60.17%)
G5 Participation (63.98%)	(62.50%)	(46.35%) Low productivity	Difficulties (52.34%)	Motivated (61.91%)	Compromised (61.91%)	–	–	(58.17%)
G6 Participation (63.98%)	–	(46.35%) Low productivity	–	–	–	Very little qualified (52.64)	–	(54.32%)

4.1   Analyzing Data for the OS Discipline

In the following paragraphs, we analyze data for the Operating Systems (OS) Discipline. We also explain how the values were calculated. In Table 4, we present the values for metrics M1–M8.

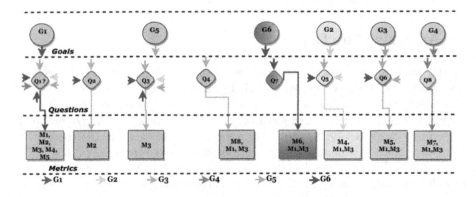

Fig. 5. Relationship among goals, questions and metrics [24].

Table 4. Collected metrics for the OS discipline [24].

Metric	Description	Value (Average)
M1	Average of students attendance (frequency)	90.49%
M2	Assignments average value	62.50%
M3	Average of activities/discussions posted on blackboard	46.35%
M4	Students' motivational level in activities	61.91%
M5	Level of commitment to students in activities	61.91%
M6	Qualification level of students to deal with cloud computing activities	52.64%
M7	Student preparedness level for cloud computing challenges	56.36%
M8	Percentage of difficulties students had in the activities with cloud resources	52.34%

Answering the Questions for the OS Discipline. In the following, we present the calculations for the eight questions aiming at providing conditions to characterize the goals stated in this study.

Question Q1 - Participation of the Students in OS. According to Figs. 3 and 5, the metrics M1–M5 were designated to answer Question Q1. In Table 5, we present the results of metrics M1, M2 and M3 to answer Q1. In Table 6, we present the results of metrics M4 and M5 collected from questions 3.1 to 3.9 of the questionnaire of discipline Operating Systems (Table 7).

Table 5. M1, M2 and M3 in OS discipline.

Metrics	Description	Average
M1	Average of students attendance (frequency) (total 1088 h/103.50 h Faltas)	90.49%
M2	Average rating	62.50%
M3	Average of activities/discussions posted on blackboard	46.35%

Table 6. M4 and M5 in OS discipline - question 3.1 a 3.9.

Question	Not approached	Insufficient	Little enough	Enough	More than enough
3.1	0%	15.38%	15.38%	69.23%	0%
3.2	0%	7.69%	15.38%	61.54%	15.38%
3.3	0%	7.69%	23.08%	61.54%	7.69%
3.4	0%	15.38%	30.77%	38.46%	15.38%
3.5	0%	15.38%	7.69%	46.15%	30.77%
3.6	0%	7.69%	7.69%	53.85%	30.77%
3.7	0%	15.38%	15.38%	61.54%	7.69%
3.8	7.69%	23.08%	46.15%	15.38%	7.69%
3.9	0%	7.69%	15.38%	61.54%	15.38%
Average	**0.85%**	**12.82%**	**19.66%**	**52.14%**	**14.53%**

Table 7. Answering Q1 through M1–M5 for OS discipline.

Metric	Average (%)	Weight	Result (%)
M1	90.49%	3	271.47%
M2	62.50%	2	125%
M3	46.35%	3	139.05%
M4 and M5	52.14%	2	104.28%
		Average	**63.98%**

The value obtained for Q1 of 63.98% classified students from the Operating Systems (OS) as Participatives. This is consistent with the feedback students provided describing their motivation to perform the activities contextualized in cloud computing scenarios.

Question Q2 - Results of the Assignments/Evaluations - OS. According to Figs. 3 and 5, only the metric M2 was designated to answer Question Q2. In Table 8, we present the results of metric M2 to answer Q2 for the first semester of 2017. We considered the medterm and final exam to calculate M2 to answer Q2. The value of 63.98 is considered regular, near 70 that was the expected result.

Question Q3 - Activities Posted in Blackboard - OS. According to Figs. 3 and 5, the metric M3 was designated to answer Question Q3. In Table 9, we present the results of metric M3 to answer Q3. As can be seen in the table, a participation of 46.35% in the activities of the course was an evidence that it can be improved. The reason for this occurrence was obtained by feedback in which students declared that also used email and instant message services in their mobile for discussions.

Question Q4 - Difficulties Faced by Students - OS. According to Figs. 3 and 5, the metrics M1, M3 and M8 were designated to answer Question Q4. Considering that M1 and M3 for the OS discipline were already discussed and listed in Table 5, we present in Table 10 the result for metric M8 as 52.34% related to difficulties faced by students while performing cloud computing activities in the discipline. Considering together metrics M1, M3 and M8, in Table 11 we present the result for Question Q4 as 52.34%. This highlight the challenges faced by students to perform cloud related activities in the context of the OS discipline. However, analyzing evidence from the students feedback, we realized that despite the difficulties, students strove to achieved the goals.

Question Q5 - Motivation to Perform Cloud Activities - OS. According to Figs. 3 and 5, the metrics M1, M3 and M4 were designated to answer Question Q5. In Table 12, we present the results of metrics M1, M3. The metric M4 is presented in Table 13. Considering together metrics M1, M3 and M4, in Table 14 we present the result for Question Q5 as 61.91%. This is considered a regular level of motivation for this discipline with an increasing tendency as verified in the feedback provided by the students.

Question Q6 - Commitment to Perform Cloud Activities - OS. According to Figs. 3 and 5, the metrics M1, M3 and M5 were designated to answer Question Q6. In Table 12, we present the results of metrics M1 and M3. In Table 15, we present the results of metrics M5. Finally, in Table 16, we calculate the value for Q6 as 61.91%. This is an interesting evidence of commitment, reporting that majority of students are engaged in the cloud activities in the context of the discipline.

Table 8. Answering Q2 through M2 for OS discipline.

k	Average	Frequency	Frequency relative	Percentage (%)
1	3.4	1	0.06	6
2	3.7	1	0.06	6
3	4.8	2	0.13	12
4	5.2	1	0.06	6
5	6.0	1	0.06	6
6	6.8	3	0.19	19
7	7.0	1	0.06	6
8	7.1	1	0.06	6
9	7.2	3	0.19	19
10	8.0	2	0.13	12
			Average	**62.50**

Table 9. Answering Q3 through M3 for OS discipline.

Data	Activities	Scenarios	Participation students (%)
15/03/2017	Activity 1	Machine resources virtual and container	63%
15/03/2017	Activity 2	wiki.openmrs.org	50%
22/03/2017	Activity 3	http://www.open-emr.org	50%
22/03/2017	Activity 3	Web applications	25%
12/04/2017	Activity 4	Virtualization	43.75%
	Average		**46.35%**

Table 10. Difficulties faced in activities (M8 - OS).

Elements	Qty	Percentage (%)
(a) Understanding the proposed strategy for using cloud-computing scenarios	3	23.08%
(b) Assimilate basic concepts (OS, programs, processes, memory, CPU, files, devices, etc.)	1	7.69%
(c) Assimilate the concepts of Process Management, Memory Management, File Management, Input and Output Management	3	23.08%
(d) Understand memory hierarchy Registers, Cache (L1 and L2), Main, Auxiliary/Secondary	3	23.08%
(e) Use Virtualization techniques (Virtual Machine, Container, images)	3	23.08%
(f) Analyze Process Management - Process Life Cycle: (interrupt, Block, System Call, Apt, Creation, Running, Destruction), Deadlock	1	7.69%
(g) Understand process scalability algorithms, Access Levels (User and Kernel), Process Profiles: CPU Bound and I/O Bound	6	46.15%
(h) Use simulators to analyze key process scheduling algorithms, memory management, and input/output	4	30.77%
(i) Understand memory allocation management, First-Fit partition selection policy; Best-fit-only; Best-available-fit, Internal vs. External Fragmentation	3	23.08%
(j) Implement First-Fit Memory Allocation Algorithms; Best-fit-only; Best-available-fit	8	61.54%
(k) Use Cloud Computing Resource Monitoring Tools	7	53.85%
	Average	28.21%

Table 11. Answering Q4 through M1, M3 and M8 for OS discipline.

Metric	Average (%)	Weight	Result (%)
M1	90.49%	3	271.47%
M3	46.35%	3	139.05%
M8	28.21%	4	112.84%
		Average	**52.34%**

Table 12. M1 and M3 in OS discipline.

Metrics	Description	Value
M1	Frequency (total 1088 h/103.50 h Fouls)	90.49%
M3	Average of activities/discussions posted on blackboard	3.6%

Table 13. M4 in OS discipline.

Question	Not approached	Insufficient	Little enough	Enough	More than enough
3.1	0%	15.38%	15.38%	69.23%	0%
3.2	0%	7.69%	15.38%	61.54%	15.38%
3.3	0%	7.69%	23.08%	61.54%	7.69%
3.4	0%	15.38%	30.77%	38.46%	15.38%
3.5	0%	15.38%	7.69%	46.15%	30.77%
3.6	0%	7.69%	7.69%	53.85%	30.77%
3.7	0%	15.38%	15.38%	61.54%	7.69%
3.8	7.69%	23.08%	46.15%	15.38%	7.69%
3.9	0%	7.69%	15.38%	61.54%	15.38%
Average	**0.85%**	**12.82%**	**19.66%**	**52.14%**	**14.53%**

Table 14. Answering Q5 through M1, M3 and M4 for OS discipline.

Metric	Average (%)	Weight	Result (%)
M1	90.49%	3	271.47%
M3	46.35%	3	139.05%
M4	52.14%	4	208.56%
		Average	**61.91%**

Table 15. M5 in OS discipline.

Question	Not discussed	Insufficient	Little enough	Enough	More than enough
3.1	0%	15.38%	15.38%	69.23%	0%
3.2	0%	7.69%	15.38%	61.54%	15.38%
3.3	0%	7.69%	23.08%	61.54%	7.69%
3.4	0%	15.38%	30.77%	38.46%	15.38%
3.5	0%	15.38%	7.69%	46.15%	30.77%
3.6	0%	7.69%	7.69%	53.85%	30.77%
3.7	0%	15.38%	15.38%	61.54%	7.69%
3.8	7.69%	23.08%	46.15%	15.38%	7.69%
3.9	0%	7.69%	15.38%	61.54%	15.38%
Average	**0.85%**	**12.82%**	**19.66%**	**52.14%**	**14.53%**

Table 16. Answering Q6 through M1, M3 and M5 for OS discipline.

Metric	Average (%)	Weight	Result (%)
M1	90.49%	3	271.47%
M3	46.35%	3	139.05%
M5	52.14%	4	208.56%
		Average	**61.91%**

Question Q7 - Level of Qualification - OS. According to Figs. 3 and 5, the metrics M1, M3 and M6 were designated to answer Question Q7. In Table 12, we present the results of metrics M1 and M3. In Table 17, we present the results of the metric M6. Finally, in Table 18, we calculate the value for Q7 as 52.64%. This value indicates that students have the perception that they need to improve their qualification to deal with challenges and opportunities related to cloud computing in the market. This is in fact an evidence that students are aware of improvement opportunities they need to strive in order to be a qualified professional.

Table 17. M6 in OS discipline.

Question	No activity	Little activity	Activity
Performed activities	78%	0%	22%

Question Q8 - Level of Preparation - OS. According to Figs. 3 and 5, the metrics M1, M3 and M7 were designated to answer Question Q8.

Table 18. Answering Q7 through M1, M3 and M6 for OS discipline.

Metric	Average (%)	Weight	Result (%)
M1	90.49%	2	180.98%
M3	46.35%	4	185.40%
M6	40.00%	4	160.00%
		Average	**52.64%**

Table 19. M7 in OS discipline.

Question	Not prepared	Very little prepared	Little prepared	Prepared	Very prepared
5.1	23.08%	15.38%	23.08%	38.46%	0%
5.2	15.38%	23.08%	30.77%	23.08%	7.69%
5.3	15.38%	15.38%	61.54%	7.69%	0%
5.4	7.69%	15.38%	38.46%	30.77%	7.69%
5.5	30.77%	7.69%	38.46%	23.08%	0%
5.6	7.69%	46.15%	30.77%	15.38%	0%
5.7	7.69%	23.08%	38.46%	23.08%	7.69%
5.8	15.38%	23.08%	23.08%	38.46%	0%
Average	**15.38%**	**21.15%**	**35.58%**	**25.00%**	**2.88%**

Table 20. Answering Q8 through M1, M3 and M7 for OS discipline.

Metric	Average (%)	Weight	Result (%)
1	90.49%	3	271.47%
3	46.35%	4	185.40%
7	35.58%	3	106.74%
		Average	**56.36%**

In Table 12, we present the results of metrics M1 and M3. In Table 19, we present the results of the metric M7. Finally, in Table 20, we calculate the value for Q8 as 56.36%. Similarly to Q7, this value indicates that students have the perception that they need to improve their preparation to deal with challenges and opportunities related to cloud computing in the market. This is in fact an evidence that students are aware of improvement opportunities they need to strive in order to perform effectively cloud related activities.

In Table 23, we summarize the results for all Goals, Questions and Metrics for the OS discipline.

Table 21. Collected metrics for the SAD discipline [24].

Metric	Description	Value (average)
M1	Average of students attendance (frequency)	89.66%
M2	Assignments average value	64.80%
M3	Average of activities/discussions posted on blackboard	47.00%
M4	Students' motivational level in activities	61.73%
M5	Level of commitment to students in activities	61.73%
M6	Qualification level of students to deal with cloud computing activities	40.73%
M7	Student preparedness level for cloud computing challenges	56.61%
M8	Percentage of difficulties students had in the activities with cloud resources	55.54%

Table 22. Comparing the Metrics of SAD and OS Disciplines [24].

Metric	APS (%)	SO (%)
M1 - Average of students attendance (frequency)	89.66%	90.49%
M1 - Average of students attendance	64.32%	63.98%
M2 - Average students grade	64.80%	62.50%
M3 - Average of the activities/discussions posted at blackboard	47.00%	46.35%
M4 - Level of student motivation in activities	61.73%	61.91%
M5 - Level of commitment of students in the activities	61.73%	61.91%
M6 - Level of qualification of pupils to act with cloud computing (virtualization activities)	40.73%	52.64%
M7 - Level of preparation of students for the challenges of cloud computing	56.61%	56.36%
M8 - Percentage of difficulties faced by students in cloud computing activities	55.54%	52.34%

4.2   Analyzing Data for the OS Discipline

Considering that the Operating System discipline has the same goals, questions and metrics as the SAD discipline and that it follows the sama analysis as presented in the previous subsection, we present Table 3 where we summarize the results for all Goals, Questions and Metrics for this discipline.

Table 23. Goals, questions and metrics for SAD discipline [24].

| Research issues | | | | | | | | Results |
Q1 Participation	Q2 Evaluation	Q3 Activities	Q4 Difficulties	Q5 Motivated	Q6 Committed	Q7 Qualification	Q8 Challenges	
G1 Participation (64.32%)	(64.80%)	(47%) Low productivity	–	Motivated (61.73%)	Compromised (61.73%)	–	–	(59.92%)
G2 Participation (64.32%)	–	(47%) Low productivity	–	Motivated (61.73%)	–	–	–	(57.68%)
G3 Participation (64.32%)	–	(47%) Low productivity	–	–	Compromised (61.73%)	–	–	(57.68%)
G4 Participation (64.32%)	–	–	–	–	–	–	Little prepared (56.61)	(60.47%)
G5 Participation (64.32%)	(64.80%)	(47%) Low productivity	Difficulties (55.54%)	Motivated (61.73%)	Compromised (61.73%)	–	–	(59.19%)
G6 Participation (64.32%)	–	(47%) Low productivity	–	–	–	Very little qualified (40.73)	–	(50.68%)

4.3 Analysis of the Results of APS and OS Disciplines

In Table 22, we compare the results for metrics M1–M8 for the disciplines SAD and OS. In Tables 23 and 3, we present a panoramic view for the goals, questions and metrics for the disciplines SAD and OS. Analyzing these values, we can conclude that both disciplines have similarities based on their Goals, Questions and Metrics. Hence, despite being different disciplines, they reacted uniformly to the proposed approach that includes cloud computing scenarios in the activities of the disciplines.

4.4 The Engagement of the Students

As can be seen in the results presented in the fields Q5 and Q6 (Motivated/Committed: 61.73% SAD/61.91% OS) of Tables 23 and 3, students from both disciplines manifested engagement and also commitment to perform the activities contextualized in cloud computing scenarios. This is an initial evidence that in fact classes in Computer Science undergraduate courses can be enriched with these scenarios when applied using active learning techniques such as flipped classroom to provide students the opportunity to be the main participants in the learning process. On the other hand, teachers can identify improvement opportunities in each student and guide them to fill gaps in topics they are not so confident. This is an iterative and incremental process that can be conducted with real scenarios from the market (Table 21).

5 Conclusions

The cloud computing paradigm has increasingly provided a better value for money for organizations. To support companies in architectural design to execute and make available their assets in the cloud, as well as their legacy systems and at the same time contribute to the abstraction and qualification of students in these concepts, cloud computing scenarios were used to prepare students, future professionals in this area to perform tasks in this scenario. In this paper, we analyze the use of cloud computing scenarios in two undergraduate courses. The data of the analysis makes it possible to understand statistically how the learning process of these scenarios contributes in the educational process. Thus, the results suggest that the adoption of cloud computing scenarios is important in the education process for the future professional cloud formation. As a future work, there is the possibility of conducting a new version of this research in collaboration with industry [9] as well as applying the described instruments of the field research and inverted action approach in the training industry [6]. Another possibility is to conduct this study in other universities to compare results and obtain better conditions to generalize results and findings.

Acknowledgments. The first author of this paper received a scholarship from the Bahia Research Foundation (FAPESB) registered as BOL0731/2016.

References

1. Armbrust, M., et al.: A view of cloud computing. Commun. ACM **53**(4), 50–58 (2010)
2. Bahill, A.T., Madni, A.M.: Discovering system requirements. In: Bahill, A.T., Madni, A.M. (eds.) Tradeoff Decisions in System Design, pp. 373–457. Springer, Cham (2017). https://doi.org/10.1007/978-3-319-43712-5_4
3. Basili, V., Caldiera, G., Rombach, H.: Goal question metric approach paradigm (1994)
4. Bishop, J.L., Verleger, M.A.: The flipped classroom: a survey of the research. In: ASEE National Conference Proceedings, Atlanta, GA, pp. 1–18 (2013)
5. Bond, J.: The Enterprise Cloud: Best Practices for Transforming Legacy IT. O'Reilly Media, Sebastopol (2015). https://books.google.com.br/books?id=NIL5oAEACAAJ
6. Borges, H., Hora, A., Valente, M.T.: Predicting the popularity of github repositories. In: Proceedings of the 12th International Conference on Predictive Models and Data Analytics in Software Engineering, PROMISE 2016, pp. 9:1–9:10. ACM, New York (2016). https://doi.org/10.1145/2972958.2972966
7. Fernando, N., Loke, S.W., Rahayu, W.: Mobile cloud computing: a survey. Future Gener. Comput. Syst. **29**(1), 84–106 (2013)
8. Santos Green, L., Banas, J.R., Perkins, R.A. (eds.): The Flipped College Classroom. Springer, Cham (2017). https://doi.org/10.1007/978-3-319-41855-1
9. Hendricks, C.C.: Improving Schools Through Action Research: A Reflective Practice Approach. Pearson Higher Education, Upper Saddle River (2012)
10. Holwell, S.: Themes, iteration, and recoverability in action research. In: Kaplan, B., Truex, D.P., Wastell, D., Wood-Harper, A.T., DeGross, J.I. (eds.) Information Systems Research. IIFIP, vol. 143, pp. 353–362. Springer, Boston (2004). https://doi.org/10.1007/1-4020-8095-6_20
11. Jararweh, Y., Alshara, Z., Jarrah, M., Kharbutli, M., Alsaleh, M.N.: Teachcloud: a cloud computing educational toolkit. Int. J. Cloud Comput. **12**(2–3), 237–257 (2013)

12. Jones, S., Irani, Z., Sivarajah, U., Love, P.E.: Risks and rewards of cloud computing in the UK public sector: a reflection on three organisational case studies. Inf. Syst. Front. 1–24 (2017)
13. Lin, Y.T., Wen, M.L., Jou, M., Wu, D.W.: A cloud-based learning environment for developing student reflection abilities. Comput. Hum. Behav. **32**, 244–252 (2014)
14. Marston, S., Li, Z., Bandyopadhyay, S., Zhang, J., Ghalsasi, A.: Cloud computing-the business perspective. Decis. Support Syst. **51**(1), 176–189 (2011)
15. McNiff, J.: You and Your Action Research Project. Routledge, London (2016)
16. Mokhtar, S.A., Ali, S.H.S., Al-Sharafi, A., Aborujilah, A.: Cloud computing in academic institutions. In: Proceedings of the 7th International Conference on Ubiquitous Information Management and Communication, p. 2. ACM (2013)
17. Newman, D.L., Deyoe, M.M., Connor, K.A., Lamendola, J.M.: Flipping stem learning: impact on students' process of learning. In: Curriculum Design and Classroom Management: Concepts, Methodologies, Tools, and Applications, pp. 23–41 (2015)
18. Oliveira, T., Thomas, M., Espadanal, M.: Assessing the determinants of cloud computing adoption. Inf. Manag. **51**(5), 497–510 (2014)
19. de Paula, A.C.M., de Figueiredo Carneiro, G., Maciel, R.S.P.: A characterization of cloud computing adoption based on literature evidence. In: ICEIS 2017 - Proceedings of the 19th International Conference on Enterprise Information Systems, Porto, Portugal, 26–29 April 2017, vol. 1, pp. 53–63 (2017). https://doi.org/10.5220/0006264600530063
20. Petcu, D., Vasilakos, A.V.: Portability in clouds: approaches and research opportunities. Scalable Comput. Pract. Exp. **15**(3), 251–270 (2014)
21. Ryan, M.D.: Cloud computing privacy concerns on our doorstep. Commun. ACM **54**(1), 36–38 (2011)
22. Sadiku, M.N., Musa, S.M., Momoh, O.D.: Cloud computing: opportunities and challenges. IEEE Potentials **33**(1), 34–36 (2014)
23. Silberschatz, A., Galvin, P.B., Gagne, G.: Operating System Concepts Essentials. Wiley, Hoboken (2014)
24. da Silva Filho, H.C., de Figueiredo Carneiro, G.: An action research study towards the use of cloud computing scenarios in undergraduate computer science courses. In: Proceedings of the 13th International Conference on Evaluation of Novel Approaches to Software Engineering, ENASE 2018, Funchal, Madeira, Portugal, 23–24 March 2018, pp. 15–25 (2018). https://doi.org/10.5220/0006644800150025
25. Smith, A., Bhogal, J., Sharma, M.: Cloud computing: adoption considerations for business and education. In: 2014 International Conference on Future Internet of Things and Cloud (FiCloud), pp. 302–307. IEEE (2014)
26. Sultan, N.: Cloud computing for education: a new dawn? Int. J. Inf. Manag. **30**(2), 109–116 (2010)
27. Tucker, B.: The flipped classroom. Educ. Next **12**(1), 82–83 (2012)
28. Vaquero, L.M.: EduCloud: PaaS versus IaaS cloud usage for an advanced computer science course. IEEE Trans. Educ. **54**(4), 590–598 (2011)
29. Wang, Y., Wang, S., Zhou, D.: Retrieving and indexing spatial data in the cloud computing environment. In: Jaatun, M.G., Zhao, G., Rong, C. (eds.) CloudCom 2009. LNCS, vol. 5931, pp. 322–331. Springer, Heidelberg (2009). https://doi.org/10.1007/978-3-642-10665-1_29
30. Williams, A., et al.: Flipping STEM. In: Santos Green, L., Banas, J.R., Perkins, R.A. (eds.) The Flipped College Classroom. ECTII, pp. 149–186. Springer, Cham (2017). https://doi.org/10.1007/978-3-319-41855-1_8

Involvement of Business Roles
in Auditing with Process Mining

Ella Roubtsova[1]($\boxtimes$) and Niels Wiersma[2]

[1] Open University of the Netherlands, Heerlen, The Netherlands
ella.roubtsova@ieee.org
[2] Municipality Eindhoven, Eindhoven, The Netherlands
nwiersma@gmail.com
http://www.open.ou.nl/elr/

Abstract. Acceptance of novel formal methods-based approaches by businesses depends on involvement of the existing (not imaginary) business roles in the process of their application. This paper presents an extension of frameworks for auditing with process mining with a series of participatory workshops involving three business roles: Business Expert, Audit Expert and IT specialist. Such workshops produce the necessary input to apply frameworks of auditing with process mining: normative business process, audit statements in a controlled natural language and the logs needed for mining of process instances that do not conform audit statements.

The proposed extension of frameworks for auditing with process mining has been tested with two case studies of processes in different domains. The case studies show the need of participatory workshops, the percentage of possible audit automation, the advantages of using workshops and possible difficulties, and the types of artifacts needed to apply process mining for audit in organizations. The presented results can be used for expectation management of the businesses attempting an application of auditing with process mining.

Keywords: Audit · Audit statements · Compliance patterns ·
Frameworks for audit with process mining · Auditor ·
Business Analyst · IT specialist

1 Introduction

Auditing is a standard business practice with many applications. Traditionally, the first thing that comes to mind when thinking about auditing is a financial context, aimed for example at examining compliancy of a business to tax rules and regulations. The growing volume of services provided by government and businesses increases attention to their audit. It is already suggested by Gartner to make steps towards real time audit or assurance [7]. Today, one can audit maintenance engineering practices, health and safety issues, ethical conduct,

© Springer Nature Switzerland AG 2019
E. Damiani et al. (Eds.): ENASE 2018, CCIS 1023, pp. 24–44, 2019.
https://doi.org/10.1007/978-3-030-22559-9_2

and a wide variety of IT-related practices such as information systems security and access control [1,8,9].

An audit is defined as an "independent and documented system for obtaining and verifying audit evidence, objectively examining the evidence against audit criteria, and reporting the audit findings, while taking into account audit risk" [10]. Traditionally, an audit is a work-intensive and time-consuming procedure involving taking samples of documents and interviews and allowing one to verify a small part of all process cases.

There are different types of audits. The most often used is the Compliance Audit and Operational Audit, i.e. examination of the policies and procedures and business processes of an organization, to find if it is in compliance with internal or regulatory standards. According to [17] business process audits are used to measure conformance to standards and requirements of the product that is delivered through the process. Another objective of audit may be measuring the effectiveness of the process and the instructions that deliver the product.

In all these types of audit, the object of analysis is a business process instance. Business process instances are recorded in event logs. Event logs can be used to discover processes and to check conformance of processes against a predefined model [21]. Recently, the necessary techniques have implemented in the ever-increasing number of process analysis tools, such as [5,6,14] and many others. Still, process mining is rarely used for audit in practice.

This paper analyses the reasons, identifies the missing steps and proposes a practical extension for auditing frameworks with process mining. The proposed extended framework is validated by two case studies of audit of a grant application process and a process of handling invoices.

The structure of the paper is the following.

- Section 2 describes related work, including process mining, audit statements, conformance patterns and existing frameworks for audit with process mining. This section contains our findings about possible reasons of rare practical use of process mining for audit in practice.
- In Sect. 3 we propose a practical extension for auditing frameworks with process mining and a method of its evaluation by case studies.
- Section 4 contains results of the case study Audit of a Grant Application Process.
- Section 5 contains results of the case study Audit of a Invoice Handling Process.
- Section 6 discusses the results of evaluation of the proposed extension of frameworks for process mining and its possible future application within the existing frameworks and within the education of business students.

2   Related Work

2.1   Process Mining

Process mining is defined as the activity of discovering, monitoring and improving real processes by extracting knowledge from event logs that are present in Information Systems [22].

Central to process mining is an event log, which contains log entries of events that are captured by an information system.

Each entry of a log presents an event and consists of at least the following information: *(case designation, activity label, time stamp)*. In practice, logs may contain more information; so an event can be presented as an instance of a tuple *(case designation, activity label, time stamp, resource, performer, product description, order size...)*.

An event log of a process can be seen as a record of all events of all cases of the process within a certain time interval. Each case of the given process is a sequence of events.

There are different types of process mining [21]:

- *Process Discovery.*
  Process mining may be organized as a process discovery from a log. "For example, well-known algorithms such as the Alpha algorithm can automatically extract a Petri net that gives a concise model of the behavior seen in the event log. This gives the auditor an unbiased view on what has actually happened" [23]. The model extracted from a log maybe too detailed for the level of abstraction needed to the auditor.
- *Model Conformance.*
  Process mining may be organized as model conformance checking that uses a predefined process model and compares this model with the data in the event log. By doing this, one can answer questions regarding conformance of a real-world process as recorded in the event log to the model of the process as it should be. A predefined model is a prerequisite for conformance checking.
- *Rules Conformance.*
  Process mining may validate the compliance of a logged process with the rules specified for a given business process. Compliance with various laws, regulations and standards is a well known problem in business process development and management. The compliance can be checked at the design time [2] and at run-time [3].

2.2   Process Audit, Audit Statements

Such process mining types as process discovery and conformance checking do not completely correspond to the process audit in its traditional sense.

Process audit in practice is defined as obtaining evidence that a process is in compliance with predefined rules called audit statements. Practical audit usually does not demand the existence of a given business process model, as some adhocracy and adaptivity are considered acceptable [12]. Practical audit is executed unexpectedly or periodically. Its major goal is to find evidence of violations of predefined rules and possibly find the reasons of violations [10]. The audit evidence is often obtained manually, by conducting interviews with users about the process they follow, or taking samples of cases that are executed in the system. This evidence must then be compared against documented procedures. The documented procedures can be presented as a number of written rules and regulations called audit criteria that pertain to the business process and should be observed while executing it [10]. In other words, the whole business process is usually not specified in the documented procedures of audit.

Process audit risk influences the scope of audit statements. The auditor focuses his or her effort on formulating audit statements in the areas where most risk is perceived. The risk is calculated as a function depending upon the number of cases (process instances) that non-compliant with the audit statement, and as the financial loss associated with all non-compliant cases.

Audit statements specify the important rules as principles which are not ready for process mining as they do not name the process activities and data items in the log structure.

For example, a simple ordering based rule is specified as "no change to a request can be made after it is approved" [21]. In order to automate the compliance checks to this rule, the auditor needs some knowledge or assumption about the business process activities that can be found in the log. She can assume that there are activities *Order Approved* and *Request Order Change*. The auditor should see a case as a sequence of events where the activities have ordering relations, say one activity can follow another. If these assumptions are made, then the audit statement can be formulated as: "Activity *Order Approved* must never be followed by activity *Request Order Change* (for the same Order)".

2.3 Compliance Patterns

Audit statements are the rules that should be checked for the business process under the audit, so the classification of rules as process compliance patterns used by the compliance checking [11] is applicable for audit.

The compliance patterns have been conceptually presented in [3]. A compliance pattern is "an abstract specification of monitoring requirements and it covers the major structural facets of business processes: (1) Occurrence, (2) Order (with or without time span) and (3) employed resources" [3].

The group of Occurrence Patterns presents Existence or Absence of activities with given values of process data.

The group of Order Patterns often includes the time span information and presents a sequence of actions often with time stamps to define a time span, a precedence or a response.

The group of Resource Patterns presents Binding of Duty, Separation of Duty or Responsibility (Performed By). This group is often called Agent Based.

There is a group of Product Patterns that names the states of the products handled or produced by the business process.

The compliance patterns can be logically composed. In general, a process compliance pattern is an expression supported with the temporal logic that informally means "there are (or there are no) cases where an Order Pattern defined on activities is met, and(or) the Time Span between activities is within the norm, and(or) the given Resource was used and(or) by the given Role, and(or) the specified Product is produced (or ordered) ..." [15].

The concept of anti-patterns (pattern negations, or negation of sub-expressions of a pattern) can be also used as the process instances that violate the rules are the target of audit [3].

Legal infringements, risk management patterns, change management patterns are presented by Becker et al. in [4].

Compliance patterns are implemented in process mining tools as log-filters. The role of an audit statement in audit with process mining is twofold. On the one hand, an audit statement is an instantiation of a compliance pattern or a composition of patterns. On the other hand, an audit statement is a means of communication of experts with different backgrounds. So, the replacing the formal expression of audit statements with expressions in a Controlled Natural Language [20] should definitely support analysis of audit results. A Controlled Natural Language preserves the terminology used by auditors and business process experts and preserves the structure of compliance patterns in expressions of audit statements.

2.4   Existing Frameworks for Audit with Process Mining

The existing frameworks for audit with process mining assume that the business process model is given or is built for the audit. It is assumed that the audit statements are ready for process mining.

Indeed, the framework presented by [18] suggests to find a business process model in the log and check the compliance of the logged process with audit statements. The straightforward application of this framework is problematic. The real-world process instances in the event log may not contain the activities and other data mentioned in audit statements.

The framework [23] is principally designed to mine and compare de-jure and de-facto business process models.

The BP-MaaS framework [3] (see Fig. 1) for run-time compliance checking supposes that "Business process management practice commences with the Business Expert defining and modelling business process requirements using BPMN. ...The BPMN model follows multiple iterations of design and refinement to faithfully represent business logic and requirements. The outcome is a BPMN model capturing the control and the dataflow of the business logic." The BPMN model is used to filter only cases of the audited process from logs. Another role, is the role of Compliance Expert, who is responsible for formulating audit statements using the compliance patterns.

We may evidence the presence of Business Experts in the practice of iterative building of a process model suitable for audit. However, we do not agree that each company has a Compliance Expert. The traditional role of an Auditor, who formulates audit statements as principles and may be not acquainted with compliance patterns and details of the business process, is not present within the BP-MaaS framework.

We observed the roles of an Audit Expert, and an IT Expert involved in organizing an audit with process mining. This observation has led us to a proposal of an extension for frameworks for audit with process mining.

3 Participatory Workshop of Three Business Roles for Frameworks for Audit with Process Mining

The practice shows that the auditors see the audited process abstractly, see only important principles. The auditors often use different terminology than the terminology of business process experts. Audit statements almost always need refinement to the process activities existing in a business process and recorded in logs.

However, the logs usually record activities of many business processes. Moreover, the names of activities in the logs may deviate from the names used by business experts (for example, they may be abbreviated). Sometimes, one business process is recorded in different logs. So, the logs need to be prepared and filtered for the audited business process.

The research question of this work is the following:

What steps should be included into the frameworks for audit with process mining to relate the audit statements formulated by Audit Experts, the business process known by Business Experts, and the logged process activities available for IT Experts, and enable audit with process mining?

We have found in the literature a recommendation that "A participatory modeling workshop is appropriate for the situations where the facilitated

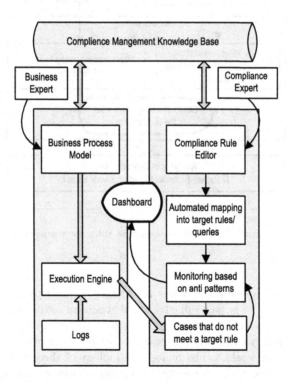

Fig. 1. BP-MaaS framework for run-time compliance checking [3].

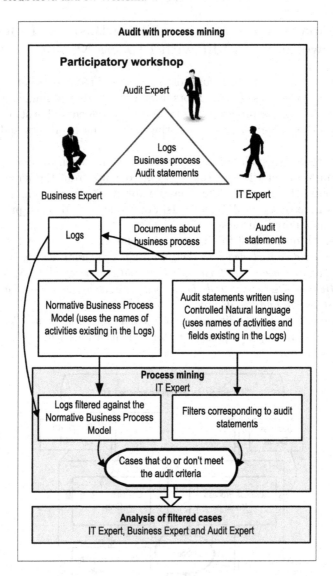

Fig. 2. Participatory workshop of three business roles for frameworks for audit with process mining.

modeling with a group of stakeholders is crucial for the implementation of new business technology. It is particularly useful when an agreement and solution can be completely covered if all stakeholders participate in discussion" [19].

We have proposed to extend the frameworks for audit with process mining with a participatory workshop to relate terminology of three groups of experts. Figure 2 shows our extension for audit with process mining with a participatory workshop.

The expected results of the workshop are

- A set of logs recording the process under the audit fund by the IT Expert;
- A Normative Business Process Model of the process under the audit, as it is seen by the Business Expert. The business process should use names of activities and fields existing in the Logs.
- A set of Audit Statements formulated by the Audit Expert and rewritten in a Controlled Natural Language, so that the statements use names of activities and fields existing in the Logs.

Achievement of these expected results demands iterative interaction of three experts.

3.1 Evaluation of the Proposed Extension

We have conducted two case studies in different business domains. Both cases are representative. A Grant Application Process is used in municipalities (and other fund distribution service providers). A Process of Handling of Invoices is familiar to any organization.

The case studies have been conducted in order to

- Identify the types of experts available for audit.
- Identify the need of a participatory workshop.
- Organize a participatory workshop to construct the normative process and formulate the audit statements in a Controlled Natural Language and enable audit with process mining.
- Evaluate how many audit statements can be prepared for audit with process mining.
- Fulfil audit with process mining.
- Analyse the results of participatory workshop for audit automation.

The case studies schold validate our hypothesis that

- the audit criteria formulated by Audit Experts need refinement allowing one to relate them to the process activities;
- the event logs often do not contain the names of activities used by Business Experts for process description;
- audit with process mining needs a participatory workshop combining an IT Expert, a Business Expert and an Audit Expert. The workshop should create a model of the Normative Business Process with the names of activities used in the log;
- the participants of a participatory workshop are able to reformulate the Audit statements in a Controlled Natural Language that uses the names of activities from the Normative Business Process, and phrases indicating ordering of activities, resources and other concerns used in compliance patterns.

The validation of the results of a participatory workshop can be measured as a the number of audit statements formulated after the proposed steps and checked with process mining techniques.

4   Audit of a Grant Application Process

4.1   Initial Description of a Grant Application Process

The process description found in documentation was rather informal. This is the process description:

In the process of grant applications, citizens or local institutions apply for a monetary allowance provided by the city. This is called a grant, and can be used to organize an (yearly or one-time) activity that contributes to the communal goals that the city has defined. Grants can be awarded for several small-scale goals, such as sporting events and local festivals, but also large grants for welfare support of special-interest groups are issued.

A grant application should be sent within the deadline. After that it is examined, additional information may be requested. All steps of the application and examination should be done in predefined time slots. After all the examinations, a grant can be awarded or the application can be rejected.

4.2   Initial Log

An IT Expert of the municipality took the initiative to organize the participatory workshop. He started with obtaining the process log.

To obtain the log, an IT Expert exported the log of the municipality, translated metadata, anonymized data and imported the log into the process mining application.

The log was then filtered for year of grant 2014, as this was fully contained in the exported time period of 2011–2015.

The csv-file (comma-separated values) of the log was loaded as a spreadsheet. There were found 132 unique events (activities) that are part of the grant application process. The log contains the following fields: *(1) Case Number, (2) Case Description, (3) Year of Grant, (4) Amount requested, (5) Amount granted, (6) Grant Regime, (7) Grant Type, (8) Date of payment, (9) Activity name, (10) Resource name (anonymized), (11) Activity date (time).*

The deviation of the informal process description from the log structure is already recognized. For example, it is not clear what "Grant Type" and "Grant Regime" mean. The process description does not contain names of process activities.

4.3   Normative Process as a Result of a Participatory Workshop

A participatory workshop was organized, a Business Expert and an audit Expert were invited. The first purpose of the workshop was an agreement on a normative process, containing the activities found in the log.

First, the experts agreed on the grant application process shown in Fig. 3. It contains 11 activities and the end-state of grant allocation.

However, during the workshop, the Business and IT Experts identified that each decision point of the normative process shown in Fig. 3 has in real log more

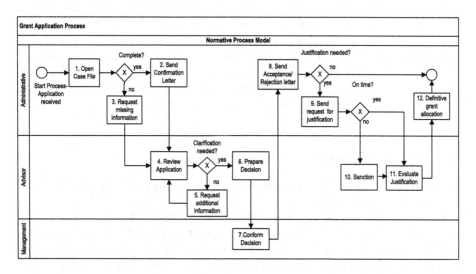

Fig. 3. Initial normative process [16].

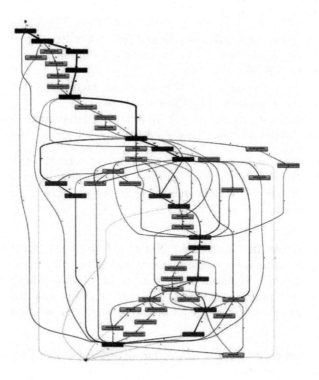

Fig. 4. Corrected grant application process [16].

outcomes. A grant may be approved, rejected, partially approved, approved with a sanction etc. When the real normative outcomes were listed, the normative process recoded in the log was filtered with the help of the Disco tool. It contains 56 activities (see Fig. 4). In the Disco tool, the colour intensity of the activity corresponds to the frequency of its use in cases (process instances). So, the grey activities are used in a smaller number of cases than the dark activities. The names of activities and the frequencies of their use were zoomed in and the list of real activities was corrected.

4.4 Control Objectives and Audit Statements

After agreement on the business process in terms of logged events, the experts moved to audit statements.

We have observed, that an Audit Expert begins his work with control objectives. A control objective is a generic statement that is applicable on the entire domain of a law or regulation. Among such objectives are respecting the deadlines, classification of cases, prioritizing of particular properties of a process case.

In order to support process mining, any control objective should be formulated in terms of the audited business process. The first versions of 52 audit statements found in documents were also rather informal. We present examples of the initial audit statements.

- $ST1$: Every grant application is required to be submitted on time.
- $ST13$: The activities that will be executed if the grant is approved must be described in a SMART manner.
- $ST14$: During the grant approval process, the financial review and content review cannot be performed by the same employee.
- $ST25$: If the grant amount that is approved is larger than 50.000 EUR, a semi-annual progress report is required by July, 1st at the latest.

Analyzing these audit criteria, one can think of activities that can be presented in the log, like submission, approval, review, progress report. However, one can never be sure, if these names of activities are present in the business process and the log.

Audit Statements in Controlled Natural Language (CNL). After the agreement on the normative business process expressed using the names of activities found in the log and showing the ordering of activities, the 52 audit statements were revised and reformulated to be used in the process mining tool. We present examples of audit statements. All statements can be found in [24].

- Example 1.
  $ST1$ (informal): Every grant application is required to be submitted on time. got the new formulation:
  $ST1(CNL)$: For every case where the grant regime equals "average" or "large", the timestamp of activity "proposal received" must be earlier than 31-10-2013.

– Example 2.

ST7 (informal): If a request to supply missing information has been sent to the applicant, the missing information need to be provided by the applicant within 10 working days.

ST7 (CNL): For every case if the activity "DI datum request missing information" is executed, the time between this activity and the activity "Receipt of missing information" must be <14 days (the weekends have been added).

– Example 3.

There is a statement corresponding the so-called four-eye principle.

ST48 (informal): During the grant application process, the financial review and content review cannot be performed by the same employee.

ST48 (CNL): For all cases where activities "review context" and "review financial part" must be reviewed by two different resources.

– Example 4. Some audit criteria specify the details of specific cases.

ST36 (informal): Grants >100.000 must submit an accountant statement.

ST36 (CNL): For all cases where the attribute "amount received" >100.000, activity "additional information received" must contain an accountant statement.

– Example 5.

Some audit criteria were used to correct the normative process. For example, it was found that two reviews (context and finance) were required to be performed in the real process.

S11: Every application is reviewed with respect to content by the grant expert. The review is documented.

S12: Every application is reviewed with respect to finance by the grant account manager. The review is documented.

There were initial audit statements containing events (activities) that were not present in the log.

– Example 6.

ST8: For every case where activity "Request additional information" is performed, a notification of suspension is included in the letter. All letters that can be sent to grant applicants are digitally available, and can be checked for inclusion of the suspension notice.

It was found that letters remain a human one-time activity and not reflected in the log.

There were audit statements that could be seen as principles for a group of other audit statements.

– Example 7.

"ST47: The activities that will be executed if the grant is approved, must be described in a SMART manner".

ST47 is a principle for a group of audit statements "that will be executed if the grant is approved" to be Specific, Measurable, Assignable, Realistic and Time-related.

4.5   Results of the Audit with Process Mining

In total, 27 statements out of 52 were made suitable for process mining. This shows the degree of audit support that can be achieved with process mining. In case of the design of logs of processes for automated audit, the degree of support can be increased.

Results of the audit with process mining are the following. 23 of 27 filters of all verifiable audit statements did have one or more non-compliant cases that were included in the event log. In the Disco-tool, the non-compliant cases can be visually identified by applying the appropriate filter for the audit statement.

For example, after application of the $ST7$ filter (about deadlines for receiving missing information), the process map, containing four cases, can be analyzed to find the reasons of non-compliance [24].

$ST7$ has four cases that are non-compliant. Is this good or bad? This depends on the risks associated with compliance to this statement. The analysis should be done by the Audit and Business Experts.

4.6   Results of the Case Study on Grand Application Process

The audit of the Grant Application Process has shown that a participatory workshop is the key step to the success of frameworks for audit with process mining.

In the participatory workshop, the business model described by business experts was corrected by confronting with the activities recorded in the log. Audit statements were rewritten using the names of activities in the log, and the norms used in the business process.

After such preparations, the process mining was used for compliance checks of the business process to the audit statements.

5   Audit of a Process of Handling Invoices

The second case study was conducted in a financial department, because the processes in this domain are a subject to law regulations and have guidance proscribed by the national professional accountants organizations, like, for example, [13]. The question was if the identified need for a participatory workshop depends on the domain of audit.

5.1   Initial Description of a Process of Handling Invoices and Process Logs

Municipality uses services and purchases goods. The service and goods providers send invoices as requests for payment for certain goods or services. The handling of invoices is a process under the study. This process concerns all invoices that are sent by external parties to the city of Eindhoven, as a request for payment

Nr	Name	Description	Role	Activity in log
1.	Scan invoice	Incoming invoice (by mail) is scanned as part of a batch of invoices	Department Invoices	None (Kofax system)
2.	Check / complete scanned invoice	The text on the invoice is automatically recognized (OCR) and translated to specific fields: date on the invoice, invoice no., bank account number, commitment number and amount payable. The result of the OCR is visually checked against the digital scan (and completed / corrected)	Department Invoices	None (KTM system)
3.	Send invoice to DMS	The invoice is exported from KTM and imported into the Document Management System (eDocs)	Department Invoices	Purchasing Invoices 2.0
4.	Complete invoice details	The fields required for further handling that were not imported are completed: invoice description, tax code and amount, department to authorise, number of supplier (looked up in Decade)	Financial data entry	Purchasing Invoices 2.0
5.	Invoice at block manager	The invoice is sent to the block manager for re-routing to the department	Financial data entry	1.Invoice at block manager
6.	Re-route to department	The block manager re-routes the invoice to the department for authorization	Block manager	2.Receive and reroute
7.	Encode invoice	The invoice is re-routed to the right resource for the performance check, to verify that the goods that are billed are delivered.	Department inbox	3.Encode invoice
X	Correctly Booked?	If the department thinks the invoice is incorrectly put in their inbox, it is rerouted back to the block manager.		
8.	Performance check	The performance check is executed by sending an 'Ok' and a comment in the eDocs system. This step is not enforced and sometimes skipped.	Checker	4.Performance check
9	Encode invoice	The booking details (cost centre and booking combination) are entered.	Department inbox	3. Encode invoice
10.	Check booking details	The invoice is sent to a resource that checks the booking details. This step can be skipped	Checker	5. Booking entry check
11.	Approval	The invoice is approved by the budget administrator (in case of a commitment already exists in Decade) or the budget manager. Approval is done for each invoice line.	Budget admin / budget mgr.	6. Approve invoice
12	Authorize payment / process invoice	The complete invoice and payment details are checked and payment is authorised. After authorisation, the payment is automatically processed by Decade.	Financial advisor	Process invoice

Fig. 5. Initial description of the business process of handling invoices [16].

after a certain good or service is provided for the city. Approximately 800.000 invoices are received and processed on a yearly basis, for a total amount of EUR 500 million.

We have found the following sources with some elements of the process model: (a) a process breakdown in a table of statements that is used by the internal auditors; (b) a user process instruction for specific roles.

We have collected the initial information about process activities, their relation to business roles and logs in a table (see Fig. 6) to present it during the participatory workshop. Figure 6 shows the absence of a well-described business process model of the audited process.

Figure 6 also shows that a number of IT applications is involved in the process. The column Activity in Log displays the application that is used for the activity, and contains log information that is needed for the process audit (Kofax system, KTM system, Invoice 2.0).

5.2   Normative Process

One result of the participatory workshop was a Normative Process expressed in names of activities recorded in the process logs. The process is shown in Fig. 6.

5.3   Control Objectives, Audit Statements and Logs

Control objectives come from different sources. The general procedures concerning applications to government institutions states that all requests that are made to the government are legally required to be decided within 60 days of receiving the invoices (Fig. 5).

To promote a speedy payment by the city, the council has stipulated that all invoices should be paid within 30 days (but this is not legally binding and no rights can be obtained).

In the participatory workshop, 55 audit statements have been found. (The complete list is in [16,24]). Following our framework extension, the statements were rewritten for compliance checks using a Controlled Natural Language.

We faced with the fact that not all 55 statements were unambiguous. For instance, statement *ST5.1* is ambiguous:

ST5.1. Imported invoices are re-routed to employees that can select the department for further processing of the invoice after the necessary information is added.

Our sources contained no further information that could be used to assert which data is considered necessary.

The participatory workshop has shown that no log of the *Purchasing Invoices Process* is available. The Purchasing Invoices Process workflow is implemented in the OpenText eDocs Document Management System, which is used by all departments. In addition to this system, the scanning and processing of received invoices was done in a KTM (Kofax Transformation Module) application. Finally, the actual payment order to the bank is processed by the financial system. Logging of this system was available for auditing, but was too complex to integrate in the audit. To obtain the event log of the invoices workflow, IBM Cognos BI was used to select and export the data from the eDocs Document

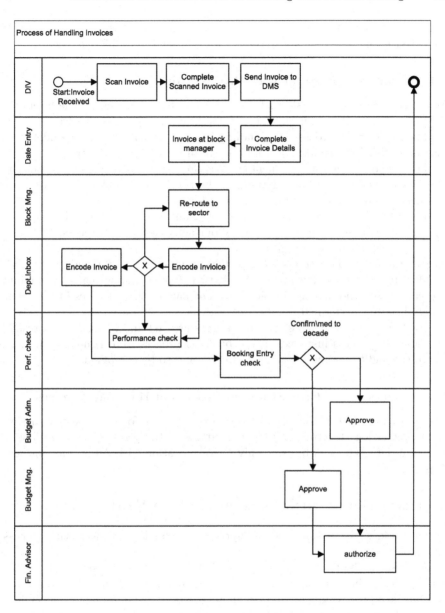

Fig. 6. Normative business process of handling invoices.

Management System. For this case, a selection is made based on the time stamps of case activities in eDocs with date values between 01-01-2015 and 31-12-2015

Even in the found log, not all audit criteria could be transformed into a filter of a process mining tool, because the log did not contain necessary information.

The first two activities of the process (scanning and importing) are not part of the activities in the event log as these are performed in a different system.

5.4   Results of the Audit with Process Mining

As a result, we could transform 11 out of 55 audit statements to the filters for the process mining and finding the compliant and non-compliant cases.

The audit of the process for Handling Invoices has shown the dependency of the audit with Process Mining from the carefully designed log structure.

The 10 from 55 audit statements in this process are related to roles, but the available logs do not contain information about roles. Other 18 audit statements also need the information that is absent in logs.

The 19 of 55 audit statements were not transformed into filters because the logs did not contain necessary records about activities in the process.

One of the 11 audit statements

ST3.1: The event log contains all steps that are described in the audit document.

identified the log deficiency. The first two steps of the normative (scanning and completing the scanned invoices) are not part of the activities in the event log as these are performed in different systems.

For ten audit statements, the filters were created and applied. As a result, one or more process instances of the business process were non-compliant. In one of the audit statements, all cases were found to be compliant.

5.5   Results of the Case Study on Process of Handling Invoices

The participatory workshop has shown a front of work for IT Experts in design of the better log structure and the procedures of the proceedings of feeling of logs with data. This can be done only in collaboration with Audit and Business Experts.

6   Discussion, Conclusions and Future Work

In this work, we have evaluated the upcoming technology of audit with process mining.

Analysis of the literature has shown that the existing frameworks for audit with process mining assume existence of business experts with the knowledge of a business process model, and compliance experts, who are able to formulate audit statements applicable for process mining tools.

Conduction case studies in different domains of municipality has shown that companies more likely have IT Experts, Audit Experts and Business Experts. The success of application of process mining for audit depends on agreement on terminology achieved by these three groups of experts. This agreement can be achieved in a participatory workshop.

Our proposal is to include such a participatory workshop in any practical audit framework with process mining in order to manage the expectations of businesses, that plan to apply process mining for audit.

We have applied the proposed participatory workshop in a framework framework for Audit with Process Mining in two case studies in different business domains. The participants of workshops were an IT Expert, an Audit Expert and a Business Expert. Both workshops succeeded to design the normative business processes and audit statements that can be used for compliance checks on logs.

The Table 1 presents the most important metrics of both case studies.

Table 1. Metrics of two case studies of auditing with process mining.

Metric	Grant application	Handling invoices
Audit period/scope	Grant year 2014 start in 2013, finish in 2015	Invoices received in 2015 (Jan–Dec)
No. of cases	780	41714
Mean activity/case	16	17
Mean case duration	19,1 month	17,5 day
No. of unique process activities	132	40
Documents for audit analysis	9	8
No. of audit statements	52	55
No. of tool filters	27	11
Non-compliancy in audit report	23 from 27 filters	10 from 11 filters

Both processes has a large amount process instances (cases), with relatively long duration respectively, Respectively, 780 process instances with the mean duration of 19,1 month and 41714 process instances with the mean duration 17,5 day. Each process instance uses only 16 (17) activities from 132 (40) unique activities.

It is interesting, that the number of audit statements is almost the same 52 (55), however, the transformation of audit statements to tool filters is different 27 (11). These numbers indicate the level of readiness of the audit experts for auditing with Process Mining, because the availability of filters means automatic search of compliant and non-compliment process instances.

Both case studies have evidenced that the direct application of process mining for audit cannot be made by the business without intermediate steps of designing the normative business processes and audit statements applicable for process mining on the process logs.

In our first case study, the Grant Application process, the business process model provided by business experts was corrected by extra outputs of decisions. The correction came from the log analysis.

In the second case study, the process of Handling Invoices, the business process model was created from a table of partial descriptions of process steps.

Both of our case studies have evidenced that such a business role as *Compliance Expert* does not exist and the initial audit statements made by *Audit Experts* should be rewritten for process mining by an *IT expert* in collaboration with an *Audit Expert* and a *Business Expert*.

Both case studies have demonstrated usefulness of our proposal to include a participatory workshop into audit frameworks for audit with process mining. They have also shown the types of artifacts that are created by the participatory workshop: a Normative Business Process Model using the activities mentioned in the log and a set of Audit Statements formulated in a Controlled Natural Language. A Controlled Natural Language uses the activities mentioned in the log and the compliance patterns that can be checked in the log by process mining tools.

Both workshops of the case studies have identified the importance of careful design of the log structure. If the log contains the needed in formation, the effectiveness of Process Mining for auditing can be increased. However, the audit will, probably, newer be automated completely. The reasons for that is changeability of business processes and adhocrasy of services meaning that some deviation of normative processes are allowed and sometimes even stimulated if it satisfies the service users. Nevertheless, there are always such indicators of process problems as too long processes, often cancellations of processes, unidirected streams of resources etc., that can and should be audited automatically.

The construct validity of our case studies is guaranteed by the many sources of information used for conduction of them (triangulation). Indeed, any business model and statement was inspected by three different specialists using different documents.

The conduct validity of our case studies can be checked by everyone as we have presented the steps of the proposed framework and results for research reproduction, as it is recommended in literature on case studies [25]. All details about case studies can be found in [24]. The logs can be provided on request.

Although we used the Disco tool for process mining, our extension is tool independent and can be applied for the frameworks that work with different process mining tools.

As future work, we invite using our extension for audit frameworks with process mining. This may result in a reusable collection of normative business processes and audit statements for specific domains of audit application.

The results of this study can be also analysed from the perspective of the university education of business students. It seems that they will be very successful if they study log structures, transaction structures and learn how to apply linear temporal logic in form of a Controlled Natural language needed for formulating audit statements that can be validated on logs and transaction structures. The best way to introduce the knowledge about logs and transactional structures is a participatory workshop in their courses, may be even with the students studying software engineering. Practicing in logical formulating of audit criteria by business students in a group with software engineering students may produce new generation of auditors using process mining for audit in practice of business organizations. However, this idea demands further investigation.

References

1. Accorsi, R., Stocker, T.: On the exploitation of process mining for security audits: the conformance checking case. In: Proceedings of the 27th Annual ACM Symposium on Applied Computing, pp. 1709–1716. ACM (2012)
2. Awad, A., Weidlich, M., Weske, M.: Specification, verification and explanation of violation for data aware compliance rules. In: Baresi, L., Chi, C.-H., Suzuki, J. (eds.) ICSOC/ServiceWave -2009. LNCS, vol. 5900, pp. 500–515. Springer, Heidelberg (2009). https://doi.org/10.1007/978-3-642-10383-4_37
3. Barnawi, A., Awad, A., Elgammal, A., Elshawi, R., Almalaise, A., Sakr, S.: An anti-pattern-based runtime business process compliance monitoring framework. Framework 7(2), 551–572 (2016)
4. Becker, J., Delfmann, P., Dietrich, H.A., Steinhorst, M., Eggert, M.: Business process compliance checking-applying and evaluating a generic pattern matching approach for conceptual models in the financial sector. Inf. Syst. Front. 18(2), 359–405 (2016)
5. Business Process Analysis in R (2017). http://bupar.net/
6. Flexicon DISCO (2016). http://fluxicon.com/disco/
7. George, S.: Simple steps internal audit can take toward real-time assurance, 15 June 2018. https://www.gartner.com/smarterwithgartner/simple-steps-internal-audit-can-take-toward-real-time-assurance/
8. Jans, M., Alles, M., Vasarhelyi, M.: The case for process mining in auditing: sources of value added and areas of application. Int. J. Account. Inf. Syst. 14(1), 1–20 (2013)
9. Jans, M., Alles, M.G., Vasarhelyi, M.A.: A field study on the use of process mining of event logs as an analytical procedure in auditing. Account. Rev. 89(5), 1751–1773 (2014)
10. Karapetrovic, S., Willborn, W.: Generic audit of management systems: fundamentals. Manag. Audit. J. 15(6), 279–294 (2000)
11. Ly, L.T., Maggi, F.M., Montali, M., Rinderle-Ma, S., van der Aalst, W.M.: A framework for the systematic comparison and evaluation of compliance monitoring approaches. In: 2013 17th IEEE International Enterprise Distributed Object Computing Conference (EDOC), pp. 7–16. IEEE (2013)
12. Mintzberg, H., McHugh, A.: Strategy formation in an adhocracy. Adm. Sci. Q. 30(2), 160–197 (1985)
13. Professional Accountants in Europe (2017). http://paie.nl
14. Process Mining Workbench ProM (2016). http://www.promtools.org
15. Roubtsova, E.E.: Property driven mining in workflow logs. In: Kłopotek, M.A., Wierzchoń, S.T., Trojanowski, K. (eds.) Intelligent Information Processing and Web Mining, vol. 31, pp. 471–475. Springer, Heidelberg (2005). https://doi.org/10.1007/3-540-32392-9_55
16. Roubtsova, E.E., Wiersma, N.: A practical extension of frameworks for auditing with process mining. In: Proceedings of the 13th International Conference on Evaluation of Novel Approaches to Software Engineering, ENASE 2018, Funchal, Madeira, Portugal, March 23–24, pp. 406–415 (2018)

17. Russell, J.: Process auditing and techniques. Qual. Prog. **39**(6), 71–74 (2006)
18. Sadiq, S., Governatori, G., Namiri, K.: Modeling control objectives for business process compliance. In: Alonso, G., Dadam, P., Rosemann, M. (eds.) BPM 2007. LNCS, vol. 4714, pp. 149–164. Springer, Heidelberg (2007). https://doi.org/10. 1007/978-3-540-75183-0_12
19. Sandkuhl, K., Stirna, J., Persson, A., Wißotzki, M.: Enterprise Modeling: Tackling Business Challenges with the 4EM Method, vol. 309. Springer, Heidelberg (2014). https://doi.org/10.1007/978-3-662-43725-4
20. Spreeuwenberg, S., Healy, K.A.: SBVR's approach to controlled natural language. In: Fuchs, N.E. (ed.) CNL 2009. LNCS (LNAI), vol. 5972, pp. 155–169. Springer, Heidelberg (2010). https://doi.org/10.1007/978-3-642-14418-9_10
21. van der Aalst, W.M.: Process Mining - Discovery, Conformance and Enhancement of Business Processes. Springer, Heidelberg (2011). https://doi.org/10.1007/978-3-642-19345-3
22. van der Aalst, W.M.: Process mining: overview and opportunities. ACM Trans. Manag. Inf. Syst. (TMIS) **3**(2), 7 (2012)
23. van der Aalst, W.M., van Hee, K.M., van der Werf, J.M., Verdonk, M.: Auditing 2.0: using process mining to support tomorrow's auditor. Computer **43**(3), 90–93 (2010)
24. Wiersma, N.: The use of process mining in business process auditing. Open University of the Netherlands (2017). http://hdl.handle.net/1820/7702
25. Yin, R.: Case study research: design and methods. Beverly Hills (1994)

Architecting Service-Dominant Digital Products

Alfred Zimmermann[1(✉)], Rainer Schmidt[2], Kurt Sandkuhl[3],
Dierk Jugel[1,3], Justus Bogner[1,4], and Michael Möhring[2]

[1] Herman Hollerith Center, Reutlingen University, Danziger Str. 6,
71034 Böblingen, Germany
{alfred.zimmermann,dierk.jugel,justus.bogner}
@reutlingen-university.de
[2] Munich University of Applied Sciences, Lothstrasse 64,
80335 Munich, Germany
{rainer.schmidt,michael.moehring}@hm.edu
[3] University of Rostock, Albert Einstein Str. 22, 18059 Rostock, Germany
kurt.sandkuhl@uni-rostock.de
[4] DXC Technology, Herrenberger Str. 140, 71034 Böblingen, Germany

Abstract. Presently, many companies are transforming their strategy and product base, as well as their culture, processes and information systems to become more digital or to approach for a digital leadership. In the last years new business opportunities appeared using the potential of the Internet and related digital technologies, like Internet of Things, services computing, cloud computing, edge and fog computing, social networks, big data with analytics, mobile systems, collaboration networks, and cyber physical systems. Digitization fosters the development of IT environments with many rather small and distributed structures, like the Internet of Things, Microservices, or other micro-granular elements. This has a strong impact for architecting digital services and products. The change from a closed-world modeling perspective to more flexible open-world composition and evolution of micro-granular system architectures defines the moving context for adaptable systems. We are focusing on a continuous bottom-up integration of micro-granular architectures for a huge amount of dynamically growing systems and services, as part of a new digital enterprise architecture for service-dominant digital products.

Keywords: Digital transformation · Service-dominant logic ·
Value-oriented digital products · Digital enterprise architecture ·
Decision management

1 Introduction

Influenced by the digital transformation many enterprises are presently transforming their strategy, culture, processes, and their information systems to become more digital. Data, information and knowledge are fundamental core concepts of our everyday activities and are driving the digital transformation of today's global society [7, 50].

© Springer Nature Switzerland AG 2019
E. Damiani et al. (Eds.): ENASE 2018, CCIS 1023, pp. 45–67, 2019.
https://doi.org/10.1007/978-3-030-22559-9_3

New services and smart connected products [31] expand physical components by adding information and connectivity services using the Internet.

Digitization [35] defines the process of digital transformation, which is promoted by important technological megatrends: Internet of Things, cloud, edge and fog computing, services computing, big data, mobile systems, and social networks. The disruptive change of current business interacts with all information systems that are important business enablers for the digital transformation. Digitized services and products amplify the basic value and capabilities, which offer exponentially expanding opportunities. Digitization enables human beings and autonomous objects to collaborate beyond their local context using digital technologies. The exchange of information enables better decisions of humans, as well as of intelligent objects. Furthermore, social networks, smart devices, and intelligent cars are part of a wave of digital economy with digital products, services, and processes, which call for an information-driven vision [54, 57].

The digital transformation deeply disrupts existing enterprises and economies. Digitization fosters the development of IT systems with many, globally available and diverse rather small and distributed structures, like Internet of Things or mobile systems. Since years a lot of new business opportunities appeared using the potential of the Internet and related digital technologies, like Internet of Things, services computing, cloud computing, big data with analytics, mobile systems, collaboration networks, and cyber physical systems. This has a strong impact for architecting digital services and products integrating high distributed systems and services.

Unfortunately, the current state of art in research and practice of enterprise architecture lacks an integral understanding of software evolution [8, 58], when integrating a huge amount of micro-granular systems and services, like Microservices and Internet of Things, in the context of digital transformation and evolution of architectures. Our goal is to extend previous quite static approaches of enterprise architecture to fit for flexible and adaptive digitization of new products and services. This goal shall be achieved by introducing suitable mechanisms for collaborative architectural engineering and by positioning open micro-granular architectures.

Our current extension of our ENASE 2018 paper [58] focuses in this paper on a fundamental research question:

How can a value-oriented digital enterprise architecture for service-dominant digital products and services be modeled to support the open-world integration and management for a huge amount of dynamically growing micro-granular digital structures, like Internet of Things and Microservices?

We will proceed as follows. First, we will set the fundamental architectural context for digital transformation. Then we present our digital modeling approach for systematically defining value-oriented service-dominant digital products in order to enable a mapping of digital business models to digital product compositions and digital architectures. Based on the target of digital architectures we are focusing on architecting micro-granular systems and services with Internet of Things and Microservices, while the next section gives the larger integration context with an original and high scalable digital enterprise architecture. In the following section we are presenting our architectural composition model for bottom-up integrating micro-granular digital products and services into a digital enterprise architecture. Then we provide insides to our methods and mechanisms for architectural decision management for multi-perspective digital architectures. Based on these steps, we sketch fundamental aspects of an architectural evolution path for digital systems and services. Finally, we conclude in the last section our research findings and mentioning our future work.

2 Digital Transformation

The digital transformation is the current dominant type of business transformation having IT both as a technology enabler and as a strategic driver. Digitized services and associated products [50], are software-intensive [35] and therefore malleable and usually service-oriented [8]. Digital products are able to increase their capabilities via accessing cloud-services and change their current behavior [53].

The service-dominant S-D logic [41–43] is a service-centered approach and to some extend opposite to the traditional goods-centered paradigm for large parts of the traditional business. The principal idea is that all economic exchanges can be defined as service-to-service exchanges considering also associated real or digital products. The origin of the service-dominant logic relies on ten fundamental axioms [42] for defining service businesses, including digital services and products. The origin of service-dominant logic was slightly extended through modifications and additional premises [43] to a body of five axioms and eleven foundational premises.

New ways of interaction with the customer are enabled [19] by combining a product consisting of hardware and software with cloud-provided services. Current research suggests that different customers will use such devices for different use cases enabling new ways of triggering and interaction with business processes. An example is Amazon Alexa [46] that consists of a physical device with microphone and speaker e.g. Echo Dot, and services, called "Alexa skills". The set of Alexa skills is dynamic and can be tailored to the customer's requirements during run-time. The lifecycle of digitized products is extended by the acquisition and decommissioning of services.

Digitized products and services [35] support the co-creation of value together with the customer and other stakeholders in different ways. First, there is a permanent feedback to the provider of the product. The internet connection of the digitized product allows to collect permanently data on the usage of the product by the customer. Second, the data provided by a large number of digitized products are able to provide new insights, which are not possible with data from a single device. Current research argues that digital products and services are offering disruptive opportunities [7, 50] for new business solutions, having new smart connected functionalities.

In the beginning, digitization was considered a primarily technical term [48]. Thus, a number of technologies is often associated with digitization [50]: cloud computing, big data often combined with advanced analytics [44], social software, and the Internet of Things [1, 29]. New technologies are associated with digitalization such as deep learning [36]. They allow computing to be applied to activities that were considered as exclusive to human beings. Therefore, the present emphasis on digitization become an important area of research. Our thesis is, that digitization embraces both a product and a value-creation [35] perspective.

Classical industrial products are static [7]. You can only change them to a limited extent, if at all. On the contrary, digitized products are dynamic. They contain both hardware, software and (cloud-)services. They can be upgraded via network connections. In addition, their functionality can be extended or adapted using external services. Therefore, the functionality of products is dynamic and can be adapted to changing requirements and hitherto unknown customer needs. In particular, it is possible to create digitized products and services step-by-step or provide temporarily unlockable functionalities. So, customers whose requirements are changing can add and modify service functionality without hardware modification.

Digitized products [35] are able to capture their own state and submit this information into linked contexts. This is the basis for the so called servitization of products. Not a physical product, but a service is sold to the customer. The service usage is measured and lays the foundation for usage-based billing models. The provider can remotely determine, whether the product is still functional and trigger, where appropriate, maintenance and repairs. Evaluation of status information and analysis of the history of use of the product can be predicted when a malfunction of the product is probable. A maintenance or replacement of the product is performed before predicted data of failure. The data collected also provide information for a repair on the spot, so that a high first-time solution rate can be achieved. At the same time, storage can be improved in this way of spare parts. By this means, preventive maintenance can be implemented. Unscheduled stoppages can this way be significantly reduced.

Digital products also enable network effects [49] that grow exponentially with the number of participating devices. An increase in the number of digitized products increases the incentive for providers of add-on services and complementary skills [7]. At the same time this increase the attractiveness for further digitized products. In summary, an exponential growth can be achieved. Therefore, significant first-mover advantages exist. Network effects emerge not only for the functionality but also for the analytical exploitation of data collected by the digitized products. These effects are called network intelligence [49]. By bringing together data from many devices and not only single devices, trends can be detected much earlier and more accurately. Further improvements can be achieved by linking data from different sources, also external one. In this way, it is possible to establish correlations that would not have been possible considering data from a single device. This effect increases with the number of devices.

The digitized products [35] become part of an information system, which accelerates the learning and knowledge processes across all products. The manufacturer can win genuine information about the use of the product. Important information for the development of new products can be obtained in this way. Therefore, a number of other beneficial effects can be achieved as network optimization, maintenance optimization, improved restore capabilities, and additional evidence against the consideration of individual systems.

Traditional products were created with a tayloristic view in mind, that emphasized the separation of production and consumer in order to enable centralized production and thus scaling effects. Now, the co-creation [42] approach of service-dominant logic [43] can be implemented because of a persisting continuous connectivity of digital products with the manufacturer. The consumer converts dynamically to be co-producer. Platforms are complementary to products, which cooperate via standardized interfaces.

3 Value-Oriented Digital Products

The business and technological impact of digitization [35] has multiple aspects, which directly affect digital architectures of service-dominant digital products. Unfortunately, our current modeling approach for designing proper digital service and product models suffers from having many uncontrolled diverse modeling approaches and structures, where value-orientation of integral composed services and systems is only partially fulfilled. High quality digital models should follow a clear value and service perspective. But today, we currently have no sound value relationship from digital strategies, to the resulting digital business modeling, and subsequently to a value-oriented enterprise architecture, which today often has seldom proper aligned service and product model representations. The core idea of the present contribution and current paper is to present and discuss a new introduced integral value-oriented model composition approach by linking digital strategies with digital business models for digital services and close aligned products by means of an extended multi-perspective digital enterprise architecture model.

Value is commonly associated with worth and aggregates potentially required categories like worth, importance, desirability and usefulness. The concept of value is important in designing adequate digital services with their associated digital products, and to align their digital business models with value-oriented enterprise architectures. From a financial perspective the value of the integrated resources and the price defines the main parts of the monetary worth.

A current conceptualization of value as a service-based view is offered by [41] and [16] considering a conceptual framework of service-dominant (S-D) logic [42, 43] and its service-ecosystem perspective. The distinction between the concepts of value-in-use and value-in-exchange dates back to the antiquity and continue to influence our today's value view. Since the work of Adam Smith and the development of economic science the value-in-exchange as a measure for price a person is willing to pay for a service or a product moved to the forefront. Smith recognized the value-in-use as the real value and value-in-exchange as the nominal value. The digital marketing discipline nowadays shifted to a nominal use of the value perspective [41] considering customer experience and customer satisfaction as important value-related concepts.

Characteristics of value modeling for a service ecosystem were elaborated by [41]. Value has important characteristics: value is phenomenological, co-created, multidimensional, and emergent. Value is phenomenological means that value is perceived experimentally and differently by various stakeholders in the varying context within a service ecosystem. Value is co-created though the integration and exchange of resources between multiple stakeholders and related organizations. Value is also multidimensional, which means that value is aggregated up of individual, social, technological and cultural components. Value results as emergent value from specific manifestations of relationships between resources and resource combinations. Therefore, the resulting real value cannot be determined ex-ante. Value propositions are value promises for a typical, but not exactly known customer at design time and should be realized later when using these digital services and associated products.

Through exploiting the base of service-dominant logic and by means of design research a focused set of four design principles for business-model-based management methods was elaborated in [4]. The first principle defines the proactive base for an ecosystem-oriented management by positioning the orchestration tasks for specific actors in a service ecosystem, defining an organization's role as focal orchestrator in the service ecosystem, and for sharing the risks, costs, and revenues among multiple actors. The second principle about a technology-based management defines responsibilities for using digital infrastructures, for decoupling informational assets from products and facilitate product exchange, and for driving value creation through digital channels. Principle three about mobilization-oriented management postulate the mobilization of operand resources, like knowledge and capabilities, which are the fundamental source of strategic benefit, and further uncovering and utilizing internal knowledge. The last principle about co-creation-oriented management demands for customer involvement, to reflect on co-creation through customer journey as dynamic interaction, and for recalibrating service bundles to optimize customer's experience.

Our current paper sketches our view of an integrated value perspective combined with a service perspective, as in Fig. 1. Today, we are experiencing a starting set of now not well consolidated digital strategy frameworks, like in [28] which are loosely associated with traditional strategy frameworks, as in [3].

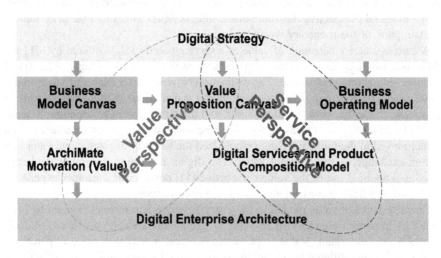

Fig. 1. Value perspective of service-dominant logic.

Our starting point is a model of the digital strategy, which provides direction and sets the base and a value-oriented framing for the digital business definition models, with the business model canvas [25], and the value proposition canvas [26]. Having the base models for a value-oriented digital business we map these base service and product models to a digital business operating model. An operating model [32] strategically defines the necessary level of business process integration and standardization for delivering services and products to customers. From the value perspective of the business model canvas [25] results suitable mappings to enterprise architecture value models [17] with ArchiMate [23]. Finally, we are setting the frame for the systematic definition of digital services and associated products by modeling digital services and product compositions following semantically related composite patterns [10].

The primary motivation of successful organizations is to provide value to one or mode stakeholders, typically considering value for clients at first. This includes the modeling of value creation, capturing, and value delivery by using discrete value producing tasks. Classical concepts of value chains and value networks are seminal for lean value streams and for applying the current fundamental TOGAF series guide on value streams [24]. Porter's value chain modeling focuses on an economic perspective while value networks primarily shows participants involved in creating value.

Value streams, as in [24], models an end-to-end value view of value-adding activities as value stream stages from the customer's or stakeholder's perspective. Therefore, value streams enable digital business models which are closer to the definition and not the implementation of organizational core activities. Value streams are defined as compositions of value stages from the value-perspective for the addressed stakeholders.

From using value stream models and mappings we can summarize important benefits. Value stream models are the base for decision making helping to envision and prioritize the impact from strategic plans, for managing the stakeholders' engagement, and supporting the deployment of new business solutions. Business capabilities enable value stages and value streams, which are focused to the viewpoint of customers. Value streams provide a framework for better requirement analysis, case management, and supports modeling of digital services. Finally, value streams are focused on how business value is achieved for specific stakeholders, particularly for customers.

4 Micro-granular Architectures

Digitalization promotes massively distributed systems, which are based on the development of IT systems with many rather small and distributed structures, like Internet of Things, mobile systems, cyber physical systems, etc. Additionally, we have to support digitalization by a dense and diverse amount of different service types, like microservices, REST services, etc. and put them in a close relationship with distributed systems, like Internet of Things. The change from a closed-world modeling perspective to more flexible open-world composition and evolution of system architectures defines the moving context for adaptable systems, which are essential to enable the digital transformation. This has a strong impact for architecting digital services and products. The implication of architecting micro-granular systems and services considering an open-world approach fundamentally changes modeling contexts, which are classical and well defined by quite static closed-world and all-times consistent and less complex models.

4.1   Internet of Things Architecture

The Internet of Things (IoT) [1, 22, 32] connects a large number of physical devices to each other using wireless data communication and interaction based on the Internet as a global communication environment. Additionally, we have to consider challenging aspects of the overall software and systems architecture to integrate base technologies and systems, like cyber-physical systems, social networks, big data with analytics, services, and cloud computing. Typical examples for the next wave of digitization [45] are smart enterprise networks, smart cars, smart industries, and smart portable devices. Objects from the real world are mapped into the virtual world. Furthermore, the important interaction with mobile systems, collaboration support systems, and service-based systems for big data as well as cloud environments is extended. Additionally, the Internet of Things is an important foundation of Industry 4.0 [34] and adaptable digital systems.

The Internet of Things [1, 15] is our typical use case for micro-granular systems, which are today not well covered by an enterprise architecture. The Internet of Things connects a large number of physical devices to each other using wireless data communication and interaction, based on the Internet as a global communication environment. Real world objects are mapped into the virtual world. The interaction with mobile systems, collaboration support systems, and systems and services for big data and cloud environments is extended. Furthermore, the Internet of Things is an important foundation of Industry 4.0 [34] and adaptable digital enterprise architectures [57].

The Internet of Things, supports smart products as well as their production enables enterprises to create customer-oriented products in a flexible manner. Devices, as well as human and software agents, interact and transmit data to perform specific tasks as parts of sophisticated business or technical processes [29]. The Internet of Things embraces not only a things-oriented vision [1] but also an Internet-oriented and a Semantic-oriented one. A cloud-centric vision for architectural thinking of a ubiquitous sensing environment is provided by [40].

A layered Reference Architecture for the Internet of Things is in [52] and Fig. 2, where layers can be implemented using suitable technologies.

The main question is, how the Internet of Things architecture fits in a context of a service-based enterprise computing environment? A service-oriented integration approach for the Internet of Things is referenced in [37]. The core issue is, how millions of devices can be flexibly connected to establish useful advanced collaborations within business processes. The service-oriented architecture abstracts the heterogeneity of embedded systems, their hardware devices, software, data formats and communication protocols. The typical setting includes a cloud-based server architecture, which enables interaction and supports remote data management and calculations. By these means, the Internet of Things integrates software and services into digitized value chains.

From the inherent connection of a magnitude of devices, which are crossing the Internet over firewalls and other obstacles, are resulting a set of generic requirements [11]. Because of so many and dynamically growing numbers of devices we need an architecture for scalability. Typically, we additionally need a high-availability approach in a 24×7 timeframe, with deployment and auto-switching across cooperating

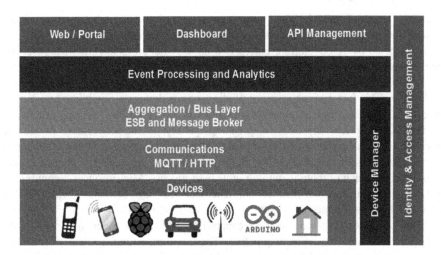

Fig. 2. Internet of things reference architecture [52].

datacenters in the case of disasters and high scalable processing demands. The Internet of Thing architecture has to support automatically managed updates and remotely managed devices. Typically, often connected devices collect and analyze personal or security relevant data. Therefore, it should be mandatory to support identity management, access control and security management on different levels: from the connected devices through the holistic controlled environment.

The contribution from [37] considers a role-specific development methodology and a development framework for the Internet of Things. The development framework specifies a set of modeling languages for a vocabulary language to be able to describe domain-specific features of an IoT-application, besides an architecture language for describing application-specific functionality and a deployment language for deployment features. Associated with programming language aspects are suitable automation techniques for code generation, and linking, to reduce the effort for developing and operating device-specific code.

The metamodel for Internet of Things applications from [29] specifies elements of an Internet of Things architectural reference model like IoT resources of type: sensor, actuator, storage, and user interface. Base functionalities of IoT resources are handled by components in a service-oriented way by using computational services. Further Internet of Thing resources and their associated physical devices are differentiated in the context of locations and regions.

4.2 Microservices Architecture

Microservices addresses our second fundamental use-case for micro-granular architectures, which are developed and operated in an open-world. The open-world approach fundamentally changes the rules of engineering and management by following a high distributed and globally metaphor for the new setting of a digital business operating model. This new bottom-up tailored digital operating model changes the perspective of a classical top-down oriented enterprise architecture.

A lot of software developing enterprises have switched to integrate Microservice architectures to handle the increase velocity [2, 5]. Therefore, applications built this way consist of several fine-grained services that are independently scalable and deployable. The fast-moving process of digitization demands flexibility to adapt to rapidly changing business requirements and newly emerging business opportunities.

The Microservices approach is spreading quickly. Defined by James Lewis and Martin Fowler, as presented in [5], it is a fine-grained, service-oriented architecture style combined with several DevOps elements. A single application is created from a set of services. Each of them is running in its own process. Microservices communicate using lightweight mechanisms. Often, Microservices are combined with NoSQL databases from on-premise and optional Cloud environments.

Microservices implement business capabilities and are independently deployable, using an automated deployment pipeline. The centralized management elements of these services are reduced to a minimum. Microservices are implemented using different programming languages. Different data storage technologies may be used. As opposed to big monolithic applications, a single Microservice tries to represent a unit of functionality that is as small and coherent as possible. This unit of functionality or business capability is often referred to as a bounded context, a term that originates from Domain-Driven Design (DDD) [5].

Microservices and Microservices Architectures (MSA), as in [2], is considered to be an important enabler for the digital enterprise and the digital transformation. The fundamental concept of architecture is defined as structure of components, their interrelationships, together with principles and guidelines for governing their design and evolution.

Both the architecture and the instantiation of these components define the architectural style as a more concrete combination of features in which architecture is expressed. Therefore, the Microservices Architecture is considered to be more an architectural style for aligning small and self-contained services with business activities. The conceptual representation of a Microservices solution delimits primarily independent and self-contained services to serve specific business functions or processes.

The Open Group's White Paper [2] sketches in Fig. 3 a Microservice Reference Architecture for the application example of a rainy-day grocer.

The problem space in [2] defines a holistic view for specific pain points, which are addressed by MSA, like decreasing the complexity of the development, operation, and management of services. A key obstacle today is that changes in a complex software produces long and complicated change cycles. Typically, the modularity of a system even built from Web Services tends to weaken over time. Therefore, Microservices promote to be both independent and self-contained. Scaling of a tightly-coupled service system requires scaling of the entire application.

Because instantiation of additional services and service instances is performed independently, Microservices Architectures could much better support scalability by providing restart and relocation of services. Further, Microservices should keep each service most independent and aligned with a single business process of a business function.

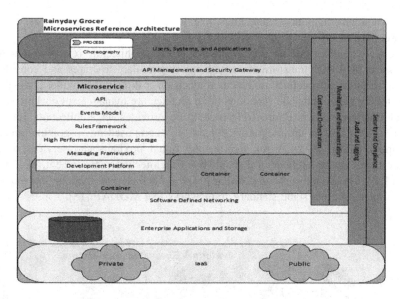

Fig. 3. Microservices reference architecture [2].

Microservices should be designed to be self-contained by integrating with specific needed platform and infrastructural elements. Microservices does not require a large pre-existing infrastructure. As exemplified by DevOps [20], Microservices support processes of Continuous Development (CD) in small environments and Continuous Integration (CI). Additionally, Microservices should also naturally support resiliency and scalability in both cloud and on-premise environments. Microservices need a strong DevOps culture [20] to handle the increased distribution level and deployment frequency. Moreover, while the single Microservice may be of reasonably low complexity, the overall complexity of the system has not been reduced at all. Microservices enable technological heterogeneity and thus reduce the possibility of lock-ins by outdated technology. Unfortunately, classical enterprise architecture approaches are not flexible enough for the kind of diversity and distribution present in a Microservice Architecture.

5 Digital Enterprise Architecture

Enterprise Architecture Management [15, 27], as today defined by several standards like [22] and [23] uses a quite large set of different views and perspectives for managing current IT. An effective architecture management approach for digital enterprises should additionally support the digitization of products and services [35] and be both holistic and easily adaptable [5]. Furthermore, a digital architecture sets the base for the digital transformation enabling new digital business models and technologies that are based on a large number of micro-structured digitization systems with their own micro-granular architectures like IoT [29, 52], mobile devices, or with Microservices [2, 20].

We are extending our service-oriented enterprise architecture reference model for the context of digital transformation with micro-granular structures and considering associated multi-perspective architectural decision-making [13] models, which are supported by viewpoints and functions of an architecture management cockpit. DEA - Digital Enterprise Architecture Reference Cube provides an architectural reference model [57] for bottom-up integrating dynamically composed micro-granular architectural models (Fig. 4). DEA for architecting digital products and services is more specific than existing architectural standards of architecture management, like in [22] and in [23]. The bottom-up composition of living architectural models fundamentally extends existing quite static standard frameworks like MODAF [18].

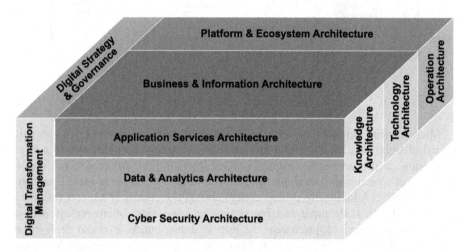

Fig. 4. Digital enterprise architecture reference cube.

DEA extends the research base in [53–58] and provides today in our current research ten integral architectural domains for a holistic architectural classification model, which is well aligned to embed also mirco-granular architectures for different digital services and products. DEA abstracts from a concrete business scenario or technologies, because it is applicable for concrete architectural instantiations to support digital transformations [7, 31, 56] independent of different domains. The Open Group Architecture Framework TOGAF [22] provides the basic blueprint and structure for extended service-oriented enterprise architecture domains. Metamodel extensions are additionally provided by considering and integrating ArchiMate Layer models from [23].

Metamodels and their architectural data are the core part of the enterprise architecture. Enterprise architecture metamodels [15] and [23] should enable decision making [57] as well as the strategic and IT/business alignment. Three quality perspectives are important for an adequate IT/business alignment and are differentiated as: (i) IT system qualities: performance, interoperability, availability, usability, accuracy, maintainability, and suitability; (ii) business qualities: flexibility, efficiency, effectiveness, integration and coordination, decision support, control and follow up, and organizational culture; and finally (iii) governance qualities: plan and organize, acquire and implement deliver and support, monitor and evaluate (e.g., [47]).

DEA extends by a holistic view the metamodel-based extraction and bottom-up integration for micro-granular viewpoints, models, standards, frameworks and tools of a digital enterprise architecture model. DEA frames these multiple elements of a digital architecture into integral configurations of an digital architecture by providing an ordered base of architectural artifacts for associated multi-perspective decision processes.

Architecture governance, as in [47], defines the base for well aligned management practices through specifying management activities: plan, define, enable, measure, and control. Digital governance should additionally set the frame for digital strategies, digital innovation management, and Design Thinking methodologies. The second aim of governance is to set rules for a value-oriented architectural compliance based on internal and external standards, as well as regulations and laws. Architecture governance for digital transformation changes some of the fundamental laws of traditional governance models to be able to manage and openly integrate a plenty of diverse micro-granular structures, like Internet of Things or Microservices.

6 Architectural Composition Model

Digital transformation [31, 48, 50] not only changes our personal lives but also has massive implications on the competitive landscape. To win in this new environment, established companies need to develop new digitized products and services quickly, interact across channels, analyze customer behavior in real-time, and leverage digital processes. Digitization can lower entry barriers for new players but causing long-understood boundaries between sectors to become more ambiguous and permeable. The nature of digital assets disaggregates value chains, creating openings for focused, fast-moving competitors.

Adaptability for architecting open micro-granular systems like Internet of Things or Microservices is mostly concerned with heterogeneity, distribution, and volatility. It is a huge challenge to continuously integrate numerous dynamically growing open architectural models and metamodels from different sources into a consistent digital architecture. To address this problem, we are currently formalizing small-decentralized mini-metamodels, models, and data of architectural microstructures, like Microservices and IoT into DEA-Mini-Models (Digital Enterprise Architecture Mini Model).

In general, such DEA-Mini-Models [5] consists of partial DEA-Data, partial DEA-Models, and partial EA-Metamodel. Microservices are associated with DEA-Mini-Models and/or objects from the Internet of Things [56]. Our model structures (Fig. 5) are extensions of the Meta Object Facility (MOF) standard [21] of the Object Management Group (OMG).

Basically, we have extended the base model layer M1 to be able to host additionally metadata. Additionally, we have associated the original metamodel from layer M2 with our architectural ontology with integration rules. In this way we provide a close associated semantic-oriented representation of the metamodel to be able to support

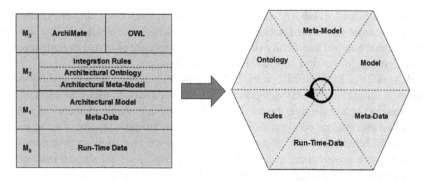

Fig. 5. Structure of EA-mini-descriptions [57].

automatic inferences for detecting model similarities, like model matches and model mappings during runtime.

Regarding the structure of EA-Mini-Descriptions, the highest layer M3 [5] represents an abstract language concepts used in the lower M2 layer. It can be also seen as the meta-metamodel layer. The following layer M2 is the metamodel integration layer. The layer defines the language entities for M1 (e.g. models from UML or ArchiMate [23]). The models can be seen as a structured representation of the lowest layer M0 [21].

Volatile technologies, requirements, and markets typically drive the evolution of business and IT services. Adaptation is a key success factor for the survival of digital enterprise architectures [56], platforms, and application environments. Weil and Woerner introduces in [48] the idea of digital *ecosystems* that can be linked with main strategic drivers for system development and system evolution. Reacting rapidly to new technology and market contexts improves the fitness of such adaptive ecosystems.

During the integration of DEA-Mini-Models as micro-granular architectural cells (Fig. 6) for each relevant object, e.g., Internet of Things object or Microservice, the step-wise composed time-stamp dependent architectural metamodel becomes adaptable [5] and [53–55]. Furthermore, it can be mostly be automatically synthesized by respecting the integration context from a growing number of previous similar integrations [56].

Being a bit closer to the architecture and design of systems, Trojer et al. coined in [39] the *Living Models* paradigm that is concerned with the model based creation and management of dynamically evolving systems. Adaptive Object-Modelling and its patterns and usage provide useful techniques to react to changing user requirements, even during the runtime of a system. Moreover, we have to consider model conflict resolution approaches to support automated documentation of digital architectures and to summarize integration foundations for federated architectural model management.

In case of new integration patterns, we have to consider additional manual support. Currently, the challenge of our research is to federate these DEA-Mini-Models to an integral and dynamically growing DEA model and information base by promoting a mixed automatic as well as collaborative decision process, introduced and developed by Jugel in [13] and [14], as in the following Section.

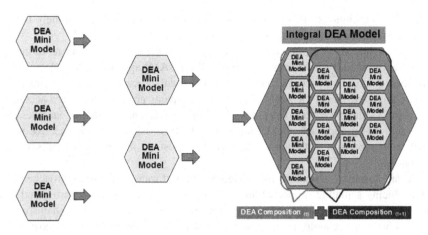

Fig. 6. Architectural federation by composition [57].

The Enterprise Services Architecture Model Integration (ESAMI) [53] (see Fig. 7) method is based on correlation analysis, which provides an instrument for a systematic manual integration process. Typically, this process of pair wise mappings is of quadratic complexity. We have linearized the complexity of these architectural mappings by introducing a neutral and dynamically extendable architectural reference model, which is supplied and dynamically extended from previous mapping iterations. Furthermore, we have adopted modeling concepts from ISO/IEC 42010 [9], like *Architecture Description*, *Viewpoint*, *View*, and *Model*.

Reference Model			Correlation Index			Integration Options		
Viewpoint	**Model**	**Element**	**OrderSrv**	**ShippingSrv**	**BillingSrv**	**OrderSrv**	**ShippingSrv**	**BillingSrv**
Business Actor	Customer	CustomerID	2	1	1	m	p	p
		Name	3	0	2	m	r	p
		Address	0	2	1	r	p	p
		Payment						r
		...	0 no correlation			r reject		...
Passive Structure	Product	ProdID	1 low correlation			p partially		p
		ProdName	2 medium correlation			m mandatory		m
		ProdDescr	3 strong correlation			(leading model)		m
		ProdComp						r
		Rate	...	...	...	...	...	...
...	...	...	...	...	...	...	...	...

Fig. 7. Correlation analysis and integration matrices [57]. (Color figure online)

The *Correlation Index* for different IoTs or microservices (red middle columns) with respect to the current *Reference Model* (yellow columns on the left) is created. Based on these Correlation *Indices*, the *Integration Options* for each service (green columns on the right) are chosen and the selection is integrated into the *Reference*

Model. This continuous model refinement allows to integrate even extremely heterogeneous microservices that may not even share a complete metamodel.

These architectural metamodels are composed of their elements and relationships and are represented by architecture diagrams. The ESAMI approach is based on special correlation matrices, which are handled by a manual process to identify similarities between analyzed model elements. The chosen elements are then integrated according to their most valuable contribution towards a holistic reference model. In each iteration of this bottom-up approach, we are analyzing the fit of each new microservice metamodel in comparison with the context of the existing integrated set of services' metamodels.

We are currently extending model federation and transformation approaches [39] by introducing semantic-supported architectural representations, from partial and federated ontologies and associate mapping rules with special inference mechanisms.

Fast changing technologies and markets usually drive the evolution of ecosystems. Therefore, we have extracted the idea of digital ecosystems from [38] and linked this with main strategic drivers for system development and their evolution. Adaptation drives the survival of digital architectures, platforms, and application ecosystems.

7   Decision Management

Our current research links decision objects and processes to multi-perspective architectural models and data. We are extending the more fundamentally approach of decision dashboards for Enterprise Architecture [15, 27, 33] and integrate this idea with an original Architecture Management Cockpit [13, 14] for the context of decision-oriented digital architecture management for a huge amount of micro-granular architectural models from the open-world.

A cockpit presents a facility or device via which multiple viewpoints on the system under consideration can be consulted simultaneously. Each stakeholder who takes place in a cockpit meeting can utilize a viewpoint that displays the relevant information. Thereby, the stakeholders can leverage views that fit the particular role, like Application Architect, Business Process Owner or Infrastructure Architect. The viewpoints applied simultaneously are linked to each other such that the impact of a change performed in one view can be visualized in other views as well.

As shown in Fig. 8, the architectural cockpit [13] enables analytics as well as optimizations using different multi-perspective interrelated viewpoints on the system under consideration [54, 55]. Multiple perspectives of architectural models and data result from a magnitude of architectural objects, which are typed according the dimension categories of a digital enterprise architecture. Additionally, we have to consider analytics and decision viewpoints in a close association with the architectural core information.

The ISO Standard 42010 [9] defines, how the architecture of a system can be documented through architecture descriptions. Jugel et al. [14] develops and introduces a special annotation mechanism adding additional needed knowledge via an architectural model to an architecture description.

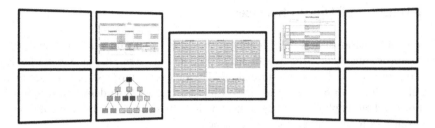

Fig. 8. Architecture management cockpit [13, 14].

The advantage of architectural decision mechanisms is a close link between architectural artefacts and architectural models with explicit decisions, both from a classical Enterprise Architecture Management perspective and a new way of managing micro-granular structures and systems as well.

In addition, the fundamental work in [13] reveals a viewpoint concept by dividing it into an Atomic Viewpoint and a Viewpoint Composition. Therefore, coherent viewpoints can be applied simultaneously in an architecture cockpit to support stakeholders in decision-making [14]. Figure 9 illustrates the decision metamodel, as extension of [30], showing the conceptual model of main decisional objects and their relationships.

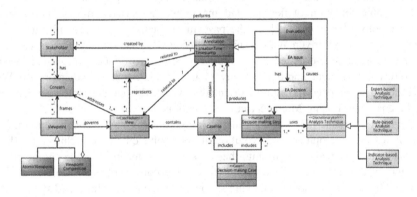

Fig. 9. Architecture decision metamodel [14].

According to the architecture management cockpit [13, 14], each possible stakeholder can utilize a viewpoint that shows the relevant information. Furthermore, these viewpoints are connected in a dynamically way to each other, so that the impact of a change performed in one view can be visualized in other views as well.

8   Evolution of Digital Services

The digital transformation [7, 35] highly increased the competitive pressure and urges enterprises to quickly develop new digitized products and services. Time to market is a key differentiator in digital transformation. The quicker a business is, the more successful it is likely to be. But more established businesses have delivered technology solutions to their employees and customers on lengthy release schedules that no longer make sense in today's accelerated environment.

The nature of digital assets disaggregates value chains, creating openings for focused, fast-moving competitors. Furthermore, the customer expects to interact seamlessly across different channels. Enterprises have to analyze customer behavior in real-time. At the same time digitization lowers the market entry barriers for new competitors, by dissolving long-understood boundaries between sectors. These challenges require a better support for software evolution.

Principally we can identify, as in [51], two broad perspectives of software evolution: First, software can be designed anticipating change by the original software developer to make evolution easier by predicting possible change perspectives of a new software. The main mechanism of proactive change is based on modularity structures of services. Secondly, software evolution can be handled during the maintenance phase by using special tools and methods. The intention here is to support understanding of software structures of the existing code, as fast and easy as possible.

The implementation of flexible and maintainable services strongly depends on service quality of services [12]. In the past, most quality of service indicators were designed for method-driven Web Services with SOAP. Today, many new services are designed in a resource-oriented way using REST or Microservices, to follow an easier technology-independent approach. Many of the existing quality indicators for Web Services can be mapped to resource-oriented services. Resource-oriented services can also be engineered using Microservices, as mentioned.

Decision analytics [55] provides increasingly complex and decision support, particularly for the development and evolution of sustainable enterprise architectures (EA), and this is duly needed. Tapping into these systems and techniques, the engineers and managers of the software and system architecture become part of a viable enterprise, i.e. a resilient and continuously evolving service-oriented architectures and systems that enable and drive innovative business models.

Main challenges of service computing for the next ten years guide a redefinition of service computing, which are postulated by [6]. The service computing manifesto (Fig. 10) maps out in a strategy that positions emerging concepts and technologies to support the service paradigm. The service computing manifesto recommends focusing on four main research directions by specifying both challenges and a research roadmap: service design, service composition, crowdsourcing based reputation, and the Internet of Things.

An important prerequisite for building and analyzing sound service systems and architectures is a formal understanding of the nature of services and their model-supported relationships. We have to currently consider a big change from traditional

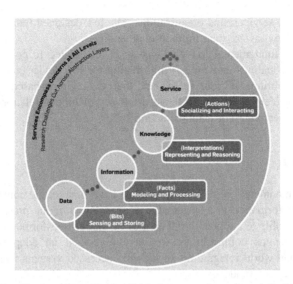

Fig. 10. Service evolution along the computing value chain [6].

closed-world software engineering approaches to the open-world of service systems with autonomous parts [6].

An important prerequisite for building and analyzing sound service systems and architectures is a formal understanding of the nature of services and their model-supported relationships. Cloud computing as a new service delivery model, which gives inspiration to integrate service computing and cloud computing. So, cloud computing is a main influencing factor for the service computing manifesto in [49], while other important influencers for service computing are mobile computing, big data, and social computing.

In the next wave of service composition [6], we have to integrate a fast growing and large set of non-WSDL-described services: REST services, Microservices, and partial services, like IoT or Android apps. In an open-world setting of big data existing static service selection, composition, and recommendation are inadequate and should be extended by large-scale Web and cloud service composition, big data driven service composition, and social network-based service compositions.

Trust [35] plays an important role for a functional service ecosystem. Crowdsourcing provides effective means for collecting data through collaborations within communities. Reputation mechanisms and crowdsourcing in social networks support predicting credibility, which is important for derive trust. Artificial intelligence technologies, like deep learning [36], allow computers to behave in specific usage scenarios to behave like human beings.

Innovative models are required for the composition of Internet of Things (IoT) [2] and [29]. IoT poses two fundamental challenges: communication with things, and management of things. One additional challenge is that things are resource-constrained, making it practical impossible to combine IoT with heavy standards like, SOAP and BPEL. The IoT component model is further heterogeneous and multi-layered, typically with devices, data, services, and organizations. The IoT designed functionality is more dynamic and context-aware than in traditional settings.

The resulting fundamental IoT challenges [2] are related to continuously maintaining cyber personalities and context information for IoT devices, and continuously discovering, integrating, and reusing IoT and their data. Graph-based approaches and machine-learning techniques can facilitate discovery of hidden relationships between IoT and helping detecting correlations among IoT.

9   Conclusion

Based on our fundamental research question we have first set the context proceeding from digital transformation to a systematic value-oriented digital product and service modeling. To be able to support the dynamics of digital transformation with flexible software and systems compositions we have leveraged an adaptive architecture approach for open-world integrations of globally accessed systems and services with their local architecture models.

We contribute to the literature in different ways. Looking to our results, we have identified the need and solution mechanisms for a value-oriented integration of digital strategy models through suitable digital business models up to models for service-dominant products as part of a value-based digital enterprise architecture. We have developed a bottom-up integration approach for a huge amount of dynamically growing micro-granular systems and services, like mobile systems, Microservices or the Internet of Things. To integrate micro-granular architecture models from an open-world we have extended traditional enterprise architecture reference models and enhanced them with state of art elements from agile architectural engineering to support the digitalization of products, services, and processes. This is a major extension of our seminal work on reference enterprise architectures, to be able to openly integrate through a continuously bottom-up approach a huge amount of global available and heterogeneous micro-granular systems, having their own local architectures. Additionally, we have investigated current and next elements of service-oriented technologies to point to main influence factors, challenges and research areas for the evolution of enterprise architecture and the evolving discipline of the service economy.

Strength of our research results from our novel integration of micro-granular structures and systems, while limits are still resulting from an ongoing validation of our research and open issues in managing inconsistencies and semantic dependencies.

Future research addresses mechanisms for flexible and adaptable integration of digital enterprise architectures. Similarly, it may be of interest to extend human-controlled dashboard-based interaction and visualizations by integrating automated decision making by AI-based systems like, ontologies with semantic integration rules, and architectural data and model analytics with deep learning mechanisms as well as mathematical comparisons (similarity, Euclidean distance) and statistical methods.

References

1. Atzori, L., Iera, A., Morabito, G.: The internet of things: a survey. J. Comput. Netw. **54**, 2787–2805 (2010)
2. Balakrushnan, S., et al.: Microservices architecture. White Paper, The Open Group (2016)
3. Benson, R.J., Bugnitz, T.L., Walton, W.B.: From Business Strategy to IT Action. Wiley, Hoboken (2004)
4. Blaschke, M., Haki, M.K., Riss, U., Aier, S.: Design principles for business-model-based management methods—a service-dominant logic perspective. In: Maedche, A., vom Brocke, J., Hevner, A. (eds.) DESRIST 2017. LNCS, vol. 10243, pp. 179–198. Springer, Cham (2017). https://doi.org/10.1007/978-3-319-59144-5_11
5. Bogner, J., Zimmermann, A.: Towards integrating microservices with adaptable enterprise architecture. In: Dijkman, R., Pires, L.F., Rinderle-Ma, S. (eds.) IEEE – EDOC Conference Workshops EDOCW, Vienna, pp. 158–163. IEEE (2016)
6. Bouguettaya, A., et al.: A service computing manifesto: the next 10 years. Commun. ACM **60**(4), 64–72 (2017)
7. Brynjolfsson, E., McAfee, A.: The Second Machine Age: Work, Progress, and Prosperity in a Time of Brilliant Technologies. W. W. Norton & Company, New York (2014)
8. El-Sheikh, E., Zimmermann, A., Jain, L.C. (eds.): Emerging Trends in the Evolution of Service-Oriented and Enterprise Architectures. ISRL, vol. 111. Springer, Cham (2016). https://doi.org/10.1007/978-3-319-40564-3
9. Emery, D., Hilliard, R.: Every architecture description needs a framework: expressing architecture frameworks using ISO/IEC 42010. In: 2009 Joint Working IEEE/IFIP Conference on Software Architecture and European Conference on Software Architecture, pp. 31–39 (2009)
10. Gamma, E., Helm, R., Johnson, R., Vlissides, J.: Design Patterns. Addison Wesley, Boston (1995)
11. Ganz, F., Li, R., Barnaghi, P., Harai, H.: A resource mobility scheme for service-continuity in the Internet of Things. In: 2012 IEEE International Conference on Green Computing and Communications (GreenCom), pp. 261–264 (2012)
12. Gebhart, M., Giessler, P., Abeck, S.: Flexible and maintainable service-oriented architectures with resource-oriented web services. In: El-Sheikh, E., Zimmermann, A., Jain, L. (eds.) Emerging Trends in the Evolution of Service-Oriented and Enterprise Architectures. ISRL, vol. 111, pp. 23–39. Springer, Cham (2016). https://doi.org/10.1007/978-3-319-40564-3_3
13. Jugel, D., Schweda, C.M.: Interactive functions of a cockpit for enterprise architecture planning. In: International Enterprise Distributed Object Computing Conference Workshops and Demonstrations (EDOCW), Ulm, Germany, pp. 33–40. IEEE (2014)
14. Jugel, D., Schweda, C.M., Zimmermann, A.: Modeling decisions for collaborative enterprise architecture engineering. In: Persson, A., Stirna, J. (eds.) CAiSE 2015. LNBIP, vol. 215, pp. 351–362. Springer, Cham (2015). https://doi.org/10.1007/978-3-319-19243-7_33
15. Lankhorst, M.: Enterprise Architecture at Work: Modelling, Communication and Analysis. Springer, Heidelberg (2017). https://doi.org/10.1007/978-3-662-53933-0
16. Lüftenegger, E.R.: Service-Dominant Business Logic. Technische Universiteit Eindhoven, Eindhoven (2014)
17. Meertens, L.O., et al.: Mapping the business model canvas to ArchiMate. In: SAC 2012, pp. 1694–1701. ACM (2012)
18. MODAF: The British Ministry of Defence Architecture Framework Views. https://www.gov.uk/guidance/mod-architecture-framework. Accessed 24 Feb 2018

19. Möhring, M., et al.: Using smart edge devices to integrate consumers into digitized processes: the case of amazon dash-button. In: Teniente, E., Weidlich, M. (eds.) BPM 2017. LNBIP, vol. 308, pp. 374–383. Springer, Cham (2018). https://doi.org/10.1007/978-3-319-74030-0_28

20. Newman, S.: Building Microservices: Designing Fine-Grained Systems. O'Reilly, Sebastopol (2015)

21. OMG: Meta Object Facility (MOF) Core Specification. Version 2.5 (2011)

22. Open Group: TOGAF Version 9.2. The Open Group (2018)

23. Open Group: ArchiMate 3.0 Specification. The Open Group (2016)

24. Open Group: Value Streams. The Open Group (2017)

25. Osterwalder, A., Pigneur, Y.: Business Model Generation. Wiley, Hoboken (2010)

26. Osterwalder, A., Pigneur, Y., Bernarda, G., Smith, A., Papadokos, T.: Value Proposition Design. Wiley, Hoboken (2014)

27. Op't Land, M., Proper, H.A., Waage, M., Cloo, J., Steghuis, C.: Enterprise Architecture Creating – Value by Informed Governance. Springer, Heidelberg (2009). https://doi.org/10.1007/978-3-540-85232-2

28. Outram, C.: Digital Stractics. Palgrave MacMillan, London (2016)

29. Patel, P., Cassou, D.: Enabling high-level application development for the internet of things. J. Syst. Softw. **103**, 62–84 (2015)

30. Plataniotis, G., De Kinderen, S., Proper, H.A.: EA anamnesis: an approach for decision making analysis in enterprise architecture. Int. J. Inf. Syst. Model. Des. **4**(1), 75–95 (2014)

31. Porter, M.E., Heppelmann, J.E.: How smart connected products are transforming competition. Harvard Bus. Rev. **92**(11), 64–88 (2014)

32. Ross, J.W., Weill, P., Robertson, D.: Enterprise Architecture as Strategy – Creating a Foundation for Business Execution. Harvard Business School Press, Brighton (2006)

33. Saat, J., Fanke, U., Lagerström, R., Ekstedt, M.: Enterprise architecture meta models for IT/business alignment situations. In: 2010 IEEE International Enterprise Distributed Object Computing Conference, Vitoria, Brazil (2010)

34. Schmidt, R., Möhring, M., Härting, R.C., Reichstein, C., Neumaier, P., Jozinović, P.: Industry 4.0 - potentials for creating smart products: empirical research results. In: Abramowicz, W. (ed.) BIS 2015. LNBIP, vol. 208, pp. 16–27. Springer, Cham (2015). https://doi.org/10.1007/978-3-319-19027-3_2

35. Schmidt, R., Zimmermann, A., Möhring, M., Nurcan, S., Keller, B., Bär, F.: Digitization – perspectives for conceptualization. In: Celesti, A., Leitner, P. (eds.) ESOCC Workshops 2015. CCIS, vol. 567, pp. 263–275. Springer, Cham (2016). https://doi.org/10.1007/978-3-319-33313-7_20

36. Schmidthuber, J.: Deep learning in neural networks: an overview. Neural Netw. **61**, 85–117 (2015)

37. Spiess, P., et al.: SOA-based integration of the internet of things in enterprise services. In: ICWS 2009, pp. 968–975 (2009)

38. Tiwana, A.: Platform Ecosystems: Aligning Architecture, Governance, and Strategy. Morgan Kaufmann, Waltham (2013)

39. Trojer, T., Farwick, M., Häusler, M., Breu, R.: Living modeling of IT architectures: challenges and solutions. In: De Nicola, R., Hennicker, R. (eds.) Software, Services, and Systems. LNCS, vol. 8950, pp. 458–474. Springer, Cham (2015). https://doi.org/10.1007/978-3-319-15545-6_26

40. Uckelmann, D., Harrison, M., Michahelles, F.: Architecting the Internet of Things. Springer, Cham (2011). https://doi.org/10.1007/978-3-642-19157-2

41. Vargo, S.L., Akaka, M.A., Vaughan, C.M.: Conceptualizing value: a service-ecosystem view. J. Creat. Value **3**(2), 1–8 (2017)

42. Vargo, S.L., Lusch, R.F.: Service-dominant logic: continuing the evolution. J. Acad. Mark. Sci. **36**(1), 1–10 (2008)
43. Vargo, S.L., Lusch, R.F.: Institutions and axioms: an extension and update of service-dominant logic. J. Acad. Mark. Sci. **44**(4), 5–23 (2016)
44. Veneberg, R.K.M., Iacob, M.E., van Sinderen, M.J., Bodenstaff, L.: Relating business intelligence, and enterprise architecture – a method for combining operational data with architectural metadata. J. Coop. Inf. Syst. **25**(2), 1–36 (2016)
45. Walker, M.J.: Leveraging enterprise architecture to enable business value with IoT innovations today. In: Gartner Research (2014). http://www.gartner.com/analyst/49943
46. Warren, A.: Amazon Echo: The Ultimate Amazon Echo User Guide 2016 Become an Alexa and Echo Expert Now!. CreateSpace Independent Publishing Platform, Scotts Valley (2016)
47. Weill, P., Ross, J.W.: IT Governance: How Top Performers Manage IT Decision Rights for Superior Results. Harvard Business School Press, Brighton (2004)
48. Weill, P., Woerner, S.: Thriving in an increasingly digital ecosystem. MIT Sloan Manag. Rev. **56**(4), 27 (2015)
49. Weitzel, T., Wendt, O., Westarp, F.V.: Reconsidering network effect theory. In: Proceedings of European Conference on Information Systems (ECIS), pp. 484–491 (2000)
50. Westerman, G., Bonnet, D.: Revamping your business through digital transformation. MIT Sloan Manag. Rev. **56**(3), 10 (2015)
51. Wilde, N., Gonen, B., El-Sheikh, E., Zimmermann, A.: Approaches to the evolution of SOA systems. In: El-Sheikh, E., Zimmermann, A., Jain, L. (eds.) Emerging Trends in the Evolution of Service-Oriented and Enterprise Architectures. ISRL, vol. 111, pp. 5–21. Springer, Cham (2016). https://doi.org/10.1007/978-3-319-40564-3_2
52. WSO2: A reference architecture for the internet of things. Version 0.9.0 (2015). https://wso2.com. Accessed 8 Sept 2018
53. Zimmermann, A., Schmidt, R., Sandkuhl, K., Wißotzki, M., Jugel, D., Möhring, M.: Digital enterprise architecture – transformation for the internet of things. In: Kolb, J., Weber, B., Hall, S., Mayer, W., Ghose, A.K., Grossmann, G. (eds.) EDOC 2015 with SoEA4EE, 21–25 September 2015, Adelaide, Australia, pp. 130–138. IEEE (2015)
54. Zimmermann, A., Jugel, D., Sandkuhl, K., Schmidt, R., Schweda, C.M., Möhring, M.: Architectural decision management for digital transformation of products and services. J. Complex Syst. Inf. Model. Q. **6**, 31–53 (2016)
55. Zimmermann, A., et al.: Leveraging analytics for digital transformation of enterprise services and architectures. In: El-Sheikh, E., Zimmermann, A., Jain, L. (eds.) Emerging Trends in the Evolution of Service-Oriented and Enterprise Architectures. ISRL, vol. 111, pp. 91–112. Springer, Cham (2016). https://doi.org/10.1007/978-3-319-40564-3_6
56. Zimmermann, A., Schmidt, R., Sandkuhl, K., Wißotzki, M., Jugel, D., Möhring, M.: Digital enterprise architecture – decision management for micro-granular digital architecture. In: Hallé, S., Dijkman, R.M., Lapalme, J. (eds.) EDOC 2017 with SoEA4EE, pp. 29–38. IEEE Computer Society (2017)
57. Zimmermann, A., Schmidt, R., Sandkuhl, K., Jugel, D., Bogner, J., Möhring, M.: Decision-controlled digitization architecture for the internet of things and microservices. In: Czarnowski, I., Howlett, R., Jain, L.C. (eds.) Intelligent Decision Technologies 2017, pp. 82–92. Springer, Cham (2018). https://doi.org/10.1007/978-3-319-59424-8_8
58. Zimmermann, A., Schmidt, R., Sandkuhl, K., Jugel, D., Bogner, J., Möhring, M.: Software evolution for digital transformation. In: Damiani, E., Spanoudakis, G., Maciaszek, L. (eds.) Proceedings of ENASE 2018, Funchal, Madeira/Portugal, pp. 205–212. SCITEPRESS Science and Technology Publications (2018)

Software Engineering

Risk-Based Elicitation of Security Requirements According to the ISO 27005 Standard

Roman Wirtz[1]([✉]), Maritta Heisel[1], Angela Borchert[1], Rene Meis[1],
Aida Omerovic[2], and Ketil Stølen[2]

[1] University of Duisburg-Essen, Duisburg, Germany
roman.wirtz@uni-due.de
[2] SINTEF Institute Oslo, Oslo, Norway
http://swe.uni-due.de

Abstract. Security is of great importance for software intensive systems. Security incidents become more and more frequent in the last few years. Such incidents can lead to substantial damage, not only financially, but also in term of reputation loss. The security of a software system can be compromised by threats, which may harm assets with a certain likelihood, thus constituting a risk. All such risks should be identified, and unacceptable risks should be reduced. The task of dealing with risks is called risk management and should be performed right from the beginning of the software development process. Security requirements can be used to address security aspects during requirements engineering. We propose a risk-based method to elicit security requirements based on functional requirements. Our method complies to the ISO 27005 standard for security risk management. We provide guidance for all steps of that process, and the results are collected in a model. We also define validation conditions to support the identification of errors when carrying out the process as early as possible.

Keywords: Risk management · Security requirements ·
Requirements engineering · Compliance · ISO 27005

1 Introduction

In a connected world, almost every piece of software may be subject to attacks. Such attacks can cause great harm to enterprises and individuals. Almost every week, media report on attacks against public or private organizations. Therefore, software should be developed with security issues in mind. Nevertheless, organizations can only spend a limited amount of resources on security. These resources should be spent in a way that maximizes return on investment, i.e., that provides the best possible protection against attacks.

In this paper, we describe a risk-based method to elicit security requirements that complies with the ISO 27005 standard. Given the functional requirements

© Springer Nature Switzerland AG 2019
E. Damiani et al. (Eds.): ENASE 2018, CCIS 1023, pp. 71–97, 2019.
https://doi.org/10.1007/978-3-030-22559-9_4

for a software system, possible threats to security and the corresponding risks are identified and evaluated. A risk is determined by two factors: the likelihood of the threat leading to harm of an asset, and the severity of the harm, i.e., the consequence. For each identified risk, it has to be determined whether it is acceptable or not. Only unacceptable risks need to be treated, thus leading to corresponding security requirements for the software system to be developed. Moreover, our method supports the selection of treatments that are suitable to achieve the necessary risk reduction. The result of our method is a set of functional and corresponding security requirements that form the basis for the subsequent software development process.

Our method is model-based, so that the results of the risk analysis can be smoothly integrated in a model-based software development process. The name of the method is *ProCOR – Problem-based CORAS*, because it combines parts of the model-based risk management method CORAS [1] with Jackson's problem frames approach [2]. The initial model consists of functional requirements that are expressed using problem diagrams. We developed a new type of diagram to extend this model with security requirements. The so enhanced requirements model forms the starting point for a software development that adequately balances functionality and security.

The paper is structured as follows: In Sect. 2, we explain problem frames, CORAS and the underlying ISO 27005 standard. We present the terminology for our method in Sect. 3 with a conceptual model. In Sect. 4, we describe all steps of the ProCOR method in detail. We apply the ProCOR method to an example application in Sect. 5. The results of the evaluation of our method are described in Sect. 6. The paper concludes with related work in Sect. 7, and we discuss our method along with future work in Sect. 8.

2   Fundamentals

We briefly summarize the concepts on which our work is based. First, we introduce the ISO 27005 standard [3], which describes a high-level security risk management process. Second, we describe problem frames by Michael Jackson [2] to document requirements in a model. Last, we introduce the elements of the CORAS language to document security incidents.

2.1   ISO 27005

The ISO 27005 standard [3] (based on ISO 31000 [4]) describes a high-level risk management process, which aims to manage risks for some asset. An asset represents some kind of value for an organization, e.g. a piece of information. *A risk is a combination of the consequences [for an asset] that would follow from the occurrence of an unwanted event and the likelihood of the occurrence of the event* [3].

In the following, we briefly explain the four steps we address in this paper.

(1) **Establishing the Context.** The first step is used to collect basic evaluation criteria and to define scope and boundaries. A well-defined scope ensures that all relevant assets will be considered during the risk assessment. The boundaries define the parts of the environment that are considered in the following steps.

(2) **Risk Assessment.** The risk assessment part of a risk management process is divided into three sub-activities.

  (2.1) **Risk Identification.** First, the assets to be protected and possible threats, which might harm those assets, are identified. To avoid unnecessary costs and effort, existing controls, e.g. security mechanisms, need to be identified. Vulnerabilities are exploited by a threat to harm an asset and have to be documented. Last, the consequences, which might arise for an asset, are identified.

  (2.2) **Risk Analysis.** To analyze risks, it is possible to consider qualitative or quantitative approaches to assess likelihoods and consequences. For each previously identified consequence, a specific value has to be determined. For each incident that might have a consequence for an asset, its likelihood has to be determined, too. To determine the risk, the assigned values for consequences and likelihoods are combined.

  (2.3) **Risk Evaluation.** Each identified risk is evaluated with regard to the defined risk evaluation criteria and risk acceptance criteria. The output of that activity is a prioritized list of risks that need to be addressed by controls.

(3) **Risk Treatment.** During the treatment of the identified risks, controls have to be selected to reduce the risk, if possible, to an acceptable level. The output is a plan for treating all risks and the documentation of the residual risks.

(4) **Risk Acceptance.** The organization's managers need to accept the risk treatment plan and the residual risks. In case that the plan is not accepted, another iteration of the process is necessary.

2.2 Problem Frames

To model requirements, we make use of Michael Jackson's problem frames [2]. Problem frames are patterns to describe subproblems of a complex software development problem in the early stages of the software development life-cycle. An instance of such a pattern is called problem diagram and contains a functional requirement (dashed ovals) for the system-to-be. Examples are given in Figs. 3 and 4. A requirement is an optative statement, which describes how the environment of the software should behave when the software is in action. The entities related to a requirement are represented as domains (rectangles). There are different types of domains: biddable domains (e.g., persons), causal domains (e.g., technical equipment), machine domains (representing the software to be developed, rectangle with vertical bars) and lexical domains (data representations). A causal domain can take the role of a connection domain. Such a domain is used to connect other domains, for example representing a network.

There are symbolic phenomena, representing some kind of information or a state, and causal phenomena, representing events, actions, operations and so on. Each phenomenon is controlled by exactly one domain and can be observed by other domains. A phenomenon controlled by one domain and observed by another is called a shared phenomenon between these two domains. Interfaces (solid lines) contain sets of shared phenomena. Such a set contains phenomena controlled by the same domain (indicated by $A!\{...\}$, where A is an abbreviation for the controlling domain). Some domains are *referred to* by a requirement (dashed line) via some phenomena, and at least one domain is *constrained* by a requirement (dashed lines with arrowhead) via some phenomena. The domains and their phenomena that are referred to by a requirement are not influenced by the machine, whereas we build the machine to influence the constrained domain's phenomena in such a way that the requirement is fulfilled.

Fig. 1. CORAS language [1].

2.3   CORAS

CORAS [1] is a model-based method for risk management. It consists of a stepwise process and different kinds of diagrams. The method follows the ISO 31000 risk-management standard [4]. Each step provides guidelines for the interaction with the customer on whose behalf the risk management activities are carried out. The results are documented in a model using the CORAS language. The method starts with the establishment of the context and ends up with the suggestion of treatments to address the risk.

In our risk management process, we use the CORAS language to document security incidents, which may lead to a harm for an asset. The symbols we make use of are shown in Fig. 1. *Direct Assets* are items of value. There are *Human-threats deliberate*, e.g. a network attacker, as well as *Human-threats accidental*, e.g. an employee pressing a wrong button accidentally. To describe technical issues *Non-human threats* are used, e.g. power loss of a server. A *Threat scenario* describes a state, which may possibly lead to an unwanted incident, where an *Unwanted incident* describes the action that harms an asset. Risk is defined as the combination of a likelihood and a consequence according to ISO 31000 [4]. *Treatment scenarios* are used to describe countermeasures to reduce the risk. In Sect. 3.2, we provide a mapping of CORAS to the terminology of the ISO 27005 standard.

3   Terminology

In this section, we present a conceptual model for the terminology of the ISO 27005 standard we use in the following sections. CORAS differs to that terminology. We address this issue by providing a mapping of both terminologies.

3.1   Conceptual Model

We first introduce a conceptual model to describe the terminology and the relations between the different items we make use of in the following sections. The conceptual model is based on the ISO 27005 standard [3] and is shown in Fig. 2. The ISO 27005 standard has a special focus on security and is based on the ISO 31000 standard.

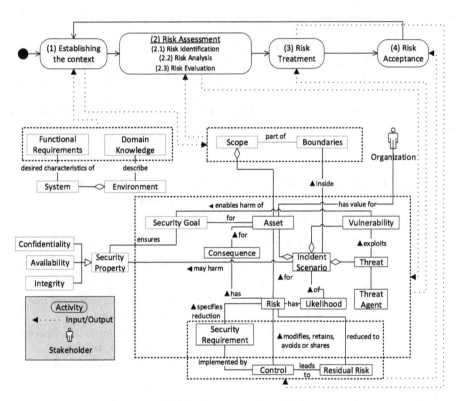

Fig. 2. Conceptual model.

As mentioned in Sect. 2.1, a risk management process consists of four steps: (1) Establishing the context, (2) Risk Assessment, (3) Risk Treatment, and (4) Risk Acceptance. Risk Assessment contains three sub activities: (2.1) Risk Identification, (2.2) Risk Analysis and (2.3) Risk Evaluation. The initial input to our process is a set of *Functional Requirements*, which describes the desired characteristics of the *System*. The system is part of the *Environment*, which is described by *Domain Knowledge*. An *Asset* is part of the *Scope*, and the scope is inside the *Boundaries* of the analysis. An asset has some value for an *Organization*. In the following, we consider a piece of information as an asset. For an asset, there are *Security Goals* which ensure *Security Properties* for an asset. We consider the following types of properties: (1) *Confidentiality*: Some piece of information shall not be disclosed to unauthorized third parties. (2) *Integrity*: Some piece of information shall not be altered by unauthorized third parties. (3) *Availability*: Some piece of information shall be available for authorized parties. A security goal might be harmed when a *Threat* exploits a *Vulnerability*. According to ISO 27005, a threat might be human or natural (for instance a thunderstorm), and deliberate or accidental. In the Common Criteria [5], a *Threat Agent* is explicitly mentioned. A threat is the action which has a negative influence on assets, and a threat agent performs that action. An *Incident Scenario* includes a threat, a vulnerability and an asset that might be harmed. Such a scenario has a likelihood which is further used to evaluate risks. A *Risk* is related to that likelihood and the specific consequence for the asset. A risk can be treated (e.g. modified, retained, avoided or shared) by some *Controls*. After applying controls, there is still a *Residual Risk* because usually a risk cannot be eliminated. The risk reduction is specified by a *Security Requirement* which is implemented by some controls.

Table 1. Mapping CORAS and problem frames to our conceptual model.

CORAS	Conceptual model	Remark
Human-threat deliberate	Threat agent	–
Human-threat accidental	Threat agent	–
Non-human threat	Threat agent	Used to represent environmental influences like a thunderstorm
Direct asset	Security goal	A piece of information (asset) shall be protected with regard to a specific goal
Threat scenario	Threat	–
Treatment scenario	Control	–
Unwanted incident	Part of incident scenario	Illustrating harm of security goal for an asset

3.2 Mapping

The terminology of the ISO 27005 standard is not consistent with the CORAS language. For each element of the language we make use of in ProCOR, we provide a mapping to the corresponding terms of the conceptual model. The mapping is shown in Table 1. A path in a CORAS diagram from a threat agent to a direct asset describes an incident scenario.

4 Process

In an earlier paper [6], we proposed a problem-based method to elicit security requirements based on functional requirements. The method follows the principles of risk management described by the ISO 31000 standard but does not provide compliance. In the present paper, we revised that method to comply with the ISO 27005 standard. We adjusted the terminology (see Sect. 3, and we restructured the method according to the high-level process described by the standard. The outputs of each step meet the requirements defined by the standard to document the results of the risk management. For each step, we present an overview based on the agenda concept by Heisel [7]. Such an overview consists of the input, output and procedure of the specific step briefly describing the activities that need to be carried out. In addition, we identified *validation conditions* for each step that check the coherence of the results of each step, thus helping to identify errors in the application of the method as early as possible. We give examples of such validation conditions in the following.

Table 2. Process: context establishment.

Context establishment	
Input	• Description of software and environment (informal) • List of functional requirements
Output	• Problem diagrams • Security concerns as risk evaluation criteria (informal)
Procedure	• Create problem diagrams for functional requirements • Identify and document security concerns of organization as initial risk evaluation criteria
Validation conditions	• All functional requirements are covered by at least one problem diagram • All connection domains have been identified and are added to the problem diagrams

4.1 Context Establishment

Table 2 gives an overview of the initial step for the risk management process. With ProCOR, we present a risk management process based on functional requirements. Problem diagrams can be used to illustrate functional requirements as explained in Sect. 2.2. We request an informal description of the environment and a list of functional requirements as an input for the creation of those diagrams.

To identify all risks in the following, it is essential to collect all domains which might enable harm for an asset. Faßbender et al. [8] describe a way to create problem diagrams with regard to security, so that no domain is left out which might be relevant for the analysis. We suggest to use this approach to create problem diagrams.

Connection domains play a specific role for the analysis because they represent connections between domains. Those connections are often subject to attacks. Hence, a validation condition is to identify all domains of that type. Additionally, all functional requirements need to be covered by at least one problem diagram.

The security concerns of the organization serve as initial risk evaluation criteria. We document those concerns as an informal enumeration.

The output of the context establishment is a set of problem diagrams and a list of security concerns.

4.2 Risk Assessment

The step for risk assessment consists of three sub-activities that we now describe in more detail.

Risk Identification. In Table 3, we show the overview for the step of risk identification. With ProCOR, we aim to support the protection of information in a software-based system with regard to the three security properties confidentiality, integrity and availability. In problem diagrams, a piece of information is represented by a symbolic phenomenon, whereas commands or events are represented by causal phenomena. Hence, we define a security goal as a combination of a symbolic phenomenon and a security property. A piece of information related to such a security goal needs to be protected. The identified security goals are documented in a table, such as Table 8. We also document the value of the asset for the organization with regard to the specific property to make it comparable to the costs of a control.

Information Flow Graph. To assist the analysts in identifying security incidents, we automatically identify domains where the information to be protected is available. "Available" means that the domain observes or controls the symbolic phenomenon representing the information to be protected, as specified in the set of problem diagrams that is part of the input for this step. However, it does not suffice to only consider symbolic phenomena, because valuable information

Table 3. Process: risk identification.

Risk identification	
Input	• Security goals of customer (informal) • Information about processed data • Knowledge about incident scenarios
Output	• List of assets and corresponding value • CORAS threat diagram
Procedure	• Identify information considered as an asset based on security goals of customer • Create information flow graph • Document incident scenarios with CORAS
Validation conditions	• For all information to be protected, the desired security goals (confidentiality, integrity, availability) are documented • All interfaces contained in the set of problem diagrams are considered for the information flow graph • All domains on which an asset-related information are inspected for risk identification

can also be part of commands or events, i.e., causal phenomena. For example, there may be an interface with a causal phenomenon to store some user data. This phenomenon is a command, but contains information in form of user data. Hence, it is necessary to document that a phenomenon is contained in another to decide whether an interface contains some information or not.

To document the availability of information at a domain and the information flow between domains, we developed the concept of an *Information Flow Graph*, which is a directed graph. Its nodes are domains, and its edges denote the information flowing from one domain to another. To create this graph, we consider all interfaces contained in the set of problem diagrams. A domain is contained in the graph only if it observes or controls a phenomenon that is related to an asset. Either, the phenomenon is a symbolic one, which contains the asset directly, or the phenomenon is related to such a symbolic phenomenon, as explained earlier.

The directed edges of the graph indicate an asset-related information flow. The starting nodes of the edges are the domains which control the asset-related symbolic phenomenon or the one in which it is contained. The end nodes are the domains that observe the respective phenomenon. All domains contained in the graph need further inspection for possible risks. To ensure that the graph is complete, we define a validation condition that all interfaces contained in the problem diagram are considered for the graph generation.

CORAS Threat Diagram. To identify risks, we make use of a structured brainstorming process as proposed by Lund et al. [1]. The analysts moderate a meeting with experts, who have different expertise. The results of this brainstorming session are documented in a *threat diagram*. Such a diagram (see Fig. 7) contains CORAS elements as described in Sect. 2.3 and relations between them, as described in the conceptual model given in Sect. 3.1.

The domains that are contained in the information flow graph are inspected in this meeting, and possible attacks on these domains have to be elicited. We define a validation condition that all domains of the information flow graph need to be inspected. For example, a domain representing an employee needs investigation for social engineering attacks. However, it might be the case that additional domains have to be considered for risk identification. This is because the information flow graph has been created based on the functional requirements. These requirements only describe the desired behavior. For example, the attacker who performs a social engineering attack on the employee is not part of the desired behavior and is hence not contained in the information flow graph. This threat is then newly introduced in the threat diagram, even though it is not contained in any problem diagram.

Table 4. Process: risk analysis.

Risk analysis	
Input	• CORAS threat diagram
	• Qualitative/quantitative risk analysis methodology
	• Knowledge about incident scenarios
Output	• Scales for likelihoods and consequences
	• Annotated CORAS threat diagram
Procedure	• Select appropriate analysis methodology
	• Define scales
	• Assess likelihood and consequences
	• Annotate threat diagram
Validation conditions	• All likelihoods and consequences are documented in the threat diagram to ensure a correct estimation of the risks

Risk Analysis. Table 4 provides an overview of the step for risk analysis. Depending on the chosen analysis method, we define qualitative or quantitative scales for likelihoods and consequences. Scales can for example be expressed using intervals. Based on the threat diagram and the knowledge of experts, we then estimate and document likelihoods and consequences. There is a likelihood for the following elements of the threat diagram: (1) for a threat agent to initiate a threat, (2) for a threat to occur, (3) for a threat leading to an unwanted incident and (4) for an unwanted incident to occur. The likelihoods for (2) and (4) are derived from the likelihoods of the incoming edges (i.e., (1) and (3)) based on empirical knowledge about the dependencies between the different likelihoods. The consequences for an asset are annotated on the relation between an unwanted incident and an asset. Thus, it describes what consequence an unwanted incident has on an asset.

To evaluate the risks in the next step, it is essential to document all likelihoods and consequences. Hence, we define a corresponding validation condition.

Table 5. Process: risk evaluation.

Risk evaluation	
Input	• Annotated CORAS threat diagram
	• Security concerns of customer
Output	• Risk matrices
	• (Un-)acceptable risks
	• High-level security requirements
Procedure	• Create a risk matrix for each security goal
	• Using the risk matrices, decide about acceptable and unacceptable risks
	• Assign a priority to each unacceptable risk and define a corresponding high-level security requirement
Validation Conditions	• The likelihood scales and consequence scales used for the documentation in the threat diagram are consistent with the ones used in the risk matrices
	• There is a risk matrix for each security goal
	• For each risk that is considered as unacceptable according to the corresponding risk matrix, exactly one high-level security requirement is set up

Risk Evaluation. In this step, we evaluate the identified risks and set up a high-level security requirement for each unacceptable risk, based on a given risk matrix. The overview of this step is shown in Table 5.

The likelihoods and consequences are expressed using scales. These scales can for example be defined based on intervals. To evaluate the risks, we make use of a risk matrix. For each security goal, a risk matrix must be defined. Annotated on the x-axis of the matrix are the different values of the consequence, while on the y-axis the values for the likelihood scale are annotated. Since a risk consists of a likelihood and a consequence, a cell in the matrix denotes a risk level. Each risk of the threat diagram, represented as the likelihood of an unwanted incident and the corresponding consequence on an asset, is added to the risk matrix. Using

Table 6. Process: risk treatment.

Risk treatment	
Input	• CORAS threat diagram with consequences and likelihoods
	• Knowledge about controls
Output	• CORAS threat diagram with controls
	• Concretized security requirements
	• Treatment problem diagrams
	• List of risks that remains unacceptable
Procedure	• Select appropriate controls to reduce risks to acceptable
	• Document risks that cannot be sufficiently reduced along with justification
	• Instantiate a concretized security requirement for each sufficiently reduced risk
	• Create treatment problem diagrams
Validation Conditions	• The costs for controls are not higher than the value of the asset to be protected
	• Risks that cannot be reduced to an acceptable level are documented for the risk acceptance decision
	• For each high-level security requirement, there is at most one concretized security requirement
	• Each concretized security requirement is represented by exactly one treatment problem diagram
	• Only domains that are related to the concretized security requirement are contained in the treatment problem diagram
	• A domain in a treatment problem diagram is constrained only if a control is applied to it
	• For each applied control, a control domain is contained in the treatment problem diagram

the matrix, a decision regarding a risk's acceptance is now possible. For each unacceptable risk, a *high-level security requirement (HL-SR)* is set up, which describes the necessary risk reduction. Such a requirement is expressed by using the following textual pattern:

Ensure that the risk for **A** with regard to *[Confidentiality, Integrity, Availability]* due to **UI** caused by $\mathcal{T}$ and initiated by $\mathcal{TA}$ is acceptable according to the risk matrix of the asset.

A stands for the asset, UI for the unwanted incident, $\mathcal{T}$ for the set of threats that lead to the unwanted incident and $\mathcal{TA}$ for the set of threat agents that initiate the threats.

For each risk represented by an HL-SR, we define a priority based on the security concerns of the customer. The number of the HL-SR denotes its priority.

To achieve the required risk reduction and thereby fulfill the HL-SR, we select controls in the next step.

4.3   Risk Treatment

In this step, we first select controls based on the threat diagram to fulfill the previously determined high-level security requirements. Afterwards, we evaluate the costs of the treatments. The costs shall not be higher than the value of the asset to be protected. In Table 6, we give an overview of the present step.

For each high-level security requirement, controls have to be selected to achieve the necessary risk reduction. The elements, which might be possibly addressed by a control, are described in the high-level security requirement (threat agents and threats) and can also be found in the threat diagram. As shown in the conceptual model (see Sect. 3.1), a threat agent or threat, respectively, is associated with a domain. Therefore, a control is applied at that domain. A control either leads to a likelihood or a consequence reduction. To express this in a threat diagram, we extend the CORAS language with a new arrow type for a control, called *addresses*, which points to the likelihood or consequence on an edge to be reduced, whereas the *treats* arrow points to the domain on which the control is applied.

The controls can be selected in a brainstorming session. The goal is to add controls until all risks have been reduced to an acceptable level. The priorities define the order in which risks are treated. If such a reduction is not possible, the high-level security requirement cannot be fulfilled which has to be documented. In the step *Risk Acceptance*, the customer has to decide whether to accept a higher risk (changing the risk matrix), change the functional requirements, e.g. by not offering risky services any more or search for other possibilities to mitigate the unacceptable risk.

Furthermore, the controls should not cost more than the value of the asset they protect. Therefore, it is necessary to calculate the overall costs for all controls that are related to a high-level security requirement. The overall costs are then compared to the value of the asset to be protected. If the costs are higher than the value, the customer has to decide how to proceed with the development, similarly as described above. If the overall costs of all controls are higher than the money to be spent for risk treatment, the priorities are considered to select the most severe risks.

Based on the previously determined high-level security requirements and the proposed controls, we concretize the security requirements and close the circle to the functional requirements.

A *Concretized Security Requirement (C-SR)* adds information about selected controls to a high-level security requirement. For this reason, there is one C-SR for each risk that has been reduced to an acceptable level. A C-SR has the following form:

> The risk for **A** with regard to *[Confidentiality, Integrity, Availability]* due to **UI** caused by $\mathcal{T}$ and initiated by $\mathcal{TA}$ is reduced to an acceptable level according to the risk matrix of the asset by applying $\mathcal{TR}$.

There, $\mathcal{TR}$ describes the required controls as a set of tuples *domain × control*, where *domain* describes the domain to which the *control* is applied. To align the concretized security requirements with the functional ones, we introduce a new type of problem diagram, called *Treatment Problem Diagram*. In contrast to a functional requirement, a C-SR is not implemented by a machine but by a control. This control can be technical. In this case, it could lead to a software development problem, similar to the functional requirements. But controls can also be non-technical, for example training personnel to resist social engineering attacks. Therefore, a new type of problem diagrams is needed to specify the controls to be implemented and their effects on the relevant domains. We call this diagram type *Treatment Problem Diagram*.

Table 7. Process: risk acceptance.

Risk acceptance	
Input	• List of high-level security requirements that cannot be reduced to acceptable
	• List of concretized security requirements
Output	• Documentation and reasoning about accepted risks
Procedure	• For each risk, decide whether it has been sufficiently reduced
	• Document the results of the review
Validation Conditions	• For each risk, it is documented if it has been accepted by the organization
	• A justification is given for unacceptable risks that will not be treated

As a counterpart of the machine domain in problem diagrams, we introduce a new domain type called *Control* for treatment problem diagrams. For each C-SR, one treatment problem diagram must be set up. All domains and controls given by the C-SR are added to the diagram. To indicate that a control treats a domain, we add an interface between the control domain and treated domain. These domains share a phenomenon controlled by the control domain, which describes how the treated domain is influenced. The C-SR constrains the treated domain and refers to all other domains related to the elements mentioned in the C-SR. The referring edges of the requirement are annotated with a phenomenon that is controlled by the domain and describes the harm on the asset. Each concretized security requirement is represented by exactly one treatment diagram.

The result of the present step is an extended requirement model consisting of a set of functional requirements, expressed as problem diagrams, and a set of security requirements, expressed as treatment problem diagrams. In subsequent phases of a software development lifecycle, it is now possible to consider both types of requirements directly and to ensure that the security requirements are considered right from the beginning of the software development process instead of treating them as an add-on.

The validation conditions for the present step are concerned with the creation of the treatment problem diagrams, the documentation of risks that remains unacceptable, and the evaluation of the costs of the selected controls.

4.4 Risk Acceptance

An overview of the last step is given in Table 7. In Sect. 4.3, we described how to identify controls to reduce risks to an acceptable level according to the risk evaluation. During risk acceptance, those results are presented to the organization. The organization has to agree on the selected controls and the risks that cannot be reduced to an acceptable level.

We suggest a table to document the decisions, as shown in Table 11. In the left column, we list the high-level security requirements and concretized security requirements. A concretized security requirement indicates that the risk has been reduced to an acceptable level whereas a high-level security requirement remains for risks that cannot be reduced. In the middle column, the organization documents the acceptance and in the right column it is possible to add some remarks and justifications.

In case that a risk treatment is not accepted by the organization, a further iteration of risk assessment is necessary.

The stated validation conditions ensure a consistent documentation of the final decisions of the performed risk management.

In the next section, we apply our process for an example application.

5 Case Study

To exemplify our proposed risk management process, we use the example of a smart grid. First, we give an informal description of the scenario followed by a list of functional requirements.

5.1 Scenario

The used example is a subsystem of a smart grid system inspired by the OPEN meter project [9]. A smart grid is an intelligent power supply network in which different participants are able to interact and control the grid. For example, it is possible to retrieve the measurements of the power consumption remotely. In the following, we describe the main components of the scenario. The system-to-be (i.e., the machine) is the *Communication Hub*. It serves as the connection between all other components and actors and is used to perform some calculations, e.g. to provide invoices to the customer for consumed energy. *Smart Meters* measure the consumption of energy using sensors. They are connected to the Communication Hub by a local metrological network (LMN), which might be wired or realized with a wireless connection. The *Energy supplier* is the provider of the smart grid. It is able to do an initial setup locally on the communication hub to be able to initiate a remote connection for later interaction. The *End customer* is the one, who pays the energy supplier's invoices and in whose home the communication hub is installed.

5.2   Context Establishment

The organization for which the risk management process is carried out is the energy supplier. We applied our method for eight functional requirements specified in the specification document [9]. In the following, we focus on a selection of two requirements:

Setup. The energy supplier performs an initial setup for the communication hub. The personal data of the client and tariff parameters are stored in a configuration. Figure 3 shows the problem diagram for *Setup*. The requirement refers to a phenomenon of *EnergySupplier* and constrains a phenomenon of *Configuration*.

Measuring. In given intervals, the communication hub receives measured data from smart meters and stores it persistently. Figure 4 shows the problem diagram for *Measuring*. The requirement refers to a phenomenon of *SmartMeter* and constrains a phenomenon *MeterData*.

The ProCOR method is carried out based on the problem diagrams shown in Figs. 3 and 4.

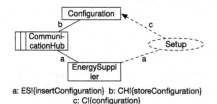

a: ESI{insertConfiguration} b: CHI{storeConfiguration}
c: CI{configuration}

Fig. 3. Case study: problem diagram for setup [6].

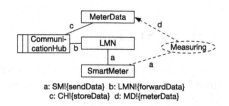

a: SMI{sendData} b: LMNI{forwardData}
c: CHI{storeData} d: MDI{meterData}

Fig. 4. Case study: problem diagram for measuring [6].

The security concerns (SC) for the stated functional requirements of the energy supplier are the following:

SC1. Wrong tariff parameters lead to a value loss because of incorrect invoicing.
SC2. Inconsistent measured data will lead to a value loss because of incorrect invoicing.

5.3 Risk Assessment

We carry out the three sub steps of risk assessment in the following.

Risk Identification. The ProCOR method is carried out based on the problem diagrams shown in Figs. 3 and 4. The organization defined the security goals as stated in Table 8. The values of the assets are estimated in Euros per year according to the following reasoning: (1) The integrity of tariff parameters has a value of 20.000 Euros because without correct parameters, the invoicing cannot be performed correctly. Because of periodical updates of the parameters, incorrect parameters will be overwritten at some time. Therefore, the incorrect values exist only for a limited amount of time. This results in a relatively small value of the asset. (2) The availability of measured data is important for invoicing, too. The absence of measured data leads to the case that an invoicing is not possible. In this case, an employee needs to collect the data manually. For this reason, we estimate the overall costs for all clients to 10.000 Euros. (3) A harm of the integrity of stored measured data leads to an incorrect invoicing. Due to the high number of clients of an energy supplier, the financial consequences are estimated with 50.000 Euros.

Next, we identify the phenomena in Figs. 3 and 4 that are related to the assets given in Table 8. The results of that identification process are shown in Fig. 5. The symbolic phenomena, which are considered as an asset, are shown in gray. An arrow pointing from one phenomenon to another means that it is contained in the other one. For example, the symbolic phenomenon *ES!{clientData}* representing the personal information of a client is contained in the causal phenomenon *ES!{insertConfiguration}*.

The corresponding information flow graph is shown in Fig. 6. Below a domain name, the available asset-related information is given in gray. For example, at the domain *Configuration* the information *tariffParameters* is available, and there is a corresponding information flow to this domain from the *CommunicationHub*.

Figure 7 shows the outcome of the risk identification process for our case study. There is one deliberate threat agent *EndCustomer*, who bribes the energy supplier (threat) to change the tariff parameters (unwanted incident). This harms the integrity of the tariff parameters (asset). The end customer is also an accidental threat agent, who disrupts the frequency of the local metrological network (threat), for example by using the same frequency for other purposes. This leads to two unwanted incidents. First, the integrity of measured data (asset) is harmed by an incorrect transmission of data (unwanted incident). Second, the availability of measured data (asset) is harmed by no transmission of data (unwanted incident).

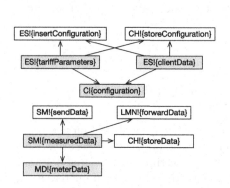

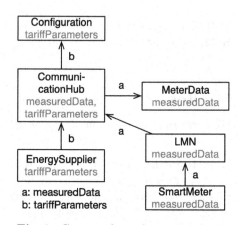

Fig. 5. Case study: phenomena relations [6].

Fig. 6. Case study: information flow graph [6].

Risk Analysis. In Fig. 8, we show the threat diagram with annotated likelihoods and consequences. We express the likelihood of an event as the frequency of the event per year. We assume that ten times a year some end customer tries to bribe the energy supplier, which is successful in 2% of the cases and leads to a change of tariff parameters. The consequence is given in Euros as a value loss, here 20.000 Euros. There are 10.000 disruptions of the local metrological network by the end customer per year, because the local metrological network and most of the wireless equipment used in private areas make use of the 2.4 GHz band. In 50% of the cases, this leads to an incorrect transmission of data and a value loss of 50.000 Euros for the integrity of measured data. In one percent of the cases it leads to no transmission of data, which harms the availability of measured data completely and hence, produces a value loss of 10.000 Euros.

Table 8. Case study: asset documentation [6].

Symbolic phenomenon	Security property	Value
TariffParameters	Integrity	20.000 Euros
MeasuredData	Availability	10.000 Euros
MeasuredData	Integrity	50.000 Euros

Risk Evaluation. Since there is only at most one incoming edge per element, the likelihood for each unwanted incident is calculated by multiplying both previous likelihoods. The risk for each pair of unwanted incident and asset is documented in Table 9. Afterwards, the risks are added to the risk matrix as shown in Table 10. Here, we assume that the values for the risk matrix are the same for

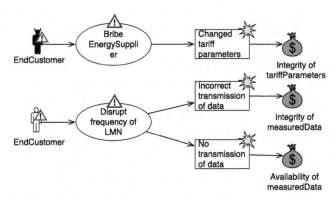

Fig. 7. Case study: threat diagram [6].

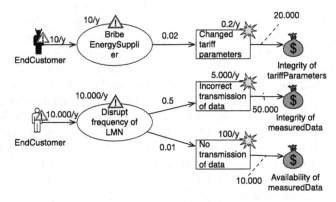

Fig. 8. Case study: threat diagram with annotated risks [6].

each asset. Unacceptable risks are marked in gray. Hence, there are three unacceptable risks, and it is necessary to provide a high-level security requirement for each of them:

HL-SR1. Ensure that the risk for *tariffParameters* with regard to *Integrity* due to *Changed tariff parameters* caused by {*Bribe EnergySupplier*} and initiated by {*EndCustomer*} is acceptable according to the risk matrix of the asset.

HL-SR2. Ensure that the risk for *measuredData* with regard to *Integrity* due to *Incorrect transmission of data* caused by {*Disrupt frequency of LMN*} and initiated by {*EndCustomer*} is acceptable according to the risk matrix of the asset.

HL-SR3. Ensure that the risk for *measuredData* with regard to *Availability* due to *No transmission of data* caused by {*Disrupt frequency of LMN*} and initiated by {*EndCustomer*} is acceptable according to the risk matrix of the asset.

Table 9. Case study: risk calculation [6].

No	Unwanted incident	Security goal	Risk ($frequ./y \times consequ.$)
(1)	Changed tariff parameters	Integrity of tariffParameters	(0.2, 20.000)
(2)	Incorrect transmission of data	Integrity of measuredData	(5.000, 50.000)
(3)	No transmission of data	Availability of measuredData	(100, 10.000)

5.4   Risk Treatment

We selected three treatments to illustrate the fourth step of our method using fictitious values for their costs. (1) To reduce the likelihood that bribing the energy supplier will be successful, there is a treatment providing better working conditions, e.g. more money. There are only few employees, who are able to change the tariff parameters. Hence, the costs of the treatment are 5.000 Euros. This is less than the value loss of 20.000 Euros. The likelihood reduction is estimated to be 80%. The residual likelihood for the unwanted incident is then $10 * (1 - 0.8) * 0.02 = 0.04$. According to the risk matrix (see Table 10), the risk is now acceptable. (2) To avoid disruption of the local metrological network (LMN), the frequency is replaced by a 5 GHz band. As there are major changes to the LMN, the costs are estimated with 40.000 Euros. This treatment addresses two likelihoods, because the threat scenario leads to two unwanted incidents. Both likelihoods are reduced by 99,9%, because the 5 GHz band allows many more concurrent connections. The value loss for an incorrect transmission of data is 50.000 Euros, and for no transmission of data it is 10.000 Euros. Hence, the costs of the treatment are less than the value loss. Recalculating the likelihoods for the unwanted incidents leads to $5/y$ for an incorrect transmission and $0.1/y$ for no transmission. According to the risk matrix, the likelihood for an incorrect transmission is still too high, so we need an additional treatment. (3) The implementation of a checksum can be realized by an existing component that can be applied at the LMN. The costs are 1.000 Euros. Since a checksum makes it possible to detect modifications of data, the consequences for the

Table 10. Case study: risk matrix [6].

		Consequence / Euros				
		[0,100[	[100,1000[	[1000,2000[	[2000,5000[	[5000,∞]
frequency / year	[0,0.1]					
	]0.1,1]					(1)
	]1,10]					
	]10,100]					
	]100,∞]					(2),(3)

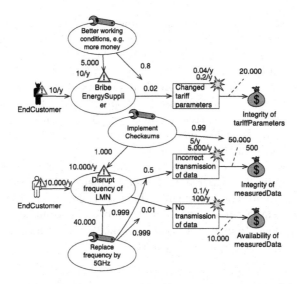

Fig. 9. Case study: threat diagram with treatments [6].

integrity of measured data are reduced by 99%. In fact, the incorrect data is still transmitted, but the communication hub is able to detect the incorrectness. The incorrect data will not be used for the invoicing. There is still a value loss, because the data has to be retrieved in a different way. The residual consequence is $(1 - 0.99) * 50000$ Euros $= 500$ Euros. According to the risk matrix and the likelihood reduction by the second treatment, the risk is now acceptable.

There are no unacceptable risks left in our example, and hence all high-level security requirements can be fulfilled. The augmented threat diagram containing all treatment scenarios is shown in Fig. 9.

We had identified three high-level security requirements. Hence, we have to set up three concretized security requirements (C-SR).

C-SR1. The risk for *tariffParameters* with regard *Integrity* due to *Changed tariff parameters* caused by *{Bribe EnergySupplier}* and initiated by *{EndCustomer}* is reduced to an acceptable level according to the risk matrix of the asset by applying *{(EnergySupplier, Better working conditions e.g. more money)}*.

C-SR2. The risk for *measuredData* with regard to *Integrity* due to *Incorrect transmission of data* caused by *{Disrupt frequency of LMN}* and initiated by *{EndCustomer}* is reduced to an acceptable level according to the risk matrix of the asset by applying *{(LMN, Implement checksums), (LMN, Replace frequency by 5 GHz)}*.

C-SR3. The risk for *measuredData* with regard to *Availability* due to *No transmission of data* caused by *{Disrupt frequency of LMN}* and initiated by *{EndCustomer}* is reduced to an acceptable level according to the risk matrix of the asset by applying *{(LMN, Replace frequency by 5 GHz)}*.

We have to set up three treatment problem diagrams, one per concretized security requirement. A machine domain is represented by a rectangle with two vertical bars. Similarly, we represent the newly introduced treatment domain with two horizontal bars.

Figure 10 shows the treatment problem diagram for *C-SR1*. The domain *EnergySupplier* is constrained, because the application of the treatment *WorkingConditions*, describing a better payment for the employees, influences that domain. The domain *EndCustomer* is referred to by C-SR1, because the end customer is mentioned in the requirement.

Figure 11 shows the treatment problem diagram for *C-SR2*. Since there is no treatment for domain *EndCustomer*, the requirement only refers to it. For the domain *LMN*, there are two treatments. Thus, it is constrained by the requirement. The treatment *NewFrequency* enables the LMN to make use of a 5 GHz band. The treatment *ImplementChecksums* allows the generation of message codes to verify the correctness of transmitted data.

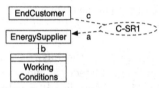

a: ES!{insertConfiguration} b: WC!{payMoreMoney}
c: EC!{bribeEnergySupplier}

Fig. 10. Case study: treatment problem diagram for C-SR1 [6].

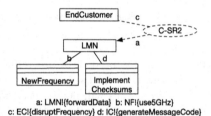

a: LMN!{forwardData} b: NF!{use5GHz}
c: EC!{disruptFrequency} d: IC!{generateMessageCode}

Fig. 11. Case study: treatment problem diagram for C-SR2 [6].

Figure 12 shows the treatment problem diagram for *C-SR3*. It is similar to the one for *C-SR2*, except that the implementation of a new frequency suffices to fulfill the requirement.

5.5   Risk Acceptance

All identified risks are reduced to an acceptable level. Hence, we only state concretized security requirements, which are all accepted by the organization without any remarks. The results are documented in Table 11.

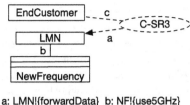

a: LMN!{forwardData} b: NF!{use5GHz}
c: EC!{disruptFrequency}

Fig. 12. Case study: treatment problem diagram for C-SR3 [6].

Table 11. Case study: risk acceptance.

Security requirement	Accepted	Rem.
C-SR1	Yes	–
C-SR2	Yes	–
C-SR3	Yes	–

6 Evaluation

For future improvement of the ProCOR method, we conducted an empirical study. The study is inspired by the work of Scandariato et al. [10], who evaluated Microsoft's STRIDE threat modeling technique in the context of an university course. Using the same context, students were asked to apply the ProCOR method with the research goal to especially extract their perception about the method and its performance afterwards.

For this reason, 15 students from the fields of computer science and applied cognitive science were educated in the ProCOR method for one semester to become familiar with it. In the end of the course, the students were divided into five groups consisting of three students whereby gender and field affiliation were respected to build counterbalanced interdisciplinary groups. In the style of a final assessment, the groups had to apply the ProCOR method on an electronic health care scenario. There, multiple stakeholders have access to personal data of patients that are collected via wireless devices and stored in a database. The groups' task was to identify as many threats and associated treatments as possible for a secure health care system. Giving them the opportunity to contact an expert, the groups can ask for necessary information like for example during the risk evaluation. Altogether, each group has had 45 min to become familiar with the scenario and two times two hours with a break of 45 min in-between to apply the ProCOR method on the scenario. Afterwards, the students were asked to answer a feedback questionnaire anonymously.

The feedback questionnaire consists of 14 items. Derived from the questionnaire of Scandariato et al., the perceived difficulty of the method was asked with a scale from 1 (very easy) to 5 (very hard). The other items are presented with a five-point *Likert-scale* from "strongly disagree" to "strongly agree". In the end, the participants could answer freely to four open questions addressing the ProCOR method as a whole.

To examine the average opinion of the participants, the descriptive statistics of the items were calculated. In addition, the same items of each step were also merged in order to gain knowledge about the participants' opinion about the ProCOR method in general. For every item, the sample size is $N = 15$. Regarding the perceived difficulty of the ProCOR method, the participants rated it as medium ($M = 2.93$, $SD = .38$), which is aligned to ProCOR's perceived simplicity being agreed to be partly simple ($M = 3.07$, $SD = .52$). Other aspects to which the participants partly agree are that ProCOR provides new perspectives on the scenario ($M = 3.25$, $SD = .45$), that other risk analysis techniques are more effective ($M = 3.27$, $SD = .79$) and that ProCOR is too complex in its execution ($M = 3.33$, $SD = .72$). Moreover, the participants are undecided whether using ProCOR is fun or partly fun ($M = 3.51$, $SD = .61$). Similar to that is the participants' opinion about a better comprehension of the scenario due to the Pro-COR method ($M = 3.69$, $SD = .36$) and that without ProCOR, less threats would have been discovered ($M = 3.67$, $SD = .97$). Furthermore, the participants tend to agree concerning the self-confidence in solving the tasks ($M = 3.80$, $SD = .57$), ProCOR'S support in a structured work within the group ($M = 3.87$, $SD = .834$) and the usefulness of previous ProCOR steps during working on a ProCOR step ($M = 3.90$, $SD = .52$). A tendency to strong agreement can be found regarding the usefulness of groupwork for the ProCOR method ($M = 4.63$, $SD = .57$). This result is in alignment with the findings towards the participants' rating to better work on the tasks alone ($M = 1.49$, $SD = .63$), so that a high negative correlation between both is correspondent ($r = -.838$, $p < .001$).

Other correlations can be found between self-confidence and perceived simplicity ($r = .646$, $p < .01$), self-confidence in using ProCOR and gaining new perspectives of the scenario ($r = -.550$, $p < .05$), and a better comprehension of the scenario and fun ($r = .712$, $p < .05$). Moreover, there is a high negative correlation between the perception of finding less threats without ProCOR and the perception of ProCOR being too complex in the execution ($r = -.539$, $p < .05$). Hence, it can be concluded that the less complicated an operator assesses Pro-COR, the more he/she is convinced in finding many threats.

Regarding the open feedback of the participants, they were asked about advantages and disadvantages of ProCOR, which ProCOR steps could be enhanced and how such an enhancement could look like. Their opinion is that ProCOR's multiple steps lead to a lucid, structured and detailed risk analysis. Furthermore, they mention that by following the single steps, the probability of disregarding aspects is decreased, and it is possible to put different aspects into context whereby new conclusions can be drawn. Therefore, the operator is led step by step to an in-depth solution approach. However, it is criticized that ProCOR is an intricate method, which employs multiple diagrams leading to an increased effort. Especially the risk evaluation and risk treatment were experienced as complex in method and calculation. Hence, the participants proposed an automation of these processes. We will address this issue in future work to reduce the effort to perform the risk management with ProCOR. Nevertheless, a detailed documentation is required by standards.

In total, the study identified the ProCOR method as being perceived in a positive and promising way to detect threats and their treatment. It has to be mention though that the sample is small and consists of students, who participated in the study during a university course. They most probably felt observed and assessed. Therefore, a bias can be assumed, which might be the reason for the partly high standard deviations of the statistics. In the future, it is planned to repeat the study with a larger sample and experts regarding risk analysis. Until then, the given remarks will be realized, as for example building a data base to enable automatized processes.

7 Related Work

Faßbender et al. [8] propose the PresSuRE method. The method provides a process to elicit security requirements. The starting point of the process is a set of functional requirements, represented as problem diagrams. The authors define an elicitation process, which consists of an identification of assets and an elicitation of attackers and their abilities based on attacker templates. The security requirements are derived from graphs that are created based on the information about the functional requirements and the elicited knowledge about attackers. The process does not cover a risk estimation or risk evaluation. The selection of treatments is not part of the method, as well.

The CORAS method [1] (see Sect. 2.3) is a model-based method for risk management. For each step, the input and output is defined as well as a language to describe the results in a model. The method is used for existing software. The security requirements are not explicitly stated, but there is a risk-based selection of treatments to achieve an acceptable risk level.

MAGERIT [11] is a methodology for Information Systems Risk Analysis and Management. It consists of several books. *Book 1* describes the risk management method itself, which covers all steps of the risk management process and provides detailed mechanisms to evaluate the risk. There are no security requirements, and the method is not model-based.

Mayer et al. provide a risk-based security engineering framework [12]. It describes a way to extend existing requirements engineering methods with security aspects. The framework describes an iterative way to perform this extension. The framework is used in the earliest stages of a software development life-cycle but does not make security requirements explicit. Moreover, it is not model-based.

Herrmann et al. propose a method for managing IT risks [13]. This method provides a risk identification with a corresponding risk prioritization and a selection of countermeasures to address the identified risk. The security requirements are elicited based on business goals. Business goals describe the expectations of different stakeholders for the software. For each business goal, one has to decide whether it is related to security. The method is not based on functional requirements and is applied to an existing software. It is not model-based.

Microsoft's STRIDE [14] is a popular security framework, which is used to identify security threats. Using data flow diagrams for modeling the system and its behavior, threats are elicited based on existing threat categories. In the end, threats are documented as a basis for the instantiation of security requirements. The security requirements are not part of STRIDE.

8   Discussion and Future Work

In this paper, we have described a step-wise risk management method to derive security requirements from functional requirements to protect valuable information. Our method provides compliance with the ISO 27005 standard for security risk management. We make use of models to document the results of each step and to express the relations between the functional requirements and the identified risks. The risk evaluation and the resulting high-level security requirements ensure that only unacceptable risks are treated. This is achieved by selecting appropriate controls and setting up concretized security requirements that specify how the necessary risk reduction can be achieved. To ensure that the security requirements can be taken into account in the software development process in a similar way as the functional requirements, we represent the elicited security requirements in a similar way as the functional ones. Finally, we identified validation conditions for our method assisting analysts in detecting errors in the application of the method as early as possible. Currently, we elaborate how to assist analysts in identifying relevant risks based on problem diagrams. Our vision is to provide a pattern-based library of relevant incident scenarios and a semi-automatic method to suggest relevant scenarios. We already submitted a paper that describes the pattern format and the basic idea of the method.

In the future, we plan to work out a similar template to build a library for controls. Using both libraries in combination will limit the effort for the analysts and provides a common format to describe incident scenarios and controls for different projects. Additionally, we will investigate in more detail how the controls are considered in the subsequent design and implementation phases. To ensure that controls are not in conflict with functional requirements, we will elaborate a feasibility analysis. We consider petri nets or automata as a first starting point for such an analysis.

Moreover, we intend to provide a web-based tool, which assists analysts in enacting the method. The results of each step are documented in a model. This allows the analysts to generate a documentation automatically and to ensure consistency between the different diagrams. Some of the proposed validation conditions can be checked automatically. The documentation can be used to certify the developed software according to a standard. The tool will provide a walkthrough of the steps described in Sect. 4. For adding new diagrams, we will provide a graphical diagram creation tool.

References

1. Lund, M.S., Solhaug, B., Stølen, K.: Model-Driven Risk Analysis. The CORAS Approach. Springer, Heidelberg (2010). https://doi.org/10.1007/978-3-642-12323-8
2. Jackson, M.: Problem Frames: Analyzing and Structuring Software Development Problems. Addison-Wesley Longman Publishing Co., Inc., Boston (2001)
3. International Organization for Standardization: ISO 27005:2011 Information technology - Security techniques - Information security risk management. Standard (2011)

4. International Organization for Standardization: ISO 31000:2018 Risk management - Principles and guidelines. Standard (2018)
5. Common Criteria: Common Criteria for Information Technology Security Evaluation v3.1. Release 5. Standard (2017)
6. Wirtz, R., Heisel, M., Meis, R., Omerovic, A., Stølen, K.: Problem-based elicitation of security requirements - the ProCOR method. In: Proceedings of the 13th International Conference on Evaluation of Novel Approaches to Software Engineering. ENASE, INSTICC, vol. 1, pp. 26–38. SciTePress (2018)
7. Heisel, M.: Agendas - a concept to guide software development activities. In: Proceedings of the IFIP TC2 WG2.4 Working Conference on Systems Implementation: Languages, Methods and Tools, pp. 19–32. Chapman and Hall London (1998)
8. Faßbender, S., Heisel, M., Meis, R.: Functional requirements under security pressSuRE. In: ICSOFT-PT 2014 - Proceedings of the 9th International Conference on Software Paradigm Trends, Vienna, Austria, 29–31 August 2014. SciTePress (2014)
9. OPEN meter Consortium: Report on the identification and specification of functional, technical, economical and general requirements of advanced multi-metering infrasturcture, including security requirements (2009)
10. Scandariato, R., Wuyts, K., Joosen, W.: A descriptive study of Microsoft's threat modeling technique. Requir. Eng. **20**, 163–180 (2015)
11. Ministerio de Administraciones Publicas: MAGERIT - version 3.0. Methodology for Information Systems Risk Analysis and Management. Book I - The Method. Ministry of Finance and Public Administration (2014)
12. Mayer, N., Rifaut, A., Dubois, E.: Towards a risk-based security requirements engineering framework. In: Proceeding of REFSQ 2005 (2005)
13. Herrmann, A., Morali, A., Etalle, S., Wieringa, R.: Risk and business goal based security requirement and countermeasure prioritization. In: Niedrite, L., Strazdina, R., Wangler, B. (eds.) BIR 2011. LNBIP, vol. 106, pp. 64–76. Springer, Heidelberg (2012). https://doi.org/10.1007/978-3-642-29231-6_6
14. Shostack, A.: Threat Modeling: Designing for Security. Wiley, Hoboken (2014)

Incremental Bidirectional Transformations: Comparing Declarative and Procedural Approaches Using the Families to Persons Benchmark

Bernhard Westfechtel[✉] and Thomas Buchmann

Applied Computer Science I, University of Bayreuth, 95440 Bayreuth, Germany
{bernhard.westfechtel,thomas.buchmann}@uni-bayreuth.de

Abstract. Model transformations constitute a key technology for model-driven software engineering. In round-trip engineering processes, model transformations are performed not only in forward, but also in backward direction. In this paper, we compare declarative and procedural approaches to defining bidirectional transformations. More specifically, we use the well-known Families to Persons benchmark to evaluate two approaches. The declarative approach is based on QVT Relations (QVT-R), a declarative language which allows to specify incremental bidirectional transformations by defining a set of relations which need to hold among the participating models. The procedural approach makes use of BXtend, a light-weight framework for bidirectional transformations which are implemented in Xtend, a procedural and object-oriented programming language. Surprisingly, the comparative evaluation demonstrates that the procedural approach outperforms the declarative approach with respect to different criteria such as correctness of the solution, implementation effort, or cognitive complexity.

Keywords: Model transformation · Bidirectional transformation · Benchmark · QVT Relations · BXtend

1 Introduction

Model transformations [11] constitute a key technology for model-driven software engineering. A model transformation takes a set of source models as input and creates or updates a set of target models. A transformation operates in *batch* mode if it generates the target models from scratch; in contrast, an *incremental* transformation propagates changes from sources to targets. Furthermore, we may distinguish between *unidirectional* transformations which are executed only from source to target, and *bidirectional transformations* which are executed also in the opposite direction. Bidirectional transformations occur in a wide variety of application domains [10], including, but not restricted to model-driven software engineering. In this paper, we focus specifically on incremental bidirectional transformations, as they are required e.g. in round-trip engineering processes.

A bidirectional transformation problem may be solved in a *unidirectional transformation language* by specifying both transformation directions separately. In contrast,

© Springer Nature Switzerland AG 2019
E. Damiani et al. (Eds.): ENASE 2018, CCIS 1023, pp. 98–118, 2019.
https://doi.org/10.1007/978-3-030-22559-9_5

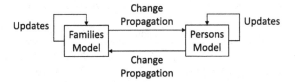

Fig. 1. The Families to Persons case [29].

a *bidirectional transformation language* is a language which allows to define bidirectional transformations with the help of a single transformation definition being executable in both directions; see [14] for a survey.

In the light of the diversity of languages and tools for bidirectional transformations, the need for *benchmarks* was identified early [10]. Later, a proposal for structuring benchmarks for bidirectional transformations was published [2]. Only recently, this proposal was materialized into an implementation called *Benchmarx*, which constitutes a practical benchmark framework for bidirectional transformations [3].

Based on this framework, a popular case from the literature—the Families to Persons case—was implemented [1]; see Fig. 1. Two related, but differently structured models have to be kept consistent: A families model with parents and children, and a persons model containing a flat set of males and females. Updates may be performed on both models, and have to be propagated in both directions.

While the Families to Persons case is rather small and thus implementable with acceptable effort, it poses a number of challenges such as heterogeneous metamodels, loss of information, the absence of keys (uniquely identifying properties of model elements), non-determinism, configurability (of the backward transformation), renamings and moves, and application-specific requirements to change operations.

So far, a wide range of solutions to the Families to Persons case has been implemented in the Benchmarx framework. The case [1] was submitted to the *Transformation Tool Contest* 2017 [12]. Table 1 provides an overview of the solutions, which are classified into TTC reference implementations and solutions submitted to the TTC itself. The employed languages are based on considerably different paradigms[1]. The solutions are based partly on unidirectional and partly on bidirectional languages.

This paper compares two solutions to the Families to Persons benchmark which were developed by the authors and constitute extremes on the spectrum of solutions summarized in Table 1:

1. The first solution [29] is written in *QVT Relations (QVT-R)* [20], a *declarative language* for the relational specification of transformations. In QVT-R, a transformation developer may specify a set of relations among participating models, which are executed as directed transformations. Bidirectional transformations may be specified by a single transformation definition being executable in both directions, making QVT-R a bidirectional transformation language. The implementation is based on *medini QVT* [17], a tool which supports editing and execution of transformations written in QVT-R (with some deviations from the standard defining the QVT-R language which will be discussed later).

---

[1] TGG denotes triple graph grammars, GT stands for graph transformations.

Table 1. Solutions to the Families-to-Persons benchmarx.

	Language	Bidirectional	Paradigm	Reference
TTC reference	**BIGUL**	×	Functional	[3]
implementations	**eMoflon**	×	TGG-based	[3]
	QVT-R	×	Relational	[3,29]
	BXtend		Procedural	[7]
TTC solutions	**EVL+STrace**		Constraint-based	[22]
	FunnyQT	×	Relational	[16]
	NMF	×	Functional	[15]
	SDMLib		GT-based	[30]

2. The second solution is written in *Xtend*, a *procedural langauge* with an abstraction level slightly higher than Java. In fact, Xtend is a multi-paradigm language supporting not only procedural, but also object-oriented and functional programming. The solution is based on *BXtend* [7], a light-weight framework for bidirectional incremental transformations. In BXtend, both directions of a bidirectional transformations are realized separately, based on a common correspondence model of links between source and target elements of the transformation.

In addition to presenting our solutions, we will also compare them with respect to different criteria. These criteria include *correctness* of the solution, *implementation effort*, the *level of abstraction* on which the solution is provided, *redundancies* in the solution, and the *cognitive complexity* of understanding the solution.

The rest of this paper is structured as follows: Sect. 2 presents the Families to Persons case. Sections 3 and 4 present the declarative solution in medini QVT and the procedural solution in BXtend, respectively. Section 5 compares these solutions. Section 6 discusses related work, and Sect. 7 concludes the paper.

2 Transformation Case

Different variants of the Families to Persons case have been proposed. To make this paper self-contained, we describe the variant on which our work is based, following [1]. The case is rather small such that it is implementable with acceptable effort. On the other hand, it includes several challenges to be summarized at the end of this section.

2.1 Metamodels and Consistency

The Families to Persons case deals with the synchronization of a families model with a persons model. The underlying *metamodels* are displayed in Fig. 2 as class diagrams. For metamodeling, we employ Ecore - an implementation of Essential MOF, a subset of

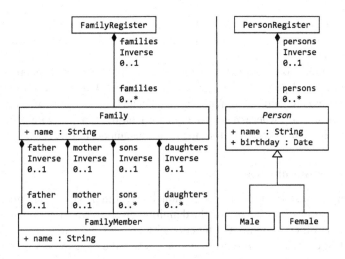

Fig. 2. Metamodels [29].

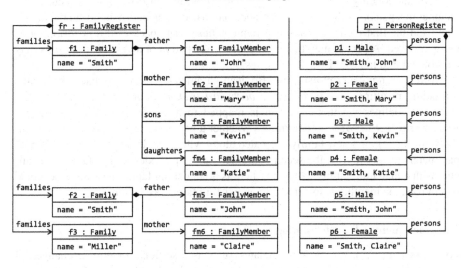

Fig. 3. Example of mutually consistent models.

MOF, provided by the Eclipse Modeling Framework [24]. Please note that we adopt the following terminology: A *model* represents a collection of instance data. A *metamodel* is a "model for models" and defines the types of objects, attributes, and links, as well as the rules for their composition.

We assume a unique root in each model. A family register stores a collection of families. Each family has members who are distinguished by their roles. The metamodel allows for at most one father and at most one mother as well as an arbitrary number of daughters and sons. A person register maintains a flat collection of persons who have a birthday and are either male or female. Note that key properties may be assumed in neither model: There may be multiple families with the same name, name clashes are even allowed within a single family, and there may be multiple persons with the same name and birthday.

A families model is *consistent* with a persons model if a bijective mapping between family members and persons can be established such that (i) mothers and daughters (fathers and sons) are paired with females (males), and (ii) the name of every person p is "$f.name, m.name$", where m is the member (in family f) paired with p. An example of mutually consistent models, conforming to the metamodel of Fig. 2, is given in Fig. 3.

2.2 Batch Transformations

After running a transformation in any direction, it is required that the participating models are mutually consistent according the definition given above. However, this requirement does not suffice to define the functionality of transformations in a unique way. Below, we first consider *batch transformations*, where the target model is created from scratch.

The functionality of a *forward transformation* is straightforward: Map each family member to a person of the same gender and compose the person's name from the family name and the first name; the birthday remains unset. The backward transformation is more involved: A person may be mapped either to a parent or a child, and persons may be grouped into families in different ways.

To reduce non-determinism, two Boolean parameters control the backward transformation, resulting in a *configurable backward transformation*: preferParent-ToChild defines whether a person is mapped to a parent or a child. prefer-ExistingToNewFamily determines whether a person is added to an existing family (if available), or a new family is created along with a single family member. If both parameters are set to true, the second parameter takes precedence: If a family is available with a matching family name, but there is no matching family with an unoccupied parent role, the member is inserted into an existing family as a child.

2.3 Incremental Transformations

For *incremental transformations*, updates such as insertions, deletions, changes of attribute values, and move operations have to be considered. In *forward direction*, insertion of a family has no effect on the target model. Insertion of a member results in insertion of a corresponding person; likewise for deletions. If a family is deleted, all persons corresponding to its members are deleted. If a member is renamed, the corresponding person is renamed accordingly. If a family is renamed, all persons corresponding to family members are renamed. If a member is moved, different cases have to be distinguished. If the gender is retained, the corresponding person object is preserved; otherwise, it is deleted, and a new person object with a different gender is created whose attributes are copied from the old person object. A local move within a family does not affect the corresponding person's name; a move to another family results in a potential update of the person's name.

In *backward direction*, the effect of an update depends on the values of the configuration parameters which may vary between different transformation executions.

Please note that the parameter settings must not affect already established correspondences; rather, they apply only to future updates. Deletion of a person propagates to the corresponding family member. If a person is inserted, it depends on the configuration parameters how insertion propagates to the families model (see above). Persons cannot be moved because the persons model consists of a single, flat, and unordered collection. Changes of birthdays do not propagate to the opposite model. If the first name of a person is changed, the first name of the corresponding family member is updated accordingly. Finally, if the family name of a person is changed, this change does not affect the current family and its members: The family preserves its name even if it does not contain other members; thus, the update has no side effects on the existing family. Rather, the corresponding family member is moved to another family, which may have to be created before the move; the precise update behavior depends on the parameter settings.

2.4   Challenges

The Families to Persons case includes a number of *challenges* which are summarized below:

Heterogeneous Metamodels. The transformation has to perform a mapping between heterogeneous metamodels, where the same information is represented in different ways (concerning e.g. names and genders).

Loss of Information. The family structure is lost in the forward transformation; birthdays are lost in the backward transformation.

No Keys. There are no uniquely identifying properties for family members or persons, which makes propagation of changes difficult.

Non-determinism. The families model does not contain information for defining birthdays in the persons model. Conversely, the persons model does not contain information about the family structure. The forward and backward transformations have to resolve non-determinism.

Configurability. Non-determinism in the backward transformation is handled by configuration parameters which affect the family structure. The parameters may be changed from execution to execution and should affect only new elements of the persons model in each run.

Renamings and Moves. Change operations to be propagated include not only creations and deletions, but also renamings and moves which must not be reduced to deletions and creations (otherwise, the principle of *least change* [18], which demands that the changes are propagated in a minimally invasive way, would be violated).

Specific Requirements to Change Operations. The case description includes specific requirements to change operations. For example, if the family name of a person is changed, the person should be moved to another family (rather than having the family name updated, with side effects on other members).

3 Declarative Approach

This section describes our declarative solution to the Families to Persons benchmark. Before presenting the actual solution, we introduce the QVT Relations language (QVT-R) as well as the tool (medini QVT) used for implementation.

3.1 QVT-R and Medini QVT

QVT Relations (QVT-R) is a transformation language which is defined in an OMG standard [20]. The tool *medini QVT* [17] partially implements the QVT-R language. With respect to syntax, only a few restrictions apply in medini QVT compared to the standard. The semantics implemented in medini QVT deviates from the standard in several respects. The following description refers to QVT-R as implemented in medini QVT, since the comparison in Sect. 5 is based on the implementation in medini QVT rather than on the standard. To the best of our knowledge, currently there is no standard-conformant implementation of QVT-R available.

In QVT-R, a *transformation* is defined for a set of $n \geq 2$ *candidate models*, which are typed over *MOF*-based metamodels [21]. A transformation is always executed in the direction of exactly one target model, i.e., the target model is modified, and the remaining models are read. In general, *multi-directional transformations* may be written in QVT-R; in this paper, we consider *bidirectional transformations*.

A transformation is composed of a set of *relations*, which are used to describe correspondences between patterns in different models. The keyword `top` indicates a *top-level relation*, implying that the respective relation must hold between all instances of patterns which may be retrieved in the respective models. In contrast, a *called relation*—for which the keyword `top` is absent—needs to hold only for the arguments on which it is called.

In QVT-R, a pattern is called a *domain*. Each domain is attached to exactly one of the candidate models and is composed of a rooted graph of objects which are connected by links and are decorated by attribute values. The potential roles of a domain are indicated by modifiers: A `checkonly` domain can only be read, while a domain with modifier `enforce` can be read or written (depending on the direction in which the transformation is executed).

In addition to domains, relations may be equipped with *pre-* and *postconditions*. A `when` *clause* determines the conditions under which a relation must hold, a `where` *clause* is composed of conditions which need to hold after the relation has been executed.

In addition to relations, a transformation may contain definitions of *queries*, which are functions without side effects. Queries are specified in *OCL* [19], which is generally used as expression language in QVT-R.

In QVT-R, *batch transformations* are considered as special cases of *incremental transformations*: A batch transformation is a transformation which is executed against an initially empty target model. After having executed a transformation, all top-level relations must hold in the direction of the target model. This means that for all source pattern instances there must be a target pattern instance such that the relation holds.

Listing 1. QVT-R transformation with root relation.

```
transformation families2personsconfig
                (famDB : Families, conf : Config,  perDB : Persons) {
    top relation FamilyRegister2PersonRegister {
        enforce domain famDB familyRegister : Families::FamilyRegister {};
        enforce domain perDB personRegister : Persons::PersonRegister {};
    }
    -- Further relations and queries
}
```

medini QVT deviates from the semantics defined in the standard by employing *traces* of transformations. A trace records which relations have been applied in the transformation. In medini QVT, traces are stored persistently. When a transformation is executed, the trace is consulted in order to determine which source pattern instances have already been transformed. For source patterns which have not been transformed yet, corresponding target patterns are instantiated. In case of inconsistencies between source and target pattern instances, changes in the source patterns may be propagated as long as only values of attributes are inconsistent. In the case of more fundamental inconsistencies (on the level of objects and links), inconsistent target pattern instances are deleted, and new (consistent) target pattern instances are created.

3.2 Solution

Since only models may be passed as parameters to a transformation, the parameters needed to realize a configurable transformation are stored in an auxiliary *configuration model*. Thus, the transformation operates on three models rather than two. In each execution, the configuration model is read, and either the families model or the persons model is updated (or created from scratch). The configuration model is composed of a single configuration object holding three Boolean attributes for determining the transformation direction and the preferences of the backward transformation.

Listing 1 shows the head of the transformation, which defines the candidate models typed by their respective metamodels. Altogether, the transformation consists of seven relations and a set of auxiliary queries. Listing 1 displays the top-level relation for mapping the root objects of the respective models. In forward direction, a person register is created if it does not yet exist, and a relation to the corresponding family register is established; likewise for the backward direction.

Two top-level relations are provided for which relate members to males and females, respectively. Listing 2 shows the relation Member2Female as example; the relation Member2Male may be obtained by replacing gender-specific parts of the relation. Altogether, the relation defines five domains which are distributed over three models; the attributes of the configuration object are read to control the behavior of the relation.

The when clause requires that the family register object must be related to the person register object: Only family members and persons may be related which are stored in corresponding registers. The conditional expression evaluates to true in backward direction, and ensures that the family member is female in forward direction.

When the relation is applicable, a female person is created (or matched) in forward direction; likewise, a family member is created or matched in backward direction. The where clause is responsible for calling further relations which handle role-specific details: Either the relation MothertoFemale or the relation Daughter2Female is

Listing 2. Relation between family members and females.

```
top relation Member2Female {
    fromPersonsToFamilies, preferParentToChild,
        preferExistingToNewFamily : Boolean;
    createDaughter : Boolean;
    enforce domain famDB member : Families::FamilyMember {};
    enforce domain famDB familyRegister : Families::FamilyRegister {};
    checkonly domain conf configuration : Config::Configuration {
        fromPersonsToFamilies = fromPersonsToFamilies,
        preferParentToChild = preferParentToChild,
        preferExistingToNewFamily = preferExistingToNewFamily
    };
    enforce domain perDB female : Persons::Female {};
    enforce domain perDB personRegister : Persons::PersonRegister {};
    when {
        FamilyRegister2PersonRegister(familyRegister, personRegister);
        if fromPersonsToFamilies then
            true
        else
            not isMale(member)
        endif;
    }
    where {
        if not fromPersonsToFamilies and
            member.motherInverse.oclIsUndefined() then
            Daughter2Female(member, configuration, female)
        else
            true
        endif;
        if not fromPersonsToFamilies and
            member.daughtersInverse.oclIsUndefined() then
            Mother2Female(member, configuration, female)
        else
            true
        endif;
        if fromPersonsToFamilies and not preferParentToChild then
            Daughter2Female(member, configuration, female)
        else
            true
        endif;
        if fromPersonsToFamilies and preferParentToChild and
            not preferExistingToNewFamily then
            Mother2Female(member, configuration, female)
        else
            true
        endif;
        createDaughter =
        (familyWithoutMother
            (familyRegister, familyName(female.name)).oclIsUndefined() and
        not family(familyRegister, familyName(female.name)).oclIsUndefined());
        if createDaughter and fromPersonsToFamilies and preferParentToChild
            and preferExistingToNewFamily then
            Daughter2Female(member, configuration, female)
        else
            true
        endif;
        if not createDaughter and fromPersonsToFamilies and preferParentToChild
            and preferExistingToNewFamily then
            Mother2Female(member, configuration, female)
        else
            true
        endif;
    }
}
```

Listing 3. Relation between daughters and females.

```
relation Daughter2Female {
    fromPersonsToFamilies, preferParentToChild,
        preferExistingToNewFamily : Boolean;
    firstName, familyName, fullName : String;
    enforce domain famDB daughter : Families::FamilyMember {
        name = firstName,
        daughtersInverse = family : Families::Family {
            name = familyName,
            familiesInverse = familyRegister : Families::FamilyRegister {}
        }
    };
    checkonly domain conf configuration : Config::Configuration {
        fromPersonsToFamilies = fromPersonsToFamilies,
        preferParentToChild = preferParentToChild,
        preferExistingToNewFamily = preferExistingToNewFamily
    };
    enforce domain perDB female : Persons::Female {
        name = fullName,
        personsInverse = personRegister : Persons::PersonRegister {}
    };
    when {
        FamilyRegister2PersonRegister(familyRegister, personRegister);
        fullName = familyName + ', ' + firstName;
        firstName = firstName(fullName);
        familyName = familyName(fullName);
        family = if fromPersonsToFamilies and preferExistingToNewFamily then
                    family(familyRegister, familyName)
                else
                    family
                endif;
    }
}
```

called. Altogether, the transformation defines four called relations for fathers, mothers, daughters, and sons, all of which are structured analogously.

The expressions in the where clause encode a decision table. To keep them simple, deeply nested subexpressions are avoided. Since each expression will be evaluated at runtime, care must be taken to keep the conditions for calling relations mutually exclusive. To keep the presentation short, we explain only the first of these expressions: If the transformation is executed in forward direction and the member is not a mother, the relation Daughter2Female is called (returning true if the call is successful). Otherwise, nothing happens, and the expression evaluates to true, as well, such that execution continues with the evaluation of the next expression.

Finally, the relation Daughter2Female (Listing 3) links the female person to the person register and assigns its full name if it is executed in forward direction. The full name is calculated in the when clause from the first name and the family name. In backward direction, the full name is decomposed into the first name and the family name, which again happens in the when clause. Furthermore, it is attempted in the when clause to bind the variable family if the member has to be inserted into an existing family. Otherwise, the variable remains unbound, and a new family is created into which the family member is inserted.

4   Procedural Approach

4.1   BXtend

BXtend [7] is a procedural and object-oriented framework implemented in the programming language *Xtend*[2]. BXtend allows to specify forward and backward rules for
bidirectional and incremental model-to-model transformations. Besides its procedural
and object-oriented character, Xtend also provides powerful functional parts, as lambda
expressions. The procedural constructs allow for a greater flexibility in transformation
specifications. Our BXtend framework is a light-weight solution helping transformation developers to easily specify a *Triple Graph Transformation System* (*TGTS*) as an
internal DSL. It is easy to use for Java developers, as Xtend directly builds upon Java
and makes it less verbose. Thus, the transformation developer does not need to learn
a new programming language. Furthermore, the resulting M2M transformation may
be integrated seamlessly with any other Java application without requiring additional
dependencies, which makes it particularly interesting for tool integrators.

Transformation directions are specified independently in a *unidirectional language*,
which provides a greater flexibility for the transformation developer, but provides no
support to check if the backward transformation actually matches the forward direction. Nevertheless, our case studies [8,9,13] showed that, although both transformation
directions need to be specified separately, the overall transformation script is still dense
and compact and does not require more lines of code than approaches allowing to derive
both forward and backward transformation from a single bidirectional specification.

In order to support incremental transformations and propagate updates to already
existing model elements, BXtend uses a generic *correspondence model*, depicted in
Fig. 4. The correspondence model contains a list of correspondence objects, each of
which maintains links to the respective source and target model element. Please note
that the 1:1 correspondences may be altered to 1:n or even m:n ones if required. For the
transformation problem discussed in this paper, 1:1 correspondences between source
and target model elements are sufficient.

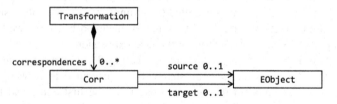

Fig. 4. BXtend correspondence model [7].

Besides the correspondence model, the BXtend framework comprises a set of
generic operations, maintaining the correspondence model and updating or creating
source and target model elements, respectively. I.e., whenever a model element has to
be transformed, the correspondence model is checked whether the current element is
already referred to in a correspondence element. If this is the case, the opposite model
element is retrieved from the correspondence model, and its properties are altered.

---

[2] http://www.eclipse.org/xtend.

Listing 4. BXtend rule class for transforming the root elements of both models.

```
class Register2Register extends Elem2Elem{
  override sourceToTarget() {
    sourceModel.allContents.filter(typeof(FamilyRegister)).forEach[ c |
      val corr = c.getOrCreateCorrModelElement()
      val target = corr.getOrCreateTargetElem(PersonsPackage.
        eINSTANCE.personRegister) as PersonRegister
      if(!targetModel.contents.contains(target))
        targetModel.contents.add(target)
    ]
  }

  override targetToSource() {
    targetModel.allContents.filter(typeof(PersonRegister)).forEach[ c |
      val corr = c.getOrCreateCorrModelElement()
      val source = corr.getOrCreateSourceElem(FamiliesPackage.
        eINSTANCE.familyRegister) as FamilyRegister
      if(!sourceModel.contents.contains(source))
        sourceModel.contents.add(source)
    ]
  }
}
```

Thus, the transformation developer only has to supply the respective forward and backward rules for the model elements that need to be transformed. Typically, for each meta class of the source model, a BXtend class is supplied, which is derived from the generic transformation base class, and two operations, each specifying one transformation direction need to be specified by the transformation developer.

4.2 Solution

In contrast to the QVT-R solution discussed above, only source and target model are required. The configuration options for the transformation are stored as Boolean attributes in a special configurator class supplied with the transformation rules. The respective configuration parameters are used only when the transformation is executed in the backward direction. In total, the transformation consists of four transformation classes containing rules for forward and backward transformation of the respective source and target model elements. The BXtend solution follows the containment hierarchy of both source and target models. The start rule shown in Listing 4 is responsible for transforming a FamilyRegister into a PersonRegister and vice versa. In forward direction (sourceToTarget()), a PersonRegister is created in case it does not exist yet, and a correspondence relationship to the respective FamilyRegister is established. The backward transformation (targetToSource()) works analogously.

The transformation of a FamilyMember into a Person is split into two BXtend rules, since the abstract class Person in the Person metamodel has two concrete subclasses Male and Female. The two transformation rules share common code except the creation of the respective target model classes and thus, inheritance is used to factor out the common parts of those transformation rules. The abstract rule class FamilyMember2Person shown in Listing 5 is used for this purpose. The common parts of the forward transformation are rather straightforward and just involve creating a Person element and setting its properties accordingly. In the backward direction, the configuration of the transformation is taken into account. The abstract rule class contains methods for returning an existing family with the given name, or creating a new one and adding FamilyMembers as parents or children.

Listing 5. BXtend abstract rule class for transforming `FamilyMembers` to `Persons`.

```
abstract class FamilyMember2Person extends Elem2Elem {
  def protected getOrCreateFamily(Family sourceFamily, Person p,
      FamilyRegister fregister) {
    val familyname = p.name.split(", ").get(0)
    val families = fregister.getFamilies(familyname)
    var family = decision.getFamily(families, p, sourceFamily)
    if (family == null) {
      family = createFamilyElement(FamiliesPackage.
        eINSTANCE.family) as Family => [name = familyname]
      fregister.families += family
      decision.linkPersonToFamily(p, family)
    }
    family
  }

  def protected void addToFamily(Person p, Family family,
    FamilyMember newMember, ()=>FamilyMember parentGetter,
    (FamilyMember)=>void parentSetter,
    (FamilyMember)=>void childSetter) {
    if (decision.setAsParent(p, family)) {
      val parent = parentGetter.apply()
      if (parent != null)
        childSetter.apply(parent)
      parentSetter.apply(newMember)
    } else {
      childSetter.apply(newMember)
    }
  }

  def protected getOrCreatePersonElement(String name, Corr corrPerson,
      EClass personClass) {
    val birthday = ((corrPerson.personElement as Person)?.birthday) ?:
    PersonsPackage.eINSTANCE.person_Birthday.defaultValue as Date
    if (corrPerson.personElement != null &&
      corrPerson.personElement.eClass != personClass) {
      EcoreUtil.delete(corrPerson.personElement, true)
      corrPerson.personElement = null
    }
    val person = corrPerson.getOrCreateTargetElem(personClass) as Person
    person.name = name
    person.birthday = birthday
    person
  }

  def private getFamilies(FamilyRegister fregister, String familyname) {
    val size = decision.getFamilyListSize
    val families = newArrayList
    switch size {
      case size < 0:
        families += fregister.families.filter[name == familyname]
      case size == 0:
        families.clear
      case size == 1:
        families += fregister.families.findFirst[name == familyname]
      default:
        fregister.families.forEach [ f |
          if (f.name == familyname)
            families += f
          if (families.size > size)
            return
        ]
    }
    families
  }
}
```

Two concrete subclasses of `FamilyMember2Person` are used to transform `Males` and `Females`. Listing 6 depicts the rule which is responsible for the transformation of `Females`. In the forward direction (`sourceToTarget()`), all female `FamilyMembers` are retrieved for each `Family` in the source model. Afterwards, for each `Female` the corresponding counterpart in the Persons model is created if it does not exist yet, or updated using the operation `getOrCreatePersonElement`, which is defined in the abstract rule class shown in Listing 5.

In the backward direction (`targetToSource()`), the corresponding `Family-Member` element is created or updated. Afterwards, the `Family` which the person belongs to is retrieved, depending upon the configuration parameters. The operation `getOrCreateFamily` defined in the abstract rule class is used for this purpose. The operation `addToFamily` is responsible for adding the `FamilyMember` to the proper reference in the containing `Family` (either `mother` or `daughters`, depending on the chosen configuration option). Finally, empty families without any family member are deleted from the source model. The transformation of male persons is performed analogously.

5 Discussion

In the following, the solutions presented in the preceding sections are compared against each other according to various criteria (correctness, implementation effort, level of abstraction, redundancies in the solutions, and cognitive complexity). We conclude this section with a discussion of potential threats to validity.

5.1 Correctness

The test suite supplied with the benchmark contains different test cases for each transformation direction, as well as test cases carried out in batch and incremental mode of operation. In total, the Families to Persons benchmark comprises 34 test cases.

The BXtend solution successfully passes all test cases—in forward and backward direction as well as in batch and in incremental mode. Since the application code is written in Xtend, the full flexibility of a procedural programming language may be exploited. Thus, the solution may be programmed precisely according to the requirements imposed by the benchmark.

The QVT-R solution successfully passes all test cases in batch mode, but fails in most of the incremental test cases. Thus, the incremental behavior of the transformation does not meet the requirements of the benchmark. Altogether, the QVT-R solution fails in 12 out of 34 test cases. In contrast to the BXtend solution, the transformation developer has to "buy" the built-in incremental behavior and cannot adjust it in such a way that the requirements are satisfied.

In forward direction, 4 out 8 incremental test cases succeed for the QVT-R solution. The failures reveal some deficits in propagating changes. While it is possible to propagate changes of attribute values (name changes in the case of the Families to Persons

Listing 6. BXtend rule class for transforming Mothers or Daughters to Female.

```
class MotherDaughter2Female extends FamilyMember2Person {
  override sourceToTarget() {
    sourceModel.allContents.filter(typeof(Family)).forEach [ family |
      val corrregister = family.eContainer.getCorrModelElem
      val females = ECollections.newBasicEList()
      females.addAll(family.daughters)
      if (family.mother != null)
        females.add(family.mother)
        females.forEach [ member |
          val corrFemale = member.getOrCreateCorrModelElement()
          val female = getOrCreatePersonElement(family.name + ", "
              + member.name, corrFemale, PersonsPackage.eINSTANCE.female)
          (corrregister.personElement as PersonRegister).
            getPersons().add(female)
        ]
    ]
  }

  override targetToSource() {
    targetModel.allContents.filter(typeof(Female)).forEach [ p |
      val corr = p.getOrCreateCorrModelElement(s);
      val source = corr.getOrCreateSourceElem(
        FamiliesPackage.eINSTANCE.familyMember) as FamilyMember
      val firstname = p.name.split(", ").get(1)
      val familyname = p.name.split(", ").get(0)
      val sourceFamily = source.eContainer() as Family
      val fregister = p.eContainer().getCorrModelElem().
        getFamilyElement() as FamilyRegister

      source.name = firstname
      if (sourceFamily == null || sourceFamily.name != familyname) {
        val family = getOrCreateFamily(sourceFamily, p, fregister)
        p.addToFamily(family, source, [family.mother],
          [family.mother = it], [family.daughters += it])
        if (sourceFamily != null && sourceFamily.father == null
            && sourceFamily.mother == null && sourceFamily.sons.empty
            && sourceFamily.daughters.empty
            && decision.deleteEmptyFamily(sourceFamily, source)) {
          EcoreUtil.delete(sourceFamily, true)
        }
      }
    ]
  }
}
```

benchmark), medini QVT cannot propagate changes of links. For example, the move of a member to another family cannot be propagated; rather, the corresponding person is deleted and re-created.

In backward direction, all incremental test cases fail. Rather than applying the configuration parameters just to new model elements (new persons added to the person register), they are applied globally. For example, let us reconsider Fig. 3. Starting from the family register, the forward transformation creates the person register as shown in the figure. After any incremental change to the person register, any backward transformation destroys the family structure regardless of the parameter settings because it is not possible to generate two families with the same name ``Smith''.

5.2 Implementation Effort

Although QVT-R provides support for bidirectional and incremental model-to-model transformations, significant effort was required to specify the bidirectional rules for our use case. To a large extent, this effort is due to redundancies in the rule set (see also Sect. 5.4). For this reason, the BXtend solution outperforms the QVT-R solution in terms of lines of code. **211** lines of BXtend code are required compared to **320** lines of QVT-R code. The fact that in the BXtend solution both transformation directions have to be specified and incremental behavior has to be programmed explicitly, whereas in the QVT-R specification a single rule may be executed in both directions both in batch and incremental mode, renders the obtained numbers even more impressive.

5.3 Level of Abstraction

The QVT-R rules are highly declarative. Since QVT-R supports bidirectional relations between source and target elements, only one single rule set is sufficient for transformations in both directions in batch and incremental mode. QVT-R employs OCL statements in both queries and `when` and `where` clauses, which allows for a compact and concise specification of constraints and model traversals. It should be noted, however, that in QVT-R the transformation developer needs to consider the operational behavior of the transformation in detail, i.e., the operational behavior cannot be simply abstracted away.

The BXtend solution resides on a lower level of abstraction, as the Xtend programming language primarily is a procedural object-oriented language which is augmented with some declarative language constructs like lambda expressions. However, in our use case this fact did not cause negative effects on the required implementation effort or on the complexity of the resulting forward and backward rules.

5.4 Redundancies in the Solutions

As already mentioned in Subsect. 3.2, the QVT-R solution suffers from *redundancies in the rule set*. Two similar top-level relations are required for mapping family members to male and female persons, respectively. Likewise, four similar call relations are required for handling the different roles of family members. These redundancies are primarily due to differences in types of objects and links. In QVT-R, reuse mechanisms such as parameterization and inheritance of relations are not available. It is merely possible to factor common parts out into called relations. Since relations need to be executed in both directions in the case of bidirectional transformations, the related domains must not contain any variation points, such as e.g. objects of an abstract class.

In contrast to the declarative approach supported by QVT-R, language features like inheritance, genericity or control structures are available in BXtend and are extensively exploited in our solution. Compared to the QVT-R approach, the number of rules can be reduced significantly in BXtend. Only one rule per model element is required here. Furthermore, reuse and modularization is supported by object-oriented paradigms, as complex and recurring assignments may be easily extracted to operations which are called whenever appropriate.

5.5 Cognitive Complexity

Due to the declarative specification of bidirectional transformations being executable both in batch and incremental mode, one might expect that QVT-R imposes a low cognitive complexity on its user. However, the transformation developer has to accomplish more than merely the specification of a declarative consistency relation: The transformation has to be written in such a way that it can be actually executed in both directions and behaves as required. The relations which make up the transformation are typically overloaded since they contain parts which are relevant for only one transformation; consider e.g. the `where` clause of the relation `MemberToFemale` in Listing 2. The transformation developer has to check that direction-specific parts do not get in the way when the transformation is executed in the opposite direction. Furthermore, since there is no control flow, it has to be verified that execution steps are executed in the appropriate order, leaving e.g. no unbound variables in an expression that needs to be evaluated.

On the one hand, cognitive complexity in BXtend should be higher since the user has to program incremental behavior explicitly and also has to encode both transformation directions. The latter has to be performed in such a way that the forward and the backward transformation are mutually compatible. On the other hand, the transformation developer may control the behavior of the transformation precisely, using familiar concepts of object-oriented and procedural programming. Furthermore, considering one transformation direction at a time significantly reduces cognitive complexity.

5.6   Threats to Validity

The conclusions drawn in the previous section are subject to various threats of validity. To some extent, they are based on metrics such as the number of passed test cases (correctness) and lines of source code (implementation effort). For other criteria such as level of abstraction, redundancies in the solutions, and cognitive complexity, we cannot offer suitable metrics. With respect to these criteria, our discussion is purely qualitative (but, as we hope, well supported by arguments).

It might also be argued that our findings are confined to the specific use case—the Families to Persons benchmark—and cannot be generalized. However, our findings are also supported by other case studies. For example, we implemented round-tripping between UML and Java models both in QVT-R [13] and in BXtend [8]; the QVT-R solution covers 1905 lines of code, while the BXtend solution requires only 1032 lines of code. In addition, we implemented the transformation cases solved for QVT-R in [28] also in BXtend. Again, these case studies confirm the conclusions drawn above.

6   Related Work

This paper is based on two predecessor publications. The first one [29] discusses the application of QVT-R to the Families to Persons benchmark. In that paper, the QVT standard [20] was used strictly as the sole point of reference. In this paper, we referred to a solution executed in medini QVT, which reuses QVT-R syntax, but implements a deviating semantics. This solution was not published before and constitutes our best effort solution for medini QVT. The second predecessor [7] focused on the presentation of the BXtend framework and used small fragments of the solution to the Families to

Persons benchmark merely as an example. In addition, the current paper compares the declarative and the procedural solution, which we consider as its key contribution.

As far as QVT-R is concerned, our work complements previous case studies having been performed with QVT-R [8,13,26–28]. Altogether, our work is unique inasmuch as it targets the evaluation of QVT-R with the help of case studies. A detailed comparison with related work on QVT-R is given in [28]. Generally, we may observe that a great detail of research into QVT-R focuses on its semantics definition [5,6,18,25] rather than on its application.

The BXtend framework differs from declarative bidirectional and incremental model-to-model transformation approaches considerably. Previous case studies using an industrial-sized bidirectional incremental transformation for round-tripping between UML and Java models, implemented using Triple Graph Grammars (TGG) [9], QVT-R [13], and BXtend [8], revealed that common declarative approaches have limitations when conditional creations of target elements are required. In this case, procedural approaches like BXtend are more powerful.

Common declarative approaches may be classified into grammar-based approaches and constraint-based ones. The most prominent representative of the first group are Triple Graph Grammars (TGG) [23], implemented by various tools, such as, e.g. eMoflon [4]. QVT-R belongs to the group of constraint-based approaches. The BXtend approach relies on common object-oriented and procedural programming, enriched with powerful functional parts. The procedural character allows for a greater flexibility in transformation specifications. In BXTend, the transformation developer effectively handcrafts a Triple Graph Transformation System (TGTS) as an internal DSL.

7   Conclusion

We applied QVT-R, a declarative language for bidirectional transformations, and BXtend, a framework for bidirectional transformations written in the procedural and object-oriented language Xtend, to the Families to Persons case, a well-known benchmark for bidirectional transformations. We implemented the benchmark in a novel framework (Benchmarx) for bidirectional transformations. Finally, we compared the developed solutions with respect to a set of criteria (correctness, implementation effort, level of abstraction, redundancies in the solution, and cognitive complexity).

One might have expected QVT-R as a clear winner in this comparison: In QVT-R, a bidirectional transformation may be specified at a high level of abstraction in a single transformation definition which is executable in both directions in both batch and incremental mode. Thus, the transformation developer is relieved from specifying the operational details of consistency restoration, and is not exposed to problem of ensuring the mutual compatibility of forward and backward transformations. However, our comparison in Sect. 5 of the declarative and the procedural solution reveals a number of problems of QVT-R:

Correctness. Due to the flexibility of procedural and object-oriented programming, the BXtend solution passes all test cases. Due to the built-in semantics of incremental transformations in QVT-R, our solution fails in 12 out of 34 test cases (and so far we have found no way to improve this figure).

Implementation Effort. Although each transformation direction has to be programmed explicitly and incremental consistency restoration has to be defined explicitly, as well, the BXtend solution is much shorter than the QVT-R solution.

Level of Abstraction. QVT-R is located at higher level of abstraction than Xtend. However, the operational behavior of transformations needs to be considered in detail, which breaks the originally intended level of abstraction in QVT-R.

Redundancies in the Solution. In BXtend, all reuse mechanisms known from procedural and object-oriented programming are available. In contrast, relation calls (and queries) are the only reuse mechanisms available in QVT-R. As a result, the QVT-R solution suffers from considerable redundancies (similar relations obtained by copy-paste-modify).

Cognitive Complexity. In BXtend, both directions as well as the operational details of incremental consistency restoration need to be considered. However, the semantics of the programs written on top of the BXtend framework are comparatively easy to understand. In contrast, in QVT-R the transformation developer employs a declarative language, but must understand in detail how transformations are executed. In particular, it proves difficult to understand a bidirectional transformation, which simultaneously serves for the execution in forward and backward direction.

As it stands, the declarative bidirectional transformation language QVT-R did not provide us with the power which we expected. Improved reuse mechanisms such genericity or inheritance could reduce redundancies signficantly, implying also a reduced implementation effort. However, the semantics definition has to be improved, as well: First, it must be possible to solve bidirectional transformation problems such as the Families to Persons case completely rather than merely partially. Second, cognitive complexity has to be reduced considerably, resulting in an operational execution behavior which is much easier to understand and predict. Thus, by identifying problems in the application of QVT-R, we hope to contribute to its further improvement.

Acknowledgments. The BXtend solution for the Families to Persons case was developed by Sebastian Kaske in a Bachelor thesis under the supervision of both authors. Furthermore, the authors are indebted to Anthony Anjorin for providing the Benchmarx framework, as well as to Erhan Leblebici for integrating medini QVT into the framework.

References

1. Anjorin, A., Buchmann, T., Westfechtel, B.: The families to persons case. In: Garcia-Dominguez et al. [12], pp. 27–34
2. Anjorin, A., Cunha, A., Giese, H., Hermann, F., Rensink, A., Schürr, A.: BenchmarX. In: Candan, K.S., Amer-Yahia, S., Schweikardt, N., Christophides, V., Leroy, V. (eds.) Workshop Proceedings of the EDBT/ICDT 2014 Joint Conference. CEUR Workshop Proceedings, Athens, Greece, vol. 1133, pp. 82–86, March 2014
3. Anjorin, A., Diskin, Z., Jouault, F., Ko, H.S., Leblebici, E., Westfechtel, B.: BenchmarX reloaded: a practical framework for bidirectional transformations. In: Eramo, R., Johnson, M. (eds.) Sixth International Workshop on Bidirectional Transformations (BX 2017). CEUR Workshop Proceedings, Uppsala, Sweden, vol. 1827, pp. 15–30, April 2017

4. Anjorin, A., Lauder, M., Schürr, A.: eMoflon: a metamodelling and model transformation tool. In: Störrle, H., et al. (eds.) Joint Proceedings of the Co-located Events at the 8th European Conference on Modelling Foundations and Applications (ECMFA 2012), p. 348. Technical University of Denmark (DTU), Copenhagen (2012)
5. Bradfield, J., Stevens, P.: Recursive checkonly QVT-R transformations with general *when* and *where* clauses via the modal mu calculus. In: de Lara, J., Zisman, A. (eds.) FASE 2012. LNCS, vol. 7212, pp. 194–208. Springer, Heidelberg (2012). https://doi.org/10.1007/978-3-642-28872-2_14
6. Bradfield, J., Stevens, P.: Enforcing QVT-R with mu-calculus and games. In: Cortellessa, V., Varró, D. (eds.) FASE 2013. LNCS, vol. 7793, pp. 282–296. Springer, Heidelberg (2013). https://doi.org/10.1007/978-3-642-37057-1_21
7. Buchmann, T.: BXtend—a framework for (bidirectional) model transformations. In: Hamoudi, S., Pires, L.F., Selic, B. (eds.) Proceedings of the 6th International Conference on Model-Driven Engineering and Software Development: MODELSWARD (MODELSWARD 2018), Funchal, Madeira, vol. 1, pp. 336–345. SciTePress, January 2018
8. Buchmann, T., Greiner, S.: Bidirectional model transformations using a handcrafted triple graph transformation system. In: Cabello, E., Cardoso, J., Ludwig, A., Maciaszek, L.A., van Sinderen, M. (eds.) ICSOFT 2016. CCIS, vol. 743, pp. 201–220. Springer, Cham (2017). https://doi.org/10.1007/978-3-319-62569-0_10
9. Buchmann, T., Westfechtel, B.: Using triple graph grammars to realize incremental round-trip engineering. IET Softw. **10**(6), 173–181 (2016)
10. Czarnecki, K., Foster, J.N., Hu, Z., Lämmel, R., Schürr, A., Terwilliger, J.F.: Bidirectional transformations: a cross-discipline perspective. In: Paige, R.F. (ed.) ICMT 2009. LNCS, vol. 5563, pp. 260–283. Springer, Heidelberg (2009). https://doi.org/10.1007/978-3-642-02408-5_19
11. Czarnecki, K., Helsen, S.: Feature-based survey of model transformation approaches. IBM Syst. J. **45**(3), 621–645 (2006)
12. Garcia-Dominguez, A., Hinkel, G., Krikava, F. (eds.): Proceedings of the 10th Transformation Tool Contest (TTC 2017). CEUR Workshop Proceedings, Marburg, vol. 2026, July 2017
13. Greiner, S., Buchmann, T., Westfechtel, B.: Bidirectional transformations with QVT-R: a case study in round-trip engineering UML class models and Java source code. In: Hammoudi, S., Pires, L.F., Selic, B., Desfray, P. (eds.) Proceedings of the 4th International Conference on Model-Driven Engineering and Software Development (MODELSWARD 2016), pp. 15–27. SciTePress (2016)
14. Hidaka, S., Tisi, M., Cabot, J., Hu, Z.: Feature-based classification of bidirectional transformation approaches. Softw. Syst. Model. **15**(3), 907–928 (2016)
15. Hinkel, G.: An NMF solution to the families to persons case at the TTC 2017. In: Garcia-Dominguez et al. [12], pp. 35–39
16. Horn, T.: Solving the TTC families to persons case with funnyQT. In: Garcia-Dominguez et al. [12], pp. 47–51
17. IKV++ technologies: medini QVT (2017). http://projects.ikv.de/qvt
18. Macedo, N., Cunha, A.: Least-change bidirectional model transformation with QVT-R and ATL. Softw. Syst. Model. **15**(3), 783–810 (2016)
19. Object Management Group: Object Constraint Language Version 2.4. Needham, MA, formal/2014-02-03 edn, February 2014
20. Object Management Group: Meta Object Facility (MOF) 2.0 Query/View/Transformation Specification Version 1.3. Needham, MA, formal/2016-06-03 edn, February 2016
21. Object Management Group: OMG Meta Object Facility (MOF) Core Specification Version 2.5.1. Needham, MA, formal/2016-11-01 edn, November 2016
22. Samimi-Dehkordi, L., Zamani, B., Rahimi, S.K.: Solving the families to persons case using EVL+Strace. In: Garcia-Dominguez et al. [12], pp. 54–62

23. Schürr, A.: Specification of graph translators with triple graph grammars. In: Mayr, E.W., Schmidt, G., Tinhofer, G. (eds.) WG 1994. LNCS, vol. 903, pp. 151–163. Springer, Heidelberg (1995). https://doi.org/10.1007/3-540-59071-4_45
24. Steinberg, D., Budinsky, F., Paternostro, M., Merks, E.: EMF Eclipse Modeling Framework. The Eclipse Series, 2nd edn. Addison-Wesley, Upper Saddle River (2009)
25. Stevens, P.: Bidirectional model transformations in QVT: semantic issues and open questions. Softw. Syst. Model. **9**(1), 7–20 (2010)
26. Westfechtel, B.: A case study for evaluating bidirectional transformations in QVT relations. In: Filipe, J., Maciaszek, L. (eds.) In: Proceedings of the 10th International Conference on the Evaluation of Novel Approaches to Software Engineering (ENASE 2015), Barcelona, Spain, pp. 141–155. SciTePress, April 2015
27. Westfechtel, B.: A case study for a bidirectional transformation between heterogeneous metamodels in QVT relations. In: Maciaszek, L.A., Filipe, J. (eds.) ENASE 2015. CCIS, vol. 599, pp. 141–161. Springer, Cham (2016). https://doi.org/10.1007/978-3-319-30243-0_8
28. Westfechtel, B.: Case-based exploration of bidirectional transformations in QVT relations. Softw. Syst. Model. **17**(3), 989–1029 (2018)
29. Westfechtel, B.: Incremental bidirectional transformations: applying QVT relations to the families to persons benchmark. In: Damiani, E., Spanoudakis, G., Maciaszek, L. (eds.) Proceedings of the 13th International Conference on the Evaluation of Novel Approaches to Software Engineering (ENASE 2018), Funchal, Madeira, pp. 39–53. SciTePress, March 2018
30. Zündorf, A., Weidt, A.: The SDMLib solution to the TTC 2017 families 2 persons case. In: Garcia-Dominguez et al. [12], pp. 41–45

Adopting Collaborative Games into Agile Software Development

Mateusz Zakrzewski[1], Dagmara Kotecka[1], Yen Ying Ng[2],
and Adam Przybyłek[1(✉)]

[1] Faculty of Electronics, Telecommunications and Informatics,
Gdańsk University of Technology, Gdańsk, Poland
matzak91@gmail.com, dagkotecka@gmail.com,
adam.przybylek@gmail.com
[2] Department of English Studies, Nicolaus Copernicus University,
Toruń, Poland
nyysang@gmail.com

Abstract. Although the emergence of agile methods has triggered a growing awareness that social factors have a crucial impact on the success of software projects, neither the Scrum Guide nor the Agile Manifesto prescribe techniques that aid the human side of software development. To address this challenge, we enriched the Scrum process with a set of collaborative games. Collaborative games refer to techniques inspired by game play, but designed for the purpose of solving practical problems. Our approach was evaluated in two companies. The feedbacks received from Scrum teams indicate that the implementation of collaborative games leads to a variety of measurable societal outcomes. In particular, the adopted games improved participants' communication, involvement, and creativity, make participants more willing to attend Scrum meetings, and produce better results than the standard approach. This paper is an extended version of our previous work [60].

Keywords: Collaborative games · Agile software development · Scrum

1 Introduction

Traditionally, Requirements Engineering (RE) is the process of identifying right stakeholders and eliciting their needs, documenting these needs as explicit requirements, and then, communicating and validating the requirements [51, 54].

Przybyłek [55] enumerated a number of inherent difficulties in the requirements engineering process. Such difficulties, despite being well known, are still encountered in present industrial practice [33]. Customers rarely know what they really need [20] and usually they have only a vague picture of their needs at the beginning of the project [8, 41]. In addition, their needs may be difficult to articulate [14]. Moreover, stakeholders may be numerous and distributed [70]. Their needs may vary and conflict, depending on their perspectives of the environment in which they work and the tasks they wish to accomplish [51]. Furthermore, effective communication among stakeholders may be difficult as a consequence of their different vocabularies and

© Springer Nature Switzerland AG 2019
E. Damiani et al. (Eds.): ENASE 2018, CCIS 1023, pp. 119–136, 2019.
https://doi.org/10.1007/978-3-030-22559-9_6

professional backgrounds [7, 68]. What is more, the ways requirements are documented and communicated may be chosen inappropriately with respect to stakeholders' profiles [34]. Finally, requirements evolve during the project due to exploration in the problem space, and dynamics of a business environment formed and reformed by the interactions of the stakeholders [27, 62]. As a response to some of these problems, agile methods were proposed and over the years have become dominant in the software industry.

In Agile software development, requirements engineering activities are present over the whole life cycle of a project. Thereby, the role of stakeholders is expanded within the entire development process by involving them in writing user stories, discussing product features, prioritizing the product backlog, and providing feedback to the development team on a regular basis [26, 49]. This requires that the customers work with developers as active team members [35, 58, 71]. The idea of having a customer as a member of a development team has grown from a single on-site customer, which was dismissed by Kent Beck himself as "an error of early XP thinking" [12], to a customer team "equal to or larger in size than the programming team" [46]. Since there is a wide range of potential customers, it would be difficult for a single person to represent them all [4]. The representation of stakeholders may be also achieved with the role of a product manager or an entire product management team [73]. Moreover, in agile software development stakeholders are expected to be collaborative [6]. Unfortunately, agile methods do not provide techniques to promote these attitudes. Therefore, inadequate stakeholder participation, inability to obtain consensus among various stakeholders and lack of effective knowledge sharing are still challenges confronting agile RE [8, 11, 13, 26, 49, 53, 61].

In the meantime, many researchers and practitioners have acknowledged and agreed on the importance and the role of creativity in RE [27, 45]. As a result, a substantial body of knowledge has been established, which can be summarized as follows. Requirements are no longer considered to exist in an implicit manner in the mind of stakeholders [39], while the stakeholders are no longer viewed as a passive source of requirements information but rather as active participants in requirements engineering process [50, 58]. Active participation means forward thinking, creating new visions, suggesting IT innovations, and shaping solutions [64]. Thus, finding the "right" requirements is not only about capturing requirements, but is also about helping stakeholders to discover requirements they were not aware of, and solving problems they did not know they had [31]. According to Robertson [64], requirements analysts should invent requirements based on their understanding of the organisation's competitive business goals and context. Such requirements are not often things that requirements analysts directly asked for [44]. Furthermore, Mahaux et al. [42] and Svensson and Taghavianfar [67] suggest that RE is not simply a creative process, but a collaboratively creative process, where interdisciplinary group of stakeholders work together to create ideas, solve conflicts, and reach a consensus on a novel and valuable system they want to build [60]. Thus, traditional requirements gathering techniques such as interviews, questionnaires, focus groups, participant observation, or document analysis [52] are insufficient to elicit the whole range of requirements [14].

Unfortunately, agile methods do not provide new requirements gathering techniques nor they explicitly support creativity [60]. Even though Highsmith and

Cockburn [25] mention that "creativity, not voluminous written rules, is the only way to manage complex software development problems and diverse situations", agile methods make little reference to established creativity techniques [30].

Responding to the above-mentioned challenges, we propose to equip agile teams with a set of collaborative games. A game is collaborative if two or more players must work together to achieve its goal, which is to solve a practical problem [21]. Collaborative games are designed to leverage multiple dimensions of communication that let participants engage the full power of their brains, resulting in richer, deeper, and more meaningful exchanges of information [28]. At the same time, they emphasize the concepts of teamwork and collaboration which are highly valued by agile practices [32]. They can also bring numerous benefits to the requirement elicitation process since they typically provide immediate feedback, activate participants and increase participant's motivation [19, 63].

In our study, we selected 8 games and implemented them in commercial projects. Based on the received feedback, we proposed a framework that specifies how to integrate a set of collaborative games into the Scrum process. There are number of methods and process (i.e. Scrum, Kanban, Scrumban, Spotify model etc.) used in software industry [1, 2, 72]. However, we chose Scrum, since it is one of the most widely adopted in industry [65, 72].

2   Research Method

Our study was conducted as Action Research [5]. Action Research is a partnership of the researchers with the study participants who use an iterative process to initiate improvement and investigate it. The researchers bring their knowledge of action research while the participants bring their practical knowledge and context [5]. Action Research simultaneously assists in practical problem solving, increases participants competencies, and improves scientific knowledge [15, 16]. A precondition for action research is to have a problem owner willing to collaborate to both identify a problem, and engage in an effort to solve it [18]. We conducted two Action Research projects. The problem owner in the first study was an internal software development department of the world's recognized leading food processing company with 150 years of tradition (the company wishes to remain anonymous). The department was experiencing typical challenges faced by Agile teams, such as the inability to gain access to the customer and the lack of customer involvement. The second problem owner was Intel Technology Poland. The company was interested in revising its work practices related to Sprint Retrospective. Authorities of both companies were open to new ideas and willing to deploy our framework in practice.

3   Adapted Games

3.1   Cover Story

In Cover Story [24, 29], customers imagine an ideal future system so spectacular that it gets published on the front page of a newspaper. The customers must pretend as though this future has already taken place. The game encourages people to ignore all limits and "think big". As a result, it uncovers shared goals and can lead to realizing true possibilities that were once unimaginable. To play the game, the customers are divided into teams of four to six and each team is given a template (see [60]) that include six components:

- Cover – states the spectacular success of the software system;
- Headlines – reveal what the cover story is about;
- Sidebars – reveal interesting facets of the cover story;
- Quotes – testimonials about the accomplishment;
- Brainstorm – is used for documenting initial ideas;
- Images – pictures that support the cover story.

After taking 5 min for individuals to silently think over the system, the team should collaborate to fill in each component. Next, each team presents their chart.

3.2   Whole Product

Originally, the game aims to help the team discover new ideas about what can be done to make the product distinct and find ways to gain more customers [40]. However, it can be also useful for prioritizing a product backlog or for defining a product roadmap. The game board comprises four concentric circles that represent different aspects of the product [29]:

- Inner Circle: Generic Product – the fundamental features that define the product;
- Circle 2: Expected Product – the features that customer considers absolutely essential;
- Circle 3: Augmented Product – the features that go beyond customer expectations;
- Outer Circle: Potential Product – everything that might be done to attract and hold customers.

Participants write ideas on sticky notes related to each circle, and then post the ideas on the chart. After all of the ideas are posted, the significance of the resulting chart is discussed. This allows developers to understand what the customers truly want from the product.

3.3   AVAX Storming

AVAX Storming [69] is based on brainstorming. Its aim is to identify the desired functional requirements for the system. The participants write down each functional requirement on a single sticky note and place it on a flipboard. This practice helps customers to figure out the size of their project because soon the flipboard starts to be filled up. There are two note colors. One for "needed" requirements and the other for "desired" requirements. When all notes are posted on the flipboard, each requirement is explained in detail by the author and discussed by the team. Overlapped requirements are merged. Later, the notes are grouped in order to sketch the system modules. The final result is a mind map demonstrating the size of the project.

3.4 Buy a Feature

Buy-a-Feature [28] is a way of choosing the right set of features to be developed in the next Sprint. In this game, customers collaborate to purchase their most desired features. Strictly speaking, they jointly prioritize their desires as a group. Each feature should include a meaningful label, a short description, and an enumeration of benefits. Features are also assigned a price depending on their development costs and a number according to their position in the product backlog. Customers buy features that they want in the subsequent Sprint using game money. Some features may be priced so high that no single player can buy them individually. This motivates negotiations among players because they have to pool their money to buy the feature [28]. Listening to the negotiations improves the understanding of what the customers really need. The total amount of money for all players involved in the exercise should allow them to purchase as many features as the developers are able to implement within a sprint.

3.5 Agile Game Incubator

This game [29] allows participants to teach each other the tangle of factors involved in certain dilemmas while gaining a deeper understanding of the predicament themselves. Its goal is to create a way to explain complex problems so that others will genuinely understand it and be able to form solutions. The game board consists of 5 sections, representing the 5 steps of the game-creation strategy, which conveniently form the acronym PLAID (pronounced "played"). There are also colorful sticky notes that symbolize the ideas for each section:

- Problem – what you want to solve (red notes);
- Lead Objectives – what you hope to gain from solving the problem (green notes);
- Aspects – the different parts of the problem (purple notes);
- Invent – the game created to solve the problem (blue notes);
- Debrief – how the game worked out (yellow notes).

The team should brainstorms ideas related to each of the 5 steps, write them on sticky notes, and then post on the board in the respective sections.

3.6 How-Now-Wow Matrix

When people want to develop new ideas, they most often think out of the box in the creative idea generation phase. However, when it comes to convergence, people often end up picking ideas that are most familiar to them (tastycupcakes.org). The How-Now-Wow Matrix game [60] helps stakeholders select features that make the product unique and distinguish it from the competition. It naturally follows the brainstorming session, where the features that were initially flushed out are now discussed. The features are listed down on a large poster. The game board is a 2 × 2 matrix with

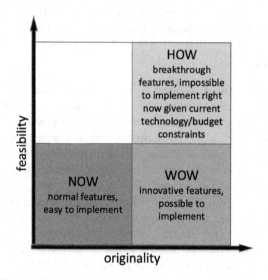

Fig. 1. How-Now-Wow Matrix [60]. (Color figure online)

"originality" on the x-axis and "feasibility" on the y-axis as shown in Fig. 1. Each player is given 9 colored dot stickers (3 yellow, 3 blue, 3 green) that correspond to the quadrants of the matrix. Then, players place the respective stickers next to the three ideas that they believe are best for each category. After all the dots have been used, the number of dots under each idea are counted. The highest number of dots of a certain color categorizes the idea under that color.

3.7 Speedboat

Speedboat [58] explicitly asks customers to say what they do not like about the product. Nonetheless, it lets the facilitator stay in control of how the complaints are stated. The game starts by drawing a boat. The boat represents the software system. Everyone wants the boat to move fast. Unfortunately, the boat has a few anchors holding it back. Customers write what they don't like on an index card and place it under the boat as an anchor. The lower an anchor is placed, the more significant the issue is. Although most customers have complaints, some of them do not feel comfortable expressing their frustrations verbally, while others complain a lot about the little details. Speedboat creates a relatively safe environment where customers can say what is wrong. By asking people to verbalize their issues in writing, the game motivates them to reflect on what is genuinely most troublesome. In this way, many of them will self-identify trivial issues as just that – trivial issues. When customers are finished posting their anchors, the facilitator reviews each one, carefully confirming the understanding of what they want to see changed in the system.

3.8   Prune the Product Tree

Prune the Product Tree [28, 60] helps to develop a balanced product roadmap by looking at the set of features that compose the product in a holistic manner. In this game, customers collaborate to shape the evolution of the product (i.e., the system to be developed). The product is represented by a large tree on a whiteboard. Branches correspond to major areas of functionality within the software system, while leaves correspond to features. The differently colored canopies stand for various product releases. The oldest features should therefore go near the trunk. Players write a short description for each new feature on an index card, ideally shaped as leaves, and places the card on the tree. This short description generally represents a valued functionality that satisfies customers' needs. Features to add in the next Sprint are attached in the area near the edge considered as the current release. Leaves at the outer edge of the canopy are considered longer term. Participants may group leaves or draw lines between leaves to clarify relationships among features. They may also "prune" features that are not working for them by taking them off the tree.

3.9   Sailboat

The Sailboat game [23, 56, 57] is quite similar to the Speedboat game but instead of engines, there are sails and wind. In addition, there are rocks which represent the risks the team might encounter along the way, an island which represents the team's objectives. Then, the attendances write down their ideas on post-it notes and put them into the different areas according to the picture. After that, they discuss all the categories on the picture.

3.10   Mad/Sad/Glad

Mad/Sad/Glad [17] uncovers the emotional content of the past iteration and helps teams to look for things that:

- drive them mad;
- make them feel sad;
- they are glad of.

The game starts with creating poster divided into three areas labeled Mad, Sad, and Glad. Next, attendees should write one issue per sticky note and put the sticky notes on the corresponding area. Then, the team groups related sticky notes into logical themes. In the end, each theme is discussed, a consensus is found, and corrective actions are proposed [57].

3.11   Starfish

The Starfish game [23, 57] is a technique that helps people to reflect on different degree of things and helps team members to understand each other. Instead of the typical three questions i.e. what worked well, what did not work, and what did we learn, the game board comprises a circle divided into five equal areas:

- Stop Doing – something that has not brought value, or even worse, which hindered the progress;
- Less Of – something that has been done and with added value, but the effort required is bigger than the benefit;
- Keep Doing – something that the team is doing well and wants to continue;
- More Of – something that is useful but could be exploited even more to bring more value;
- Start Doing – something new that the team wants to bring to the game.

To play the game, participants write their ideas on post-it notes, and then proceed in a manner analogous to that for Mad/Sad/Glad.

3.12   5Ls

The 5Ls game [57] handles both the positive and negative aspects of the past iteration but also brings forth the continuous development. Before the game starts, the moderator divides the poster into five categories:

- Liked – what did the team members really like about the iteration?
- Learned – what new things did the team members learn during the iteration?
- Lacked – what things could the team members have done better in the iteration?
- Longed For – what things did the team members wish for but were not present during the iteration?
- Loathed – what things did the team members dislike in the iteration?

Again, the next steps are analogous to those of Mad/Sad/Glad.

4   Proposed Framework

Figure 2 shows the typical Scrum life cycle with collaborative games superimposed. There are three meetings where collaborative games may occur: Product Planning, Sprint Planning, and Sprint Review.

The purpose of Product Planning is to establish the vision of what customers wish to build and accordingly the initial Product Backlog. Three games that can support this phase are Cover Story, AVAX Storming, and Whole Product. Cover Story enables Scrum teams to understand (1) the customer's vision of the system to be developed, (2) the customers' imagination of success, and (3) how the system will create business value.

In turn, Whole Product discovers features at a very high level and categorizes them into four main categories. Features belonging to the two first categories should be implemented first. Lastly, AVAX Storming identifies functional requirements and categorizes each as either needed or desired.

Before the start of each Sprint two consecutive meetings are held. In the first, stakeholders meet to refine and re-prioritize the Product, and to choose goals for the next iteration, usually driven by highest business value [38]. In the second meeting, the team and Product Owner meet to consider how to achieve the goals, and to create a

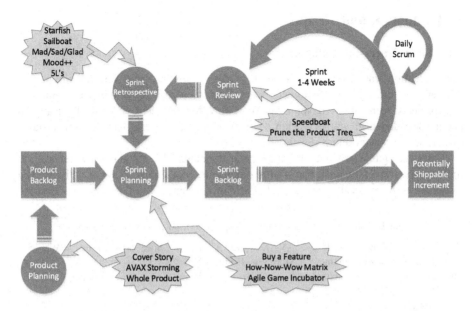

Fig. 2. Scrum life cycle with collaborative games superimposed [60].

Sprint Backlog. The team asks enough questions that they can break down user stories of the product backlog into the more detailed tasks of the sprint backlog.

The essential game to prioritize the Product Backlog enough for the next Sprint is Buy-a-Feature. It identifies the customer's highest-priority features that can be completed within the Sprint period. The game also helps several customer representatives reach a consensus if they have conflicting interests. Likewise, How-Now-Wow Matrix aims at selecting the most valuable features as a group. On the other hand, Agile Game Incubator let the Scrum Team understand complex and unclear requirements.

The Sprint Review is held to inspect the Increment and to adapt the Product Backlog if needed. Typically, after the team demonstrates new features to the Product Owner or to the business stakeholders, all attendees collaborate on what could be done to deliver more business value to the customer. Two games – Speedboat and Prune the Product Tree – may be deploy to elicit the feedback and foster collaboration. Both games give the team the opportunity to identify those features that are simply not meeting customer needs. Speedboat solely focuses on features that need to be addressed, while Prune the Product Tree additionally provides customers with a way to indicate the directions in which to evolve the system. By observing how customers shape the tree's growth, the team has the opportunity to refine the requirements to ensure they maintain cohesion with the business.

At the end of each sprint, the team conducts a retrospective to look back at events that already have taken place, discuss what went right and wrong and decide how to improve these items for the next sprint [57]. We adopted the following games to facilitate this meeting: Sailboat, Starfish, Mad/Sad/Glad, Mood++, 5L's.

5   Evaluation and Results

5.1   Food Processing Company

The evaluation was made on two projects carried out by the same Scrum team, but for different customers. The customers were other departments within the company. The projects were about developing Workflow Management System. Typically, 8 people attended each game session. Among them there were 3 customers, product owner, scrum master and 3 developers.

After each game session, we issued a questionnaire. The attendances were asked to indicate their level of agreement with statements about game-playing activity. The responses were on a Likert scale of: 1 – Strongly disagree; 2 – Disagree; 3 – Neutral;

Table 1. Summary of questionnaire responses (food processing company).

Rating scale: 1 – Strongly disagree 2 – Disagree 3 – Neutral 4 – Agree 5 – Strongly agree	Cover Story	Agile Game Incubator	AVAX Storming	Buy a Feature	How-Now-Wow Matrix	Speedboat	Prune the Product Tree	Whole Product
The game produces better results than the standard approach	3.5	3.9	4.2	4.0	3.5	4.3	3.9	3.6
The game makes participants more willing to attend the meeting	4.3	4.0	4.0	4.0	4.0	4.2	4.0	4.0
The game fosters participants' creativity	2.7	2.9	3.4	3.4	3.0	3.5	2.9	2.4
The game fosters participants' commitment	3.7	3.7	4.2	4.3	4.0	4.4	3.9	3.7
The game is easy to understand	4.0	3.6	4.4	4.4	3.9	4.5	4.1	4.0
All facets together	3.6	3.6	4.0	4.0	3.7	4.2	3.8	3.5

4 – Agree; 5 – Strongly Agree. Table 1 presents average values for each game and statement across both projects and all attendances. The corresponding standard deviation was always less than 1.

At the end of the survey, the attendances were also invited to specify any additional remarks. Several of them reported a high level of enjoyment when using the games, while those who represented the customer side reported that the games were useful and motivated them to contribute to requirements gathering.

Generally all games were evaluated positively, because they achieved the average score between 3.5 and 4.2. The only issue that was not appreciated was the impact on creativity, since four games obtained score below the baseline (neutral). This can be explained by the fact that both projects were designed for internal customers, so the business needs were well known and the requirements gathering process did not require much creative thinking. In addition, the implemented software was a standard Workflow Management System and was not expected to provide any innovative features. On the contrary, willingness to attend the meeting was significantly stimulated by every game.

Whole Product, Cover Story and Agile Game Incubator performed the worst, but still above the baseline. Again, the internal customer factor probably prevented Cover Story to demonstrate its full power. In turn, Agile Game Incubator was the most difficult to understand. Indeed, it required the attendances to create their own game to communicate a complex problem. How-Now-Wow Matrix also performed below expectations, probably due to a lack of innovative features in the system.

Prune the Product Tree was considered a bit childish and its output was not perceived as meaningful even though it obtained quite high scores in all facets except creativity. On the other hand, 3 top rated games were Speedboat, AVAX Storming, and Buy-a-Feature. Each of them generated very tangible output that was considered valuable by the attendances.

Note, that some games are substitutes for others, e.g. Speedboat is a substitute for Prune the Product Tree. The attendances preferred AVAX Storming over Whole Product, Buy-a-Feature over How-Now-Wow Matrix, and Speedboat over Prune the Product Tree.

5.2   Intel Technology Poland

The evaluation (for details look at [57]) was conducted by 3 teams, which are characterized in Table 3. We collaborated with the Scrum Master to properly implement the games into the teams. After evaluation in the first company, we reflected that our question set needed to be refined, since it did not captured all essential aspects of game sessions. The new question set is presented in Table 2. For each question, we first took the average per retrospective session, then based on these averages we took the average per team, and finally per game. All games except Mad/Sad/Glad were evaluated positively with respect to all categories. Even if they hardly scored above 3 for one category, they scored around 4 for other categories.

The Sailboat Game. Although the attendances agreed that Sailboat produces better results than the standard approach, they believed it should not be used too often due to

Table 2. Summary of questionnaire responses (Intel Technology Poland).

Rating scale: 1 – Strongly disagree 2 – Disagree 3 – Neutral 4 – Agree 5 – Strongly agree	Sailboat	Starfish	Mad/Sad/Glad	Mood++	5L's
The game produces better results than the standard approach	4.0	4.0	3.0	3.7	4.0
The game should be implemented permanently instead of the standard approach	3.0	4.3	3.2	3.4	4.0
The game may be considered as complementary to the standard approach	3.5	3.6	4.2	4.0	4.2
The game fosters participants' creativity	3.3	3.7	3.7	3.9	4.0
The game fosters participants' involvement	3.8	4.1	3.2	3.9	4.4
The game improves participants' communication	3.5	3.1	2.3	3.7	4.2
The game is easy to understand and play	3.2	4.0	4.2	4.1	4.0
All facets together	3.5	3.8	3.4	3.8	4.1

Table 3. Participating teams.

Team	Description
T1, 9 people	The team had worked on the project for 18 months, when we started our research. Team members had typically 2 years of Scrum development experience
T2, 3 people	The team had just joined a new project, but all team members had over 3 years of experience with Scrum
T3, 8 people	The team had worked on the project for 7 months. All team members had over 3 years of experience with Scrum

three reasons. Firstly, it would be boring to consider the vision and risks every time because they hardly change over the life cycle of a project. Secondly, using a sailboat as a metaphor was too abstract for some attendances, so the game was quite difficult to play. Finally, the attendances claimed that the discussion was not effective on improving the teamwork and the process. In contrast, they were satisfied that the game fostered their participation and built a friendly environment where they were able to express and discuss their frustrations [57].

The Starfish Game. Starfish functioned well in all categories but "communication among team members", which was not affected. Since the game covers all topics of traditional retrospective and fosters attendances' involvement at the same time, the attendances favored the substitution of the game for the standard approach. They also recognized that the game was effective in helping them to understand each other perceived value on the way they worked [57].

Mad/Sad/Glad and Mood++. Mad/Sad/Glad was perceived as the easiest to understand and play, even though it performed the worst overall. In particular, its influence on communication between team members has received negative rate. The cause was likely that the game is too simple and does not cover all topics that are usually discussed during a retrospective. Nonetheless, after improving the game with two new categories, the communication aspect was substantially enhanced, while the new version performed as well as the Starfish game [57].

The 5L's Game. Overall, 5L's received high rate in each category and surpassed all other games. When compared to Starfish and Mood++, it also covers all aspects of the Retrospective, but was perceived as excellent especially in improving attendances' communication. The other strength of the game is that the attendances' involvement was boosted [57].

6 Related Work

Gelperin [21] defined six collaborative games that support requirements understanding by improving communication and cooperation between customers and developers. He also defined a mapping system to help developers choose the best game to play in any situation. His games could be used complementary to the games used in our framework during Sprint Planning.

Trujillo et al. [69] proposed a game-based workshop (ActiveAction) used as an alternative for the software project's Inception phase. ActiveAction combines classical and game-based techniques to foster stakeholders' involvement and a collaborative identification of objectives, constraints and risks.

Ghanbari et al. [22] proposed a new approach for gathering requirements from distributed software stakeholders. Their approach employs two collaborative games (Prune the Product Tree and Buy-a-Feature) provided by a web-based tool designed by Hohmann [29].

Besides, considerable research has been directed at adopting collaborative games to support agile developers. Przybyłek and Olszewski [56] proposed an extension to Open Kanban, which contains 12 collaborative games that help inexperienced teams better understand the principles of Kanban. Ahmad et al. [3] highlighted that collaborative learning and Kanban board play important role in software engineering students learning and professional skills gaining. In turn, Derby and Larsen [17], Gonçalves and Linders [23], Caroli and Caetano [9], and Krivitsky [37] presented collaborative games that can be used to facilitate the Sprint Retrospective. In this study, we evaluated some of these games.

On the other hand, numerous creativity fostering techniques have been proposed to improve the quality of requirements deliverables and to increase customer satisfaction with the final product. The most popular ones are probably brainstorming and Joint Application Development [10]. More recently, Maiden et al. [44] proposed RESCUE, a scenario-driven requirements engineering process that includes workshops that integrate creativity techniques with different types of use case and system context modeling. The process was successful applied to encourage creative thinking about requirements for an air traffic control system [43].

Mich et al. [47] developed and evaluated EPMcreate – a creativity enhancement technique that is based on the Elementary Pragmatic Model. EPMcreate can be applied in any situation in which ideas need to be generated, e.g., at any time one might apply brainstorming [48]. The feasibility of applying EPMcreate to idea generation in requirements gathering was established by two experiments. EPMcreate demonstrated to be very effective in finding requirements that had not been known to the managers of the projects involved. Moreover, EPMcreate proved to generate more ideas and, in particular, more useful ideas than the familiar brainstorming [47]. Furthermore, Mich et al. [48] showed that EPMcreate is also effective when used by individuals.

Sakhnini et al. [66] proposed POEPMcreate, which is an optimization of EPMcreate that requires fewer steps than EPMcreate. The effectiveness of POEPMcreate was demonstrated in two controlled experiments by comparing it to both brainstorming and EPMcreate. The results indicate that POEPMcreate is more effective, by the quantity and quality of the ideas generated, than EPMcreate, which is, in turn, more effective than brainstorming.

Karlsen et al. [36] integrated ART-SCENE, a tool designed to discover more complete requirements with scenarios, with combinFormation, a tool that supports people in creating new ideas while finding and collecting information. As pointed out by the authors [36], their approach was designed to support individual creativity.

Hollis and Maiden [30] extended Ambler's agile process with three creativity techniques: brainstorming, Partners in Creative Learning, and a new technique inspired by Hall-of-Fame. The evaluation shows that requirements generated from the extended process were rated more novel then requirements in the original product backlog.

Svensson and Taghavianfar [67] evaluated four different creativity techniques, namely Hall of Fame, Constraint Removal, Brainstorming, and Idea Box, using creativity workshops. The creativity workshops followed the structure and the design of the creativity workshops in RESCUE [44]. The results indicate that Brainstorming can generate by far the most ideas, while Hall of Fame generates most creative ideas. Idea Box generates the least number of ideas, and the least number of creative ideas. Finally, Hall of Fame is the technique that generates the most practical ideas [67] companies were open to new ideas and willing to deploy our framework in practice.

7 Summary

This paper reports on two Action Research projects carried out in two different companies to explore the ways in which collaborative games could benefit Scrum teams. Collaborative games represent a powerful tool in improving interactions among the development team and between the team and the customer. Their social and entertaining aspects provide an alternative to traditional Scrum meetings. The received feedbacks obtained through questionnaires show that the adopted games improved participants' communication, involvement, and creativity; make participants more willing to attend Scrum meetings; and produce better results than the standard approach. Moreover, the participated teams intended to continue playing the proposed games after the project finished. We also learnt that the issues that teams deals with may be different in each Sprint and project, so the Scrum Master should have a set of possible games to be able to pick the most effective one depending on the situation at hand.

As future work, we will continue implementing collaborative games in other companies. Moreover, we will try to integrate collaborative games with other agile methods. We also plan to add more games to saturate each Scrum meeting in a balanced way. Furthermore, we want to develop a digital version of some games using the framework presented by Przybyłek and Kowalski [58]. Finally, we want to study the effect of collaborative games on social aspects of software development in a controlled experiment with settings similar to [59].

References

1. Ahmad, M.O., Dennehy, D., Conboy, K., Oivo, M.: Kanban in software engineering: a systematic mapping study. J. Syst. Softw. **137**, 96–113 (2018)
2. Ahmad, M.O., Kuvaja, P., Oivo, M., Markkula, J.: Transition of software maintenance teams from Scrum to Kanban. In: 49th Hawaii International Conference on System Sciences (HICSS 2016), Koloa, HI (2016)
3. Ahmad, M.O., Liukkunen, K., Markkula, J.: Student perceptions and attitudes towards the software factory as a learning environment. In: Global Engineering Education Conference (EDUCON 2014), Istanbul, Turkey (2014)
4. Ambler, S.W.: Scaling on-site customer. Dr. Dobbs Journal, 63–66, January 2008
5. Baskerville, R., Myers, M.D.: Special issue on action research in information systems: making IS research relevant to practice—foreward. MIS Q. **28**(3), 329–335 (2004)
6. Boehm, B., Turner, R.: Balancing Agility and Discipline: A Guide for the Perplexed. Addison-Wesley, Boston (2004)
7. Bormane, L., Gržibovska, J., Bērziša, S., Grabis, J.: Impact of requirements gathering processes on success of information system development projects. Inf. Technol. Manag. Sci. **19**(1), 57–64 (2016)
8. Cao, L., Ramesh, B.: Agile requirements engineering practices: an empirical study. IEEE Softw. **25**(1), 60–67 (2008)
9. Caroli, P., Caetano, T.: Fun Retrospectives - Activities and Ideas for Making Agile Retrospectives More Engaging. Leanpub, Layton (2016)
10. Carmel, E., Whitaker, R., George, J.: PD and joint application design: a transatlantic comparison. Commun. ACM **36**(4), 40–48 (1993)
11. Chan, F.K.Y., Thong, J.Y.L.: Acceptance of agile methods: a critical review and conceptual framework. Decis. Support Syst. **46**(4), 803–814 (2009)
12. Conboy, K., Wang, X., Fitzgerald, B.: Creativity in agile systems development: a literature review. In: Dhillon, G., Stahl, B.C., Baskerville, R. (eds.) Information Systems – Creativity and Innovation in Small and Medium-Sized Enterprises. IFIP Advances in Information and Communication Technology, vol. 301, pp. 122–134. Springer, Heidelberg (2009). https://doi.org/10.1007/978-3-642-02388-0_9

13. Conboy, K., Coyle, S., Wang, X., Pikkarainen, M.: People over process: key people challenges in agile development. IEEE Softw. **99**, 47–57 (2010)
14. Davis, C.J., Fuller, R.M., Tremblay, M.C., Berndt, D.J.: Communication challenges in requirements gathering and the use of the repertory GRID technique. J. Comput. Inf. Syst. **47**, 78–86 (2006)
15. Davison, R.M., Martinsons, M.G., Kock, N.: Principles of canonical action research. Inf. Syst. J. **14**(1), 65–86 (2004)
16. Dawson, C.: Practical Research Methods: A User-Friendly Guide to Mastering Research Techniques and Projects. How To Books Ltd., Oxford (2002)
17. Derby, E., Larsen, D.: Agile Retrospectives: Making Good Teams Great. Pragmatic Programmers (2006)
18. Easterbrook, S.M., Singer, J., Storey, M.A., Damian, D.: Selecting empirical methods for software engineering research. In: Shull, F., Singer, J., Sjøberg, D.I.K. (eds.) Guide to Advanced Empirical Software Engineering, pp. 285–311. Springer, London (2006). https://doi.org/10.1007/978-1-84800-044-5_11
19. Fernandes, J., Duarte, D., Ribeiro, C., Farinha, C., Pereira, J., da Silva, M.M.: iThink: a game-based approach towards improving collaboration and participation in requirement elicitation. Procedia Comput. Sci. **15**, 66–77 (2012)
20. Faulk, S.: Software requirements: a tutorial. In: Thayer, R., Dorfman, M. (eds.) Software Requirements Engineering. IEEE Computer Society Press, Washington (1997)
21. Gelperin, D.: Increase requirements understanding by playing cooperative games. In: INCOSE International Symposium, Denver, CO (2011)
22. Ghanbari, H., Similä, J., Markkula, J.: Utilizing online serious games to facilitate distributed requirements gathering. J. Syst. Softw. **109**, 32–49 (2015)
23. Gonçalves, L., Linders, B.: Getting Value Out of Agile Retrospectives: A Toolbox of Retrospective Exercises. Leanpub, Layton (2014)
24. Gray, D., Brown, S., Macanufo, J.: Gamestorming: A Playbook for Innovators, Rulebreakers, and Changemakers. O'Reilly Media, Sebastopol (2010)
25. Highsmith, J., Cockburn, A.: Agile software development: the business of innovation. IEEE Comput. **34**(9), 120–122 (2001)
26. Hoda, R., Noble, J., Marshall, S.: The impact of inadequate customer collaboration on self-organizing agile teams. Inf. Softw. Technol. **53**, 521–534 (2011)
27. Hoffmann, O., Cropley, D., Cropley, A., Nguyen, L., Swatman, P.: Creativity, requirements and perspectives. Aust. J. Inf. Syst. **13**(1), 159–175 (2005)
28. Hohmann, L.: Innovation Games: Creating Breakthrough Products Through Collaborative Play. Addison-Wesley Professional, Boston (2006)
29. Hohmann, L.: Innovation Games Website (2017). www.innovationgames.com
30. Hollis, B., Maiden, N.: Extending agile processes with creativity techniques. IEEE Softw. **30**(5), 78–84 (2013)
31. Horkoff, J., Maiden, N.: Creativity and conceptual modeling for requirements engineering. In: 5th International Workshop on Creativity in Requirements Engineering, Essen, Germany (2015)
32. International Institute of Business Analysis (IIBA): Agile Extension to the BABOK®Guide. Toronto, Canada (2011)
33. Jarzębowicz, A., Marciniak, P.: A survey on identifying and addressing business analysis problems. Found. Comput. Decis. Sci. **42**(4), 315–337 (2017)
34. Jarzębowicz, A., Połocka, K.: Selecting requirements documentation techniques for software projects: a survey study. In: 1st International Conference on Lean and Agile Software Development, pp. 1189–1198 (2017). http://dx.doi.org/10.15439/2017F387

35. Jarzębowicz, A., Ślesiński, W.: Assessing effectiveness of recommendations to requirements-related problems through interviews with experts. In: 2018 Federated Conference on Computer Science and Information Systems (FedCSIS 2018), Poznan, Poland (2018). http://dx.doi.org/10.15439/2018F85

36. Karlsen, K., Maiden, N.A.M., Kerne, A.: Inventing requirements with creativity support tools. In: 15th International Working Conference, REFSQ 2009, Amsterdam, The Netherlands (2009)

37. Krivitsky, A.: Agile Retrospective Kickstarter. Leanpub, Layton (2015)

38. Larman, C.: Agile and Iterative Development: A Manager's Guide. Addison Wesley, Boston (2003)

39. Lemos, J., Alves, C., Duboc, L., Rodrigues, G.: A systematic mapping study on creativity in requirements engineering. In: 27th ACM SAC - Requirements Engineering Track, Riva Del Garda, Italy (2012)

40. Levitt, T.: Marketing success through differentiation – of anything. Harvard Bus. Rev. 20–28 (1980) . http://www.confianzys.com/Marketing%20Sucess%20-%20Differentiation%20of% 20anything.PDF. The January-February 1980 Issue

41. Maciaszek, L.: Requirements Analysis and Systems Design. Addison-Wesley, Boston (2005)

42. Mahaux, M., Nguyen, L., Gotel, O., Mich, L., Mavin, A., Schmid, K.: Collaborative creativity in requirements engineering: analysis and practical advice. In: 7th IEEE International Conference on Research Challenges in Information Science (RCIS), Paris, France (2013)

43. Maiden, N., Gizikis, A., Robertson, S.: Provoking creativity: imagine what your requirements could be like. IEEE Softw. 21(5), 68–75 (2004)

44. Maiden, N., Manning, S., Robertson, S., Greenwood, J.: Integrating creativity workshops into structured requirements processes. In: 5th Conference on Designing Interactive Systems: Processes, Practices, Methods, and Techniques, Cambridge, MA (2004)

45. Maiden, N., Jones, S., Karlsen, I.K., Neill, R., Zachos, K., Milne, A.: Requirements engineering as creative problem solving: a research agenda for idea finding. In: 18th IEEE International Conference on Requirements Engineering, Sydney, Australia (2010)

46. McBreen, P.: Questioning Extreme Programming. Addison-Wesley, Boston (2003)

47. Mich, L., Anesi, C., Berry, D.M.: Applying a pragmatics-based creativity-fostering technique to requirements gathering. Requir. Eng. 10(4), 262–275 (2005)

48. Mich, L., Berry, D.M., Alzetta, A.: Individual and end-user application of the EPMcreate creativity enhancement technique to website requirements gathering. In: Workshop on creativity in requirements engineering at REFSQ 2010, Essen, Germany (2010)

49. Nerur, S., Mahapatra, R., Mangalaraj, G.: Challenges of migrating to agile methods. Commun. ACM 48, 72–78 (2005)

50. Nguyen, L., Cybulski, J.: Into the future: inspiring and stimulating users' creativity. In: 12th Pacific Asia Conference on Information Systems, Suzhou, China (2008)

51. Nuseibeh, B., Easterbrook, S.: Requirements engineering: a roadmap. In: Conference on the Future of Software Engineering, Limerick, Ireland (2000)

52. Ossowska, K., Szewc, L., Weichbroth, P., Garnik, I., Sikorski, M.: Exploring an ontological approach for user requirements elicitation in the design of online virtual agents. In: Wrycza, S. (ed.) SIGSAND/PLAIS 2016. LNBIP, vol. 264, pp. 40–55. Springer, Cham (2016). https://doi.org/10.1007/978-3-319-46642-2_3

53. Owoc, M., Weichbroth, P., Żuralski, K.: Towards better understanding of context-aware knowledge transformation. In: 2017 Federated Conference on Computer Science and Information Systems (FedCSIS 2017), Prague, Czech Republic (2017). http://dx.doi.org/10. 15439/2017F383

54. Przybyłek, A.: The integration of functional decomposition with UML notation in business process modelling. Adv. Inf. Syst. Dev. **1**, 85–99 (2007)
55. Przybyłek, A.: A business-oriented approach to requirements gathering. In: 9th International Conference on Evaluation of Novel Approaches to Software Engineering (ENASE 2014), Lisbon (2014)
56. Przybyłek, A., Olszewski, M.: Adopting collaborative games into Open Kanban. In: 2016 Federated Conference on Computer Science and Information Systems (FedCSIS 2016), Gdansk, Poland (2016). http://dx.doi.org/10.15439/2016F509
57. Przybyłek, A., Kotecka, D.: Making agile retrospectives more awesome. In: 2017 Federated Conference on Computer Science and Information Systems (FedCSIS 2017), Prague, Czech Republic (2017). http://dx.doi.org/10.15439/2017F423
58. Przybyłek, A., Kowalski, W.: Utilizing online collaborative games to facilitate agile software development. In: 2018 Federated Conference on Computer Science and Information Systems (FedCSIS 2018), Poznan, Poland (2018). http://dx.doi.org/10.15439/2018F347
59. Przybyłek, A.: An empirical study on the impact of AspectJ on software evolvability. Empir. Softw. Eng. **23**(4), 2018–2050 (2018). https://doi.org/10.1007/s10664-017-9580-7,2018
60. Przybyłek, A., Zakrzewski, M.: Adopting collaborative games into agile requirements engineering. In: 13th International Conference on Evaluation of Novel Approaches to Software Engineering (ENASE 2018), Funchal, Madeira, Portugal (2018)
61. Ramesh, B., Cao, L., Baskerville, R.: Agile requirements engineering practices and challenges: an empirical study. Inf. Syst. J. **20**(5), 449–480 (2010)
62. Redlarski, K., Weichbroth, P.: Hard lessons learned: delivering usability in IT projects. In: 2016 Federated Conference on Computer Science and Information Systems (FedCSIS 2016), Gdansk, Poland (2016). http://dx.doi.org/10.15439/2016F20
63. Ribeiro, C., Farinha, C., Pereira, J., da Silva, M.M.: Gamifying requirement elicitation: practical implications and outcomes in improving stakeholders collaboration. Entertain. Comput. **5**(1), 335–345 (2014)
64. Robertson, J.: Requirements analysts must also be inventors. IEEE Softw. **22**(1), 48–50 (2005)
65. Rodriguez, P., Markkula, J., Oivo, M., Turula, K.: Survey on agile and lean usage in Finnish software industry. In: ACM-IEEE International Symposium on Empirical Software Engineering and Measurement, Lund, Sweden (2012)
66. Sakhnini, V., Mich, L., Berry, D.M.: The effectiveness of an optimized EPMcreate as a creativity enhancement technique for website requirements gathering. Requir. Eng. **17**(3), 171–186 (2012)
67. Svensson, R.B., Taghavianfar, M.: Selecting creativity techniques for creative requirements: an evaluation of four techniques using creativity workshops. In: 23rd IEEE International Requirements Engineering Conference, Ottawa, Canada (2015)
68. Taylor-Cummings, A.: Bridging the user-IS gap: a study of major information systems projects. J. Inf. Technol. **13**, 29–54 (1998)
69. Trujillo, M.M., Oktaba, H., González, J.C.: Improving software projects inception phase using games: activeaction workshop. In: 9th International Conference on Evaluation of Novel Approaches to Software Engineering (ENASE 2014), Lisbon, Portugal (2014)
70. Weichbroth, P.: Facing the brainstorming theory. A case of requirements elicitation. Studia Ekonomiczne **296**, 151–162 (2016)
71. Weichbroth, P.: Delivering usability in IT products: empirical lessons from the field. Int. J. Softw. Eng. Know. (2018). https://doi.org/10.1142/S0218194018500298
72. VersionOne, 12th Annual State of Agile Report (2018). https://stateofagile.versionone.com
73. Springer, O., Miler, J.: The role of a software product manager in various business environments. In: 2018 Federated Conference on Computer Science and Information Systems (FedCSIS 2018), Poznan, Poland (2018). http://dx.doi.org/10.15439/2018F100

Detecting Behavioral Design Patterns from Software Execution Data

Cong Liu[1]([✉]), Boudewijn F. van Dongen[1], Nour Assy[1],
and Wil M. P. van der Aalst[1,2]

[1] Eindhoven University of Technology, 5600 MB Eindhoven, The Netherlands
{c.liu.3,b.f.v.dongen,n.assy}@tue.nl
[2] RWTH Aachen University, 52056 Aachen, Germany
wvdaalst@pads.rwth-aachen.de

Abstract. Design pattern detection techniques provide useful insights
to help understand the design and architecture of software systems.
Existing design pattern detection techniques require as input the source
code of software systems. Hence, these techniques may become not applicable in case the source code is not available anymore. Large volumes
of data are recorded and stored during software execution, which is very
useful for design pattern detection of software systems. This chapter
introduces a general framework to support the detection of behavioral
design patterns by taking as input the software execution data. To show
the effectiveness, the proposed framework is instantiated for the observer,
state and strategy patterns. The developed pattern detection techniques
are implemented in the open-source process mining toolkit ProM. The
applicability of the proposed framework is evaluated using software execution data containing around 1.000.000 method calls that are generated
by running both synthetic and real-life software systems.

Keywords: Behavioral design pattern · Pattern instance detection ·
Software execution data · General framework · Observer pattern ·
State and strategy patterns

1 Introduction

Design patterns describe reusable solutions to recurrent design problems in the
software development process. The use of design patterns leads to the construction of well-structured, maintainable and reusable software systems [22]. Generally speaking, design patterns are descriptions of communicating objects and
classes that are customized to solve a general design problem in a particular context [11]. The detection of implemented design pattern instances during reverse
engineering can be useful for a better understanding of the design decisions
and architectures of the underlying software system. In addition, software developers can consequently reuse and extend software units from code snippets to
architectures based on the detected pattern instances. Therefore, researchers

© Springer Nature Switzerland AG 2019
E. Damiani et al. (Eds.): ENASE 2018, CCIS 1023, pp. 137–164, 2019.
https://doi.org/10.1007/978-3-030-22559-9_7

have developed a lot of design pattern detection techniques and tools, e.g., [1–5,8,10,20,21], to locate design patterns for software systems.

A design pattern is regarded as a tuple of software elements, for example classes and methods, conforming to a set of constraints or rules. Constraints are categorized as structural constraints and behavioral constraints. The former defines classes and their inter-relationships while the latter specifies how classes and objects interact with each other. Many techniques have been proposed to detect design pattern instances in the past two decades. Based on the analysis type, these techniques are classified as static analysis techniques, dynamic analysis techniques and combination analysis techniques.

- **Static Analysis Techniques** (e.g., [3–5,7,8,10,20–22]) take the source code as input and only consider the structural connections among classes of the design patterns. Therefore, the detected pattern instances based on static analysis techniques only satisfy structural constraints.
- **Dynamic Analysis Techniques** (e.g., [1,2]) can detect design pattern instances directly from the software execution data by considering sequences of the method calls and interactions of the objects that are involved in the patterns.
- **Combination Analysis Techniques** (e.g., [6,12,19,23,24]) take as input the candidate design pattern instances that are detected by static analysis tools and software execution data, and check whether the detected candidate pattern instances conform to the behavioral constraints. Therefore, the identified pattern instances using combination techniques match both structural and behavioral constraints. Compared with static analysis techniques, the combination techniques can eliminate some of the false positives caused by static analysis techniques because the candidate pattern instances are examined with respect to the behavioral constraints.

To the best of our knowledge, both the static analysis and combination analysis techniques require source code of a software system as input. They are not applicable anymore if the source code is not available (e.g., in case of legacy software systems). For this scenario, dynamic analysis techniques are needed. However, existing research into dynamic analysis techniques is limited and mainly suffers from the following problems that restrict the application: (1) they do not provide explicit description of detected pattern instances; (2) they miss explicit definition of pattern instance invocation; (3) they are unable to support novel design patterns; and (4) they lack tool support. For more detailed explanations of the limitations, readers can refer to [17].

In this chapter, we introduce a general framework to support the detection of design pattern instances from software execution data with full consideration of eliminating the limitations of existing dynamic analysis techniques. More accurately, we explicitly define a pattern instance as a set of roles that each involves a class or a method. In addition, we precisely define the notion of a pattern instance invocation and propose a refactoring of the execution data in such a way that the refactored data represents a pattern instance invocation to ensure an accurate behavioral constraint checking. Our proposed framework is generic and can be instantiated to support new design patterns (or pattern variants). To validate the proposed approach, we have developed a tool, named *DEsign PAttern Detection from execution data* (*DePaD*), which supports observer, state and strategy design patterns.

The remainder of this chapter is organized as follows. Section 2 presents a brief review of the related work. Section 3 defines some preliminaries. Section 4.1 formalizes the general framework to detect design patterns from software execution data. Section 5 shows the instantiation of the framework by taking the observer pattern as an example. Section 6 introduces the instantiation of state and strategy pattern for the framework. Section 7 introduces the tool support. Section 8 performs experimental evaluation. Section 9 discusses some threats that affect the validity of our approach. Finally, Sect. 10 concludes the chapter and presents some further research directions.

2   Related Work

In this section, we discuss related work on design pattern detection for java-based software systems. Table 1 summarizes some typical design pattern detection approaches by considering the type of analysis (i.e., static, dynamic and combination of both), artifacts that are required as input (e.g., source code and execution data), the description of pattern instances (i.e., what roles are used to describe the pattern), tool support, and the extensibility of the approach.

According to Table 1, we have following observations for existing work:

- **Less Attention to Dynamic Analysis Techniques.** Most existing work employed the static analysis techniques or the combination analysis techniques. Pure dynamic analysis techniques received less attention. Because both static analysis techniques and combination analysis techniques require source code as input, they are not applicable anymore if the source code is not available (e.g., legacy software systems).
- **Inability to Support Novel Design Patterns.** An approach is extensible if it can be easily adapted to some novel design patterns rather than only supporting a sub-group of existing patterns. Existing dynamic analysis techniques do not provide effective solutions to support new emerging design patterns with novel structural and behavioral characteristics. This limits the applicability and extensibility of existing approaches in the large.
- **Lack of Tool Support.** The usability of an approach heavily relies on its tool availability. Existing dynamic analysis techniques do not provide reusable tools that implement their techniques. This unavailability prohibits other researchers to reproduce the experiment and compare techniques.

Based on the above observations, we provide a general framework to detect behavioral design patterns by only taking the execution data as input. Note that this framework can easily be extended to support novel design patterns or variants. In addition, we implemented this framework in an open-source platform.

Table 1. Existing design pattern detection approaches [17].

Reference	Analysis type	Required artifacts	Pattern instance	Tool	Extensibility
[20]	static	source code	class roles	✓/✗	✗
[21]	static	source code	class & method roles	✓	✓
[22]	static	source code	class roles	✓	✗
[8]	static	source code	class roles	✓/✗	✗
[7]	static	source code	class roles	✓/✗	✗
[10]	static	source code	class roles	✓	✗
[4]	static	source code	class roles	✓	✗
[5]	static	source code	class roles	✓	✗
[3]	static	source code	class roles	✓	✗
[1,2]	dynamic	execution data	unclear	✗	✗
[12]	combination	source code & execution data	class & method roles	✗	✗
[24]	combination	source code & execution data	class & method roles	✗	✗
[23]	combination	source code & execution data	class roles	✓/✗	✗
[19]	combination	source code & execution data	class roles	✗	✗
[6]	combination	source code & execution data	class roles	✓/✗	✗

Note: ✓/✗ means the tool is introduced in the paper but is unavailable or does not work any more because of outdated dependencies.

3   Preliminaries

Given a set S, $|S|$ denotes the number of elements in S. $\emptyset$ denotes the empty set. We use $\cup$, $\cap$ and $\setminus$ for the union, intersection and difference of two sets. The powerset of S is denoted by $\mathcal{P}(S) = \{S'|S' \subseteq S\}$. $f : X \to Y$ is a total function, i.e., $dom(f) = X$ is the domain and $rng(f) = \{f(x)|x \in dom(f)\} \subseteq Y$ is the range. $g : X \nrightarrow Y$ is a partial function, i.e., $dom(g) \subseteq X$ is the domain and $rng(g) = \{g(x)|x \in dom(g)\} \subseteq Y$ is the range.

Let $\mathcal{U}_M$ be the method call universe, $\mathcal{U}_N$ be the method universe, $\mathcal{U}_C$ be the universe of classes and interfaces, $\mathcal{U}_O$ be the object universe where objects are instances of classes, $\mathcal{U}_R$ be the role universe and $\mathcal{U}_T$ be the time universe. To relate these universes, we use the following notations: For any $m \in \mathcal{U}_M$, $\widehat{m} \in \mathcal{U}_N$ is the method of which m is an instance. For any $o \in \mathcal{U}_O$, $\widehat{o} \in \mathcal{U}_C$ is the class of o. $pc : \mathcal{U}_N \to \mathcal{P}(\mathcal{U}_C)$ defines a mapping from a method to its parameter class set. $ms : \mathcal{U}_C \to \mathcal{P}(\mathcal{U}_N)$ defines a mapping from a class to its method set. $iv : \mathcal{U}_N \to \mathcal{P}(\mathcal{U}_N)$ defines a mapping from a method to its invoked method set.

In this chapter, we mainly reason based on the software execution data. A method call is the basic unit of software execution data [13–18] and its attributes can be defined as follows:

Definition 1 (Method Call, Attribute) [17]. *For any $m \in \mathcal{U}_M$, the following standard attributes are defined:*

- $c : \mathcal{U}_M \to \mathcal{U}_M \cup \{\bot\}$ *is the calling relation among method calls. For any $m_i, m_j \in \mathcal{U}_M$, $c(m_i) = m_j$ means that m_i is called by m_j, and we name m_i*

as the callee and m_j as the caller. Specially, for $m \in \mathcal{U}_M$, if $c(m) = \perp$, then $\widehat{m}$ is a main method.

- $\eta : \mathcal{U}_M \to \mathcal{U}_O$ *is a mapping from method calls to objects such that for each method call $m \in \mathcal{U}_M$, $\eta(m)$ is the object containing the instance of the method $\widehat{m}$.*
- $p : \mathcal{U}_M \to \mathcal{P}(\mathcal{U}_O)$ *is a mapping from method calls to their (input) parameter object set such that for each method call $m \in \mathcal{U}_M$, $p(m)$ is a set of (input) parameter objects of the instance of the method $\widehat{m}$.*
- $t_s : \mathcal{U}_M \to \mathcal{U}_T$ *is a mapping from method calls to their timestamps such that for each method call $m \in \mathcal{U}_M$, $t_s(m)$ is start timestamp of the instance of method $\widehat{m}$.*
- $t_e : \mathcal{U}_M \to \mathcal{U}_T$ *is a mapping from method calls to their timestamps such that for each method call $m \in \mathcal{U}_M$, $t_e(m)$ is end timestamp of the instance of method $\widehat{m}$.*

Definition 2 (Software Execution Data) [17]. *Software execution data are defined as a set of method calls, i.e., we have $SD \subseteq \mathcal{U}_M$.*

4 A General Framework to Detect Design Patterns from Software Execution Data

This section introduces the general framework to support the detection of behavioral design patterns from software execution data. An overview of the framework is shown in Fig. 1. It mainly involves two phases, i.e., candidate pattern instance discovery and behavioral constraint checking. Software execution data and a design pattern specification are required as the two input artifacts. In the following, the design pattern specification and the two involved phases are explained in detail. In addition, the instantiation of the framework is also discussed.

4.1 Design Pattern Specification

A design pattern specification defines the role set that is involved in the design pattern, the definition of pattern instance, a set of structural constraints, the definition of pattern instance invocation, and a set of behavioral constraints.

Definition 3 (Design Pattern Specification) [17]. *A design pattern is defined as a 5-tuple $DP = (U_R^P, rs, sc, pii, bc)$ such that:*

- **Role Set.** $U_R^P \subseteq \mathcal{U}_R$ *is the role set of a design pattern.*
- **Pattern Instance.** $rs : U_R^P \to \mathcal{U}_N \cup \mathcal{U}_C$ *is a mapping from the roles to their values (methods or classes). Essentially, it is an implementation of the pattern.*
- **Structural Constraints.** $sc : (U_R^P \to \mathcal{U}_N \cup \mathcal{U}_C) \to \mathbb{B}$ *with $\mathbb{B} = \{true, false\}$ is used to check the structural constraints of a pattern instance.*

– **Pattern Instance Invocation Identification.** $pii : \mathcal{P}(\mathcal{U}_M) \to \mathcal{P}(\mathcal{P}(\mathcal{U}_M))$ *is a function that identifies a set of pattern instance invocations from the method call set of a pattern instance.*
– **Behavioral Constraints.** $bc : \mathcal{P}(\mathcal{P}(\mathcal{U}_M)) \to \mathbb{B}$ *is used to check the behavioral constraints of all invocations of a pattern instance.*

This definition specifies how a design pattern should be organized, and we show its instantiation for observer, state and strategy patterns in the next sections.

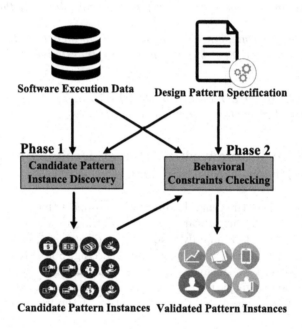

Fig. 1. An overview of the framework.

4.2   Phase 1: Candidate Pattern Instance Discovery

As shown in Fig. 1, *Phase 1* aims to discover a set of candidate pattern instances by exploring the execution data. The exploration will find the values (e.g., classes or methods) that play certain roles in the pattern instances. Formally, we have $crs : U_R^P \nrightarrow \mathcal{U}_N \cup \mathcal{U}_C$, i.e., a partial function that maps a sub-set of roles to their corresponding methods or classes. In our case, we have $dom(crs) = \emptyset$, i.e., none of the roles have values and we need to brute force all possibilities from the execution data. To prune and reduce the search space, some information from the structural constraints of the design pattern specification is available. For example, we only need to consider the case that register and unregister methods belong to the same class and this class plays the role of subject. If the source code is available, then static analysis techniques can be used to help narrow down the search scope of execution data to classes and methods that are only related to the detected candidates.

$dis\colon (U_R^P \nrightarrow \mathscr{U}_N \cup \mathscr{U}_C) \rightarrow \mathcal{P}(U_R^P \rightarrow \mathscr{U}_N \cup \mathscr{U}_C)$ is the discovery function that maps an empty pattern instance to a set of complete pattern instances. For any $crs \in U_R^P \nrightarrow \mathscr{U}_N \cup \mathscr{U}_C, rs \in dis(crs)$, we have $sc(rs) = true$, i.e., the structural constraints hold for all candidate pattern instances discovered from the execution data.

Similar to static analysis techniques that focus on structural analysis of classes, class operations and some of the relationships (e.g., dependency and inheritance relationships), can be recovered from the execution data. However, realization relationships cannot be discovered as interfaces cannot be instantiated and are not recorded during execution. Hence, some of the roles that are played by interfaces that would be detected from source code will be replaced by the implemented classes from the execution data.

4.3   Phase 2: Behavioral Constraint Checking

The pattern instance discovery takes as input the execution data and returns a set of candidate pattern instances by considering only the structural constraints of the pattern, i.e., relationships among classes and methods. Hence, the discovered candidate pattern instances inevitably contain false positives, especially for behavioral design patterns. For each candidate pattern instance rs and execution data SD, *Phase 2* checks whether the behavioral constraints given in the specification are satisfied with respect to all invocations of a pattern instance, i.e., $bc(pii(SD)) = true$. A candidate pattern instance is valid if there exists at least one invocation that satisfies all behavioral constraints, otherwise, it is not valid according to the execution data. This is common knowledge according to [24].

4.4   Instantiation of the Framework

Suppose we have a novel design pattern. In that case, a design pattern specification and software execution data that cover the behavior of such a pattern are required to execute the framework. Software execution data are collected by automatically instrumenting method calls during software execution. To test the applicability, we instantiate the proposed framework to discover the observer, state and strategy patterns in the following sections.

5   Detection of Observer Design Pattern

In this section, we introduce the instantiation of the framework for the observer design pattern. Specifically, we first provide an example piece of software that implements an observer pattern instance.

5.1   Introduction of Observer Design Pattern

The *observer design pattern* [11] defines an one-to-many dependency between objects so that when one object changes state, all its dependents are automatically notified. The key participants of this pattern are *Subject* and *Observer*. For this pattern, there are many observer objects that are observing a particular subject object. Observers have to be notified when the subject undergoes a change. Therefore, they register themselves to that subject. When an observer loses interest in the subject they simply unregister from it. For more details of the observer pattern, readers can refer to [17].

AISWorld is academic community software for researchers and practitioners. All *AISWorld* members subscribe to the news updates by registering to a public mailing server. When new events in the community occur, the mailing server will push these news items to all subscribed members. Community members can unsubscribe if they do not want to follow any more. During the execution of this software, we collected the execution data. An excerpt of the execution data are shown in Table 2. This dataset is used as an illustrating example to detect the observer pattern in this section.

5.2   Candidate Observer Pattern Instance Discovery

In this subsection, we introduce how to discover candidate observer pattern instances from software execution data. To do so, we first give a complete description, including the role set and pattern instance definition, of the observer pattern.

Definition 4 (Role Set and Pattern Instance of Observer Pattern).
The role set of the observer pattern is $U_R^O = U_{RC}^O \cup U_{RM}^O$ where $U_{RC}^O = \{Sub, Obs\}$ is a set of class-level roles and $U_{RM}^O = \{not, upd, reg, unr\}$ is a set of method-level roles. $rs^o : U_R^O \to \mathcal{U}_C \cup \mathcal{U}_N$ is a mapping from the role set to values such that $\forall r \in U_{RC}^O : rs^o(r) \in \mathcal{U}_C$ and $\forall r \in U_{RM}^O : rs^o(r) \in \mathcal{U}_N$.

According to Definition 4, an observer pattern instance is an implementation of the observer pattern and it defines a binding from the role set to its values. The discovery process aims to find the missing values for all involved roles from the execution data based on the structural constraints of the observer pattern.

Definition 5 (Structural Constraints of Observer Pattern). *For each observer pattern instance rs^o, its structural constraints $sc^o(rs^o) = true$ iff:*

- $rs^o(not) \in ms(rs^o(Sub))$, *i.e., notify is a method of Subject; and*
- $rs^o(reg) \in ms(rs^o(Sub))$, *i.e., register is a method of Subject; and*
- $rs^o(unr) \in ms(rs^o(Sub))$, *i.e., unregister is a method of Subject; and*
- $rs^o(upd) \in ms(rs^o(Obs))$, *i.e., update is a method of Observer; and*
- $rs^o(Obs) \in pc(rs^o(reg))$, *i.e., register should contain a parameter of Observer type; and*
- $rs^o(Obs) \in pc(rs^o(unr))$, *i.e., unregister should contain a parameter of Observer type; and*

Table 2. An excerpt of software execution data of AISWorld [17].

ID	(Callee) Method	(Callee) P	O(Callee) O	Caller Method	Caller O	Start Time	End Time
...	...	...	...	...	...	...	...
m_1	Member.init	–		1807970113	mainclass.main	–	709020268	709120368
m_2	Member.init	–		1807567788	mainclass.main	–	709244786	709267786
m_3	Member.init	–		1488142454	mainclass.main	–	709378641	709378641
m_4	MS.init	–		1333401746	mainclass.main	–	717761066	717961966
m_5	MS.register	1807970113		1333401746	mainclass.main	–	718086509	718086619
m_6	MS.register	1807567788		1333401746	mainclass.main	–	718261847	718361447
m_7	MS.register	1488142454		1333401746	mainclass.main	–	718420506	718588315
m_8	MS.notifyMembers	–		1333401746	mainclass.main	–	718686715	719110738
m_9	Member.update	–		1807970113	MS.notifyMembers	1333401746	718788715	718880715
m_{10}	Member.update	–		1807567788	MS.notifyMembers	1333401746	718929841	718929941
m_{11}	Member.update	–		1488142454	MS.notifyMembers	1333401746	719050867	719100467
m_{12}	MS.unregister	1807970113		1333401746	mainclass.main	–	719270253	719370253
m_{13}	MS.unregister	1807567788		1333401746	mainclass.main	–	719408812	719507712
m_{14}	MS.unregister	1488142454		1333401746	mainclass.main	–	719570465	719880462
m_{15}	Member.init	–		1491288577	mainclass.main	–	719712873	719722873
m_{16}	Member.init	–		805469502	mainclass.main	–	719843307	719943908
m_{17}	MS.init	–		1936493073	mainclass.main	–	720398401	720698461
m_{18}	MS.register	1491288577		1936493073	mainclass.main	–	720719568	720919968
m_{19}	MS.register	805469502		1936493073	mainclass.main	–	721077514	721276516
m_{20}	MS.notifyMembers	–		1936493073	mainclass.main	–	721526122	721976868
m_{21}	Member.update	–		1491288577	MS.notifyMembers	1936493073	721526122	721626122
m_{22}	Member.update	–		805469502	MS.notifyMembers	1936493073	721825906	721875908
m_{23}	MS.unregister	1491288577		1936493073	mainclass.main	–	722279646	722379646
m_{24}	MS.unregister	805469502		1936493073	mainclass.main	–	722579858	722779768
m_{25}	TestMail.mainclass.main	5336152135	–	–	–	–	703720242	723873758
...	...	...	...	...	...	...	...

Note: MS is short for MailingServer, O is short for object, P is short for parameter and – means the value is unavailable.

- $rs^o(Obs) \notin pc(rs^o(not))$, i.e., notify should not contain a parameter of Observer type; and
- $rs^o(upd) \in iv(rs^o(not))$, i.e., update should be invoked by notify; and
- $rs^o(reg) \neq rs^o(unr)$, i.e., register and unregister can not be the same method.

Based on the structural constraints, we propose an algorithm to discover candidate observer pattern instances from software execution data. Given the software execution data SD, we first define the following notations:

- $cs(SD) = \{\widehat{\eta(m)}|m \in SD\}$ is the class set involved in the software execution data SD;
- For any $c \in \mathcal{U}_C$, $ms(c, SD) = \{\widehat{m}|\widehat{\eta(m)} = c\}$ is the method set of class c in execution data SD;
- For any $n \in \mathcal{U}_N$, $pc(n, SD) = \{\widehat{o}|\exists m \in SD : \widehat{m} = n \wedge o \in p(m)\}$ is the parameter class set of method n in the software execution data SD; and
- For any $n \in \mathcal{U}_N$, $iv(n, SD) = \{\widehat{m}|m \in SD \wedge \widehat{c(m)} = n\}$ is the invoked method set of method n in the software execution data SD.

To discover candidate pattern instances from execution data, we need to identify a set of possible values for each role as intermediate results. Let U_R^W be the role set of design pattern W. We have $rs_*^w : U_R^W \to \mathcal{P}(\mathcal{U}_C \cup \mathcal{U}_N)$, i.e., each pattern role may have multiple values. Then, we define a function ϖ that generates a set of candidate pattern instances by exploiting all possible combinations of different role values. Formally, we have $\varpi : (U_R^W \to \mathcal{P}(\mathcal{U}_N \cup \mathcal{U}_C)) \to \mathcal{P}(U_R^W \to \mathcal{U}_N \cup \mathcal{U}_C)$. For any $rs_*^w \in U_R^W \to \mathcal{P}(\mathcal{U}_C \cup \mathcal{U}_N)$, we have:

- for any candidate pattern instance $rs^w \in \varpi(rs_*^w)$: $dom(rs^w) = U_R^W$;
- for any role $r \in U_R^W : rs_*^w(r) = \bigcup\limits_{rs^w \in \varpi(rs_*^w)} rs^w(r);$
- $\nexists rs^w, rs^{w\prime} \in \varpi(rs_*^w)$: $\forall r \in U_R^W,\ rs^w(r) = rs^{w\prime}(r)$, i.e., we do not have two identical candidate pattern instances; and
- $|\varpi(rs_*^w)| = \prod\limits_{r \in U_R^W} |rs_*^w(r)|.$

Considering for example design pattern W. We have (1) $U_R^W = \{X, Y\}$ is its role set where X and Y represent two different roles; and (2) $rs_*^w(X) = \{a, b\}$ and $rs_*^w(Y) = \{c, d\}$, i.e., role X can be assigned to classes/methods a and b, and role Y can be assigned to classes/methods c and d. Then, we generate four pattern instances $\varpi(rs_*^w) = \{\{rs_1^w(X) = \{a\}, rs_1^w(Y) = \{c\}\}, \{rs_2^w(X) = \{a\}, rs_2^w(Y) = \{d\}\}, \{rs_3^w(X) = \{b\}, rs_3^w(Y) = \{c\}\}, \{rs_4^w(X) = \{b\}, rs_4^w(Y) = \{d\}\}$. The pseudocode description of the observer pattern instance discovery is given in Algorithm 1.

As the algorithm discovers a set of candidate observer pattern instances using only the structural constraints and the software execution data, it inevitably produces false positive results. For example, by taking the software execution data in Table 2 as input, we obtain two candidate observer pattern instances using Algorithm 1 as shown in Table 3. As the methods that play the roles of register and unregister are undistinguishable by only considering the structural constraints, therefore we consider also behavioral constraints.

5.3 Behavioral Constraint Checking for Observer Pattern

This section introduces how to check whether a discovered candidate observer pattern instance conforms to the behavioral constraints. Because one or more invocations may be involved in the execution data, we need to identify independent observer pattern instance invocations from the execution data.

According to the specification, an observer pattern instance invocation starts with the creation of one *Subject* object and involves all method calls such that: (1) the method plays a role in the observer pattern instance; and (2) its object is the Subject object or its caller object is the *Subject* object and the object is an *Observer* object. By taking the execution data and an observer pattern instance as input, its invocations are defined in the following definition.

Definition 6 (Observer Pattern Instance Invocation). *Let rs^o be an observer pattern instance and SD be the execution data. $SD^O = \{m \in SD\ |$*

Algorithm 1. Candidate observer pattern instance discovery.[17].

Input: Software execution data SD.

Output: Observer pattern instance set OS.

1 $OS \leftarrow \emptyset$, $ClassSet \leftarrow cs(SD)$. /**initialization.**/

2 **for** $c_i \in ClassSet$ **do**

3   /**subject class should at least contain three methods**/

4   **if** $|ms(c_i, SD)| \geq 3$ **then**

5   **for** $c_j \in ClassSet$ **do**

6   /**observer class should at least contain one method.**/

7   **if** $c_i \neq c_j$ & $|ms(c_j, SD)| \geq 1$ **then**

8   /**create intermediate result op.**/

9           $op(Sub) \leftarrow \{c_i\}$, $op(Obs) \leftarrow \{c_j\}$, $op(not) \leftarrow \emptyset$,

10          $op(upd) \leftarrow \emptyset$, $op(reg) \leftarrow \emptyset$, $op(unr) \leftarrow \emptyset$;

11   **for** $m_i \in ms(c_i, SD)$ **do**

12   /**register and unregister are played by methods with a parameter of observer class.**/

13   **if** $c_j \in pc(m_i, SD)$ **then**

14   /**set values for register and unregister roles of op.**/

15             $op(reg) \leftarrow op(reg) \cup \{m_i\}$;

16             $op(unr) \leftarrow op(unr) \cup \{m_i\}$;

17

18   **if** $|op(reg)| \geq 2$ **then**

19   **for** $m_j \in ms(c_i, SD)$ **do**

20   /**notify should not contain a parameter of observer class.**/

21   **if** $m_j \notin op(reg)$ & $c_j \notin pc(m_j, SD)$ **then**

22   **for** $m_k \in iv(m_j, SD)$ **do**

23   /** update is invoked by notify.**/

24   **if** $m_k \in ms(c_j, SD)$ **then**

25                $op(not) \leftarrow op(not) \cup \{m_j\}$;

26                $op(upd) \leftarrow op(upd) \cup \{m_k\}$;

27

28

29   /** for each op, we generate all possible role to value combinations as candidate observer instances.**/

30   **for** $rs \in \varpi(op)$ **do**

31   **if** $rs(reg) \neq rs(unr)$ **then**

32   /**add candidate observer pattern instances to RS.**/

33            $OS \leftarrow OS \cup \{rs\}$;

34

35

36

37 **return** *All detected observer pattern instances RS.*

Table 3. Two observer candidate pattern instances [17].

	Sub	Obs	not	upd	reg	unr
rs_1^o	MailingServer	Member	notifyM	update	register	unregister
rs_2^o	MailingServer	Member	notifyM	update	unregister	register

$\exists r \in U_R^O : rs^o(r) = \widehat{m}\}$ *are the execution data of observer pattern instance* rs^o.
We define invocation set of rs^o *as* $pii^o(SD^O) = \{I_1, I_2, \ldots, I_n\} \subseteq \mathcal{P}(SD^O)$, *such that:*

- *for any* $I_i \in pii^o(SD^O)$, $m \in I_i$ *where* $1 \leq i \leq n$, *there exists* $o \in \mathcal{U}_O$ *and* $rs^o(Sub) = \widehat{o}$ *such that:*
  - $(\widehat{m} = rs^o(reg) \vee \widehat{m} = rs^o(unr) \vee \widehat{m} = rs^o(not)) \wedge$ $(\eta(m) = o)$, *i.e., the object of each method call is the Subject object and the method should play the role of register, unregister or notify; or*
  - $\widehat{m} = rs^o(upd) \wedge \eta(c(m)) = o \wedge rs^o(Obs) = \widehat{\eta(m)}$, *i.e., the caller object of each method call is the Subject object and the method should play the role of update.*
- *for any* $I_i, I_j \in pii^o(SD^O)$, $m \in I_i$, $m' \in I_j$ *where* $1 \leq i < j \leq n$, $\nexists o \in \mathcal{U}_O$ *and* $rs^o(Sub) = \widehat{o}$ *such that* $(\eta(m) = o \vee \eta(c(m)) = o) \wedge (\eta(m') = o \vee \eta(c(m')) = o)$.

Considering the software execution data in Table 2, we identify two observer pattern instance invocations $I_1^O = \{m_i | 5 \leq i \leq 14\}$ and $I_2^O = \{m_i | 18 \leq i \leq 24\}$.

After obtaining candidate observer pattern instances and identifying pattern instance invocations, we can check whether a candidate conforms to the behavioral constraints. To this end, the following notations and operators are first introduced on the basis of each identified invocation.

Given an invocation $I \subseteq SD$, we define:

- For any $n \in \mathcal{U}_N$, $N(I, n) = \{m \in I | \widehat{m} = n\}$ is a set of method calls with n being its method in I;
- For any $M \subseteq I$, $CO(M) = \{o \in \mathcal{U}_O | \exists m \in M : \eta(m) = o\}$ is the object set of M;
- For any $n \in \mathcal{U}_N$, $c \in \mathcal{U}_C$, $PS(I, n, c) = \{o \in \mathcal{U}_O | \exists m \in I : \widehat{m} = n \wedge o \in p(m) \wedge \widehat{o} = c\}$ is a set of (input) parameter objects of method calls with n being their method and these objects are of class type c in I;
- For any $m \in \mathcal{U}_M$, $I_v(I, m) = \{m' \in I | c(m') = m\}$ is the invoked method call set of method call m in I; and
- For any $m \in \mathcal{U}_M$, $Pre(I, m) = \{m' \in I | t_e(m') < t_s(m)\}$ is the set of method calls that are invoked before method call m in I.

Then, the behavioral constraints of observer pattern are defined as follows:

Definition 7 (Behavioral Constraints of Observer Pattern). *For each observer pattern instance* rs^o, *the behavioral constraints* $bc^o(pii^o(SD^O)) = true$ *iff there exists an invocation* $I \in pii^o(SD^O)$ *such that:*

- $|N(I, rs^o(not))| \geq 1 \wedge |N(I, rs^o(upd))| \geq 1 \wedge |N(I, rs^o(reg))| \geq 1 \wedge |N(I, rs^o(u$ $nr))| \geq 1$, i.e., for each observer pattern invocation, notify, update, register and unregister methods should be invoked at least once; and

- $\underset{o \in PS(I, rs^o(reg), rs^o(Obs)) \cup PS(I, rs^o(unr), rs^o(Obs))}{\forall} (\underset{m \in I}{\exists} \widehat{m} = rs^o(reg) \wedge o \in p(m)) \wedge$ $(\underset{m \in I}{\forall} \underset{m' \in I}{\exists} \widehat{m} = rs^o(reg) \wedge \widehat{m'} = rs^o(unr) \wedge o \in p(m) \wedge o \in p(m') \wedge t_e(m) < t_s(m'))$, i.e., for each observer pattern invocation an observer object should be first registered to the Subject object and then unregistered from it; and

- $\underset{m \in I \wedge \widehat{m} = rs^o(upd)}{\forall} CO(N(I_v(I, m), rs^o(upd))) = (PS(Pre(I, m), rs^o(reg), rs^o(Obs)) \backslash$ $PS(Pre(I, m), rs^o(unr), rs^o(Obs)))$, i.e., a notify method should invoke the update methods of all Observer objects that are currently registered to the Subject object.

According to Definition 7, a candidate observer pattern instance is valid if there exists at least one invocation that satisfies all behavioral constraints, otherwise, it is not valid. Considering the observer pattern candidates in Table 3 and its invocations I_1^O and I_2^O, rs_1^o is a valid observer pattern instance but rs_2^o is not. This is because the second behavioral constraint is violated, i.e., some unregister methods are invoked before the register methods for both invocations of rs_2^o.

6   Detection of State and Strategy Design Pattern

This section takes both the state and strategy patterns as examples to illustrate the generic nature of the proposed framework. We selected these two patterns since they cannot be distinguished using static analysis techniques.

6.1   Introduction of State and Strategy Design Pattern

The state design pattern [11] allows an object to change its behavior when its internal state changes. The structure of the state pattern is shown in Fig. 2, based on which we can see that the key participants of this pattern are *Context* and *State*. *Context* is a class that keeps a *State* object as its state and it has two methods. One is the *setState* method that is used to update the current state of *Context* and the other one is the *request* method that is responsible for delegating requests to the current *State* object. *State* is an interface for handling the behavior and *handle* is the concrete method.

The strategy design pattern [11] is used when we have multiple algorithms for a specific task and the client decides the actual implementation to be used. The structure of the strategy pattern is shown in Fig. 3, based on which we can see that the key participants of this pattern are *Context* and *Strategy*. *Context* is a class that keeps a *Strategy* object and it has two methods. One is the *setStrategy* method that is used to change the current strategy object and the other one is the *contextInterface* method that is responsible for delegating requests to the *Strategy* object. *Strategy* is an interface for handling the behavior and *algorithmInterface* is the concrete implementation.

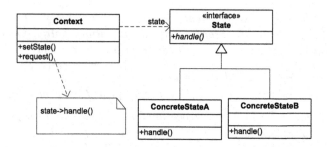

Fig. 2. Structure of state design pattern.

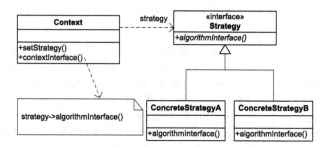

Fig. 3. Structure of strategy design pattern.

We give two software examples that implement a state pattern and a strategy pattern respectively. The first one is a payment software that allows to pay by cash or by card. The second one is a light control software that can be used to change the light from on to off and vice visa. We collected their execution data by monitoring executions of these two software examples. Excerpts of the execution data of these two software are shown in Tables 4 and 5.

Table 4. An excerpt of software execution data of the payment software.

ID	(Callee) method	(Callee) P O	(Callee) O	Caller method	Caller O	Start time	End time
...	...	...	...	...	...	...	...
m_{21}	LightControl.init	–	2807970113	mainclass.main	–	749020268	749120368
m_{22}	LightStatus.init	–	2807567788	mainclass.main	–	749244786	749247786
m_{24}	LightControl.switch	–	2807970113	mainclass.main	–	749378641	749378641
m_{25}	LightControl.setStatus	2807567788	2807970113	LightControl.switch	2807970113	757761066	757961966
m_{26}	LightStatus.concreteSwitch	–	2807567788	LightControl.switch	2807970113	758086509	758086619
...	...	...	...	...	...	...	...

Note: O is short for object, P is short for parameter and – means the value is unavailable.

Table 5. An excerpt of software execution data of the light control software.

ID	(Callee) method	(Callee) P O	(Callee) O	Caller method	Caller O	Start time	End time
...	...	...	...	...	...	...	...
m_{31}	PayMethod.init	–	1907567788	mainclass.main	–	719244786	719267786
m_{32}	Payment.init	–	1588142454	mainclass.main	–	719378641	719378641
m_{33}	Payment.setPayment	1907567788	1588142454	mainclass.main	–	737761066	737961966
m_{34}	Payment.pay	–	1588142454	mainclass.main	–	738086509	738086619
m_{35}	PayMethod.concretePay	–	1907567788	Payment.pay	1588142454	738261847	738361447
...	...	...	...	...	...	...	...

Note: O is short for object, P is short for parameter and – means the value is unavailable.

6.2   Candidate State Pattern Instance Discovery

In this section, we introduce how to discover candidate state pattern instances from software execution data. To do so, we first give a complete description, including the role set and pattern instance definition, of the state pattern.

Definition 8 (Role Set and Pattern Instance of State Pattern). *The role set of the state pattern is defined as $U_R^S = U_{RC}^S \cup U_{RM}^S$ where $U_{RC}^S = \{Con, Sta\}$ is a set of class-level roles and $U_{RM}^S = \{req, han, setS\}$ is a set of method-level roles. $rs^s : \mathcal{U}_R^S \to \mathcal{U}_C \cup \mathcal{U}_N$ is a mapping from the role set of state pattern to their values such that $\forall r \in U_{RC}^S : rs^s(r) \in \mathcal{U}_C$ and $\forall r \in U_{RM}^S : rs^s(r) \in \mathcal{U}_N$.*

According to Definition 8, a state pattern instance is an implementation of the state pattern and it defines a binding from the role set to its values. The discovery process aims to find the missing values for all involved roles from the execution data based on the structural constraints of the state pattern.

Definition 9 (Structural Constraints of State Pattern). *For each state pattern instance rs^s, its structural constraints $sc^s(rs^s) = true$ iff:*

- *$rs^s(req) \in ms(rs^s(Con))$, i.e., request is a method of Context; and*
- *$rs^s(setS) \in ms(rs^s(Con))$, i.e., setState is a method of Context; and*
- *$rs^s(han) \in ms(rs^s(Sta))$, i.e., handle is a method of State; and*
- *$rs^s(Sta) \in pc(rs^s(setS))$, i.e., setState should contain a parameter of State; and*
- *$rs^s(han) \in iv(rs^s(req))$, i.e., handle should be invoked by request.*

Based on the structural constraints, we propose an algorithm to discover candidate state pattern instances from software execution data shown in Algorithm 2 .

As the algorithm discovers a set of candidate state pattern instances using the structural constraints and the software execution data, it inevitably produces false positive results. As expected, by taking the software execution data of the two examples as input, we obtain two candidate state pattern instances using Algorithm 2 as shown in Table 6. Hence, we need to consider behavioral constraints to differentiate them.

Algorithm 2. Candidate state pattern instance discovery.

Input: Software execution data SD.

Output: State pattern instance set TS.

1 $TS \leftarrow \emptyset$, $ClassSet \leftarrow cs(SD)$. /**initialization.**/
2 **for** $c_i \in ClassSet$ **do**
3 | /**context class should at least contain two methods**/
4 | **if** $|ms(c_i, SD)| \geq 2$ **then**
5 | | **for** $c_j \in ClassSet$ **do**
6 | | | /**state class should at least contain one method.**/
7 | | | **if** $c_i \neq c_j$ & $|ms(c_j, SD)| \geq 1$ **then**
8 | | | | /**create intermediate result sp.**/
9 | | | | $sp(Con) \leftarrow \{c_i\}$, $sp(Sta) \leftarrow \{c_j\}$, $sp(setS) \leftarrow \emptyset$, $sp(req) \leftarrow \emptyset$, $sp(han) \leftarrow \emptyset$;
10 | | | | **for** $m_i \in ms(c_i, SD)$ **do**
11 | | | | | /**setS is played by method with a parameter of state class.**/
12 | | | | | **if** $c_j \in pc(m_i, SD)$ **then**
13 | | | | | | /**set values for setS role of sp.**/
14 | | | | | | $sp(setS) \leftarrow sp(setS) \cup \{m_i\}$;
15 | | | | |
16 | | | | **if** $|sp(setS)| \geq 1$ **then**
17 | | | | | **for** $m_j \in ms(c_i, SD) \setminus sp(setS)$ **do**
18 | | | | | | **for** $m_k \in iv(m_j, SD)$ **do**
19 | | | | | | | /** handle is invoked by request.**/
20 | | | | | | | **if** $m_k \in ms(c_j, SD)$ **then**
21 | | | | | | | | $sp(req) \leftarrow sp(req) \cup \{m_j\}$;
22 | | | | | | | | $sp(han) \leftarrow sp(han) \cup \{m_k\}$;
23 | | | | | |
24 | | | | /** for each sp, we generate all possible role to value combinations as candidate state instances.**/
25 | | | | **for** $rs \in \varpi(sp)$ **do**
26 | | | | | /**add candidate state pattern instances to TS.**/
27 | | | | | $TS \leftarrow TS \cup \{rs\}$;
28 | | | |
29 | |
30 **return** *All detected state pattern instances TS.*

6.3 Behavioral Constraint Checking for State Pattern

This section introduces how to check whether a candidate state pattern instance conforms to the behavioral constraints. As one or more invocations may be involved in the execution data, we need to identify independent state pattern instance invocations from the execution data.

Definition 10 (Invocation of State Pattern Instance). *Let rs^s be a state pattern instance and SD be the execution data. $SD^S = \{m \in SD | \exists r$*

$\in \mathcal{U}_R^S : rs^s(r) = \widehat{m}\}$ *is defined as the execution data of* rs^s. *The invocation set of* rs^s *is* $pii^s(SD) = pii^s(SD^S) = \{I_1, I_2, \dots, I_n\} \subseteq \mathcal{P}(SD^S)$ *such that:*

- *for any* $I_i \in pii^s(SD^S)$, $m \in I_i$ *where* $1 \leq i \leq n$, *there exists* $o \in \mathcal{U}_O$ *and* $rs^o(Con) \in \widehat{o}$ *such that:*
  - $(\widehat{m} = rs^s(req) \vee \widehat{m} = rs^s(setS)) \wedge (\eta(m) = o)$, *i.e.,* *the object of each method call is the Context object and the method should play the roles of request or setState; or*
  - $\widehat{m} = rs^s(han) \wedge \eta(c(m)) = o \wedge rs^s(Sta) \in \widehat{\eta(m)}$, *i.e., the caller object of each method call is the Context object and the method should play the role of handle.*
- *for any* $I_i, I_j \in pii^s(SD^S)$, $m \in I_i$, $m' \in I_j$ *where* $1 \leq i < j \leq n$, $\nexists o \in \mathcal{U}_O$ *and* $rs^s(Con) \in \widehat{o}$ *such that* $(\eta(m) = o \vee \eta(c(m)) = o) \wedge (\eta(m') = o \vee \eta(c(m')) = o)$.

Table 6. Two Discovered candidate state pattern instances.

	Con	Sta	setS	req	han
rs_1^s	Payment	PayMethod	setPayment	pay	concretePay
rs_2^s	LightControl	LightStatus	setStatus	switch	concreteSwitch

According to Definition 10, a state pattern instance invocation starts with the creation of one *Context* object and involves all method calls, such that (1) the method plays a role in the state pattern instance; and (2) its object is the *Context* object or its caller object is the *Context* object and the object is a State class object.

To check whether a candidate state pattern instance conforms to the behavioral constraints of the pattern specification, we need to define the behavioral constraints of the state pattern. Given an invocation $I \subseteq SD$, we first define the following operators:

- For any $n \in \mathcal{U}_N$, $Fir(I, n)$ is the first method call with n being its method in I. $Fir(I, n) = m$ if there exists $m \in I$ such that $\widehat{m} = n \wedge \nexists m' \in I : t_s(m') < t_s(m)$, otherwise $Fir(I, n) = null$;
- For any $m \in \mathcal{U}_M$ and $c \in \mathcal{U}_C$, $PO(m, c) = \{o \in \mathcal{U}_O | \widehat{o} \in c \wedge \exists o' \in p(m) : o' = o\}$ is the (input) parameter object set of m and these objects are of class type c; and
- For any $m \in \mathcal{U}_M$, $Suc(I, m) = \{m' \in I | t_s(m') > t_e(m)\}$ is the method call set that are invoked after m in I.

Definition 11 (Behavioral Constraints of State Pattern). *For each state pattern instance* rs^s, *the behavioral constraints* $bc^s(pii^s(SD^S))$ =*true iff there exists an invocation* $I \in pii^s(SD^S)$ *such that:*

- $|N(I, rs^s(req))| \geq 1 \wedge |N(I, rs^s(han))| \geq 1 \wedge |N(I, rs^s(setS))| \geq 1$, *i.e., for each state pattern invocation, request, handle and setState methods should be invoked at least once; and*

$$- \qquad \bigvee_{m \in Suc(I, Fir(I, rs^s(req))) \wedge \widehat{m} = rs^s(setS)} \eta(\widehat{c(m)}) \in rs^s(Con) \cup rs^s(Sta), \; i.e., \; for \; each$$

state pattern invocation the state change can only be done by either the State or the Context; and

$$- \qquad \bigvee_{m \in I \wedge \widehat{m} = rs^s(setS)} \exists_{m' \in Suc(I, m)} : \widehat{m'} = rs^s(req) \wedge PO(m, rs^s(Sta)) = CO(N(I_v(I, m'), rs^s(han))),$$

i.e., for each state pattern invocation, after each state change the handle method of the new State object should be invoked by the request method.

Consider candidates in Table 6, rs_2^s is checked to be a valid state pattern instance but rs_1^s is not. This is because the *setPayment* method is invoked by the *mainclass* as shown in Table 5, i.e., the second constraint is violated for rs_1^s. If rs_1^s is valid, the *setPayment* method should be invoked by either the *Payment* class or the *PayMethod* class.

6.4   Candidate Strategy Pattern Instance Discovery

In this section, we introduce how to discover candidate strategy pattern instances from software execution data. To do so, we first give a complete description including the role set and pattern instance definition of the strategy pattern.

Definition 12 (Role Set and Pattern Instance of Strategy Pattern). *Role set of the strategy pattern is defined as $U_R^Y = U_{RC}^Y \cup U_{RM}^Y$ where $U_{RC}^Y = \{Con, Str\}$ is a set of class-level roles and $U_{RM}^Y = \{cont, alg, setS\}$ is a set of method-level roles. $rs^y : \mathscr{U}_R^Y \to \mathscr{U}_C \cup \mathscr{U}_N$ is a mapping from the role set of strategy pattern to their values such that $\forall r \in U_{RC}^Y : rs^s(y) \in \mathscr{U}_C$ and $\forall r \in U_{RM}^Y : rs^y(r) \in \mathscr{U}_N$.*

According to Definition 12, a strategy pattern instance is an implementation of the strategy pattern and it defines a binding from the role set to its values. The discovery process aims to find the missing values for all involved roles from the execution data based on the structural constraints of the strategy pattern.

Definition 13 (Structural Constraints of Strategy Pattern). *For each strategy pattern instance rs^y, its structural constraints $sc^y(rs^y) = true$ iff:*

- *$rs^y(cont) \in ms(rs^y(Con))$, i.e., contextInterface is a method of Context; and*
- *$rs^y(setS) \in ms(rs^y(Con))$, i.e., setStrategy is a method of Context; and*
- *$rs^y(alg) \in ms(rs^y(Str))$, i.e., algorithmInterface is a method of Strategy; and*
- *$rs^y(Str) \in pc(rs^y(setS))$, i.e., setStrategy should contain a parameter of Strategy type; and*
- *$rs^y(alg) \in iv(rs^y(cont))$, i.e., algorithmInterface should be invoked by contextInterface.*

Based on the structural constraints, we propose the Algorithm 3 to discover candidate strategy pattern instances from software execution data. Note that this algorithm is the same as Algorithm 2.

As the algorithm discovers a set of candidate strategy pattern instances using the structural constraints and the software execution data, it inevitably produces false positive results. Considering for example, by taking the software execution data of the two examples as input, we obtain two candidate strategy pattern instances using Algorithm 3 as shown in Table 7. For state and strategy patterns, their static structures are identical and they cannot be distinguished by existing static approaches [24]. Therefore, the state candidates in Table 6 and the strategy candidates in Table 7 are identical.

6.5 Behavioral Constraint Checking for Strategy Pattern

This section introduces how to check whether a discovered candidate strategy pattern instance conforms to the behavioral constraints. As one or more invocations may be involved in the execution data, we need to identify independent strategy pattern instance invocations from the execution data.

Definition 14 (Invocation of Strategy Pattern Instance). *Let rs^y be a strategy pattern instance and SD the execution data. $SD^Y = \{m \in SD | \exists r \in \mathcal{U}_R^Y : rs^y(r) = \widehat{m}\}$ are the execution data of rs^y. The invocation set of rs^y is $pii^y(SD) = pii^y(SD^Y) = \{I_1, I_2, \ldots, I_n\} \subseteq \mathcal{P}(SD^Y)$ such that:*

- *for any $I_i \in pii^y(SD^Y), m \in I_i$ where $1 \leq i \leq n$, there exists $o \in \mathcal{U}_O$ and $rs^y(Con) \in \widehat{o}$ such that:*
  - *$(\widehat{m} = rs^y(cont) \vee \widehat{m} = rs^y(setS)) \wedge (\eta(m) = o)$, i.e., the object of each method call is the Context object and the method should play the roles of contextInterface or setState; or*
  - *$\widehat{m} = rs^y(alg) \wedge \eta(c(m)) = o \wedge rs^y(Str) \in \widehat{\eta(m)}$, i.e., the caller object of each method call is the Context object and the method should play the role of algorithmInterface.*
- *for any $I_i, I_j \in pii^y(SD^Y)$, $m \in I_i$, $m' \in I_j$ where $1 \leq i < j \leq n$, $\nexists o \in \mathcal{U}_O$ and $rs^y(Con) \in \widehat{o}$ such that $(\eta(m) = o \vee \eta(c(m)) = o) \wedge (\eta(m') = o \vee \eta(c(m')) = o)$.*

Table 7. Two discovered candidate strategy pattern instances.

	Con	Str	setS	cont	alg
rs_1^y	Payment	PayMethod	setPayment	pay	concretePay
rs_2^y	LightControl	LightStatus	setStatus	switch	concreteSwitch

According to Definition 14, a strategy pattern instance invocation starts with the creation of one *Context* object and involves all method calls, such that (1) the method plays a role in the strategy pattern instance; and (2) its object is the *Context* object or its caller object is the *Context* object and the object is a Strategy object.

To check if a candidate strategy pattern instance conforms to the behavioral constraints, we define the behavioral constraints of the strategy pattern as follows.

Algorithm 3. Candidate strategy pattern instance discovery.

    Input: Software execution data SD.

    Output: Strategy pattern instance set YS.

1 $YS \leftarrow \emptyset$, $ClassSet \leftarrow cs(SD)$. /**initialization.**/

2 **for** $c_i \in ClassSet$ **do**

3   /**context class should at least contain two methods**/

4   **if** $|ms(c_i, SD)| \geq 2$ **then**

5   **for** $c_j \in ClassSet$ **do**

6   /**strategy class should at least contain one method.**/

7   **if** $c_i \neq c_j$ & $|ms(c_j, SD)| \geq 1$ **then**

8   /**create intermediate result yp.**/

9                 $yp(Con) \leftarrow \{c_i\}$, $yp(Str) \leftarrow \{c_j\}$, $yp(setS) \leftarrow \emptyset$, $yp(cont) \leftarrow \emptyset$, $yp(alg) \leftarrow \emptyset$;

10   **for** $m_i \in ms(c_i, SD)$ **do**

11   /**setS is played by method with a parameter of strategy class.**/

12   **if** $c_j \in pc(m_i, SD)$ **then**

13   /**set values for setS role of yp.**/

14                      $yp(setS) \leftarrow yp(setS) \cup \{m_i\}$;

15

16   **if** $|yp(setS)| \geq 1$ **then**

17   **for** $m_j \in ms(c_i, SD) \setminus yp(setS)$ **do**

18   **for** $m_k \in iv(m_j, SD)$ **do**

19   /** algorithmInterface is invoked by contextInterface.**/

20   **if** $m_k \in ms(c_j, SD)$ **then**

21                       $yp(cont) \leftarrow yp(cont) \cup \{m_j\}$;

22                       $yp(alg) \leftarrow yp(alg) \cup \{m_k\}$;

23

24   /** for each yp, we generate all possible role to value combinations as candidate strategy instances.**/

25   **for** $rs \in \varpi(yp)$ **do**

26   /**add candidate strategy pattern instances to YS.**/

27                  $YS \leftarrow YS \cup \{rs\}$;

28

29

30 **return** *All detected strategy pattern instances* YS.

Definition 15 (*Behavioral Constraints of Strategy Pattern*). *For each strategy pattern instance* rs^y, *the behavioral constraints* $bc^y(pii^y(SD^Y)) = true$ *iff there exists an invocation* $I \in pii^y(SD^Y)$ *such that:*

- $|N(I, rs^y(cont))| \geq 1 \wedge |N(I, rs^y(alg))| \geq 1 \wedge |N(I, rs^y(setS))| \geq 0$, *i.e., for each strategy pattern invocation the contextInterface and algorithmInterface methods should be invoked one or more times and the setStrategy method can be invoked zero or more times; and*

- $\displaystyle \mathop{\forall}_{m \in I \wedge \hat{m} = rs^y(setS)} \eta(\widehat{c(m)}) \notin rs^y(Con) \cup rs^y(Str)$, *i.e., for each strategy pattern invocation the strategy change cannot be done by neither the Strategy nor the Context; and*

- $\displaystyle \mathop{\forall}_{m \in I \wedge \hat{m} = rs^y(setS)} \mathop{\exists}_{m' \in Suc(I,m)} : \widehat{m'} = rs^y(cont) \wedge PO(m, rs^y(Str)) = CO(N(I_v(I,m'), rs^y$
$(alg)))$, *i.e., for each strategy pattern invocation, after the strategy change the algorithmInterface method of the new Strategy object should be invoked by the contextInterface method.*

Considering the candidates in Table 7, rs_1^y is a valid strategy pattern instance but rs_2^y is not. This is because the *setStatus* method is invoked by the *LightControl* class as shown in Table 4, i.e., the second constraint is violated for rs_2^y. If rs_2^y is valid, the *setStatus* method should not be invoked by neither the *LightControl* class nor the *LightStatus* class.

7   Tool Implementation

The open-source (P)rocess (M)ining framework *ProM 6* [9] has been developed as a completely plugable environment for process mining and related topics. It can be extended by simply adding plug-ins, and currently, more than 600 plug-ins are included. The framework can be downloaded online[1].

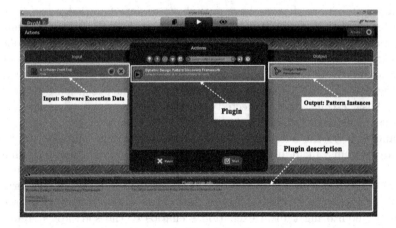

Fig. 4. Screenshot of the *DePaD* tool [17].

We have implemented the behavioral design pattern detection techniques as a plug-in, called *DEsign PAttern Discovery from execution data* (*DePaD*), in our *ProM 6* package.[2] Fig. 4 shows a snapshot of the tool, based on which we

---

[1] http://www.promtools.org/.
[2] https://svn.win.tue.nl/repos/prom/Packages/SoftwareProcessMining/.

can see that this tool takes the software execution data as input, and returns a set of detected design pattern instances. Currently, it supports observer pattern, state pattern and strategy pattern.

By taking the execution data that are generated from the *AISWorld* software as input, we run the *DePaD*. Figure 5 shows the detected observer pattern instance rs^{o1}. The *Run/Invocation Count* indicates the number of runs in the input software execution data and the number of invocations that support the current pattern instance. All experimental results in the following section are conducted on the basis of this tool.

8   Empirical Evaluation

To evaluate the effectiveness of the proposed behavioral design pattern detection approaches, we use both synthetic and open-source software systems. For these experiments, we used a laptop with a 2.40 GHz CPU, Windows 8.1 and Java SE 1.7.0 67 (64 bit) with 4 GB of allocated RAM.

8.1   Subject Software Systems and Execution Data

In this section, we introduce the execution data that we used to perform the experiments. On the one hand, we use six synthetic software systems that each implements one or more design patterns. The advantages of using synthetic software systems are that we have enough up-to-date knowledge to (1) collect execution data that cover all possible scenarios; and (2) evaluate the quality of our approach. On the other hand, we use the execution data that were collected from three open-source software systems to show the applicability and scalability of our approach for real-life scenarios. Different from the synthetic software of which we have enough knowledge to guarantee that the execution data cover all software usage scenarios, we collected execution data from typical usage scenarios of these open-source software systems.

Table 8 shows the detailed statistics of execution data collected from these software systems, including the number of packages/classes/methods that are loaded during execution and the number of method calls analyzed. In total, 1.000.000 method calls are involved in the execution data for our experiment. Please note that the execution data of *Lexi 0.1.1*[3] and *JHotDraw 5.1*[4] are collected by monitoring typical execution scenarios of the software systems. For example, a typical scenario of the *JHotDraw 5.1* is: launch JHotDraw, draw two rectangles, select and align the two rectangles, color them as blue, and close JHotDraw. For the *JUnit 3.7*[5], we monitor the execution of the project test suite with 259 independent tests provided in the *MapperXML*[6] release.

---

[3] http://essere.disco.unimib.it/svn/DPB/Lexi%20v0.1.1%20alpha/.

[4] http://www.inf.fu-berlin.de/lehre/WS99/java/swing/JHotDraw5.1/.

[5] http://essere.disco.unimib.it/svn/DPB/JUnit%20v3.7/.

[6] http://essere.disco.unimib.it/svn/DPB/MapperXML%20v1.9.7/.

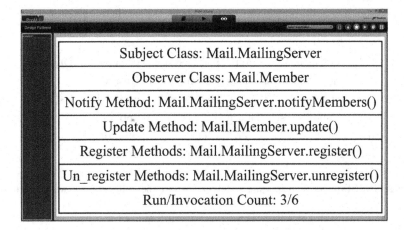

Fig. 5. A detected observer pattern instance [17].

Table 8. Statistics of subject software execution data [17].

Software		#Packages	#Classes	#Methods	#Method calls
Synthetic	Synthetic 1	1	5	9	155
	Synthetic 2	1	5	11	135
	Synthetic 3	1	5	15	160
	Synthetic 4	1	6	12	104
	Synthetic 5	1	8	14	258
	Synthetic 6	8	12	28	9728
Real-life	Lexi 0.1.1	5	68	263	20344
	JUnit 3.7	3	47	213	363948
	JHotDraw 5.1	7	1.8	549	583423

8.2 Experimental Results of Synthetic Software Systems

In this section, we report the design pattern detection results obtained by our tool for the six synthetic software systems. These synthetic software are described, including the number and type of implemented design pattern instances, as follows:

- Synthetic 1 is a calender software system that implements a state design pattern instance;
- Synthetic 2 is a testing software system that implements a state pattern instance and a strategy pattern instance;
- Synthetic 3 is a short message software system that implements an observer design pattern instance;
- Synthetic 4 is a lights control software system that implements a strategy design pattern instance;

Table 9. Observer pattern instances detected from the synthetic software systems [17].

	#1	#2	#3
Sub	GlobalClock	ActiveSensorSystem	CommentaryObject
Obs	GlobalClockObs	ActiveAlarmLis	Observer
not	run()	soundTheAlarm()	notifyObservers()
upd	periodPasses()	alarm()	update()
reg	attach()	addAlarm()	subscribe()
unr	detach()	removeAlarm()	unsubscribe()

Table 10. State pattern instances detected from the synthetic software systems.

	#4	#5
Context	TContext	Context
State	TS	State
setState	setS()	setState()
request	request()	writeName()
handle	handle()	write()

- Synthetic 5 is a sensing alarm software system that implements an observer design pattern instance; and
- Synthetic 6 is a product management software system that implements an observer pattern instance.

We executed the *DePaD* tool by taking the execution data collected from the six synthetic software systems as input. For the observer pattern, three observer pattern instances were returned. Detailed information on the discovered observer pattern instances are shown in Table 9. By manually inspecting these observer pattern instances with respect to our domain knowledge, we found that (1) all these detected observer pattern instances are valid; and (2) all observer pattern instances, i.e., #1 that is implemented in Synthetic 3, #2 that is implemented Synthetic 5, and #3 that is implemented Synthetic 6, are fully detected.

Similarly, we executed the *DePaD* tool by taking the execution data collected from the six synthetic software systems as input for state and strategy patterns, two state pattern instances and two strategy pattern instances were returned. Detailed information of the detected state and strategy pattern instances are shown in Tables 10-11. By manually inspecting these detected pattern instances with respect to the domain knowledge, we found that (1) all detected state and strategy pattern instances are valid; and (2) all state pattern instances, i.e., #4 that is implemented in Synthetic 1, and #5 that is implemented Synthetic 2, are fully detected. (3) all strategy pattern instances, i.e., #6 that is implemented in Synthetic 4, and #7 that is implemented Synthetic 2, are fully detected.

Table 11. Strategy pattern instances detected from the synthetic software systems.

	#6	#7
Context	RemoteControl	TContext
State	Command	TS
setStrategy	setCommand()	setS()
contextInterface	pressButton()	contextInterface()
algorithmInterface	execute()	algorithmI()

Based on the pattern detection results from the six synthetic software, we conclude that the proposed approach can rediscover all implemented patterns instances and does not include any false positives if the behavior of all implemented pattern instances are recorded in the execution data.

8.3 Experimental Results of Open-Source Software Systems

In this section, we report the evaluation of our approach based on three open-source software systems. We executed the *DePaD* tool by taking the software execution data as input, the number of detected observer, state and strategy pattern instances are shown in Table 12.

By manually inspecting the detected pattern instances, we found that all of them are valid, i.e., the precision of our approach is 100%. This is coincide the conclusion that our approach guarantees all detected pattern instances satisfy both structural and behavioral constraints. However, we cannot guarantee that all pattern instance in these open-source software systems are fully rediscovered as (1) we do not have the ground knowledge of all implemented pattern instances; and (2) we cannot guarantee that all the implemented pattern instances are observed in the execution data.

Table 12. Number of detected pattern instances from the three open-source software systems [17].

	Observer pattern	State pattern	Strategy pattern
Lexi 0.1.1	–	–	8
JUnit 3.7	2	2	–
JHotDraw5.1	4	22	24

Note that: – means no pattern instance is detected from the data.

9 Threats to Validity

This section discusses some main threats that may affect the validity of our approach. We separate internal threats from external threats.

9.1   Internal Threats

Internal threats refer to the limitation of the framework itself. The quality of the detection results heavily rely on the accuracy and completeness of the design pattern specification. On the one hand, if the pattern specification is over-defined (e.g., some unnecessary constraints are included), some true positives may be missing. On the other hand, if the pattern specification is under-defined (e.g., some essential constraints are not included), some false positives may be incorrectly detected.

Considering for example the observer pattern, the requirement that all registered observers need to be unregistered is a bit restrictive for some users. This constraint can be relaxed for some application cases. In addition, a candidate is valid if there exists one invocation that satisfies all behavioral constraints. This restriction may be a bit weak, some other applications may require that the behavioral constraints should be hold for all invocations.

9.2   External Threats

External threats refer to the limitations of the input of our approach. Generally speaking, our approach relies on the software execution data. Hence, the quality of the proposed approach heavily depends on the completeness of the execution data. If the data do not cover fractions of the software's behavior including all pattern candidates, the results are unreliable.

10   Conclusion

This chapter presents a general framework to support behavioral design pattern detection by taking as input the software execution data. To demonstrate the applicability, this framework is instantiated for the observer pattern, state pattern, and strategy pattern. In addition, we have implemented the proposed techniques as an integrated plugin in the open source process mining toolkit ProM. Currently, this plugin supports the observer pattern, state pattern and strategy pattern. The effectiveness and applicability of this tool are demonstrated by two groups of experiments based on both synthetic and real-life software systems.

In the future, we plan to extend this work in the following directions. The detection of other typical behavioral design patterns, such as the command pattern and visitor pattern, should be included in the framework. Moreover, we also plan to instantiate this framework for creational patterns, such as the singleton pattern and factory method pattern. Currently, we are trying to evaluate the scalability and empirically validate extensibility of the approach by analyzing more real-life software systems.

Acknowledgements. This work is supported by the *NIRICT 3TU.BSR (Big Software on the Run)* research project[7]

---

[7] http://www.3tu-bsr.nl/doku.php?id=start.

References

1. Arcelli, F., Perin, F., Raibulet, C., Ravani, S.: Jadept: dynamic analysis for behavioral design pattern detection. In: 4th International Conference on Evaluation of Novel Approaches to Software Engineering, ENASE, pp. 95–106 (2009)
2. Arcelli, F., Perin, F., Raibulet, C., Ravani, S.: Design pattern detection in java systems: a dynamic analysis based approach. In: Maciaszek, L.A., González-Pérez, C., Jablonski, S. (eds.) ENASE 2008. CCIS, vol. 69, pp. 163–179. Springer, Heidelberg (2010). https://doi.org/10.1007/978-3-642-14819-4_12
3. Bernardi, M.L., Cimitile, M., De Ruvo, G., Di Lucca, G.A., Santone, A.: Model checking to improve precision of design pattern instances identification in OO systems. In: 10th International Joint Conference on Software Technologies (ICSOFT), vol. 2, pp. 1–11. IEEE (2015)
4. Bernardi, M.L., Cimitile, M., Di Lucca, G.: Design pattern detection using a DSL-driven graph matching approach. J. Softw. Evol. Process **26**(12), 1233–1266 (2014)
5. Dabain, H., Manzer, A., Tzerpos, V.: Design pattern detection using finder. In: Proceedings of the 30th Annual ACM Symposium on Applied Computing, pp. 1586–1593. ACM (2015)
6. De Lucia, A., Deufemia, V., Gravino, C., Risi, M.: Behavioral pattern identification through visual language parsing and code instrumentation. In: 13th European Conference on Software Maintenance and Reengineering, CSMR 2009, pp. 99–108. IEEE (2009)
7. De Lucia, A., Deufemia, V., Gravino, C., Risi, M.: Design pattern recovery through visual language parsing and source code analysis. J. Syst. Softw. **82**(7), 1177–1193 (2009)
8. Dong, J., Zhao, Y., Sun, Y.: A matrix-based approach to recovering design patterns. IEEE Trans. Syst. Man Cybern. Part A Syst. Hum. **39**(6), 1271–1282 (2009)
9. van Dongen, B.F., de Medeiros, A.K.A., Verbeek, H.M.W., Weijters, A.J.M.M., van der Aalst, W.M.P.: The ProM framework: a new era in process mining tool support. In: Ciardo, G., Darondeau, P. (eds.) ICATPN 2005. LNCS, vol. 3536, pp. 444–454. Springer, Heidelberg (2005). https://doi.org/10.1007/11494744_25
10. Fontana, F.A., Zanoni, M.: A tool for design pattern detection and software architecture reconstruction. Inf. Sci. **181**(7), 1306–1324 (2011)
11. Gamma, E.: Design Patterns: Elements of Reusable Object-Oriented Software. Pearson Education, India (1995)
12. Heuzeroth, D., Holl, T., Hogstrom, G., Lowe, W.: Automatic design pattern detection. In: 11th IEEE International Workshop on Program Comprehension, pp. 94–103. IEEE (2003)
13. Leemans, M., Liu, C.: Xes software event extension. XES Working Group, pp. 1–11 (2017)
14. Liu, C., van Dongen, B., Assy, N., van der Aalst, W.: Software architectural model discovery from execution data. In: 13th International Conference on Evaluation of Novel Approaches to Software Engineering, pp. 3–10 (2018)
15. Liu, C., van Dongen, B., Assy, N., van der Aalst, W.: Component behavior discovery from software execution data. In: International Conference on Computational Intelligence and Data Mining, pp. 1–8. IEEE (2016)
16. Liu, C., van Dongen, B., Assy, N., van der Aalst, W.: Component interface identification and behavior discovery from software execution data. In: 26th International Conference on Program Comprehension (ICPC 2018), pp. 97–107. ACM (2018)

17. Liu, C., van Dongen, B., Assy, N., van der Aalst, W.: A framework to support behavioral design pattern detection from software execution data. In: 13th International Conference on Evaluation of Novel Approaches to Software Engineering, pp. 65–76 (2018)

18. Liu, C., van Dongen, B., Assy, N., van der Aalst, W.: A general framework to detect behavioral design patterns. In: International Conference on Software Engineering (ICSE 2018), pp. 234–235. ACM (2018)

19. Ng, J.K.Y., Guéhéneuc, Y.G., Antoniol, G.: Identification of behavioural and creational design motifs through dynamic analysis. J. Softw. Maint. Evol. Res. Pract. **22**(8), 597–627 (2010)

20. Niere, J., Schäfer, W., Wadsack, J.P., Wendehals, L., Welsh, J.: Towards pattern-based design recovery. In: Proceedings of the 24th International Conference on Software Engineering, pp. 338–348. ACM (2002)

21. Shi, N., Olsson, R.A.: Reverse engineering of design patterns from java source code. In: 21st IEEE/ACM International Conference on Automated Software Engineering, pp. 123–134. IEEE (2006)

22. Tsantalis, N., Chatzigeorgiou, A., Stephanides, G., Halkidis, S.T.: Design pattern detection using similarity scoring. IEEE Trans. Softw. Eng. **32**(11), 896–909 (2006)

23. Von Detten, M., Meyer, M., Travkin, D.: Reverse engineering with the reclipse tool suite. In: 2010 ACM/IEEE 32nd International Conference on Software Engineering, vol. 2, pp. 299–300. IEEE (2010)

24. Wendehals, L., Orso, A.: Recognizing behavioral patterns atruntime using finite automata. In: Proceedings of the 2006 International Workshop on Dynamic Systems Analysis, pp. 33–40. ACM (2006)

Portable Synthesis of Multi-core Real-Time Systems with Reconfiguration Constraints

Wafa Lakhdhar[1,4(✉)], Rania Mzid[2,3(✉)], Mohamed Khalgui[1,5,6(✉)],
and Georg Frey[4(✉)]

[1] LISI Lab INSAT, University of Carthage, INSAT Centre Urbain Nord BP 676,
Tunis, Tunisia
wafa.lakhdhar@live.fr

[2] ISI, University Tunis-El Manar, 2 Rue Abourraihan Al Bayrouni, Ariana, Tunisia
rania.mzid@gmail.com

[3] CES Lab ENIS, University of Sfax, B.P:w.3, Sfax, Tunisia

[4] Automation and Energy Systems, Saarland University,
66123 Saarbrucken, Germany
georg.frey@aut.uni-saarland.de

[5] Systems Control Lab, Xidian University, Xi'an, China

[6] School of Electrical and Information Engineering,
Jinan University (Zhuhai Campus), Zhuhai 519070, China
khalgui.mohamed@gmail.com

Abstract. Nowadays, multi-core architectures are increasingly being adopted in the design of emerging complex real-time systems. Meanwhile, implementing those systems as threads generates a complex system code due to the large number of threads, which may lead to a reconfiguration time overhead as well as redundancy increases. In this paper, we present a novel approach to synthesize multi-core system architectures from the specification level to the implementation level. In the design level, the proposed approach presents a mixed integer linear programming (MILP) formulation for the task mapping/scheduling problem as well as the minimizing the number of threads and the redundancy between the implementation sets while preserving the system feasibility. To address the portability issue, the optimal design is then transformed to an abstract code that may be transformed to a specific code. The viability and potential of the approach is demonstrated by a case study and a performance evaluation.

Keywords: Real-time system · Reconfigurable architecture ·
Timing constraints · Mixed integer linear programming (MILP) ·
POSIX-based code

1 Introduction

A real-time system has to respond to externally generated input stimuli within a finite and specified delay [1]. Such system may have many implementation

© Springer Nature Switzerland AG 2019
E. Damiani et al. (Eds.): ENASE 2018, CCIS 1023, pp. 165–185, 2019.
https://doi.org/10.1007/978-3-030-22559-9_8

scenarios, the transition from an implementation to another is called reconfiguration. Reconfiguration refers to the architectural or behavioral modifications of a software system during its execution [2] to meet user requirements. Currently, some real-time systems such as automotive electronics, avionics, telecommunications, and consumer electronics become more complex and need more computational power. Thus, the necessity for multi-core architecture is a common answer. The multi-core technology allows increasing the processor clock frequency, which is limited by available instruction-level parallelism and leads to challenging power requirements [3]. This paper deals with multi-core reconfigurable real-time systems.

One challenge during the development of multi-core reconfigurable real-time systems is to ensure an appropriate partitioning and scheduling of the applicative functions across the target platform such that the timing constraints are met. In that context, different scheduling policies have been proposed in the literature [4,5]. Existing multi-core scheduling policies can be classified into three different classes: the partitioned, the global and semi-partitioned approach. The partitioned scheduling allows to choose a core for all tasks and then runs a local scheduler on each core (i.e., off-line scheduling). However, the global scheduling allows to choose a task and to assign it to one of the cores (i.e., on-line scheduling). As opposed to the partitioned approach, different instances of the same task can execute on different cores. The semi-partitioned approach presents an improvement of the partitioning scheduling allowing the controlled tasks migration. It is a hybrid between partitioned and global scheduling [5]. In this paper, we adopt a partitioned approach because it is easier to implement and to analyze. Also, it allows no task migration, thus has low runtime overheads [6]. For the three multi-core scheduling approaches, several scheduling algorithms have been proposed such as Rate Monotonic RM [7] which will be adopted for tasks scheduling in this paper.

The multi-core introduces additional challenges that are still difficult to deal with in real world industrial domains. Indeed, the huge number of tasks exhibits a high complexity by increasing the energy consumption, invoking many redundancies between the different implementations, and producing a complex system code. Thus, we propose a multi-objective optimization approach that minimizes both the energy consumption and the number of tasks in order to reduce the redundancy between the implementation sets. Such optimization may reduce the time overhead and the complexity of the generated code. At the specification level, the developer defines the function sets, the condition sets, and the core sets. At the design level, this approach (i) generates the implementation sets, (ii) affects the functions to the tasks sets which are in turns assigned to the core sets, and (iii) generates a feasible and optimized task model by using the mixed integer linear programming (MILP) formulation. Finally, to address the portability issue, this approach produces from the optimal task model an abstract code "Pseudo-code" which would be converted to a specific code depending on the user choice.

The originality of the proposed approach follows from the fact that (i) it deals with the multi-core (i.e., partitioning), reconfiguration, and real-time problems simultaneously, (ii) it proposes a multi-objective optimization to minimize both the energy consumption and the number of tasks, and (iii) it defines a new abstract language to describe the multi-core real-time reconfigurable system independently from any platform to ensure a required portability.

The remainder of the article is organized as follows. Section 2 presents the state of the art on multi-core reconfigurable real-time systems. Section 3 introduces the global proposed approach and defines the system formalization. Section 4 presents the detailed methodology description. Section 5 contains the Car Collision Avoidance System (CCAS) case study and the experimental results. Section 6 summarizes our work and discuss future directions.

2   Related Works

In the area of real-time multi-core systems, some existing works focus on the synthesis problem [8–10]. In [8], the authors propose a formalization of periodic tasks adapted to engine control applications in multi-core automotive systems. The work reported in [9] presents a system level synthesis approach for multi-core system architectures from Task Precedence Graphs (TPG) models. In [10], the authors present an approach for a semi-automatic synthesis of models into a deterministic scheduling that respects real-time requirements for multi-core systems. Despite the importance of above related synthesis works, none of these solutions considers the reconfiguration property. In contrast, this paper focuses on how the feasible code may be generated for multi-core reconfigurable real-time system.

Another related area is the safe deployment to multi-core real-time systems, where approaches focus on the mapping of tasks on multi-core platforms [11–15]. In [11], the authors develop a heuristic algorithm for the function mapping on a multi-core architecture. In this work, the functions are grouped and distributed across cores, then they are mapped to tasks. Similarly to [12], which proposes a heuristic algorithm to create a task set according to the mapping of runnable entities on the cores. In [13] a linear program is developed for task partitioning, mapping, and scheduling on embedded multi-core systems. Some other related works propose an end-to-end approach to generate a full real-time system. In [14], the authors present a process for the automatic deployment of control applications on multi-core platforms and generate Java code. The work reported in [15] addresses the mapping problem of hard real-time systems composed of periodic AUTOSAR runnables in the context of the multi-core.

The proposed approach differs from the cited works in several points. First of all, it considers reconfigurable systems with real-time properties and multi-core architecture. Secondly, we address the synthesis, the partitioning, the scheduling problem, and the optimization simultaneously. Finally, the majority of them do not propose general solutions. They target a well defined system.

3 Proposed Approach and Formalization

In this section, we introduce the paper's contribution. We present in addition a formal description of the proposed approach. We summarize the outline of the proposed synthesis approach in Fig. 1. As shown in Fig. 1, at specification level, the designer provides the specification model in terms of the reconfiguration conditions and the function set which present the functional model, and the core set which presents the platform model. The design level consists of two steps: (i) initial task model generation which takes as input the functional model, and (ii) partitioning step which receives the initial task model and the platform model to produce a task model. In the implementation level, the abstract code generator transforms the optimized task model to pseudo-code. This step aims to guarantee the portability of the task model across different platforms.

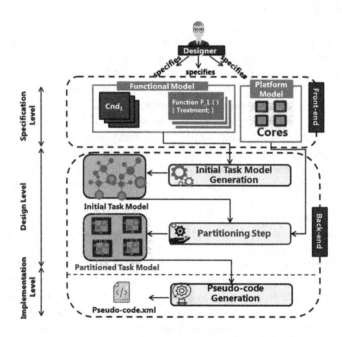

Fig. 1. Process overview.

3.1 Specification Level Formalization

The specification level is composed of (i) the functional model which is in turn composed of (i.a) condition set, and (i.b) function set with p functions that can be thought of as a C-functions. Each function F_k is characterized by static real-time parameters $(T_{F_k}, C_{F_k}, E_{F_k})$ where T_{F_k} is the activation period of the function F_k, C_{F_k} is an estimation of its worst case execution time (WCET) and E_{F_k} is the energy consumed by the function F_k during its execution. Note that these parameters are considered as inputs for the proposed approach and must be specified by the user, and (ii) the platform model consists of one processor, containing a set of M identical cores $\{\zeta_1, \zeta_2 \ldots \zeta_M\}$ that share common memory.

3.2   Design Level Formalization

In the design level, the reconfigurable real-time system system Sys is defined by: $Sys = (\xi_{imp}, C)$ where (i) ξ_{imp} presents m implementations that define the system where $\xi_{imp} = \{imp_1, \ldots imp_m\}$. Each implementation imp_i is characterized by $imp_i = \{\chi_{\tau_i}\}$ where χ_{τ_i} represents a subset of tasks describing the system at a particular instant. Each task τ_j in the implementation imp_i is characterized by: $(r_{ij}, s_{ij}, T_{ij}, C_{ij}, D_{ij}, P_{ij}, E_{ij})$ where r_{ij} is its release time, we assume that $r_{ij} = 0$, its start time s_{ij} which denotes the effective starting time of a task τ_j, its activation period T_{ij}, C_{ij} denotes the capacity or worst case execution time, its deadline D_{ij} which is assumed to be equal to its period in this work $D_{ij} = T_{ij}$, the priority P_{ij} that is inversely proportional to the period T_{ij} as we use the RM policy, E_{ij} presents the energy consumption of task τ_j which is computed as the sum of the energy consumed by the functions implemented by τ_j.

The task τ_j may implement a single or several functions which must have the same period $\tau_j = \{F_1, F_2, F_3, \ldots F_{p_j}\}$, (ii) C represents the controller which manages the moving from one implementation to another under well defined reconfiguration conditions.

Energy Model. Each function F_k is described by two parameters: (i) the function's frequency f_{F_k}, and (ii) the function's voltage V_{F_k}. The energy consumption for the execution of function F_k that we denote by E_{F_k} is computed as $E_{F_k} = f_{F_k} V_{F_k}^2 C_{F_k}$. The energy consumption E_{ij} of task τ_j is then equal to the sum of the energy consumed by the implemented functions $E_{ij} = \sum_{k \in \{1 \ldots p_j\}} E_{F_k} = \sum_{k \in \{1 \ldots p_j\}} f_{F_k} V_{F_k}^2 C_{F_k} = f_{ij} \; V_{ij}^2 C_{ij}$ where (f_{ij}, V_{ij}) are two parameters characterizing task τ_j in implementation imp_i. We assume that $f_{ij} = \sum_{k \in \{1 \ldots p_j\}} f_{F_k}$ and $V_{ij} = \sum_{k \in \{1 \ldots p_j\}} V_{F_k}$. Thus the total energy consumption [16] of implementation imp_i is given by expression 1.

$$E_i = \sum_{j \in \{0, N_i\}} E_{ij} = \sum_{j \in \{0, N_i\}} f_{ij} V_{ij}^2 C_{ij} \tag{1}$$

In expression 2, we denote by f_n and V_n the normalized frequency and voltage of the system. We denote by η_j the reduction factor of voltage when τ_j is executed, $V_{ij} = \frac{V_n}{\eta_j}$ and $f_{ij} = \frac{f_n}{\eta_j}$. In addition, we denote by C_n the computation time at the normalized processor frequency i.e., $C_{ij} = C_n \eta_j$. Thus, the total energy consumption of the implementation imp_i according to [17] is given by

$$E_i = \sum_{j \in \{0, N_i\}} \frac{f_n * V_n^2 * C_n}{\eta_j^2} = K \sum_{j \in \{0, N_i\}} \frac{C_n}{\eta_j^2} \tag{2}$$

where $K = V_n^2 f_n$.

Processor Utilization Factor. Let U_i be the processor utilization factor of the implementation imp_i is defined by: $U_i = \sum_{j=1}^{N_i} \frac{C_{ij}}{T_{ij}}$ [18]. As we perform Rate-Monotonic (RM) assignment and preemptive scheduling, the real-time system is feasible when the test given by expression 3 is verified.

$$\forall i \in \{1..m\}, U_i \leq N_i(2^{\frac{1}{N_i}} - 1). \tag{3}$$

Reconfiguration Time. We define in addition the reconfiguration time T_{reconf} [19, 20] as the sum of the time required to add/remove tasks (i.e., time spent by the system to jump from one implementation to another) and the time required for task's migration. The time for task's migration refers to the period of time required for a task to move from one core to another when the system load a new implementation. Thus, we define the reconfiguration time as follow:

$$T_{reconf} = (A + B) * T_{cost} + C * T_{migration} \tag{4}$$

where A is the number of the deleted tasks, B is the number of created tasks, T_{cost} is the spent time to delete/add a task, C is the number of migrated tasks and $T_{migration}$ is the time spent to migrate from a core to another. One objective of the present work is to reduce the reconfiguration time T_{reconf} of the multi-core reconfigurable real-time system with the aim to improve its reactivity.

3.3   Implementation Level Formalization

The pseudo-code [21] is an abstract description of the multi-core reconfigurable real-time system at the implementation level. This code may be transformed to a specific language (e.g., POSIX, RT-Java) by defining a set of transformation rules. The "pseudo-code" corresponds to a set of tags ξ_{Tags} i.e., $\xi_{Tags} = \{\chi_{Tag_{imp}}, Tag_{ctrl}, Tag_{sched}, Tag_{Mech}, Tag_{prtclAcces}\}$ where (i) $\chi_{Tag_{imp}}$ denotes the set of implementation's tag. An implementation tag is represented by $</implementation$ and is described by the following parameters: $(Name_{imp}, Cnd, IsDefault)$ where Cnd is the condition that allows to move from one implementation to another and $IsDefault$ is a boolean parameter which indicates whether the current implementation corresponds to the default one. An implementation tag is composed of $\Psi_{Tag_{Core}}$ a set of core's tag (i.e., $\chi_{Tag_{imp}} = \{\Psi_{Tag_{core}}\}$). A core's tag is representing by $</Core$ which characterized by its name. The core's tag is composed of a set of thread's tag which is represented by $</Thread$ and is characterized by the thread parameters: $(Name_{thread}, Deadline, Period, Priority)$. Each thread contains a set of function's tag $\Gamma_{Tag_{fn}}$. The function's tag represents a function executed by the current thread. A function is represented by $</Function$ tag and is only characterized by its name, (ii) Tag_{ctrl} is the Controller's tag which is represented by $</Controller$ and is composed of: (ii.a) *If-then-else* statements to move from one implementation to another, (ii.b) $Exec_{impl}(imp_i)$ is a function to execute the i-th implementation, and (iii) Tag_{sched} is the scheduler's tag which is represented

by: $</SchedulingPolicy$. This tag permits to define the adopted scheduling policy (the RM policy in our case). The correspondence between the system model and the pseudo-code is given in Fig. 2 that shows the set of tasks which are transformed into a set of threads' tag and which implement the set of functions. It shows also the set of implementation describing the system model. By using If-then-else statement, the controller executes the set of implementations' tag.

4   Detailed Methodology Description

In this section, we present in details the back-end steps. As described in Fig. 3 the approach is composed of three based steps: (i) generation of the initial task model, (ii) partitioning step, and (iii) generation of the pseudo-code.

4.1   Initial Task Model Generation

This step consists in the generating of the initial task model from the function set and the reconfiguration conditions. This step is outlined in the Algorithm 1. This algorithm ensures (i) the generation of the implementation set such as for each reconfiguration condition, it generates an implementation, and (ii) the generation of the task set from the functions. Each task will take the same parameters of the implemented function (i.e., in this step, the task number is equal to the function number). Let us note that for the generation of this model, the real-time feasibility is not considered. The complexity of this generation step is $\mathcal{O}(N^2)$.

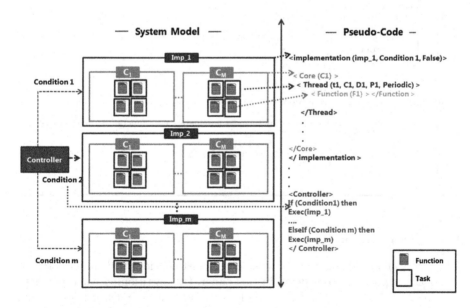

Fig. 2. Correspondence between system model and pseudo-code.

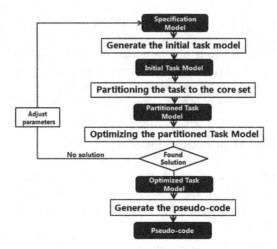

Fig. 3. Back-end description.

Algorithm 1. INITIAL TASK GENERATION.

    Input:
    - F : Functions set
    - ReconfCnd : Reconfiguration condition set
    Output:
    - InitTask : Initial Task Model
    - imp : Implementation set
1 **Notations:**
2 - Reconf_Cnd_Func: Correlation table between the reconfiguration conditions and the
    functions.
3 $k \leftarrow 0$
4 /*** Generation Of Implementations ***/
5 **for** $i \leftarrow 0$ *to* $SizeOf(ReconfCnd)$ **do**
6   **for** $j \leftarrow 0$ *to* $SizeOf(F)$ **do**
7   **if** $(F[j] \in Reconf\_Cnd\_Func[i])$ **then**
8         $imp[i][k] = F[j]$
9         $k++;$
10    $k \leftarrow 0$
11 /*** Generation Of Task Model ***/
12 **for** *each implementation* imp_i **do**
13   **for** *each function* F_j **do**
14   /* We create a task and we initialize its parameters with function F_j parameters */
15     $WcetOf(InitTask[j]) = WcetOf(F[j])$
16     $PeriodOf(InitTask[j]) = PeriodOf(F[j])$
17     $DeadlineOf(InitTask[j]) = DeadlineOf(InitTask[j])$
18     $imp[i][j] = InitTask[j]$
19 **return** imp

4.2 Task Partitioning

The partitioning of tasks into multiple cores must consider real-time feasibility. Under the hypotheses considered in this paper, the partitioning corresponds to an RM [22] scheduling problem related to periodic tasks. Each generated task must be affected to a specific core, then in each core, we run a local scheduler.

This partitioning is characterized by (i) no migration at run time (i.e., in a given implementation a task must always run on a given core), (ii) the possibility of applying end-to-end worst case response time analysis, and (iii) off-line core assignment [23]. The basic principles of an RM-based partitioning heuristic are:

1. Order tasks according to RM policy,
2. Do task assignment according to their order,
3. For each task, look for an available core, by applying one of the following policies [24],
   - Best Fit policy: for each task i, we start with core $j = 0$ and assign task i on the core on which the feasibility test is true and on which the processor utilization factor has the highest value
   - First Fit policy: for each task i, we start with core $j = 0$ and assign task i on the first core on which the feasibility test (expression 3) is true. In this paper, we use the First Fit policy.
4. Stop when all tasks are assigned.

Algorithm 2 that illustrates this step considers as inputs: the implementations, tasks and the cores set. It generates as output the partitioning task model.

Algorithm 2. PARTITIONING TASK MODEL.

    Input:
    - Imp: Implementation set
    - Task: Task set
    - Core: Core set
    Output:
    - PartTask: Partitioning Task Model

1 **Notations:**
2 - m: implementation number
3 - N_i: Number of tasks in the implementation i.
4 - M: Core number
5 **for** $i \leftarrow 0$ **to** m **do**
6   /*** Task Index ***/
7     $j \leftarrow 0$
8   /*** Core Index ***/
9     $k \leftarrow 0$
10   **for** $j \leftarrow 0$ **to** N_i **do**
11   **for** $k \leftarrow 0$ **to** M **do**
12   **if** *Feasibility is true* **then**
13            $AssignTask[j]toCore[k]$
14            $PartTask[j][k] = Core[k]$
15   **else**
16            $k++$

17 **return** *PartTask*

4.3 Optimization Step

In order to ensure a reliable implementation of the multi-core reconfigurable real-time system from the initial task model and the partitioning task model taking into consideration the different constraints (Fig. 1) (Real-time, no migration, energy), we propose in this section a MILP model which consists of a linear objective function to be optimized and a set of linear inequalities (constraints).

Variable Definition. Let (i) $Merge_{jq}$ be a boolean variable used to mention whether two tasks τ_j and τ_q are merged such that $Merge_{jq}$ is equal to 1 if task τ_j and task τ_q are merged, the merge corresponds to the situation in which τ_j absorbs τ_q, to be deleted from the model, (ii) x_{js} be a boolean variable used to mention if τ_j is executed in core s. Thus if the value of x_{js} is equal to 1, then the corresponding task τ_j is running in core s, (iii) y_{ij} be a boolean variable used to mention if τ_j is in the implementation i, (iv) T be the set of period of N task, (v) $C_{new_{ij}}$ be the new WCET of the task τ_j in imp_i, (vi) $T_{new_{ij}}$ be the new period of the task τ_j in imp_i, (vii) μ_{jq} be a binary variable where $\mu_{jq} = 1$ when τ_q is executed before τ_j.

Objective Function

$$maximize \sum_{j,q \in \{0..N\}} Merge_{jq} - \sum_{i \in \{1..m\}} \sum_{j \in \{0,N\}} E_{ij} \qquad (5)$$

The expression 5 defines the objective function. It aims to maximize the number of merges while minimizing the total energy consumption.

Merging Situation Constraints. The constraints 6 and 7 introduce the merging condition such as the two tasks $\tau_j \in \zeta_s$ and $\tau_q \in \zeta_s$ will be merged if they have the same period.

$\forall j, q \in \{1..N\}\ s \in \{1..M\}$

$$if(T_j * x_{js} - T_q * x_{qs} = 0)\ then\ Merge_{jq} = 1; \qquad (6)$$

$$if(T_j * x_{js} - T_q * x_{qs} <> 0)\quad then\ Merge_{jq} = 0; \qquad (7)$$

The constraint in 8 is used to avoid a non-meaningful situations which corresponds to the merge of a task already merged i.e., $\forall j, q, r \in \{1..N\}$,

$$Merge_{jq} \leq 1,\ , q, r \neq j, Merge_{jq} + Merge_{rj} \leq 1 \qquad (8)$$

Real-Time Constraints. In each implementation, every pair of tasks $\forall j, q \in \{1 \ldots N\}$ τ_j and τ_q, we should respect the constraints 9 and 10 to ensure that only one task will be executed at a single time. $\forall i \in \{1 \ldots m\}$

$$s_{ij} - s_{iq} >= C_{new_{iq}} - M * \mu_{jq} \qquad (9)$$

$$s_{iq} - s_{ij} >= C_{new_{ij}} - M * (1 - \mu_{jq}) \qquad (10)$$

where $C_{new_{ij}}$ and $C_{new_{iq}}$ are the WCET of the tasks τ_j and τ_q. Constraints 11, 12, and 13 give the computation formula of $C_{new_{ij}}$.

If a task $\tau_j \in imp_i$ does not be merged with any task in all implementations, the WCET of τ_i does not change. $\forall j \in \{1..N\} \ \forall i \in \{1..m\}$

$$if \left(\sum_{q \in 1..N} Merge_{qj} + \sum_{r \in 1..N} Merge_{jr} = 0 \right) then \ C_{new_{ij}} = C_{ij}; \tag{11}$$

Else if a task τ_j is merged with another task in the same implementation or not, the WCET of τ_j is calculated in two cases:(i) the task τ_j and τ_q are in the same implementation, so the resulting WCET is the sum of C_{ij} and C_{iq}, and (ii) the task τ_j and τ_q are not in the same implementation, so the resulting task has two different WCETs in the two implementations. Constraints 12, and 13 allow to compute the resulting WCET in the two cases. $\forall j, q \in \{1..N\} \ i, l \in \{1..m\}$

$if(Merge_{jq} + y_{ij} + y_{lp} = 3) \ then \ C_{new_{ij}} = C_{ij} + C_{lq}$

$$and \ C_{new_{lq}} = 0; \tag{12}$$

$if(Merge_{jq} + y_{ij} + y_{lp} = 2) \ then \ C_{new_{ij}} = C_{ij}$

$$and \ C_{new_{lq}} = C_{lq}; \tag{13}$$

Constraint 14 ensures the feasibility of the system, $\forall i \in \{1..m\}$:

$$U_i \leq N(2^{\frac{1}{N}} - 1) \tag{14}$$

where U_i is given by

$$U_i = \sum_{j=1}^{N} \frac{C_{new_{ij}}}{T_{new_{ij}}} \tag{15}$$

where $T_{new_{ij}}$ is computed as follow: $\forall j, q \in \{1..N\} \ i, l \in \{1..m\}$
$if(Merge_{jq} + y_{ij} + y_{lp} = 3) \ then T_{new_{ij}} = T_{ij}$

$$and \ T_{new_{lq}} = 0; \tag{16}$$

$if(Merge_{jq} + y_{ij} + y_{lp} = 2) \ then \ T_{new_{ij}} = T_{ij}$

$$and \ T_{new_{lq}} = T_{lq}; \tag{17}$$

The start time should respect Constraint 18 i.e.,

$$\forall j \in \{1..N\}, \forall i \in \{1..m\}, s_{ij} >= r_{ij} \tag{18}$$

Energy Constraints

$$E_{ij} = K \sum_{j \in \{1, N\}} \frac{C_n}{\eta_j^2} \tag{19}$$

The energy consumption's equation is fractional, thus we simplify this program in order to be interpretable by using the CPLEX solver that maximizes the reduction factor η_j which is inversely proportional to the energy consumption. The objective function becomes

$$Maximize \sum_{j,q \in \{1,N\}} Merge_{jq} + \sum_{i \in \{1,m\}} \sum_{j,q \in \{0,N\}} x \qquad (20)$$

To ensure the no simultaneous execution of tasks the constraints 9 and 10 become respectively 21 and 22: $\forall j, q \in \{1 \ldots N\}$ τ_j and τ_q $\forall i \in \{1 \ldots m\}$

$$s_{ij} - s_{iq} >= C_n * \eta_q - M * \mu_{jq} \qquad (21)$$

$$s_{iq} - s_{ij} >= C_n * \eta_j - M * (1 - \mu_{jq}) \qquad (22)$$

$\forall i \in \{1..m\}$, $j \in \{1..N\}$ To ensure that the start time is always greater than the release time, Constraint 23 is considered:

$$s_{ij} >= r_{ij} \qquad (23)$$

We limit the value of x by Constraint 24

$$x \leq \eta_j \qquad (24)$$

Algorithm 3. PSEUDO-CODE GENERATION.

Input:
- OTM: Optimized Task Model
- Cnd: Conditions set
Output:
$Pseudo\_codePsC = \{Thread\_tag, Function\_tag, Resource\_tag, Implement\_tag,$
$default\_tag, Control\_tag\}$
1 /*** Generation Of Thread tags ***/
2 **for** $each task \tau_i$ **do**
3      $Create(Thread\_tag\ T\_tag)$
4      $T\_tag.Deadline_i \leftarrow OTM_i.\tau_i.D_i$
5      $T\_tag.Period_i \leftarrow OTM_i.\tau_i.T_i$
6      $T\_tag.Priority_i \leftarrow OTM_i.\tau_i.P_i$
7      $T\_tag.Resource \leftarrow OTM_i.\tau_i.Resource$
8      $T\_tag.Resource.Name \leftarrow OTM_i.\tau_i.Resource.Name$
9   **for** $each Function F_j in \tau_i$ **do**
10         $Create(Function\_tag F\_tag)$
11         $F\_tag.name \leftarrow OTM_i.F_j.Name$

12 /*** Generation Of Core tags ***/
13 **for** $each Core core_i$ **do**
14     $Create(Core\_tag core\_tag)$
15     $Core\_tag.Name \leftarrow OTM_i.core_i.Name$
16     $Core\_tag.\xi = \{Task \in OTM.core_i\}$

17 /*** Generation Of Implementation tags ***/
18 **for** $each implementation imp_i$ **do**
19     $Create(Implementation\_tag imp\_tag)$
20     $imp\_tag.Name \leftarrow OTM_i.imp_i.Name$
21     $imp\_tag.\xi = \{Core \in OTM.imp_i\}$
22     $imp\_tag.Cnd = Cnd$

23 /*** Generation Of Controller tag ***/
24 $Create(Controller\_tag)$
25 /*** Generation Of Scheduling policy tag (by default RM) ***/
26 $Create(Sched\_Policy\_tag)$
27 **return** PsC

4.4 "Pseudo-code" Generation

The third main function of the proposed approach is "pseudo-code" generation from the task model produced from the optimization step. Each task is transformed into a thread' tag. Each thread implements a set of functions. The core set are represented by cores' tag. Finally, the set of implementations in the system model are implemented by the set of implementations' tag. By using If-then-else statement, the controller executes the set of implementations' tag. Algorithm 3 illustrates this generating step.

The generated "pseudo-code" may be transformed into a special code (RT-Java or POSIX).

5 Case Study

In this section, we illustrate the proposed approach through a case study: a Car Collision Avoidance System (CCAS).

5.1 Specification Level

The Car Collision Avoidance System (CCAS)detects obstacles in front of the vehicle to which it is mounted and, if an imminent collision is detected, applies the brakes to slow the vehicle. To show the applicability of our approach, we consider in this paper a simplified version of this system. For clarity, several features of the system (CCAS) were omitted. Therefore, we only define two modes of operation:

Table 1. Specification mode.

Execution mode	Condition	Function name	Period ms	WCET ms	Energy mW
Default mode	Eco = Disable	F_1: Read image	5	1	1687.5
		F_2: Discrete cosine transformation DCT	5	1	30
		F_3: Quantization	15	5	270
		F_4: Inverse DCT	15	3	2031.25
		F_5: Display	20	5	5760
Economic mode	Eco = Enable	F_1: Read image	5	1	1687.5
		F_1': Compress image	5	0.2	200
		F_2: Discrete cosine transformation DCT	5	1	30
		F_3: Quantization	15	5	270
		F_4: Inverse	15	3	2031.25
		F_4': Decompress	15	4	1000
		F_5: Display	20	5	5760

1. Default mode: represents a traditional use of CCAS,
2. Economic mode: represents a restrictive use of CCAS with safety requirement.

In the case where the economic mode must be enabled, the system jumps from the default mode to the secure one. The software architecture of the studied application is composed of five functions in default mode and of seven functions in the economic mode such that every function is characterized by a period, a WCET and an energy consumption (Table 1). It is mapped to a preemptive execution platform composed of one processor which contains two cores ζ_1 and ζ_2. A tabular description of the specification model is given in Table 1.

Table 1 depicts two execution modes *Default Mode* and *Economic Mode*. Each mode is characterized by a set of functions defined by a set of timing parameters.

5.2   Initial Task Model

The second step consists in generating the implementations and their tasks. Proceeding from the specification model, for each condition we generate an implementation so we have two implementations. Then, we assign each function to a task. The resulting task model is given in Table 2 that shows two implementations which are composed of twelve tasks. Each task is characterized by the same real-time parameters of the executed function.

Table 2. Initial task model.

Execution mode	Task	Period ms	WCET ms	Energy mW
Default mode	τ_1	5	1	1687.5
	τ_2	5	1	30
	τ_3	15	5	270
	τ_4	15	3	2031.25
	τ_5	20	5	5760
Economic mode	τ_6	5	1	1687.5
	τ_7	5	0.2	200
	τ_8	5	1	30
	τ_9	15	5	270
	τ_{10}	15	3	2031.25
	τ_{11}	15	4	1000
	τ_{12}	20	5	5760

5.3   Partitioning Task Model

The next step consists in distributing the task model into a specific multi-core architecture. The targeted multi-core architecture contains 2 cores and a shared memory. In order to assign the tasks to the cores, we apply Algorithm 2. Table 3 presents the partitioning task model.

For each implementation, we assign the tasks to the appropriate core based on the feasibility tests. The resulting partitioning task model represents the input of the optimization step.

Table 3. Partitioning task model.

Execution mode	Core	Task	Period ms	WCET ms
Default mode	ζ_1	τ_1	5	1
		τ_2	5	1
		τ_3	15	5
	ζ_2	τ_4	15	3
		τ_5	20	5
Economic mode	ζ_1	τ_6	5	1
		τ_7	5	0.2
		τ_8	5	1
		τ_9	15	5
	ζ_2	τ_{10}	15	3
		τ_{11}	15	4
		τ_{12}	20	5

5.4 Optimized Task Model

Once the initial solution is defined, we process the optimization step. This step involves the execution using CPLEX solver of the proposed linear program. We model the input of this step as two matrices: "tasks to implementation mapping matrix" (i.e., Y) and "tasks to core assignment matrix" (i.e., X). These two matrices are defined as follows:

$$
Y = \begin{pmatrix}
 & imp_1 & imp_2 \\
\tau_1 & 1 & 0 \\
\tau_2 & 1 & 0 \\
\tau_3 & 1 & 0 \\
\tau_4 & 1 & 0 \\
\tau_5 & 1 & 0 \\
\tau_6 & 0 & 1 \\
\tau_7 & 0 & 1 \\
\tau_8 & 0 & 1 \\
\tau_9 & 0 & 1 \\
\tau_{10} & 0 & 1 \\
\tau_{11} & 0 & 1 \\
\tau_{12} & 0 & 1
\end{pmatrix}
\begin{pmatrix}
 & \zeta_1 & \zeta_2 \\
\tau_1 & 1 & 0 \\
\tau_2 & 1 & 0 \\
\tau_3 & 1 & 0 \\
\tau_4 & 0 & 1 \\
\tau_5 & 0 & 1 \\
\tau_6 & 1 & 0 \\
\tau_7 & 1 & 0 \\
\tau_8 & 1 & 0 \\
\tau_9 & 1 & 0 \\
\tau_{10} & 0 & 1 \\
\tau_{11} & 0 & 1 \\
\tau_{12} & 0 & 1
\end{pmatrix} = X
$$

The linear program generates the following Merge matrix:

$$Merge = \begin{pmatrix} 0\ 1\ 0\ 0\ 0\ 1\ 1\ 1\ 0\ 0\ 0\ 0 \\ 1\ 0\ 0\ 0\ 0\ 1\ 1\ 1\ 0\ 0\ 0\ 0 \\ 0\ 0\ 0\ 0\ 0\ 0\ 0\ 0\ 1\ 0\ 0\ 0 \\ 0\ 0\ 0\ 0\ 0\ 0\ 0\ 0\ 0\ 1\ 1\ 0 \\ 0\ 0\ 0\ 0\ 0\ 0\ 0\ 0\ 0\ 0\ 0\ 1 \\ 1\ 1\ 0\ 0\ 0\ 0\ 1\ 1\ 0\ 0\ 0\ 0 \\ 1\ 1\ 0\ 0\ 0\ 1\ 0\ 1\ 0\ 0\ 0\ 0 \\ 1\ 1\ 0\ 0\ 0\ 1\ 1\ 0\ 0\ 0\ 0\ 0 \\ 0\ 0\ 1\ 0\ 0\ 0\ 0\ 0\ 0\ 0\ 0\ 0 \\ 0\ 0\ 0\ 1\ 0\ 0\ 0\ 0\ 0\ 0\ 1\ 0 \\ 0\ 0\ 0\ 1\ 0\ 0\ 0\ 0\ 0\ 1\ 0\ 0 \\ 0\ 0\ 0\ 0\ 1\ 0\ 0\ 0\ 0\ 0\ 0\ 0 \end{pmatrix}$$

We note that the MILP program allows to merge the tasks: (i) τ_1 with τ_2, τ_6, τ_7, and τ_8 (ii) τ_3 with τ_9, (iii) τ_4 with τ_{10}, and τ_{11}, and (vi) the task τ_5 with τ_{12}. The input matrices become:

$$y = \begin{pmatrix} & imp_1 & imp_2 \\ \tau'_1 & 1 & 1 \\ \tau'_2 & 1 & 1 \\ \tau'_3 & 1 & 1 \\ \tau'_4 & 1 & 1 \\ \tau'_5 & 1 & 1 \end{pmatrix} \begin{pmatrix} & \zeta_1 & \zeta_2 \\ \tau'_1 & 1 & 0 \\ \tau'_2 & 1 & 0 \\ \tau'_3 & 0 & 1 \\ \tau'_5 & 0 & 1 \end{pmatrix} = x$$

The optimized task model is presented in Table 4.

We note that the task number is reduced as well as the energy consumption.

Table 4. Optimized task model.

Execution mode	Core	Task	E_{old}	E_{new}
Default mode	ζ_1	τ_1	1717.5	1690
		τ_2	270	262
	ζ_2	τ_3	2031.25	2000.5
		τ_4	5760	5735.25
Economic mode	ζ_1	τ_1	1917.5	1902.2
		τ_7	5	0.2
		τ_8	5	1
		τ_2	270	262
	ζ_2	τ_3	3031.5	3000.12
		τ_4	5760	7550.2

5.5   "Pseudo-code" Generation

This step aims to transform the model produced by the linear program described to a "pseudo-code". Listing 1.1 represents a snippet of the abstract code describing the AV system.

```
 1  #ProtocolAcces
 2  <schedul_Policy = RM>
 3  <Mechanism = semaphore>
 4  <implementation (name_imp = DefaultMode, Cnd = Disable)>
 5  <Core (c1)>
 6  <thread (name_task= tau_1, Deadline=5, Period=5, priority=1)>
 7       <NormalFunction (name_function=F1) > </NormalFunction>
 8       <NormalFunction (name_function=F2) > </NormalFunction>
 9       ...
10       </thread>
11  </Core> ... </implementation>
12  ...
13  <Controller>
14  if (Disable) then $Exec_impl$(DefaultMode)
15  else if (Enable) then $Exec_impl$(EconomiMode)
16  </Controller>
```

Listing 1.1. AV Pseudo-code.

5.6   Evaluation

In order to generalize the performance evaluation of our strategy, we generate a random system with random task set. The experiments are carried-out on Intel Core i5-4200U processor running at 2.8 GHz with 4 GB of cache memory. The curve in Fig. 4 [20] shows the variation of the reconfiguration time of the system depending on the number of tasks and the number of implementations.

In Fig. 4 we compare the reconfiguration time using the proposed approach with the normal reconfiguration time. It can be seen that the proposed approach allows obtaining a lower reconfiguration time. This is due to the task merging technique.

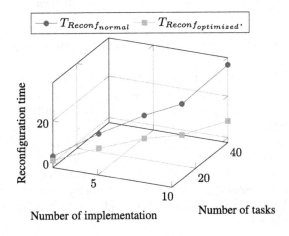

Fig. 4. Evaluation of the reconfiguration time.

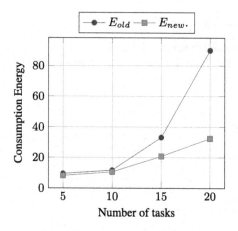

Fig. 5. Evaluation of the energy consumption.

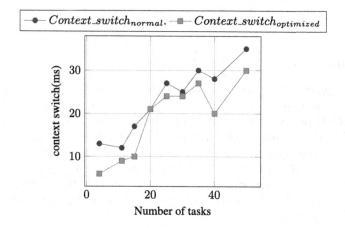

Fig. 6. Evaluation of the context switching.

Figure 5 [20] depicts the impact of our approach on the total energy consumed by the system.

In this figure, we compute the energy consumption and we compare it with the energy consumed by the system before applying the proposed approach. It is clear from this figure that we have obtained better results.

We also compare in Fig. 6 the context switching of the proposed approach to the context switching before applying this approach in a randomly generated system with a number of tasks that varies between 6 and 50. We note that this comparison shows the efficiency of the proposed approach. In Fig. 7, we evaluate the latency that we assume the it is equal to the response time. By comparing this metric in this work with that reported in [25], the efficiency of the proposed approach is confirmed.

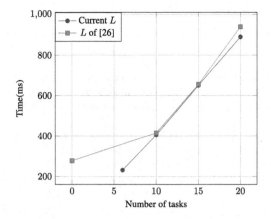

Fig. 7. Comparison in terms of latency between the proposed approach and the approach proposed in [26].

The originality of this paper is manifested in the fact that the proposed approach allows the implementation of the multi-core reconfigurable real-time systems by reducing: (i) the task number, (ii) the energy consumption, (iii) the reconfiguration time, (iv) the time overhead in terms of context switching, and (v) the redundancies between implementations.

6 Conclusion

This paper proposed a new methodology of synthesis of a Pseudo-code for multi-core reconfigurable real-time systems. We showed how from the input specification model we generate an initial task model, assign tasks to the cores while meeting timing properties. Then, we proposed a MILP formulation in order to reduce the time overhead, the energy consumption, and the redundancies between the implementations. The obtained task model would be the input of the pseudo-code generation step. We have evaluated the performance of the four-step approach by comparing the obtained results with the related works. We are interested in a future research in including the UML models to automatically generate the pseudo-code. It is interesting to develop a novel method for the considered problem in the setting of discrete event systems by using learning-based mechanism and efficient scheduling.

References

1. Burns, A., Wellings, A.: Real-Time Systems and Programming Languages: Ada, Real-Time Java and C/Real-Time POSIX, 4th edn. Addison-Wesley Educational Publishers Inc., USA (2009)
2. Polakovic, J., Mazare, S., Stefani, J.B., David, P.C.: Experience with safe dynamic reconfigurations in component-based embedded systems. In: Schmidt, H.W., Crnkovic, I., Heineman, G.T., Stafford, J.A. (eds.) CBSE 2007. LNCS, vol. 4608, pp. 242–257. Springer, Heidelberg (2007). https://doi.org/10.1007/978-3-540-73551-9_17

3. Geer, D.: Chip makers turn to multicore processors. Computer **38**, 11–13 (2005)
4. Khan, M., Hafiz, G.: Simulation of multi-core scheduling in real-time embedded systems. Master's thesis (2014)
5. Lakshmanan, K.S.: Scheduling and synchronization for multi-core real-time systems. Ph.D. thesis, Carnegie Mellon University Pittsburgh, PA (2011)
6. Funk, S., Baruah, S.: Task assignment on uniform heterogeneous multiprocessors. In: Proceedings of 17th Euromicro Conference on Real-Time Systems, pp. 219–226. IEEE (2005)
7. Liu, C.L., Layland, J.W.: Scheduling algorithms for multiprogramming in a hard-real-time environment. J. ACM (JACM) **20**, 46–61 (1973)
8. Wang, W., Camut, F., Miramond, B.: Generation of schedule tables on multi-core systems for autosar applications. In: Conference on Design and Architectures for Signal and Image Processing (DASIP), pp. 191–198. IEEE (2016)
9. Yehia, K., Safar, M., Youness, H., AbdElSalam, M., Salem, A.: A design methodology for system level synthesis of multi-core system architectures. In: Saudi International Electronics, Communications and Photonics Conference (SIECPC), pp. 1–6. IEEE (2011)
10. Geismann, J., Pohlmann, U., Schmelter, D.: Towards an automated synthesis of a real-time scheduling for cyber-physical multi-core systems. In: MODELSWARD, pp. 285–292 (2017)
11. Monot, A., Navet, N., Bavoux, B., Simonot-Lion, F.: Multisource software on multi-core automotive ECUS-combining runnable sequencing with task scheduling. IEEE Trans. Ind. Electron. **59**, 3934–3942 (2012)
12. Saidi, S.E., Cotard, S., Chaaban, K., Marteil, K.: An ILP approach for mapping autosar runnables on multi-core architectures. In: Proceedings of the Workshop on Rapid Simulation and Performance Evaluation: Methods and Tools, p. 6. ACM (2015)
13. Yi, Y., Han, W., Zhao, X., Erdogan, A.T., Arslan, T.: An ILP formulation for task mapping and scheduling on multi-core architectures. In: Proceedings of the Conference on Design, Automation and Test in Europe, pp. 33–38. IEEE (2009)
14. Vulgarakis, A., Shooja, R., Monot, A., Carlson, J., Behnam, M.: Task synthesis for control applications on multicore platforms. In: 2014 11th International Conference on Information Technology: New Generations (ITNG), pp. 229–234. IEEE (2014)
15. Faragardi, H.R., Lisper, B., Nolte, T.: Towards a communication-efficient mapping of autosar runnables on multi-cores. In: IEEE 18th Conference on Emerging Technologies & Factory Automation (ETFA), pp. 1–5. IEEE (2013)
16. Lei, H., Wang, R., Zhang, T., Liu, Y., Zha, Y.: A multi-objective co-evolutionary algorithm for energy-efficient scheduling on a green data center. Comput. Oper. Res. **75**, 103–117 (2016)
17. Chniter, H., Jarray, F., Khalgui, M.: Combinatorial approaches for low-power and real-time adaptive reconfigurable embedded systems. In: Proceedings of the 4th Pervasive and Embedded Computing and Communication Systems, pp. 151–157 (2014)
18. Klein, M.H., Ralya, T., Pollak, B., Obenza, R., Harbour, M.G.: Analyzing complex systems. In: A Practitioner's Handbook for Real-Time Analysis, pp. 535–578, Springer (1993). https://doi.org/10.1007/978-1-4615-2796-1_8
19. Lakhdhar, W., Mzid, R., Khalgui, M., Trèves, N.: MILP-based approach for optimal implementation of reconfigurable real-time systems. In: Proceedings of the International Joint Conference on Software Technologies (ICSOFT) - Volume 1: ICSOFT-EA, Lisbon, Portugal, 24–26, 11th July, pp. 330–335 (2016)

20. Lakhdhar, W., Mzid, R., Khalgui, M., Frey, G.: A new approach for optimal implementation of multi-core reconfigurable real-time systems. In: Proceedings of the 13th International Conference on Evaluation of Novel Approaches to Software Engineering, ENASE 2018, Funchal, Madeira, Portugal, 23–24 March 2018, pp. 89–98 (2018)
21. Lakhdhar, W., Mzid, R., Khalgui, M., Li, Z., Frey, G., Al-Ahmari, A.: Multiobjective optimization approach for a portable development of reconfigurable real-time systems: from specification to implementation. IEEE Trans. Syst. Man Cybern. Syst. **99**, 1–15 (2018)
22. Wang, H., Shu, L., Yin, W., Xiao, Y., Cao, J.: Hyperbolic utilization bounds for rate monotonic scheduling on homogeneous multiprocessors. IEEE Trans. Parallel Distrib. Syst. **25**, 1510–1521 (2014)
23. Tindell, K., Clark, J.: Holistic schedulability analysis for distributed hard real-time systems. Microprocessing Microprogramming **40**, 117–134 (1994)
24. Singhoff, F.: Real-Time Scheduling Analysis (2014)
25. Vulgarakis, A., Shooja, R., Monot, A., Carlson, J., Behnam, M.: Task synthesis for control applications on multicore platforms. In: 2014 11th International Conference on Information Technology: New Generations, pp. 229–234 (2014)
26. Yehia, K., Safar, M., Youness, H., AbdElSalam, M., Salem, A.: A design methodology for system level synthesis of multi-core system architectures. In: Proceedings of 2011 Saudi International Electronics, Communications and Photonics Conference (SIECPC), pp. 1–6 (2011)

From Object-Oriented to Workflow: Refactoring of OO Applications into Workflows for an Efficient Resources Management in the Cloud

Anfel Selmadji[✉], Abdelhak-Djamel Seriai, Hinde Lilia Bouziane, and Christophe Dony

LIRMM, CNRS and University of Montpellier, Montpellier, France
{selmadji,seriai,bouziane,dony}@lirmm.fr

Abstract. Cloud Computing is a technology that provides to customers computing/storage resources as services delivered through the internet. Its main characteristics are its elastic nature and its payment model (pay-as-you-go). In order to run applications in the cloud while using its resources efficiently, and thus reducing their usage costs, one of the requirements related to this type of environment is to perform dynamic configurations of these applications. Nevertheless, to dynamically configure applications determining the utilized resources, additionally to when and where they are used is needed. Workflows allow doing this. As a matter of fact, several works aiming to reduce execution costs in the cloud are based on workflows. Unlike them, the architecture of OO applications explicitly expresses little or no behavioral (temporal) information. Therefore, running an OO application in the cloud requires deploying the whole application, and thus all its used resources need to be allocated during its entire execution time. With the goal of reducing execution costs of OO applications in the cloud, we propose a re-engineering process. The process aims to restructure these applications from OO architectural style to workflow style. However, in this paper, we concentrate only on the first step of the process, which aims to generate a workflow from OO source code.

Keywords: Object-Oriented · Refactoring · Workflow · Data flow · Control flow · Cloud · Mapping model

1 Introduction

Cloud computing is a technology that provides scalable services to its customers on demand by using the internet and central remote servers [1,2]. Some of the prominent cloud computing platforms are Google App Engine, Amazon EC2, Aneka and Microsoft Azure [3].

E. Damiani et al. (Eds.): ENASE 2018, CCIS 1023, pp. 186–214, 2019.
https://doi.org/10.1007/978-3-030-22559-9_9

Usually, the provided services by the cloud can be classified into three categories: SaaS (Software as a Service), PaaS (Platform as a Service) and IaaS (Infrastructure as a Service) [4,5]. SaaS is a software delivery paradigm in which applications are developed by service providers and typically accessed by users via web browsers [6]. PaaS provides platforms for developing and deploying applications in cloud infrastructure relying on libraries, programming languages and so on [7]. IaaS providers deliver processing, storage, network and other fundamental computing resources to deploy and run customers' software [2,8].

As a matter of fact, customers can provision resources at any time they want and release them when they are no longer needed [8]. Nevertheless, according to the "pay-as-you-go" model, customers are generally billed based on the resource usage. Therefore, having the ability to adjust this usage (i.e., allocate resources only when needed and release them when they are no longer used) is essential, in order to reduce costs. This can be done by dynamically provisioning and releasing resources based on their usage [7,9]. However, the dynamic provisioning and release require specifying, for each application, which resources are utilized, as well as when and where they are used.

One of the most utilized architectural styles for developing applications is the Object-Oriented (OO) style [10,11]. However, without any prior restructuring, executing an OO application in the cloud requires deploying it entirely. Thus, all its used resources need to be allocated during its entire execution time, and therefore a customer will be charged following the utilized resources even though some of them were uselessly occupied for certain periods [7].

For the data used by particular kinds of applications, for instance, scientific ones, determining the needed resources for their manipulation is possible. More precisely, these resources are used for the storage, acquisition/transmission and processing of data (e.g., storage space, network, processor, etc.).

The data flow architectural style is well adapted for deploying this kind of applications in the cloud. Indeed, this style focuses on data transfers between the different processing elements of an application [10,12]. Therefore, these elements and their consumed/produced data are explicitly specified allowing to determine resources needed by each element. Furthermore, it enables determining when each element can be executed, and thus when its needed resources are utilized. It is worthy to note that, by extending the data flow style with a richer control flow (i.e., a control flow expressing sequences, conditional branches, and loops), an architectural style that represents a workflow [13], in which architectural components are tasks, can be obtained. Several works are based on the workflow style so as to perform dynamic configuration allowing to optimize resources usage in the cloud, and hence to reduce execution costs [3,7,9,14,15].

In order to deploy OO applications in the cloud while reducing costs, we propose a re-engineering process aiming to restructure these applications from OO architectural style to workflow style. In this paper, we concentrate on the first step of the process. The goal of this step is the generation of a workflow description from existing OO application. This generation requires the ability to map OO concepts into workflow ones. For instance, we have to specify what is the mapping of the concept task compared to the OO concepts. Once such a mapping is established, the refactoring consists in recovering the constituents of a workflow (i.e., tasks, control flow and data flow) from OO source code.

The originality of our approach can be viewed from two aspects. On the one hand, we adopt OO application to a deployment in the cloud by using source code refactoring instead of either redeveloping them from scratch, which is known as an expensive and risky task in term of time and budget [16] or executing them with high costs. On the other hand, our approach allows recovering the entire workflow, whereas a majority of the existing works (e.g., [17–21]) propose to extract only a part of a workflow (i.e., either control flow or data flow). Additionally, even if some approaches extract a description of the workflow through source code analysis, they do not generate the code of this extracted workflow (see Sect. 8).

This work is an updated and extended version of our original paper [22]. The extension includes (1) more details and deep analysis of the proposed approach, (2) an extended experimentation and (3) an extended related work analysis as well as a comparative study between existing works and ours.

The remainder of this paper is organized as follows. Section 2 shows a possible mapping from OO concepts to workflow ones and announces addressed refactoring issues. Section 3 presents a solution for task identification. Section 4 discusses control flow recovery, whereas Sect. 5 presents data flow recovery. Section 6 discusses a workflow implementation. Section 7 evaluates the proposed approach. Section 8 outlines related works. Finally, Sect. 9 concludes the paper and presents future work.

2   Object-Oriented Versus Workflow-Based Architectural Styles

2.1   Workflow-Based Architectural Style

Initially, in 1995, the WorkFlow Management Coalition (WFMC) defined the term workflow [13] as follows: "A workflow is the computerized facilitation or automation of a business process, in whole or part."

This standard definition proposes a reference model for creating, deploying and controlling workflow applications. It refers to a workflow as a solution to automate business processes. A process is defined as a coordinated set of tasks collaborating to produce a well-specified result. Coordination determines the sequencing mode of tasks, in addition to the exchanged data between them. In other words, a workflow can be viewed as an application consisting of a set of tasks, with possible dependencies specified relying on two classical formalisms: data flows and control flows. In this paper, these concepts are defined as follows:

- **Task:** a task is the basic composition unit of a workflow. Indeed, it is the smallest execution unit which represents an execution stage in an entire application. Its implementation does not depend on other tasks, and it is possible to reuse it in different contexts. A task can define input and output data. Input data represent data needed to execute the task, whereas output data,

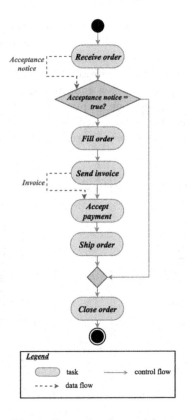

Fig. 1. Example of a workflow.

the produced ones by this execution. A task can either be primitive or composite. A composite one can be seen as a sub-workflow consisting of primitive or composite tasks.

– **Control Flow:** a control flow specifies the execution order of tasks via different constructs such as sequences, conditional branches (if and switch) and loops (for and while). In a sequence construct, a task is enabled after the competition of its predecessors. In conditional branches, based on a condition (i.e., predicate) evaluation one of several branches is chosen. In loops, one or more tasks can repeatedly be done.

– **Data Flow:** a data flow describes data dependencies between tasks. If the outputs of a task T_i are inputs of a task T_j, then T_j cannot be executed until T_i produces its outputs (i.e., the execution of T_j depends on that of T_i).

Figure 1 shows an example of a workflow describing order processing. An order can be either accepted or rejected depending on the availability of the ordered items. If it is accepted, all required information is filled in, payment is approved, and the order is shipped. Otherwise, the order is closed. As illustrated in Fig. 1, this workflow consists of six tasks. On the one hand, the control flow specifies that tasks *Fill order*, *Send invoice*, *Accept payment* and *Ship order* are executed sequentially, only if the condition *"Acceptance notice = true"* is fulfilled. On the other hand, the data flow indicates that each of the tasks *Receive order* and *Send invoice* produces one output data (resp., *Acceptance notice* and *Invoice*). The data *Acceptance notice* is utilized to evaluate the condition *"Acceptance notice = true"*, whereas *Invoice* is used by the task *Accept payment*.

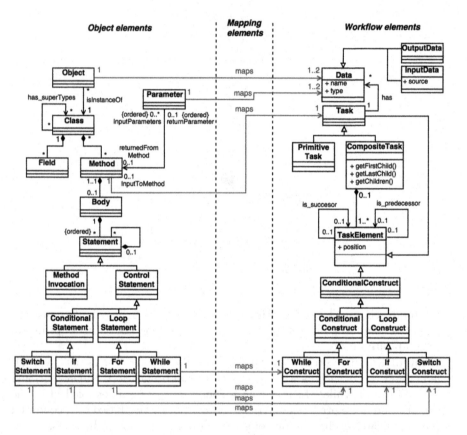

Fig. 2. From OO elements to workflow ones: the mapping model [22].

2.2 From Object-Oriented to Workflow: The Mapping Model

As explained earlier in this section, a task is the basic unit of composition of a workflow. It is the smallest execution unit which represents an execution stage in an entire application. Relying on this definition, we assume that a method in an OO source code can be mapped to a task in a workflow as illustrated in Fig. 2.

Particularly, we consider that a method containing only assignment statements or invoking only methods provided by standard libraries is mapped to a primitive task, whereas a method that includes a sequence of methods invocations and control statements is mapped to a composite task. In the case where a method includes both methods invocations, control statements and other statements, the source code has to be refactored to wrap these later in a method. As a matter of fact, a workflow, as viewed in Fig. 2, does not consider assignment statements as a unit of composition.

A task can define input and output data. Input data represent data needed to execute the task, whereas output data, the generated ones by this execution. Based on the fact that a task is the mapping of an OO method, task inputs are data required to execute the corresponding method, whereas task outputs represent the data generated from this execution. To be executed, a method requires, in addition to a receiving object, its input parameters. Once executed, the method generates its modified inputs (i.e., receiving object and/or input parameters), and/or its output parameter (i.e., returned value). Therefore, each method's generated data that represents a modified input corresponds to two data in a workflow, an input and an output data, as expressed in Fig. 2.

In a workflow, different control constructs such as sequence, conditional branches, and loops are used to express the execution order of tasks. In OO style, the execution order of methods invocations, which corresponds to the execution of tasks, depends on control statements (e.g., if statement, for statement, etc.). Thus, we consider that a control statement in OO source code can be mapped to a control construct in a workflow. Therefore, the input data of a control construct are mapped to data manipulated in the corresponding control statement (i.e., in the condition and the body of the control statement), while its output data corresponds to the data defined in the control statement and used in the following statements.

Figure 2 illustrates the presented mapping between OO concepts and workflow ones.

2.3 Refactoring Process and Addressed Issues

Our approach aims to generate a workflow based on static analysis of OO source code. For that purpose, we proposed a refactoring process, that can be viewed as a re-engineering horseshoe model illustrated in Fig. 3. On the left side of the figure, the existing OO system is represented, whereas the target system is represented on the right side.

The proposed refactoring process consists of three steps (see Fig. 3):

- **Step 1:** the aim of this step is identifying the application structural elements (e.g., classes, methods, etc.) and their links (e.g., method calls, class inheritances, etc.) by analyzing the existing source code.

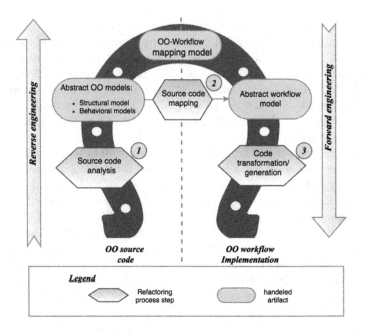

Fig. 3. OO versus workflow: the re-engineering process.

- **Step 2:** the second step consists of mapping OO concepts to workflow ones. Starting by identifying primitive and composite tasks (see Sect. 3), as well as their respective input and output data, and then recovering the control flow (see Sect. 4) and the data flow (see Sect. 5) associated to these tasks so that the identified workflow have the same behavior as the OO application.
- **Step 3:** the goal of the third step of our process is transforming the OO source code to conform to the identified workflow. More details will be presented in Sect. 6.

For this refactoring process, in order to generate the new structure of the application, we chose to preserve the object entities of the original source code. In other words, object instances will not be transformed into primitive elements (i.e., the values of their attributes). Hence, the refactoring process produces an implementation based on "task" entities. These entities are connected by input and output data and whose control flow is explicitly specified at the architectural level. This means that the target source code consists of task entities, implemented relying on the object entities of the original source code.

In order to realize this process the following questions need to be answered:

- **Q1:** what are the tasks that reflect the workflow corresponding to the existing OO application? Answering this question requires identifying, at the instance level, a matching between task entities and OO methods invoked on object instances.

– **Q2:** what is the control flow to be specified between the identified tasks to preserve the same behavior as the existing OO application? Answering this question requires, along with others, rendering explicit the implicit control flow due to OO features (e.g., polymorphism and dynamic binding, etc.).

– **Q3:** what is the data flow to be associated with the identified tasks and control flow? The aim is defining for each task its input and output data so that the application architectured as tasks (i.e., workflow) produces the same results as the application architectured as objects. In other words, given the same inputs, the two variants of the application generate the same outputs. This is mainly identifying the flow of objects associated with the tasks already identified.

– **Q4:** what model of implementation to structure the target application into new object entities that reflect the identified tasks, control flow, and data flow while preserving the object entities of the existing OO application?

3   Identifing Tasks from OO Source Code

Our mapping model between OO concepts and workflow ones establishes a unique mapping for workflow tasks. A task is mapped to an OO method (see Fig. 2). Therefore, relying on code refactoring, and more precisely extract method refactoring, all statements that do not represent method invocations in the OO source code are transformed into method invocations. Once this refactoring is done, we determine among all the methods in the OO source code those that correspond to primitive tasks from those that correspond to composite ones. Finally, we specify the input and output data for each one of them.

3.1   Extract Method Refactoring

The refactoring of OO source code consists of extracting each sequence of statements delimited by user method invocations as a new method and replacing this sequence with an invocation of the newly extracted method. In fact, only statements belonging to the same block can be extracted to guarantee the syntactical correctness of the new method.

An example of extract method refactoring is shown in Fig. 4. In this example, the statements delimited by method invocations *s.initializeInputs()* and *s.updateInputs(internalInput)* cannot be extracted as a new method because they do not belong to the same block. However, it is possible to divide this sequence into two fragments based on whether the statements belong to the same bloc or not. Each fragment is extracted as a new method (method *m1* and method *m2*).

Once the statements to be extracted are specified, the extraction starts. Variables acceded (i.e., defined or used) but not declared by these statements (i.e., the variables declaration statements do not belong to these statements) should be passed in as input parameters of the new method. Whereas, variables defined by these statements and acceded by following ones should be passed out as its output parameters. Note that, the definition of a variable means that its value is modified (i.e., writing access), while its usage implies that its value is read (i.e., reading access).

In the example shown in Fig. 4, the statement extracted as the method $m2$ uses the variables *internalInput* and *step*. Therefore, these variables are passed in as input parameters of $m2$. Moreover, the variable *internalInput* is defined by the statement to be extracted as $m2$ and used in the method invocation *s.updateInputs(internalInput)*, and thus it is an output parameter of $m2$.

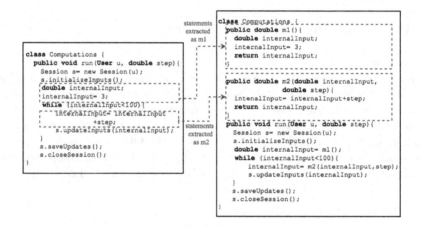

Fig. 4. Example of extract method refactoring.

Some OO languages (e.g., Java, etc.) imposes that a method can have at most one output parameter (i.e., returned value). For this reason, if a sequence of statements to be extracted has more than one output value, this sequence should be divided into multiple fragments. Each one of them is extracted as a new method and return at most one output parameter. It is worthy to note that this code fragmentation and method extraction do not re-order code statements, which excludes the possibility of breaking down program semantics (i.e., the program's behavior is preserved).

Listing 1.1. Classes *Foo, Bar and Main.*

```
1   class Foo {
2     int x;
3     void setX(int y, boolean isDifferent ){
4       if (isDifferent)
5           initializeX(y);
6       else
7           performComputations(y);}
8     void initializeX(int y) {
9       x=y;}
10    void performComputations(int y){
11      int z= multiplyX(y);
12      incX(z);}
13    int multiplyX(int y) {
14          return 2*y;}
15    int incX(int y){
16      if (x!=y)
17          setX(y, true);
18      else
19          setX(y, false);
20      return x;}
21    int getX(){
22      return x;}
23    void printX(int y) {
24        System.out.println(y);}}
25  class Bar{
26    Foo foo= new Foo();
27    void m(){
28        foo.initializeX(1);
29        int x= foo.getX();
30        while (x<20){
31            x=foo.incX(x);
32            foo.printX(x);}}}
33  class Main {
34    static Bar bar= new Bar();
35    public static void main(String[]args){
36        bar.m();}}
```

3.2 Identifying Task Based on Analysing the OO Application Call Graph

As explained earlier in Sect. 2, there are two types of tasks in a workflow: primitive and composite ones. Since a task corresponds to a method in OO source code, a method that does not contains calls to other ones is considered as a primitive task. Otherwise, it is a composite one. Therefore, the identification of primitive and composite tasks relies on analyzing the OO application's call graph.

Building a call graph requires analyzing the source code to determine for each caller method its callees. Once the call graph is built, its leaves are mapped to primitive tasks, while the remaining nodes are mapped to composite ones. Nevertheless, when analyzing the call graph to identify tasks, there is a particular case that needs to be handled. This case concerns direct or indirect recursive calls. Due to the fact that, workflows do not always support recursive transitions between tasks (i.e., the ability of a task to invoke itself directly or indirectly during its execution) [23], recursive calls between methods are transformed as follows: a method M belonging to a directed cycle is mapped to a primitive task only if all its callees (i.e., all the methods invoked by M) are in this cycle (see method *Foo.incX* in Listing 1.1). Otherwise, this method is mapped to a composite task (see method *Foo.setX* and *Foo.performComputations* in Listing 1.1).

Figure 5 represents the call graph built from the source code shown in Listing 1.1. The methods *Main.main*, *Bar.m*, *Foo.setX* and *Foo.performComputations* correspond to composite tasks, whereas the methods *Foo.initializeX*, *Foo.getX*, *Foo.incX*, *Foo.printX* and *Foo.multiplyX* are mapped to primitive ones.

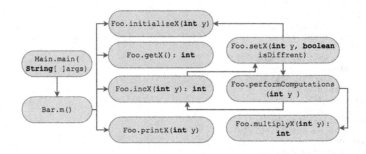

Fig. 5. Call graph built from the source code shown in Listing 1.1.

3.3   Identifying Tasks Inputs and Outputs

Each task in a workflow, primitive or composite, has input and output data. Therefore, once the tasks are identified from OO source code, their input and output data need to be specified. As explained in Sect. 2.2, task inputs are the parameters and the receiving object of the corresponding method. While its outputs correspond to the modified inputs and the returned value by this method. Note that task outputs include its modified inputs because this task generates their new values.

In order to identify the inputs that can be modified by a method, and thus the corresponding task outputs, we compute for each method M two sets: *DEF* and *USE* sets. The *DEF* (resp., *USE*) set contains parameters and attributes defined (resp., used) by M. In other words, parameters and attributes that their values are modified (resp., read) by M. A task input *INDATA* is considered as modified if either (1) *INDATA* is the receiving object of M and at least one of its attributes $\in$ *DEF(M)* or (2) *INDATA* $\in$ *DEF(M)*.

For instance, the inputs of the corresponding task to the method *initializeX* of the class *Foo*, shown in Listing 1.1, are the receiving object and the parameter y, whereas the output of this task is the receiving object because its attribute x is defined in the method *initializeX* (in Line *9*). However, for the corresponding task to the method *getX* of the class *Foo*, the receiving object is only an input since its value is not modified in this method.

Computing DEF and USE Sets. In our approach, we consider that assignment on a variable of a primitive type (i.e., a type which is not a class) as a *DEF* operation. All others operations on primitive variables are considered as *USE* ones [24]. Nevertheless, when dealing with objects, we assume that operations are *DEF* ones in three cases: (1) this operation defines at least one attribute of the object (2) it is a constructor invocation or (3) it is a call of a method that modifies this object [25]. Otherwise, these operations are of *USE* category.

Based on these cases, determining whether an input *INDATA* of a method *M* (i.e., a parameter or the receiving object) is in the *DEF* or to *USE* sets depends on the *DEF* and *USE* sets of the called methods by *M*. An input *INDATA* of *M* is considered as defined (resp., used) if it is defined (resp., used) by either (1) a statement of *M* which is not a method invocation (e.g., assignment, etc.) or (2) at least one of the methods called by *M*. More precisely, an input *INDATA* is considered as defined (resp., used) in a called method *CalledM* by *M* in two cases:

- *Case 1: INDATA* is the receiving object of the invocation of *CalledM* and at least one of the attribute of *INDATA* is in the *DEF*(resp., *USE*) set of *CalledM*. For instance, the receiving object *foo* of the invocation of the method *initilizeX* in Line *28* (see Listing 1.1) is considered as defined since the method *initializeX* defines the attribute *x* of the receiving object in Line *9*.
- *Case 2: INDATA* is passed as a parameter in the invocation of *CalledM*, and its corresponding formal parameter belong to the *DEF*(resp., *USE*) set of *CalledM*. In the example shown in Listing 1.1, the input *y* passed as parameter in the invocation of the method *initializeX* in Line *28* is considered as used because its corresponding formal parameter *y* is used in the method *initializeX* Line *9*.

The above constraints related to computing *DEF* sets can be formalized as follows [22]:

$$
\left\{
\begin{array}{ll}
\text{* *} \\
- \text{INDATA is defined in M} & (1) \\
- \exists\, stat \in \{Statements(M) - MethodCalls(M)\} & (2) \\
- \text{INDATA is defined in stat} & (3) \\
- \exists\, call \in MethodCalls(M) & (4) \\
- \text{ReceivingObj(call)= INDATA} & (5) \\
- \exists\, attribute \in AttributeOf(INDATA) & (6) \\
- \text{attribute} \in DEF(CorrespondingMethod(call)) & (7) \\
- \text{INDATA} \in ActualParameter(call) & (8) \\
- \text{FormalParameter(INDATA)} \in DEF(CorrespondingMethod(call)) & (9) \\
\text{* *} \quad \text{* * *} \\
(1) \Rightarrow ((2) \wedge (3)) \vee ((4) \wedge (((5) \wedge (6) \wedge(7)) \vee ((8) \wedge (9)))) \\
\text{* *} \quad \text{* * *}
\end{array}
\right.
$$

Where:

- *Statements*(*M*) denotes the set of statements of *M*.

- *MethodCalls(M)* represents the set of method calls in *M*.
- *ReceivingObj(call)* specifies the receiving object of a method call.
- *AttributeOf(INDATA)* denotes the set of attributes of *INDATA*.
- *ActualParameter(call)* determines the set of actual parameter in a *call*.
- *FormalParameter(INDATA)* indicates the corresponding formal parameter of an actual parameter *INDATA*.
- *CorrespondingMethod(call)* represents the called method in *call*.

Note that, by replacing the *DEF* set with *USE* set in the formula mentioned above, it specifies when an input *INDATA* is considered as used.

Based on the above constraints, it is clear that determining *DEF* and *USE* sets of any method *M* depends on the sets of its called methods. For this reason, the computation of *DEF* and *USE* sets requires an analysis order of methods. For instance, to compute *DEF* and *USE* sets of the method *m* (see Listing 1.1), *DEF* and *USE* sets of the called methods by *m* on the attribute *foo* (*initializeX*, *getX*, *incX* and *printX*) are needed to check whether *foo* is defined and/or used.

This order can be determined using the call graph. In fact, relying on the built call graph it is possible to define a total topological order of its nodes. Analyzing methods according to this order ensures that a called method is always analyzed before its callers. In the total order, the first methods are the ones that do not contain any method invocations. These methods are to the leaves of the graph.

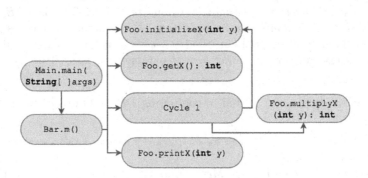

Fig. 6. Acyclic call graph.

However, in the presence of direct or indirect recursion, the call graph contains cycles. Therefore, it is not possible to define an analysis order. Replacing each cycle in the graph with a representative node allows solving this problem (i.e., allows the definition of a total order). Once the order is defined, the call graph nodes are then analyzed following this order. If a node represents a method, then *DEF* and *USE* sets are computed relying on the former constraints. If the node is a representative, *DEF* and *USE* sets of each method in the cycle represented by this node are calculated, firstly, without taking into account calls to the methods belonging to the cycle, and then these sets are re-computed while considering the calls between the methods of the cycle.

Table 1. *DEF / USE* sets of the methods shown in Listing 1.1.

Method	DEF set	USE set
InitializeX	{x}	{y}
GetX	∅	{x}
MultiplyX	∅	{y}
PrintX	∅	{y}
SetX	{x}	{x, y, isDifferent}
Perform Computations	{x}	{x,y}
IncX	{x}	{x, y}
M	{foo}	{foo}
Main	{bar}	{bar}

For example, computing *DEF* and *USE* sets of the methods shown in Listing 1.1, requires replacing the cycle containing methods *setX, perform-Computations* and *incX* with a representative node *Cycle1*, as illustrated in Fig. 6. Once the cycle is replaced, the nodes can be ordered as follows: (1) Foo.initializeX, (2) Foo.getX, (3) Foo.multiplyX, (4) Foo.printX (3) Cycle1, (4) Bar.m and (5) Main.main. Table 1 shows *DEF* and *USE* sets computed for these methods.

4   Control Flow Recovery

A workflow can be viewed as an application consisting of a set of tasks, with possible dependencies specified relying on control and data flows. Therefore, once the tasks are identified (see Sect. 3), the corresponding control flow needs to be recovered. This later specifies the execution order of tasks. When dealing with composite ones, their control flow describes the execution order of their enclosed tasks.

In our approach, we represent a control flow as a graph, named Control Flow Graph (CFG). A CFG consists of a set of nodes and a set of edges. Each node represents either a method call, a predicate or a control. A predicate specifies a condition utilized in a control statement, for instance, if statement. Note that, CFG nodes representing a method call or a predicate are labeled relying on their line number in the source code. CFG edges specify the execution order of method calls and evaluation of predicates.

To build a CFG the statements, which represents the body of the corresponding method to the composite task, are traversed and the graph is constructed incrementally. For example, the CFG corresponding to the composite task which is the mapping of the method *m* of the class *Foo*, shown in Listing 1.1, is illustrated in Fig. 7.

As explained earlier, in the CFG, a node can represent a method call. Nevertheless, if this call is dynamically dispatched, it is not possible to resolve statically

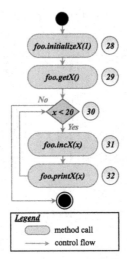

Fig. 7. The CFG of the composite task corresponding the method m of the class *Foo* shown in Listing 1.1.

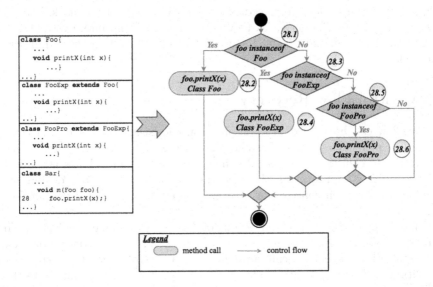

Fig. 8. Example of a CFG recovered in the presence of dynamically dispatched calls.

(i.e., at compile time) the exact method to invoke. Hence, to enable building a CFG statically, our idea is to refactor each dynamically dispatched call by replacing it with nested if-then statements. In these statements, conditions represent the possible run-time types of the receiving object of the call, whereas the branches are the different implementations of the called method in each possible receiving object type.

An example of a CFG recovered in the presence of dynamically dispatched calls is shown in Fig. 8. The method *m* of the class *Bar* calls the method *printX* of the class *Foo*, the class *FooExp* or the class *FooPro*. Therefore, the corresponding CFG contains a path for each possible run-time type of the receiver (i.e., *Foo*, *FooExp* and *FooPro*).

5   Data Flow Recovery

In addition to the identification of tasks (see Sect. 3) and control flow (see Sect. 4), the construction of a workflow also requires the recovery of data flow, which specifies the dependency links between the data of the identified tasks (i.e., which output data of a task represents an input data of another one).

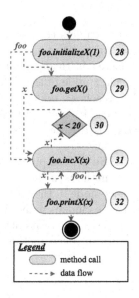

Fig. 9. The DFG corresponding to the task mapped to the method *m* of the class *Foo* shown in Listing 1.1.

In our approach, we represent a data flow as a graph, named Data Flow Graph (DFG). A DFG has the same nodes as a CFG. Nevertheless, an edge between two nodes N_i and N_j labeled using the name of the variable v means that v is defined in N_i and used in N_j. For instance, in the example shown in Fig. 9, the edge between the nodes *foo.initializeX(1)* and *foo.getX()* labeled with *foo* specifies that the variable *foo* is defined in the node *foo.initializeX(1)* and used in the node *foo.getX()*.

As explained earlier, a composite task encloses other primitive and composite ones. Hence, a data flow is recovered for each composite task to specify data dependencies between its enclosed tasks.

To build a DFG for a composite task, we compute def-use triplets for the corresponding method to this task. Each triplet *(var, def, use)* specifies the name of a variable *var*, the line number at which this variable is defined *def* and the line number at which this definition is used *use*. As explained in Sect. 4, CFG nodes are labeled relying on the corresponding line numbers in the source code. Therefore, a data flow edge is created between two nodes denoted by *k* and *l* only if the def-use triplets of the corresponding method include the triplet *(v, k, l)*.

For example, in the *DFG* represented in Fig. 9 an edge is created between the nodes denoted by *31* and *32* because the def-use triplets of the method *m* include the triplet *(foo, 31, 32)*. In the rest of this section, we will explain in details the process of computing def-use triplets.

5.1   Computing Def-use Triplets

The process of computing def-use triplets consists of three steps. The first step aims to compute *VarUsed* sets. Each set specifies the variables used in a CFG node. The goal of the second step is to determine *ReachDef* sets. Each set specifies the definitions that reach a node of the CFG. A definition of a variable v in a node N_i, denoted (v, N_i), reaches a node N_j if there is a path in the CFG between N_i and N_j without a redefinition of v. In the third step, def-use triplets are computed relying on *VarUsed* and *ReachDef* sets. We will explain in details each step in the rest of this section.

Step1: Computing *VarUsed* Sets: computing the *VarUsed* sets requires determining *USE* sets for all the methods in the source code (see Sect. 3.3). Once these sets are determined, for each node in the CFG representing a method call, the receiving object is used (i.e., included in the *VarUsed* set) if the *USE* set of the called method contains at least one of its attributes. An effective parameter is used if the *USE* set of the invoked method includes its corresponding

---

Algorithm 1. Compute reaching definitions.

> **input**   : Control flow graph CFG
> $\qquad\qquad$ Gen and $Kill$ sets for each node of the CFG
> **output**: ReachDef and ReachOut sets for each node of the CFG

1 **for** *each node n of CFG* **do**
2 $\quad$ $ReachDef(N) \leftarrow \emptyset$;
3 $\quad$ $ReachOut(N) \leftarrow \emptyset$;
4 **end**
5 **while** *any $ReachDef(N)$ or $ReachOut(N)$ changes* **do**
6 $\quad$ **for** *each node N of CFG* **do**
7 $\quad\quad$ $ReachDef(N) \leftarrow \cup_{P \in predecessor(N)} ReachOut(P)$;
8 $\quad\quad$ $ReachOut(N) \leftarrow Gen(N) \cup (ReachDef(N) - Kill(N))$;
9 $\quad$ **end**
10 **end**

---

formal parameter. The *VarUsed* of a predicate node contains variables used in the corresponding expression.

Step2: Computing *ReachDef* Sets: determining reaching definitions requires computing *DEF* sets for all the methods in the source code (see Sect. 3.3). When the *DEF* sets are computed, we specify for each node in the *CFG* its produced definitions. For a node that represents a method call, the receiving object is considered as defined (i.e., included in the produced definitions) if the *DEF* set of the called method contains at least one of its attributes. An effective parameter is considered as defined if the *DEF* set of the invoked method includes its corresponding formal parameter.

Once the definitions produced by each node are specified, reaching definition are determined using the propagation algorithm (see Algorithm 1) proposed by Aho et al. [26]. In this algorithm, each node N of the *CFG* stores the incoming and outgoing definitions respectively inside the sets *ReachDef(N)* and *ReachOut(N)*, which are initially empty. Moreover, each node N generates definitions contained in the *Gen(N)* set, and prevents the elements in the *kill(N)* set from being further propagated after the node N. Incoming definitions for a node N (i.e., *ReachDef(N)*) are obtained from its predecessors as the union of the respective *ReachOut* sets (forward propagation).

Step3: Computing Def-use Triplets: for each CFG node N, if a variable $v \in VarUsed$ (N) and $(v, def) \in ReachDef(N)$, then a triplet (v, def, N) is constructed.

For example, using *VarUsed* and *ReachDef* sets (see Table 2) computed for each node of the CFG shown in Fig. 7, def-use triplets constructed are *(foo, 28, 29), (foo, 28, 31), (foo, 31, 31), (x, 29, 30), (x, 31, 30), (x, 29, 31), (x, 31, 31)* and *(x, 31, 32)*.

Table 2. *VarUsed* and *ReachDef* computed for each node of the CFG shown in Fig. 7.

Node	*VarUsed*	*ReachDef*
28	∅	∅
29	{foo}	{(foo, 28)}
30	{x}	{(foo, 28), (foo, 31), (x, 29), (x, 31)}
31	{x, foo}	{(foo, 28), (foo, 31), (x, 29), (x, 31)}
32	{x}	{(foo, 31), (x, 31)}

6   Workflow Implementation

In the previous sections, we presented the mapping between OO concepts and workflow ones (Sect. 2.2), as well as how this mapping can be identified from source code (Sects. 3, 4 and 5). In other words, we showed how workflow constituents (i.e., tasks, control flow and data flow) can be recovered from OO source code.

To be able to run the recovered workflow, we present in this section the workflow implementation. The later is based on the implementation model shown in Fig. 10. In this model, each task is an instance of the class *Task*. It has two data lists: a list of inputs and a list of outputs. The execution of any task requires invoking the method *run* on the corresponding instance. However, the method *run* of a primitive task is not the same as a composite one:

- **Primitive Task:** the method *run* of a primitive task initializes inputs and invokes the corresponding method to this task.
- **Composite Task:** in the method *run* of a composite task, instances corresponding to the enclosed elements in this task are created and their methods *run* are executed. Note that, these elements are specified in the attribute *taskSubelements* of the class *CompositeTask*. Moreover, they can either be control constructs or other tasks. These elements are executed based on their order in the list *taskSubelements*.

Similarly, to run a control construct (i.e., if construct or while construct), an instance of the corresponding class to this construct (i.e., IfConstruct class or WhileConstruct class) is created, and the method *run* is invoked on this instance. The *run* method initializes control construct inputs and evaluates its condition. For example, in the case of while construct, if the condition is true then instances corresponding to the elements of the list *whileElements* are created, and their *run* methods are executed. In the case of if construct, when the condition is true (i.e., resp false), instances corresponding to the elements of the list *IfElements* (i.e., resp elseElements) are created, and their *run* methods are executed.

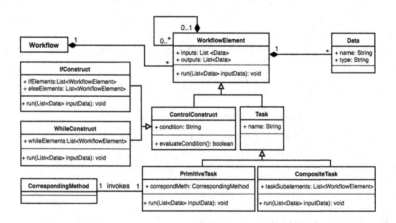

Fig. 10. Workflow implementation model [22].

7 Experimentation and Validation

7.1 Implementation

To test our approach, we implemented a plug-in within Eclipse IDE. This plug-in consists of four modules. The first module, named *Task identifier*, restructures the code by applying extract method refactoring. The *Task identifier*, firstly, determines the sequence of statements to be extracted as a new method. Then, this module uses the built-in functionality *Extract method* within Eclipse IDE. Once the OO source code is restructured, *Task identifier* recovers primitive and composite tasks, as well as their inputs and outputs. The second module, called *Control flow recoverer*, builds a control flow for each composite task. Whereas, the third module *Data flow recoverer* constructs a data flow for composite tasks. Finally, the fourth module, called *Code generator*, generates the corresponding source code. It is worthy to note that the recovered graphs (i.e., control/data flow graphs and workflow) are represented graphically using *GraphViz* [27].

7.2 Data Collection

As a proof of concept of the proposed refactoring process, we performed a case study on three applications: eLib, PostOffice, and FindSportMates. eLib is a Java application supporting the main functions operated in a library: (1) inserting and removing users/documents, searching for users/documents and loan management. The code of this application is provided in [28]. PostOffice is also a Java application that determines for each postal item (i.e., letters, parcels and express parcels) its postage fee and its reimbursement rate. Moreover, it allows printing the information of any chosen item. FindSportMates is a Java application that enables users to find groups of people with whom they can play certain sports (i.e., volleyball and basketball). Users can create a sports group or join existing ones. Table 3 provides some metrics on these applications.

Table 3. Applications metrics.

Application name	No of classes	No of methods	No of lines of code
PostOffice	6	57	231
eLib	9	80	555
FindSportMates	12	99	797

7.3 Refactoring Results

We applied the workflow refactoring process, using the developed plug-in, on the source code of each application to generate the corresponding workflow. As explained earlier in this section, the first step in our refactoring process (i.e., task identification) requires applying extract method refactoring. Table 4 shows the applications metrics after applying extract method refactoring.

As we can notice, the number of methods after applying extract method refactoring increased by an average of *25,5%* with a standard deviation of *13.75*. This can be explained by the fact that new methods were created depending on the number of fragments to be extracted (i.e., fragments consisting of statements delimited by user method invocations that belong to the same block), in the source code of the OO applications.

Table 4. Applications metrics after applying extract method refactoring.

Application	No of classes	No of methods	No of lines of code	% of the added methods
PostOffice	6	63	341	10,53%
eLib	9	115	788	43,75%
FindSportMates	12	121	889	22,22%

Once the refactoring is done, the plug-in analyzes the source code to identify tasks. Table 5 shows the results in term of the number of primitive and composite tasks for each application, as well as the total number of identified tasks.

To demonstrate that the workflow generated by our approach preserves the semantic of the analyzed OO application, we executed both the code corresponding to this workflow and the one corresponding to the analyzed OO application relying on the same test suite. Both executions produced the same results. Moreover, we identified workflows manually and compared them with the ones generated by our plug-in. Similarly, we found out that they are the same.

Table 5. Workflow refactoring results.

Application	No of primitive tasks	No of composite tasks	Total
PostOffice	51	12	63
eLib	80	35	115
FindSportMates	92	29	121

7.4   Threats to Validity

Threats to Internal Validity. Our approach may be affected by the following internal threats:

1. To restructure OO source code, we utilized *Extract method refactoring*. Nevertheless, the statements extracted as new methods are not functionally related. Therefore, as a perspective, we intend to restructure the code to obtain methods that have a purpose (e.g., their statements manipulate the same variables, etc.) [29–31].

2. As explained in Sect. 4, recovering control flow from OO source code in the presence of polymorphism and dynamic binding requires considering all the possible run-time types of a receiver. Thus, if a method includes N virtual calls and each one have M run-time types of a receiver, the CFG will contain at least $N*M$ paths. For this reason, we can not guarantee the scalability of the proposed approach. To tackle this problem, we plan to combine dynamic and static analysis. We will utilize dynamic analysis to determine the exact run-time type of a receiver, whereas static analysis collects the remaining information needed by our approach.
3. In our case studies, we recovered CFGs without taking into account exception-handling. Considering it requires extending our control flow recovery method to be able to handle implicit transfers related to exception raising.
4. The applicability of our approach is not affected by the presence of aliasing. As a matter of fact, to recover a data flow in the presence of alias, our approach requires only the availability of some alias analysis [32].

Threats to External Validity. Our approach could be concerned with the following external threats:

1. The applications utilized in our experimentation were implemented using Java programming language. Since OO languages (e.g., C++, C#, etc.) have the same structure and the same types of dependencies, experimenting on applications developed using these languages will probably produce the same results.
2. Only three case studies have been collected in the experimentation. Therefore, to consolidate and strengthen our approach, we need to experiment it on a large number of case studies, especially those of a considerably large size (i.e., thousands of classes), as well as industrial ones.

8   Related Works

In literature, several approaches were proposed to extract workflows in order to achieve specific goals (e.g., verification and validation, etc.). These approaches have as inputs the source code, the execution logs, semi-structured texts or other artifacts.

Zou et al. [17] proposed an approach to extract workflows from the source code of e-commerce applications. In this approach, to recover a workflow, a set of mapping rules was identified. These rules associate workflow entities to source code entities. However, applying them directly will probably generate a workflow that contains a large number of irrelevant entities that can not be mapped to any entities in the workflow available in the documentation. To solve this problem, a set of heuristics allowing to reduce the selected entities was proposed. An amelioration of this approach was proposed in [33]. To automate the mapping between source code entities and business process entities, Zou and Hung suggested lifting the abstraction level of the recovered control flow.

Gaaloul and Godart [18] proposed an approach to extract workflows from execution logs to improve workflow failure handling. More precisely, the proposed approach recover a control flow and a transactional flow[1]. This approach consists of three steps: (1) control flow constructs identification using logs statical analysis, (2) workflow transactional dependencies extraction and (3) improving workflow failure handling using a set of rules based on the results of the previous steps. Gaaloul et al. [34] extended the proposed approach and consolidated it with experimentations.

Ihaddadene [20] proposed another approach to extract workflows from execution logs and represent them using Petri nets. The approach has as inputs, in addition to workflow execution logs, some properties of the workflow tasks such as the minimum and maximum execution durations. The goal of the approach is to help organizations to improve the quality of their workflows. To achieve this goal, the author, firstly defined a set of rules to identify control constructs. Secondly, he proposed an algorithm which starts by identifying tasks from logs. Then, the algorithm specifies the first and the last tasks. After that, the proposed rules are applied to identify control constructs, and finally, the corresponding Petri net to the recovered workflow is constructed.

Schur et al. [35] proposed a fully automated, though configurable tool, that extract workflows from web applications to improve their development, quality assurance, and maintenance. The extracted workflows are represented using Extended Finite State Machines (EFSM). To extract such EFSM, *ProCrawl* iteratively execute actions through the UI, observes its changes and enhance the workflow.

Workflows were also extracted from semi-structured texts by Schumacher et al. [36] to support reuse of procedural knowledge[2]. The authors proposed two approaches, term-based approach, and frame-based one. These approaches rely on an extraction process consisting of three steps: (1) performing linguistic analysis, (2) extracting tasks and (3) building a workflow. The main difference between the two approaches is that the term-based approach is domain-specific, whereas the frame-based one is generic.

Besides the presented approaches related to workflow extraction, other approaches suggested reverse engineering various abstract models by analyzing source code. Actually, in literature, reverse engineering of OO source code has been widely studied. The goal is generating models allowing to understand the structure and behavior.

Diverse tools were developed to recover activity diagrams from source code. One of them is Flowgen developed by Kosower and Lopez-Villarejo [21]. Flowgen generates a set of interconnected activity diagrams from annotated C++ code. Each diagram represents a method. To recover these diagrams, the developers

---

[1] A transactional flow specifies the changes occurring in the control flow because of task failure.

[2] The procedural knowledge is also known as how to knowledge. For example, cooking recipes are considered as procedural knowledge.

have to annotate the code. The annotations along with control constructs are utilized to produce activity diagrams.

Korshunova et al. [19] developed a reverse engineering tool, called *CPP2XMI*. *CPP2XMI* extracts UML class, sequence, and activity Diagrams in XMI format from C++ code. However, the recovery process of these diagrams had not been detailed.

In our work, we constructed def-use triplets which have been widely studied in literature [24, 25, 37]. For instance, an approach was proposed by Chen and Kao [25] to construct two types of def-use triplets: (1) intra-method def-use triplets in which variable is defined and used in the same method and (2) inter-method def-use triplets in which a variable is defined in a method and used in another one. In our approach, the constructed def-use triplets are intra-method def-use triplets because we aim to determine data dependencies between the sub-tasks of each composite task.

Buy et al. [37] constructed def-use triplets for a single class. Each triplet specifies for an attribute the method that defines it and the one that uses it. Nevertheless, their approach takes into consideration only scalar attributes. This approach was extended by Martena et al. [24] to handle attributes even if they are objects. To achieve this, the methods of each class are classified into three categories: modifier, user and user-modifier, depending on whether these methods define and/or uses class attributes.

It is worthy to note that, several works rely on workflows to perform dynamic configuration for efficient resource management in the cloud, and therefore to reduce execution costs [3, 7, 9, 14, 15]. Also, several works re-engineered OO source code to achieve other goals such as code reuse and maintenance [38, 39].

8.1   Discussion

In this paper, we proposed a fully automatic approach that generates a workflow from OO source code, unlike the ones proposed by Kosower and Lopez-Villarejo [21]. Their approach requires human interactions to annotate the code which is not an easy task, especially when dealing with large applications. Besides, contrary to the approach proposed by Schur et al. [35], ours do not require any configuration.

Additionally, our approach is generic, contrary to the term-based one proposed by Schumacher et al. [36], which relies on a domain-specific dictionary. Thus, to use it in other domains, domain-specific dictionary is required.

Moreover, while generating a workflow, we recovered a control flow specifying the order of tasks through different constructs, unlike the approach proposed by Schumacher et al. [36] in which only the sequence construct was recovered. However, we did not recover parallelism constructs, contrarily to [18, 20, 34]. Also, one of the challenges that we encountered was determining the correspondent of tasks in OO source code. This challenge is not faced at all when recovering a workflow from its execution logs [18, 20, 34] which specify the tasks and other information (e.g., task end time, etc.).

Table 6. Comparative table.

	Inputs	Target	Objective	Analysis Technique	Polymorphism handling	Auto-mation	Explicit mapping
Zou et al. [17]	Source code	Workflow	Synchronising the as-specified and as-implemented workflows	Static		Auto	✓
Gaaloul and Godart [18]	Execution logs	Workflow	Improving workflow failure handling	Dynamic	Not needed	Auto	✓
Ihaddadene [20]	- Execution logs - Minimum and maximum execution durations of tasks	Workflow	Improve the quality of workflows	Dynamic	Not needed	Auto	✓
Schur et al. [35]	- Configured set of UI views - Actors - Start action executed by one of the actors	Workflow	Improving developement, quality assurance and maintenance of web applications	Dynamic	Not needed	Auto	
Schumacher et al. [36]	Semi-structured text	Workflow	Reuse of procedural knowledge	Static	Not needed	Auto	✓
Kosower and Lopez-Villarejo [21]	Source code	Activity diagram	Enhancing collaborations between programmers and algorithm or science specialists	Static		Sem	
Korshunova [19]	Source code	Class, sequence and activity diagrams	Verification and validation of software systems	?	?	Auto	?
Chen and Kao [25]	Source code	Def-use triplets	Testing OO source code	Static	✓	Auto	Not needed
Buy et al. [37]	Source code	Def-use triplets	Testing OO source code	Static	✓	Auto	Not needed
Martena et al. [24]	Source code	Def-use triplets	Testing OO source code	Static	✓	Auto	Not needed
Our approach	Source code	Workflow	Reducing execution costs of OO applications in the cloud	Static	✓	Auto	✓

Furthermore, in our approach, the generated workflow can be executed contrarily to the ones produced in [17,35,36], which can be used as documentation only. It is worthy to note that because the generated workflow has a hierarchical structure, it is possible to use it as documentation. In addition, unlike the workflow produced in [17,18,20,35], data dependencies between tasks are explicitly expressed in our workflow. To the best of our knowledge, only our approach recovers both data and control flows from source code. Table 6 recapitulates the differences between the related approaches and ours through the following criteria:

- *Inputs:* it represents the inputs required by an approach.
- *Target:* it represents the result produced by the approach.
- *Objective:* it is the objective for which the approach was proposed.
- *Analysis Technique:* it can be static, dynamic or hybrid.
- *Polymorphism Handling:* it specifies whether an approach handles polymorphism[3].
- *Automation:* an approach can be fully automatic (Auto) or semi-automatic (Sem).
- *Explicit Mapping:* it specifies whether the mapping model was explicitly presented or not. In some approaches a mapping model is not needed.

9   Conclusion

In this paper, we presented a refactoring approach aiming to generate a workflow from OO source code. To achieve that aim, we firstly set a mapping model between OO concepts and workflow ones. Then, to identify this mapping from OO source code, we proposed a refactoring process consisting of three steps. Each step recovers a workflow constituent. It is worth mentioning that the generated workflow can be utilized to deploy code and data in the cloud while reducing resources usage costs. Additionally, it can be used as documentation, due to its hierarchical structure. As a part of our future work, we intend to consolidate our approach by experimenting on other applications, especially those of a considerably large size as well as industrial ones. Additionally, since some of the identified tasks are fine-grained, we plan to enhance their granularity level so as to improve the generated workflow. Finally, we intend to run the generated workflow in the cloud while using resources efficiently to reduce costs. For that purpose, we will either use existing approaches or propose our approach inspired by the existing ones.

---

[3] Polymorphism need to be dealt with only when using static analysis.

References

1. Kaur, N., Aulakh, T.S., Cheema, R.S.: Comparison of workflow scheduling algorithms in cloud computing. Int. Adv. Comput. Sci. Appl. **2**(10), 81–86 (2011)
2. Mell, P., Grance, T., et al.: The NIST Definition of Cloud Computing (2011)
3. Masdari, M., ValiKardan, S., Shahi, Z., Azar, S.I.: Towards workflow scheduling in cloud computing: a comprehensive analysis. J. Netw. Comput. Appl. **66**, 64–82 (2016)
4. Liu, F., et al.: NIST cloud computing reference architecture. NIST Special Publication 500, pp. 1–28 (2011)
5. Wu, Z., Liu, X., Ni, Z., Yuan, D., Yang, Y.: A market-oriented hierarchical scheduling strategy in cloud workflow systems. J. Supercomput. 1–38 (2013). https://doi.org/10.1007/s11227-011-0578-4
6. Espadas, J., Molina, A., Jiménez, G., Molina, M., Ramírez, R., Concha, D.: A tenant-based resource allocation model for scaling software-as-a-service applications over cloud computing infrastructures. Future Gener. Comput. Syst. **29**, 273–286 (2013)
7. Fakhfakh, F., Kacem, H.H., Kacem, A.H.: Workflow scheduling in cloud computing: a survey. In: 2014 IEEE 18th International Enterprise Distributed Object Computing Conference Workshops and Demonstrations (EDOCW), pp. 372–378. IEEE (2014)
8. Dillon, T., Wu, C., Chang, E.: Cloud computing: issues and challenges. In: 2010 24th IEEE International Conference on Advanced Information Networking and Applications (AINA), pp. 27–33. IEEE (2010)
9. Xu, M., Cui, L., Wang, H., Bi, Y.: A multiple QoS constrained scheduling strategy of multiple workflows for cloud computing. In: 2009 IEEE International Symposium on Parallel and Distributed Processing with Applications, pp. 629–634. IEEE (2009)
10. Taylor, R.N., Medvidovic, N., Dashofy, E.M.: Software Architecture: Foundations, Theory, and Practice. Wiley, Hoboken (2009)
11. Garlan, D., Shaw, M.: An introduction to software architecture. Adv. Softw. Eng. Knowl. Eng. **2**, 1 (1993). https://www.worldscientific.com/worldscibooks/10.1142/2207#t=toc
12. Bass, L.: Software Architecture in Practice. Pearson Education, New Delhi (2007)
13. Hollingsworth, D.: Workflow Management Coalition: The Workflow Reference Model (1995)
14. Zhu, Z., Zhang, G., Li, M., Liu, X.: Evolutionary multi-objective workflow scheduling in cloud. IEEE Trans. Parallel Distrib. Syst. **27**, 1344–1357 (2016)
15. Lin, C., Lu, S.: Scheduling scientific workflows elastically for cloud computing. In: 2011 IEEE International Conference on Cloud Computing (CLOUD), pp. 746–747. IEEE (2011)
16. Sneed, H.M.: Measuring reusability of legacy software systems. Softw. Process Improv. Pract. **4**, 43–48 (1998)
17. Zou, Y., Lau, T.C., Kontogiannis, K., Tong, T., McKegney, R.: Model-driven business process recovery. In: 2004 Proceedings of 11th Working Conference on Reverse Engineering, pp. 224–233. IEEE (2004)
18. Gaaloul, W., Godart, C.: Mining workflow recovery from event based logs. In: van der Aalst, W.M.P., Benatallah, B., Casati, F., Curbera, F. (eds.) BPM 2005. LNCS, vol. 3649, pp. 169–185. Springer, Heidelberg (2005). https://doi.org/10.1007/11538394_12

19. Korshunova, E., Petkovic, M., Van Den Brand, M., Mousavi, M.R.: CPP2XMI: reverse engineering of UML class, sequence, and activity diagrams from C++ source code. In: 2006 13th Working Conference on Reverse Engineering, pp. 297–298. IEEE (2006)
20. Ihaddadene, N.: Extraction of business process models from workflow events logs. Int. J. Parallel Emergent Distrib. Syst. **23**, 247–258 (2008)
21. Kosower, D.A., Lopez-Villarejo, J.J.: Flowgen: flowchart-based documentation for C++ codes. Comput. Phys. Commun. **196**, 497–505 (2015)
22. Selmadji, A., Seriai, A., Bouziane, H., Dony, C., Tibermacine, C.: Refactoring object-oriented applications for a deployment in the cloud - workflow generation based on static analysis of source code. In: Proceedings of the 13th International Conference on Evaluation of Novel Approaches to Software Engineering, ENASE 2018, Funchal, Madeira, Portugal, 23–24 March 2018, pp. 111–123 (2018)
23. Russell, N., Ter Hofstede, A.H., Van Der Aalst, W.M., Mulyar, N.: Workflow control-flow patterns: a revised view. BPM Center Report BPM-06-22, pp. 06–22. BPMcenter (2006)
24. Martena, V., Orso, A., Pezze, M.: Interclass testing of object oriented software. In: Proceedings of Eighth IEEE International Conference on Engineering of Complex Computer Systems, 2002, pp. 135–144. IEEE (2002)
25. Chen, M.H., Kao, H.M.: Testing object-oriented programs-an integrated approach. In: 1999 Proceedings 10th International Symposium on Software Reliability Engineering, pp. 73–82. IEEE (1999)
26. Aho, A.V., Sethi, R., Ullman, J.D.: Compilers: Principles, Techniques, and Tools. Addison Wesley Publishing Company, Boston (1986)
27. Graphviz open source graph visualization software. https://www.graphviz.org/
28. Tonella, P., Potrich, A.: Reverse Engineering of Object Oriented Code. Monographs in Computer Science. Springer, New York (2005). https://doi.org/10.1007/b102522
29. Charalampidou, S., Ampatzoglou, A., Chatzigeorgiou, A., Gkortzis, A., Avgeriou, P.: Identifying extract method refactoring opportunities based on functional relevance. IEEE Trans. Softw. Eng. **4310**, 954–974 (2016)
30. Kaya, M., Fawcett, J.W.: Identification of extract method refactoring opportunities through analysis of variable declarations and uses. Int. J. Softw. Eng. Knowl. Eng. **2701**, 1–21 (2016)
31. Kaya, M., Fawcett, J.W.: Identifying extract method opportunities based on variable references (s). In: SEKE, pp. 153–158 (2013)
32. Clarke, D., Wrigstad, T., Noble, J.: Aliasing in Object-Oriented Programming: Types, Analysis and Verification, vol. 7850. Springer, New York (2013). https://doi.org/10.1007/978-3-642-36946-9
33. Zou, Y., Hung, M.: An approach for extracting workflows from e-commerce applications. In: 2006 14th IEEE International Conference on Program Comprehension, ICPC 2006 , pp. 127–136. IEEE (2006)
34. Gaaloul, W., Gaaloul, K., Bhiri, S., Haller, A., Hauswirth, M.: Log-based transactional workflow mining. Distrib. Parallel Databases **25**, 193–240 (2009)
35. Schur, M., Roth, A., Zeller, A.: Mining workflow models from web applications. IEEE Trans. Softw. Eng. **41**, 1184–1201 (2015)
36. Schumacher, P., Minor, M., Walter, K., Bergmann, R.: Extraction of procedural knowledge from the web: a comparison of two workflow extraction approaches. In: Proceedings of the 21st International Conference on World Wide Web, pp. 739–747. ACM (2012)
37. Buy, U., Orso, A., Pezze, M.: Automated testing of classes. In: ACM SIGSOFT Software Engineering Notes, vol. 25, pp. 39–48. ACM, New York (2000)

38. Chardigny, S., Seriai, A.: Software architecture recovery process based on object-oriented source code and documentation. In: Babar, M.A., Gorton, I. (eds.) ECSA 2010. LNCS, vol. 6285, pp. 409–416. Springer, Heidelberg (2010). https://doi.org/10.1007/978-3-642-15114-9_35
39. Alshara, Z., Seriai, A.D., Tibermacine, C., Bouziane, H.L., Dony, C., Shatnawi, A.: Migrating large object-oriented applications into component-based ones: instantiation and inheritance transformation. In: ACM SIGPLAN Notices, vol. 51, pp. 55–64. ACM (2015)

Crowdsourced Reverse Engineering: Experiences in Applying Crowdsourcing to Concept Assignment

Sebastian Heil$^{(\boxtimes)}$ ⓘ, Valentin Siegert ⓘ, and Martin Gaedke ⓘ

Technische Universität Chemnitz, 09107 Chemnitz, Germany
{sebastian.heil,valentin.siegert,martin.gaedke}@informatik.tu-chemnitz.de

Abstract. This article details the idea of Crowdsourced Reverse Engineering (CSRE) by analysing three major challenges: (1) automatic task extraction, (2) source code anonymization and (3) results aggregation and quality control. We re-formulate the Reverse Engineering activity of concept assignment as a crowdsourced classification task to exemplify these challenges and describe suitable methods to address them. Our overview on existing research of crowdsourcing showcases examples of successful application in the field of Software Engineering and argues that Reverse Engineering activities like Concept Assignment are likely to also benefit from crowdsourcing by determining a high similarity in eight crowdsourcing dimensions to the microtasking model. Our experiments on the crowdsourcing platform microworkers.com support this, producing 187 results by 34 crowd workers which classified 10 code fragments with decent quality. We provide an extended analysis of the observed crowd workers' behavior and report evidence of surprisingly high levels of engagement and efforts undertaken by the crowd. Concluding our experiences, this article indicates three open research challenges for future work.

Keywords: Reverse engineering · Crowdsourcing · Microtasking · Concept assignment · Classification · Web migration · Software Migration

1 Introduction

Software Migration to the Web is a crucial challenge for software developing companies with legacy systems. Changing expectations of users towards modern software pose new challenges for existing software systems that are not web-based. These challenges are particularly rooted in the diversity of user interactions of recent web applications. The continuous evolution of web technologies and the termination of support for obsolete technologies furthermore increase the pressure to modernize non-web legacy systems [7,26]. With web browsers becoming the standard interface for many applications, web applications provide a solution to platform-dependence and deployment problems [4]. Software developing companies are aware of these benefits and reasons for web migration.

ⓒ Springer Nature Switzerland AG 2019
E. Damiani et al. (Eds.): ENASE 2018, CCIS 1023, pp. 215–239, 2019.
https://doi.org/10.1007/978-3-030-22559-9_10

On the other hand, in particular Small and Medium-sized Enterprises (SMEs) face difficulties when trying to commence a web migration [12].

Our problem analysis based on LFA[1] problem trees identified a variety of sub-problems which can be summarized under two main factors: *doubts about feasibility* and *doubts about desirability* [13], which render SME-sized software developing companies hesitant to migrate their existing software products to the web. While we addressed doubts about desirability in [13], this work focuses on doubts about feasibility, which are mainly originating in the danger of losing knowledge throughout the migration process [7].

Small and medium-sized software providers often tailor their successful software products specifically to a certain niche domain, resulting from years of requirements engineering [21]. Therefore, the amount of valuable domain knowledge from the problem and solution domain [18] such as models, processes, rules, algorithms etc. encoded in the source code is vast. [26] Due to the paradigm shifts introduced through webmigration – client-server separation in the spatial and technological dimension [7], asynchronous request-response-based communication [4], explicitly addressable application states via URLs and navigation to name but a few – redevelopment methods bears the risk of losing this knowledge.

The problem and solution domain knowledge in legacy systems, however, is only implicitly represented by the source code and often poorly documented [26,27]. Therefore, *Reverse Engineering* is required to elicit this knowledge, to make it explicit and thus available for subsequent web migration processes. For small and medium-sized enterprises, existing re-documentation approaches [14] are not feasible since they cannot be integrated into day-to-day agile development activities and require additional human resources. Therefore, we introduced an approach based on in-situ source code annotations [11], allowing to enrich the legacy source code by directly linking parts of code with explicit representations of the knowledge which is contained in them. Web engineers are enabled to reference the elicited knowledge in emails, wikis, task descriptions etc. and to jump directly to their definition and location in the legacy source code, using a web-based annotation platform. The identification of domain knowledge in source code is known as *Concept Assignment* [6].

Through integration into the daily development activities of the small and medium-sized enterprise, concept assignment supported by our platform allows to incrementally re-discover and document the valuable domain knowledge. However, the concept assignment activity itself is manual. This requires a high amount of effort and time, in particular taking into account the limited resources of small and medium-sized enterprises. Moreover, the results of manual concept assignment depend solely on the migration engineer executing the activity.

The concept assignment process involves reading a part of legacy source code, selecting a relevant portion called region of interest (ROI) and determining the type of knowledge which this ROI represents, before further manual or automatic code analysis can be applied to extract model representations of the knowledge. This process can be considered a *classification task*. Crowdsourcing has been successfully applied to solve various classification tasks in areas like

---

[1] Logical Framework Approach, cf. http://ec.europa.eu/europeaid/.

image or natural language text classification. Also in the context of software engineering, crowdsourcing methods have been reported successful, in particular on smaller tasks without interdependencies [17,25], like the above. Thus, in this article we explore *Crowdsourced Reverse Engineering* (CSRE) through experimentation with the reverse engineering activity of identifying different types of knowledge in legacy codebases. This article is an extended and revised version of our previous work in [10]. Our experiments identified three main challenges. This article details these challenges, reports on how we addressed them and provides the results of our evaluation. Since these challenges are not specific to concept assignment, which is used as an example for this work and can be encountered when applying crowdsourcing to other reverse engineering activities.

Challenges of the Application of Crowdsourcing in Reverse Engineering:

1. Automatic Extraction and Creation of Crowdsourcing Tasks from the Legacy Source
2. Balancing Controlled Disclosure of Proprietary Source Code with Readability
3. Aggregation of Results and Quality Control

Existing crowdsourcing platforms require suitable classification tasks. These can be derived by splitting the legacy source code into fragments which can then be classified by the crowd workers. The fragment size has to balance context with classification, i.e. they should be large enough to provide sufficient context for a meaningful classification and small enough to allow for a unambiguous classification and a good overall recall in relation to the entire code base. Moreover, the legacy source is a valuable asset of the company. Thus, disclosure of code fragments on a public crowdsourcing platform to a potentially unknown audience needs to be controlled.

Competitors should be prevented from identifying the authoring company, the concrete software product or even the application domain, in order to not allow them to gain insights on the software product or – as worst case – replicating parts of it. On the other hand, a suitable anonymization method needs to be balanced with the source code readability. Code which is produced by traditional code obfuscation algorithms is intendedly hard to read [8]. This would jeopardize achieving high quality classification results by the crowd workers. Aggregating the crowd workers' classification results with effective quality control measures is therefore a key challenge. Fake contributions need to be filtered and contradicting classifications have to be resolved. While manual quality control by the crowdsourcing company would be effective, the advantage gained by crowdsourcing would be mitigated by the high manual effort to ensure a decent classification quality.

This article reports on our experiences when applying crowdsourcing in the reverse engineering domain. We outline the CSRE approach in Sect. 2 and detail the three challenges of automatic task extraction in Sect. 3, source code anonymization in Sect. 4 and quality control and results aggregation in Sect. 5. In Sect. 6, we position CSRE against existing work, report on and analyse the results from our experiments in Sect. 7 and conclude the article with an outlook on open issues in Sect. 8.

2   The CSRE Approach

To demonstrate the application of crowdsourcing in the domain of reverse engineering, we experimented with the reverse engineering activity of *Concept Assignment*. The original problem of concept assignment has been defined by Biggerstaff et al. in [5]. It aims at reconstructing "human-oriented expressions of computational intent" by identifying the concepts and assigning them to "the specific implementation structures within the program" [5]. The concept assignment problem is "the problem of discovering these human-oriented concepts and assigning them to their realizations within a specific program or its context" [5].

Concept assignment research has investigated a variety of different concepts: from concrete domain concepts [6] to features [18] to abstract concerns [9]. An important distinction is between *problem domain concepts* and *solution domain concepts*: while problem domain concepts (e.g. processes, rules, business entities) originate in the domain for which the software was built, solution domain concepts (e.g. algorithms, patterns) are from the domain of programming [18].

In Fig. 1, we reformulated the concept assignment process [6] as a classification problem: first the source code is read (for manual concept assignment as in [9]) or parsed (for automatic methods like [18]), regions of interest are identified and the represented concept determined. Optionally, this is followed by manual or automatic extraction of a formal representation of the concept (e.g. in UML, BPMN) to allow subsequent use of model-driven methodologies.

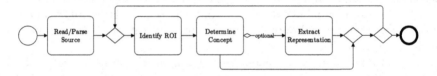

Fig. 1. Concept assignment process reformulated as classification.

Manual concept assignment often is a lexical search-based activity [24] using identifiers [18] and can be supported by tools like ConcernTagger [9] or Annotation Platform [11]. Recent automatic concept assignment approaches are Information Retrieval (IR) techniques employing Natural Language Processing (NLP) methods [24]. The filtering technique in [1] applies NLP analysis to identifiers of classes, methods and attributes to extract domain ontologies, [18] presents an approach based on Latent Semantic Indexing, [24] uses action-oriented identifier graphs. The possibility of applying crowdsourcing to concept assignment has not been considered yet. Thus, we use concept assignment as basis for our experimental application of crowdsourcing in reverse engineering.

The crowdsourcing-based classification process for concept assignment in legacy code bases presented in Fig. 2 involves three roles:

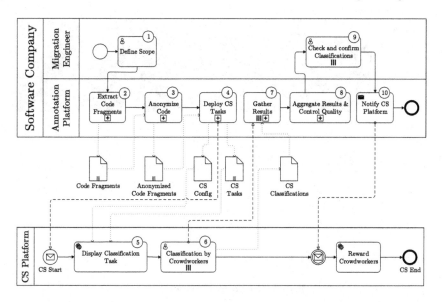

Fig. 2. Crowdsourcing-based source code classification process.

1. *Migration Engineer* is the person conducting the web migration
2. *Annotation Platform* is a system role that represents a web migration support platform [11] for the concept assignment
3. *CS Platform* represents a suitable crowdsourcing marketplace, allowing to post an open classification call to the crowd

The process starts by the migration engineer (1) defining the scope of code to be classified on the legacy code base. This scope can be defined in terms of a subset of concrete source files, software components (project/solution files) or the entire code base. The annotation platform (2) automatically extracts code fragments for classification as described in Sect. 3. The extracted fragments are (3) pre-processed to achieve the intended anonymization properties, which we describe in Sect. 4. For each of the anonymized code fragments, the annotation platform (4) deploys classification tasks in the CS Platform. The CS Configuration data passed to the CS Platform to set-up the tasks includes a brief description of the concept assignment classification task, a URL pointing to the classification view for crowdworkers (Fig. 3) in the annotation platform, the requirements for selecting suitable crowd workers and the reward configuration. Matching crowdworkers according to the crowdworker requirements are (5) presented a textual description of the available categories for classification, following our ontology for knowledge in source code [11]. Depending on the terms of use of the CS platform and its technological capabilities, the URL of the crowd worker view is either presented as a link or loaded in the CS platform using an iframe.

The crowd worker view displays the code fragment to be classified and the selection control of possible categories to the crowd worker in order to support and capture his classification result (6). In addition, it shows a list of source

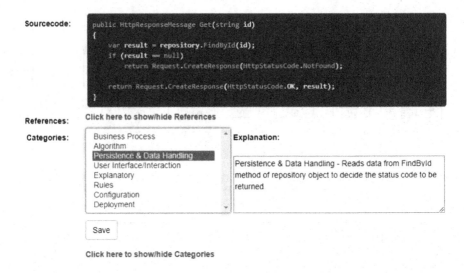

Fig. 3. Crowd worker view [10].

code references to allowing the crowdworker to review those parts of source code which are referenced in the code fragment. (7) User-specific URLs and temporary tokens are employed to capture the results per crowdworker and authenticate access to the annotation platform. In (8), the classification results are aggregated across the different crowdworkers and quality control measures are applied according to Sect. 5. The filtered results can then be (9) automatically included in the annotation platform, or marked for further review by the migration engineer, allowing to accept or reject them. Finally, the annotation platform (10) notifies the CS platform to reward the participating crowd workers according to the reward policy. The following three sections provide details about CSRE's components addressing the main challenges raised in the introduction.

3   Classification Task Extraction

3.1   Problem Analysis

According to [25], typical tasks for crowdsourcing, called *Micro-tasks*, are characterized as self-contained, simple, repetitive, short, requiring little time, cognitive effort and specialized skills. Of these characteristics, classification of code fragments as described in Sect. 2 matches the first five. Classification results are not dependent on other classification results. The classification act itself is a simple selection from a list of available options. The classification activity is highly repetitive and a single classification can be achieved in relatively low time. The last two characteristics are slightly different: The cognitive effort required is higher compared to other successfully crowdsourced classification tasks like image classification. To some extent, specialized skills are required since the crowd workers have to have a sufficient capability to read and understand source code in the legacy code base's programming language. However, only a basic understanding of programming and limited knowledge of the programming language are sufficient to read and understand enough of a given code fragment to determine the correct classification. Thus, the skill requirements are not extremly high and the concept assignment classification activity is suitable for a much wider range of crowd workers compared to crowdsourcing the entire development of an application as in [22].

To automatically extract micro classification tasks from the legacy code base, it has to be divided into code fragments for classification. These are identified through structural code analysis. Suitable methods serving this purpose must have three essential **classification task extraction properties**:

1. Automation
2. Legacy language support
3. Completeness of references

Automation. To perform the analysis and to carry out the identification of relevant code fragments for classification, no additional user interaction should be required by a suitable extraction method.

Legacy Language Support. Since structural code analysis is specific to the programming language, the method should support common programming languages. According to IEEE Spectrum[2], the ten most widely used programming languages are: Python, C++, C, Java, C#, PHP, R, JavaScript, Go and Assembly. While Go is a relatively new language (appeared in 2009) and Javascript has only recently seen an increased use in the context of web applications, R is a language mainly used for statistics and data analysis. These languages are therefore not considered relevant for a web migration. Typical languages found in legacy software to a larger extent include C, C++, Java and Assembly and should therefore be supported.

Completeness of References. To provide a crowd worker with sufficient information to properly categorize a code fragment, the control and data flow must be understandable from the code provided. To display this information to the crowd worker, the extraction method must include information about source code that is referenced in the code fragment.

3.2   Solution

We analyzed three groups of approaches for classification task extraction. *Documentation tools* are originally used to automatically create source code documentation. Existing documentation tools can be re-used for task extraction, however, instead of developing specific extraction tools. To create the documentation, the

---

[2] https://spectrum.ieee.org/at-work/innovation/the-2018-top-programming-langua ges.

structure of the source code is analyzed and transformed into representation formats. Thus, this group of methods allows to identify structural properties of a source code. *Syntactic analysis tools* explicitly analyze code regarding its structural properties. Two different types exist: regular-expression-based and parsers. Regular expressions are used to search for patterns in texts. Thus, a suitable set of regular expressions allows identifying relevant code fragments for classification. Parsers create representations of the syntactical structure of a program, based on abstract syntax trees, describing the structure and sequence of statements of the program code. Similar to documentation tools, *Syntax highlighting tools* generate custom representations of the structure of source code in order display syntax highlighting in editors and IDEs.

The applicability of these three groups for the extraction of classification tasks was systematically investigated by evaluating them against the three aforementioned essential properties as requirements. Production-grade implementations of documentation tools exist for most programming languages. Referenced parts of source code are completely traceable, ensuring good understanding for crowd workers. Through the capability to configure the extraction process by command line parameters, automation is easily achieved. Being a standardized means of extracting information from text, regular expressions are supported by all current programming languages and can thus be employed for automatic extraction, as part of a tailored extraction program. However, tracing source code references can would require very high effort and complex iterative use regular expressions. On the other hand, parsers allow to track source code references by analyzing data and control flow and are available for most programming languages. The analysis results generated in the parsing process, however, are either not exportable or they are available as graphical representations only. This makes further processing difficult. Therefore, using parsers in an automated extraction process is significantly limited. While syntax highlighting tools allow the identification of code fragments and internally create a representation of code structure, exporting these structure file to elicit source code references is restricted to certain platforms. As a result, their applicability is limited.

Based on the above considerations and supported by an internal feasibility study by students, we decided to use documentation tools as basis for the fully automated classification task extraction. The implementation runs "Doxygen"[3] on the legacy code base and parses the generated documentation to identify relevant code fragments and referenced source code.

4   Source Code Anonymization

4.1   Problem Analysis

The crowdsourcing paradigm implies that work is not assigned to individual workers, but instead crowd workers respond to an open call. The group of workers is potentially large and they are unknown to the company. [15] Thus, posting a

---

[3] https://www.stack.nl/~dimitri/doxygen/.

task on a crowdsourcing platform is equivalent to publishing the task contents, bearing the risk that competitors access the code fragments from the crowd tasks and use them uncontrolledly.

Proper *source code anonymization* means are therefore relevant to allow companies to successfully employ CSRE. *Code obfuscation* techniques adapt an existing source code to make it harder to understand/reverse engineer, while maintaining the original functionality [8]. Thus, they would provide a partial solution to prevent unintended distribution of a company's valuable source code. However, the readability is also severely impacted. [8] assesses the impact of code obfuscation techniques on the understandability through human readers.

In the context of CSRE, the challenge of source code anonymization is to balance information disclosure with readability: While a suitable anonymization method sufficiently modifies the code fragments to prevent unintended use, it has to maintain readability to a level that allows crowd workers to achieve sufficient understanding of the code to perform the reverse engineering task.

The following **anonymization properties** reflect this necessary balance. A suitable anonymization method must:

1. Prevent identification of software provider, software product and application domain
2. Maintain control flow and all information relevant for classification
3. Avoid negative impact on readability of the source code

We analyze these three anonymization properties in the following. This section is not structured per property because achievement of any of the properties influences the others. Obfuscation techniques employing code optimizations like inline expansion[4] or adding artificial branches to the control flow (cf. opaque predicates [3]) alter the syntactic sequence of expressions. As the control flow is not maintained, these obfuscation techniques are disregarded.

Identifier renaming has shown good results in source code obfuscation [8]. Identifiers are, however, not the only constituents of code containing information relevant for the identification of software provider, software product or application domain (*identification information* in the following). The three different *loci of identification information* are: identifiers, strings and comments. While traditional code obfuscation has to produce identical software from end users' perspective, anonymization for classification can apply modifications to string contents: The anonymized source code is only displayed to crowd workers for reverse engineering, but not used to compile into software and used by end users.

Another difference to traditional identifier renaming, which typically yields intendedly meaningless random combinations of characters and numbers, is that source code anynomization replacements in the context of CSRE have to sufficiently maintain readability and information content. The naïve approach would be dictionary-based replacements: creating custom blacklists of words and defining mappings to their respective replacements. However, completeness of the

---

[4] Replacing calls to usually short functions by their body.

anonymization would highly depend on the completeness of theses dictionaries and the approach requires high manual effort. This is not feasible for larger code bases as found in the professional software production context of small and medium-sized enterprises.

According to the two main origins of information in identifiers, strings and comments, research distinguishes problem and solution domain knowledge [18]. Identification information is found in identifiers or words in strings originating from the problem domain. Solution domain knowledge represents *classification information*, i.e. information relevant for classifying a code fragment. An ideal anonymization approach replaces all identification information while maintaining all classification information. Transformation of the domain model would allow this. For a legacy system, however, this model is typically not available [26].

4.2   Solution

We use static program analysis to extract the Platform Specific Model (PSM), and a list of all identifiers. Based on results from the static program analysis, we automatically generate a replacement mapping for each of the identifiers. Our anonymization algorithm (cf. Algorithm 1) generates these replacement mappings based on the identifier type. It distinguishes three basic types of identifiers: functions, variables and classes. For example, identifiers representing class names like `BlogProvider` are mapped to `Class_A`, methods like `Blogprovider.Init()` to identifiers like `Class_A.Method_A()`. Relationships between concepts are understandable to human readers through relationships in natural language between corresponding identifiers. Through identifier renaming, these relationships get lost. To improve understanding, simple relationships like generalization and class-instance can be expressed in the generated identifiers to maintain a certain level of semantics. For example, a class `class Rectangle: Shape` can be replaced as `Class_B_extends_Class_A`, an instance variable `Shape* shape = new Shape()` can be renamed to `instance_of_Class_A`. Representing further relationships like composition or aggregation would require an existing domain model. Prior creation of a domain model contradicts the aim of concept assignment, therefore these are not considered.

The pre-processing phase prepares the source code for the following renaming phase. Due to the complexity of Natural language texts contained in comments can be complex. Appropriate modifications would require high effort, thus, comments are stripped from the source code. Likewise, strings contents can contain complex natural language texts, potentially containing product or company names. Therefore, they are replaced by `"String"`. In the renaming phase, remaining strings and identifiers are replaced according to the mapping described above.

Assessing the readability of the resulting anonymized code, we conducted a brief validation experiment. Six employees of an SME-sized software provider (Age min 22, max 50, avg 32.7; Experience min 6, max 29, avg 13.2 years) rated the readability of 10 anonymized source code fragments (length min 7, max 57, avg 27.4 LOC, cf. Sect. 7.1) on a five-level Likert scale (measuring agreement between 1 and 5 to "The code is easy to read"). Expectedly, traditional obfuscation was rated near-unreadable (0.7) whereas CSRE (3.7) performed slightly better than the naïve approach (3.2).

Algorithm 1. CSRE Anonymization Algorithm.

 Input: Source Code S, Platform Specific Model PSM, Identifier List I
 Output: Anonymized Source Code

1 $m(i) = \begin{cases} \text{"instance\_of\_"} + m(c) \textbf{ if } i \text{ instance of } c \\ \text{genericName}(i) + \text{"\_extends\_"} + m(s) \textbf{ if } i \text{ subclass of } s \\ \text{genericName}(i) \textbf{ else} \end{cases}$

2 replace Strings in S by "String"
3 remove comments from S
4 replace all identifiers $i \in I$ in S with $m(i)$
5 **return** S

---

5   Results Aggregation and Quality Control

5.1   Problem Analysis

Crowdsourcing produces a set of results from different and unknown contributors. These results may even be contradicting. The quality of results from CSRE must, however, justify the resources invested by the company. Ensuring quality of crowdsourced results is a challenge. [19,25,28] Thus, proper results aggregation and quality control is crucial.

 For the classification task described in Fig. 1, the amount of correctly classified code fragments should be as high as possible, i.e. good precision is required. The precision depends on several factors: Crowd workers sometimes provide fake answers to minimize their effort, leading to poor quality. Different experience levels of the crowd workers can lead to different classification results on the same code fragment.

 To aggregate results and achieve good quality, several *quality-control design-time approaches* (Worker selection, Effective task preparation) and *quality-control run-time approaches* (Ground truth, Majority consensus) (cf. [2]) are considered.

Quality Control and Results Aggregation Properties:

1. Worker selection
2. Effective task preparation
3. Ground truth
4. Majority consensus

5.2   Solution

In the following, we outline the combination of approaches used to achieve good results quality using the schema in [2].

Worker Selection. Since experience of the crowd workers highly impacts quality of crowdsourcing results, we use reputation-based worker selection [2]. Crowd workers are rated based on their contributions to CS tasks in most crowdsourcing platforms. Their reputation is based on these ratings. Reputation-based worker selection allows only crowd workers above a specified *reputation threshold* to select a CS task. In our experiments on the bespoke [17] crowdsourcing platform microWorkers.com[5], only workers from the "best workers" group participated.

Effective Task Preparation. The reverse engineering task has to be described clearly and unambiguously. The task design must keep the effort for fake contributions similar to correctly solving the task. This is known as *defensive design* [2]. In our experiment, crowd workers are provided with a brief description of the classification task and the available classifications with examples. At any step of the process, they can access this description.

   The crowd worker view (cf. Fig. 3) displays the code fragment and references (cf. Sect. 3) with syntax highlighting, the available categories and a text input in which a brief explanation must be given to provide reasons for the classification. The minimal explanation length of 50 characters aims at reducing or at least slowing down fake contributions and allows for filtering during post-processing, e.g. filtering identically copied explanations. The *compensation policy* combines financial and non-financial rewards: For quality contributions, crowd workers receive a financial reward of 0.30 USD (platform average during the experiment) and a positive rating of their contribution as non-financial reward, adding to their reputation.

Ground Truth. To assess the quality of contributions by crowd worker, we employ the ground truth approach: Classification tasks with known correct answers form the ground truth. In this way, individual worker can be assessed based on the correctness of answers for these test questions. This information determines the *individual user score* $S(w_i) \in [0, 1]$ for each crowd worker $w_i \in W$ by comparing the amounts of correct classifications $C_{w_i}^+$ and false classifications $C_{w_i}^-$ as in Eq. (1). It can be used as weight factor during results aggregation.

$$S(w_i) = \frac{|C_{w_i}^+|}{|C_{w_i}^+| + |C_{w_i}^-|} \tag{1}$$

Majority Consensus. We employ the majority consensus technique to aggregate the crowdsourcing results. For each code fragment to be classified, the classifications $C \subset W \times A$ are tuples (w_i, c_k) of a crowd worker $w_i \in W$ and the class $c_k \in A$ which the crowd worker selected. The resulting voting distribution $V : A \mapsto [0, 1]$ is calculated for all possible classes $c_i \in A$ as in Eq. (2):

$$V(c_i) = \frac{\sum\limits_{(w,c)\in C | c = c_i} S(w)}{\sum\limits_{(w,c)\in C} S(w)} \tag{2}$$

---

[5] https://microworkers.com/.

The aggregated result c^* of all crowd classifications is defined by the highest voting value as in Eq. (3):

$$c^* = \arg\max_{c \in A} V(c) \tag{3}$$

For more control, an overview with the result distributions and explanations was implemented, so that edge cases without clear majority can be found easily and decided (cf. Figs. 4 and 5).

Statistik

Kategorie	Prozent	Umwandeln
Rules	47.06	Umwandeln
Persistence & Data Handling	17.65	Umwandeln
Explanatory	11.76	Umwandeln
Deployment	11.76	Umwandeln
Algorithm	5.88	Umwandeln
User Interface/Interaction	5.88	Umwandeln

Statistik inkl. Testfragen

Kategorie	Prozent
Rules	42.35
Persistence & Data Handling	25.98
Explanatory	10.85
User Interface/Interaction	9.96
Deployment	8.9
Algorithm	1.96

Fig. 4. Crowdsourcing results statistics view [10].

6   Related Work

In this section, we provide a brief overview on crowdsourcing research in reverse engineering and software engineering and position our CSRE approach accordingly (cf. Table 1).

6.1   Crowdsourcing in Reverse Engineering

Research applying crowdsourcing to reverse engineering is sparse. CrowdSource by Saxe et al. [23] is an approach for malware classification combining NLP with crowdsourcing. The initial data is provided by the crowd, the actual classification work, however, is performed using statistical NLP methods like full-text indexing and Bayesian networks. Based on the vast natural language corpus available on question and answer websites like StackExchange, CrowdSource creates a statistical model for malware capability detection. The model correlates low-level keywords like API symbols or registry keys with high-level malware capabilities like screencapture or network communication. In contrast to CSRE, Crowd-Source follows a *passive crowdsourcing* [16] model: Crowdsourcing is employed only to generate the required input probabilities for the Bayesian model and not directly for performing the classification work.

Crowdworker	Erklärung	Benötigte Sekunden
4f6ebfeb	As said in description of "Rules", this source code is setting and applying related rules for the " list category". So, it comes in the "rules" category.	186
	→ Rules	
57a169c1	It is used for presenting data into category after sorting according to ID.	67
	→ Explanatory	
e858273d	This category describes source code, in which general rules or rules of a specific domain are used to check or decide anything.	49
	→ Rules	
40809b34	I choose this category because of two things I noticed inside this database and first is the parent word that can explain and show the meaning of rules because when you say parent it explains many things as advice and how to live and that what means rules to process and the second one is guide and everyone knows the parent guides and explains how to deal with things and also that too specific to rules	198
	→ Rules	
0fa041b2	This method is used to create a XML file. If the file is not available than the XML file is created. List of Categories with XML files.	84
	→ Deployment	
81a80188	This code contains deployment commands and the server is hosted for the same purpose.	37
	→ Deployment	
a8ae5daa	because it defines rules of listing the entire method.	126
	→ Rules	
1e386615	the code contains rules to check if statements are true or false	65
	→ Rules	
e0aefe92	Since the methods checks if an object is not null throughout the code it belongs to Rules category. Since it processes an xml file to create a list of Category objects, which is a data structure, it belongs to Persistence & Data Handling category	323
	→ Persistence & Data Handling	
	→ Rules	
d76dbbe0	Persistence & Data Handling - the code parses an XML file and creates a list of Category objects. Rules - checks if the file with the given name exists	183
	→ Persistence & Data Handling	
	→ Rules	
8ba95609	Algorithm is a way to understand the logical facts. It helps to make program on C# or any other languages. In this process programming becomes very easy. Explanatory is also useful to understand why the particular source code is used.	14
	→ Algorithm	
	→ Explanatory	
	→ Rules	
71535d20	method, that fills a field of categories with content, so the user can interact afterwards	42
	→ User Interface/Interaction	
dba271d8	The provied function is used to save the blog details such as category and description related to it. A new category is created and stored in the categories.xml file located on server. The updated categories list is then returned as a list.	9
	→ Persistence & Data Handling	
Durchschnittszeit		106

Fig. 5. Crowdsourcing result details view for migration engineer [10].

Table 1. Overview on existing crowdsourcing approaches in reverse engineering and software engineering.

Approach	Field	CS for	Act./pass.	CS Model
CrowdSource [23]	Malware classification	Initial text corpus	Passive	Sharing and reuse
CrowdDesign [19]	Component development	Programming	Passive, active	Peer production, microtasking
CrowdAdapt [20]	HCI	Adapting and evaluating layouts	Passive	Sharing and reuse
CrowdDesign [28]	HCI	Partial UI design	Active	Microtasking
(Stol 2014) [25]	Modeling, testing	Asset modeling, test automation	Active	Microtasking
(Satzger 2014) [22]	Software development	Software development	Active	Collaborative CS

6.2 Crowdsourcing in Software Engineering

Crowdsourcing has received wider consideration in software engineering. For instance, [19] presents a platform for crowd-supported creation of composite web applications. The web engineer creates the design of the web application as mashup based on information and interface components. Nebeling et al. combine a passive with an active crowdsourcing model: *Sharing and Reuse* is used in a community-based component library. Public components can be used by the web engineer to compose the web application. *Active crowdsourcing* is used for creating new components. The web engineer defines characteristics of the required component and posts an open call to a paid, external crowd. Improving the technical quality of the crowdsourced solution candidates is reported as one of the main issues. The survey in [17] provides a good overview on crowdsourcing in software engineering, showing increased research interest since 2010.

In the HCI field, crowdsourcing was successfully employed to adapt existing layouts to different screen sizes [20]. CrowdAdapt leverages the crowd for creating adapted web layouts and to select the best layout variants. It focuses on crowd-driven end-user development web layout tools. Crowdsourcing primarily serves as a means of exploring the design space and to elicit design requirements for various viewing conditions. CrowdAdapt, unlike other CS approaches in software engineering, uses unpaid crowd work. Unpaid crowd work can be successfully employed in HCI contexts due to the high number of users indirectly providing feedback through their interactions.

Similar to CSRE, CrowdDesign [28] employs the microtasking crowdsourcing model. To solve small user interface design problems, CrowdDesign uses paid crowd workers from Amazon Mechanical Turk. It focuses on diversity, i.e. for a set of decision points in the design space, CrowdDesign creates various and diverse solution alternatives. Early results report a high diversity, but only few crowd-created solutions achieved sufficiently high quality. In contrast, for CSRE, quality is the most relevant property. Diversity in the results is not intended.

Industrial case studies on CS in software development like [25] indicate that software development activities of lower complexity and relative independence are the most successful for CS. However, even more complex software development tasks can benefit from the lower costs, faster results creation and higher quality of successful crowdsourcing application. The case study considers two areas: test automation and front end modeling. Similar to CSRE, [25] focuses on the perspective of an enterprise crowdsourcing customer. Quality is one of the main problems as seen by a significant number of defects in the produced results. Stol et al. report on continuity problems since new crowd workers lack the experience from their predecessors and even re-introduce previously fixed bugs. From an enterprise perspective, they conclude that applicability of CS in software engineering is limited to self-contained areas without interdependencies, such as GUI design.

Latoza et al. [15] identify eight foundational orthogonal *dimensions of crowdsourcing for software engineering*: crowd size, task length, expertise demands, locus of control, incentives, task interdependence, task context and replication.

Existing successful crowdsourcing models like peer production, competitions and microtasking are characterize according to these dimensions. The CSRE Classification described in this article closely matches the microtasking model, as shown in Fig. 6. The differences are in only two of the eight dimensions: while in microtasking expertise demand is generally low, we consider it low to medium for source code classification. The amount of information about the entire system required by the worker (task context) is zero for microtasking, compared to low for the classification. The high similarity makes it likely that microtasking can be similarly successful on the small, independent and easily replicatable source code classification tasks as it already has proven in software testing. Both benefit from the high number of workers and the parallel execution of tasks. The key benefit of reduced time to market through crowdsourcing can be achieved for models with two characteristics: work must easily be broken down into short tasks and each task must be self-contained with minimal coordination demands [15]. CSRE meets both of these characteristics.

Distributed software development abstracting the workforce as crowd is described by Satzger et al. [22]. The public crowd is found on crowdsourcing platforms, the private crowd consists of company employees. The approach aims at collaborative crowdsourcing of software in enterprise contexts. It proposes to start with requirement descriptions in customer language. These are transformed into developer crowd tasks by a software architect. Developed collaboratively, the tasks are delegated to private and public crowds. Tasks can recursively be divided into smaller tasks and delegated to the crowd by crowd workers. The iterative development process tries to combine properties and artifacts from agile

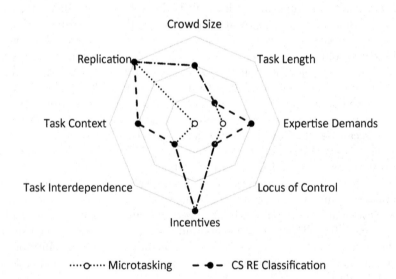

Fig. 6. Comparison of microtasking and crowdsourced reverse engineering (CS RE) classification [10].

development methodologies with collaborative crowdsourcing. Similarly, CSRE integrates with agile development, however, due to the nature of the reverse engineering classification task, it is not collaborative.

7 Evaluation

7.1 Experimental Design

We automatically extracted code fragments from BlogEngine.NET[6], an open-source ASP.NET-based blogging platform and randomly selected 10 of them. These 10 code fragments range from 7 to 57 LOC, on average 25.4 LOC. Using the following 8 categories from our source code knowledge ontology [11], we classified each of them manually:

1. Business Process
2. Algorithm
3. Persistence & Data Handling
4. User Interface & Interaction
5. Explanatory
6. Rule
7. Configuration
8. Deployment

Extending the 3 basic categories typically considered (presentation, application logic and persistence [7]), they provide a more fine-grained distinction of knowledge in source code. The implementation of CSRE was integrated into our existing source code annotation platform [11]. Crowd worker views with authentication mechanisms, classification task extraction based on doxygen (see footnote 3) and integration with crowdsourcing platform microWorkers were implemented.

Using `focus` and `blur` events, the crowd worker view tracks the time spent on it. The classification campaign ran for 14 days only with workers from the "best workers" group. 0.30 USD of financial reward were paid per 3 classifications.

7.2 Results

34 unique crowd workers contributed 187 classifications on our test data set. Table 2 shows the results. CF are the ten code fragments, Consensus indicates the result of the consensus voting. The numbers of classifications per category are stated in the categories cells. Bold values are the maxima, which are the basis for the majority consensus. Grey background marks the correct classification of the code fragment. Table 3 presents statistics to further analyze the results. $|C|$ is the number of classifications and $|W|$ the number of crowd workers. Note that the crowd worker and classification numbers differ due to multi-selections. The code fragment length in LOC is stated in l, Σt reports the overall time spent, $\bar{t}$ is the average time. Times are reported in seconds. The error rate f_e (cf. Eq. (4))

---

[6] http://www.dotnetblogengine.net/.

$$f_e = \frac{|C^-|}{|C|} \tag{4}$$

is the ratio of false classifications C^- to all classifications C of a code fragment. To investigate the degree of (dis-)agreement between the crowd worker classifications, we include entropy E (cf. Eq. 5)

$$E = -\sum_{i=1}^{k} f_i \lg f_i \tag{5}$$

and normalized Herfindahl dispersion measure H^* (cf. Eq. 6)

$$H^* = \frac{k}{k-1} \left(1 - \sum_{i=1}^{k} f_i^2 \right) \tag{6}$$

based on the relative frequencies f_i of the classifications in the $k = 8$ classes. E and H^* indicate the disorder/dispersion among crowd workers: a unanimous classification result yields $E = H^* = 0$. The higher the disagreement, the more different classifications, the closer E and H^* get to 1. Therefore, they are indicators of the classification certainty across the crowd workers. On average, 16 crowd workers created 18.7 classifications per code fragment.

7.3   Discussion

The average error rate of 0.655 seems high. With majority consensus, however, 7 of 10 code fragments were correctly classified. The minimum error rate was .25 on fragment B and the maximum 1 for fragment I. Provided a small expertise variation of the participating crowd workers, this indicates differences in the difficulty (fragment I was one of the longest) and the understanding of the categories. Rule was the most frequent classification (23.5%), Persistence & Data Handling (21.9%) s, Deployment the least voted (5.3%). No majorities

Table 2. Experimental results.

Categories

CF	1	2	3	4	5	6	7	8	Consensus
A	1	14	4	1	1	1	1	1	Algorithm
B	0	1	3	0	0	12	0	0	Rule
C	3	0	4	1	0	1	0	0	Persistence
D	2	5	6	3	0	5	2	0	Persistence
E	4	2	1	9	2	0	3	1	UIX
F	0	0	3	0	1	6	7	2	Config
G	3	1	1	2	2	6	0	0	Rule
H	0	2	12	2	4	3	2	2	Persistence
I	0	1	3	1	2	8	0	2	Rule
J	2	2	4	0	1	2	1	4	Persistence/Deployment

Table 3. Descriptive statistics.

CF	$|C|$	$|W|$	l	Σt	$\bar{t}$	f_e	E	H^*
A	24	19	18	2822	122	0.4167	0.6113	0.6906
B	16	16	20	2531	158	0.25	0.3053	0.4427
C	10	10	40	1128	112	0.6	0.6160	0.8
D	23	21	8	3033	131	0.7391	0.7402	0.8948
E	22	18	7	2580	117	0.5909	0.7228	0.8448
F	19	15	28	2857	150	0.6316	0.6146	0.8064
G	15	13	57	3225	215	0.8667	0.6891	0.8395
H	25	21	24	5249	209	0.52	0.6541	0.7893
I	17	13	40	1917	112	1	0.6504	0.7920
J	16	14	12	3393	212	0.9375	0.7902	0.9115

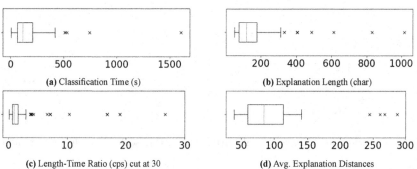

(a) Classification Time (s)

(b) Explanation Length (char)

(c) Length-Time Ratio (cps) cut at 30

(d) Avg. Explanation Distances

Fig. 7. Classification time and explanation length 1-dimensional distributions.

were achieved for Business Process and Explanatory, indicating that they might not be clear enough for the crowd workers. All other categories were correctly classified by the respective majorities.

Average entropy is 0.639 and average Herfindahl dispersion measure 0.757, their minima co-occur with minimal error rate, their maxima with the second-highest f_e. We found a significant ($\alpha = 0.05$) positive correlation (Pearson's $\rho = 0.724$, $p = 0.018$) between error rate and entropy and between error rate and Herfindahl dispersion measure ($\rho = 0.757$, $p = 0.011$), i.e. the more crowd workers vote one category, the less likely it is a wrong classification. No clear majorities for wrong classifications were observed. This supports the basic crowd-sourcing principle *"wisdom of the masses"* and the majority consensus assumption, that majorities are indicative of correct answers.

Our experiment did not show correlation between code fragment length and classification time (cf. also Fig. 8). This indicates influence of other variables and can be interpreted by assuming different levels of difficulty/clarity of the classification. Taking additionally correctness into account, correct classifications

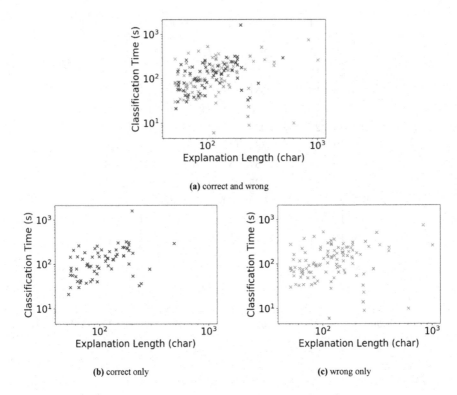

(a) correct and wrong

(b) correct only

(c) wrong only

Fig. 8. Classification time and explanation length (log scaled). (Color figure online)

showed less time outliers[7] than wrong classifications. This can be interpreted that longer classification time or longer explanations are indicative of uncertainty, leading to wrong classifications in most observed cases. Most of the outliers in Fig. 8c were *Persistance & Data Handling* code fragments, which was the second most frequently voted category and indicating, that the formulation of this category is not clear enough.

To further analyze the work of the crowd workers, we consider the distributions of time and explanation length, as well as derived length-time ratio and average explanation similarity per worker as shown in Fig. 7. Time median was 117.5 s, but the observed times varied widely: the inter quartile range was $IQR = 143.25$ s while upper outliers reached almost half an hour (1606 s). With the lower quartile at 65 s and min time 6 s, the relatively low times show that the tasks were formulated appropriately for microtasking, but also point to fake contributions as described below. Longer times, however, do not imply better accuracy as all but one time outlier in Fig. 7a belonged to C^-. Results of one specific crowd worker showed suspiciously identical time measurements (3×14 s, 3×33 s, 3×515 s), with identical explanations in all three groups which most likely resulted from the use of a record-and-replay script.

---

[7] We use $Q3 + 1.5IQR$ as outlier threshold in this article.

Explanation lengths (cf. Fig. 7b) ranged between 51 and 1017 characters (median $\tilde{d} = 119$) and were relatively close (IQR $= 100.5$) to the min threshold of 50 chars. Also, the lower quartile of 76.25 chars and outliers for time and length only appearing above the third quartile show that most of the workers wrote rather short explanations in short time. Figure 8 shows explanation length and time in relation, with correct classifications in green and wrong in red.

Time and explanation length distributions revealed that some crowd workers tried to gain the reward quickly through fake contributions. To identify these unlikely fast classifications, we calculated the length-time ratio in characters per second (cps). As shown in Fig. 7c, within a range of 0.13 to 61.2 cps, most of the values are distributed very closely (IQR 0.96 cps) around a median of 0.94 cps. The 20 outliers are likely to have copied texts. Analysis of the contents showed that these copies were most often copies of own previous explanations and sometimes from the task description. Since time does not only include writing time for justifications, but also time for source reading, understanding, deciding and selecting the classification, very high length-time ratios were only reachable if also little time was spent for thorough consideration, resulting in only 4 of 20 outliers belonging to C^+. Even when assuming fast thinking and typing capabilities, speeds are not likely to exceed the upper level of 16 cps measured at competitions[8]. However, 7 crowd workers exceeded this level. Manual analysis of explanations of the outliers determined the fastest worker who did not copy text and classified correctly at approx. 6.6 cps. The upper quartile at 1.63 cps shows that the vast majority of workers produced results in reasonable time.

To further identify workers who tried to complete the tasks very quickly through copying, we calculated average similarity of explanations per user using pairwise Levenshtein distance. The average distances range from 39 to 287 and are concentrated (IQR $= 54.5$) around a median of 83.8 (cf. Fig. 7d). Identical copies (distance 0) were received from 10 of 34 (29.4%) crowd workers, but the min average of 39 indicates that crowd workers did not exclusively copy. Note that 7 workers provided only one classification and could thus not copy their own texts. When normalized with the average explanation length, two workers had even less than 50% relative changes, copying most explanations with only minor adaptions. Manual inspection of crowd worker responses furthermore showed that 3 of 34 replied exclusively with code in their explanations, indicating a wrong understanding of the task.

In contrast to these negative cases, we also observed very thorough workers: Fragment J was split-voted as Persistence/Deployment. The explanation texts argued that J is related to persistence because the fragment is part of a class related to persistence. This observation was very interesting, because our dataset did not include the entire class. Thus, several crowd workers looked up the sample source code on the internet and read also the surrounding parts in order to classify. This level of active engagement and investment of time by the crowd workers to complete their task positively surprised us.

---

[8] cf. http://www.intersteno.org/.

In spite of the cases of low quality and fake contributions reported above – which are a known characteristic of crowdsourcing [2] – our quality control measures proved robust enough to yield 70% overall correctness. Our experiment has shown that the expertise level of the best crowd workers group on crowdsourcing platform microWorkers in combination with our quality control is sufficient to perform the reverse engineering classification activity and produce decent results. The overall degree of correctness of 70% is a good result similar to what can be achieved by a single expert performing the same task. However, with less than 20 USD expenses for classifying the ten code fragments, crowdsourcing is a significantly more cost-effective solution. The results indicate that crowdsourcing can be applied to perform specific reverse engineering activities, when they are broken down into small tasks and the process is guided by suitable quality control methods. Larger-scale experimentation could look deeper into the applicability of measures for disagreement as indicators for correctness, into suitability of other crowds from different platforms and into understanding the complexity of different reverse engineering tasks for crowd workers.

8 Conclusions and Future Work

This article motivated research in crowdsourced reverse engineering and outlined three major challenges – (1) automatic task extraction, (2) source code anonymization and (3) results aggregation and quality control – for applying crowdsourcing in the reverse engineering domain. To illustrate these challenges, we presented CSRE, our approach for concept assignment based on crowdsourced classifications. Extending our previous work in [10], we provided a detailed theoretical basis of the reverse engineering problem of concept assignment and, following an overview on existing approaches, presented a re-formulation of concept assignment as classification problem. Figure 2 refines the CSRE process [10], introducing relevant activities and artifacts and specified the anonymization algorithm in Algorithm 1. We presented a detailed problem analysis and the CSRE approach to address each of the challenges. Our classification task extraction method re-uses existing software documentation tools. To address aggregation and quality of crowdsourced results, we showcased a method combining several crowdsourcing quality control techniques. The extended review of related work of crowdsourcing in software engineering and reverse engineering shows a lack of crowdsourcing consideration in reverse engineering. At the same time, we reported examples of successful application of crowdsourcing in software engineering and demonstrated the similarity of crowdsourced concept assignment to microtasking in eight dimensions.

We reported on our experiences from an evaluation experiment on the crowdsourcing platform microWorkers, which produced 187 results by 34 crowd workers, classifying 10 code fragments at a low cost. The results' quality indicates that crowdsourcing is a suitable approach for certain reverse engineering activities. We were positively surprised by observations demonstrating an unexpectedly high level of engagement and effort by individual crowd workers to solve the tasks correctly. Calculating entropy and Herfindahl dispersion measure, we could see some evidence for the applicability of the crowdsourcing principle "wisdom of the masses" in our context, since higher levels of agreement was indicative of correctness. Extending previous evaluations [10], we added a focus on crowd worker behavior, in particular traces of fake contributions. The detailed analysis includes definitions, figures and interpretations of time and length distributions, time-length ratio and levenshtein-based similarity.

Future research challenges include achieving similar results in other areas of reverse engineering and improving the quality of the results. To identify these further reverse engineering activities and corresponding crowdsourcing paradigms, the matching procedure we used in Sect. 6 can be employed. An evaluation with a larger budget and crowd worker base should yield more insights into the applicability of crowdsourcing for reverse engineering activities, especially when combined with more specific, tailored measures of agreement in crowd worker results. An interesting research challenge is the crowd-based specification of concrete problem and solution domain models. Further investigations will show if this is possible through isolated microtasking with a more comprehensive classification ontology specific to the legacy system instance, or whether complex collaborative crowdsourcing approaches are necessary. While anonymization has been shown as the most difficult challenge, providing many opportunities for further research, application of our proposed method in contexts without anonymization requirements like intra-organization settings or open source projects will produce further insights.

Acknowledgements. The authors would like to thank Felix Förster for his valuable contributions towards this research. This research was supported by the eHealth Research Laboratory funded by medatixx GmbH & Co. KG.

References

1. Abebe, S.L., Tonella, P.: Extraction of domain concepts from the source code. Sci. Comput. Program. **98**, 680–706 (2015). https://doi.org/10.1016/j.scico.2014. 09.012
2. Allahbakhsh, M., Benatallah, B., Ignjatovic, A., Motahari-Nezhad, H.R., Bertino, E., Dustdar, S.: Quality control in crowdsourcing systems: issues and directions. IEEE Internet Comput. **17**(2), 76–81 (2013). https://doi.org/10.1109/MIC.2013. 20
3. Arboit, G.: A method for watermarking Java programs via opaque predicates. In: The Fifth International Conference on Electronic Commerce Research (ICECR-5), pp. 102–110 (2002)
4. Aversano, L., Canfora, G., Cimitile, A., De Lucia, A.: Migrating legacy systems to the web: an experience report. In: Proceedings of the Fifth European Conference on Software Maintenance and Reengineering, pp. 148–157. IEEE Computer Society Press (2001)
5. Biggerstaff, T.J., Mitbander, B.G., Webster, D.E.: Program understanding and the concept assignment problem. Commun. ACM **37**(5), 72–82 (1994). https:// doi.org/10.1145/175290.175300

6. Biggerstaff, T., Mitbander, B., Webster, D.: The concept assignment problem in program understanding. In: Proceedings of the 15th International Conference on Software Engineering, ICSE 1993, pp. 482–498. IEEE Computer Society Press (1993). https://doi.org/10.1109/ICSE.1993.346017

7. Canfora, G., Cimitile, A., De Lucia, A., Di Lucca, G.A.: Decomposing legacy programs: a first step towards migrating to client-server platforms. J. Syst. Softw. **54**(2), 99–110 (2000). https://doi.org/10.1016/S0164-1212(00)00030-3

8. Ceccato, M., Di Penta, M., Falcarin, P., Ricca, F., Torchiano, M., Tonella, P.: A family of experiments to assess the effectiveness and efficiency of source code obfuscation techniques. Empir. Softw. Eng. **19**(4), 1040–1074 (2014). https://doi.org/10.1007/s10664-013-9248-x

9. Eaddy, M., et al.: Do crosscutting concerns cause defects? IEEE Trans. Softw. Eng. **34**(4), 497–515 (2008). https://doi.org/10.1109/TSE.2008.36

10. Heil, S., Felix, F., Gaedke, M.: Exploring crowdsourced reverse engineering. In: Proceedings of the 13th International Conference on Evaluation of Novel Approaches to Software Engineering, pp. 147–158. SCITEPRESS - Science and and Technology Publications (2018)

11. Heil, S., Gaedke, M.: AWSM - Agile web migration for SMEs. In: Proceedings of the 11th International Conference on Evaluation of Novel Software Approaches to Software Engineering, pp. 189–194. SCITEPRESS - Science and Technology Publications (2016). https://doi.org/10.5220/0005869301890194

12. Heil, S., Gaedke, M.: Web migration - a survey considering the SME perspective. In: Proceedings of the 12th International Conference on Evaluation of Novel Approaches to Software Engineering, pp. 255–262. SCITEPRESS - Science and Technology Publications (2017). https://doi.org/10.5220/0006353502550262

13. Heil, S., Siegert, V., Gaedke, M.: ReWaMP: rapid web migration prototyping leveraging webAssembly. In: Mikkonen, T., Klamma, R., Hernández, J. (eds.) ICWE 2018. LNCS, vol. 10845, pp. 84–92. Springer, Cham (2018). https://doi.org/10.1007/978-3-319-91662-0_6

14. Kazman, R., Brien, L.O., Verhoef, C.: Architecture reconstruction guidelines third edition. Technical report, Software Engineering Institute, Carnegie Mellon University, Pittsburgh, PA, November 2003

15. Latoza, T.T.D., van der Hoek, A.: Crowdsourcing in software engineering: models, opportunities, and challenges. IEEE Softw. **33**(1), 1–13 (2016)

16. Loukis, E., Charalabidis, Y.: Active and passive crowdsourcing in government. In: Janssen, M., Wimmer, M.A., Deljoo, A. (eds.) Policy Practice and Digital Science. PAIT, vol. 10, pp. 261–289. Springer, Cham (2015). https://doi.org/10.1007/978-3-319-12784-2_12

17. Mao, K., Capra, L., Harman, M., Jia, Y.: A survey of the use of crowdsourcing in software engineering. J. Syst. Softw. **126**, 57–84 (2017). https://doi.org/10.1016/j.jss.2016.09.015

18. Marcus, A., Sergeyev, A., Rajlich, V., Maletic, J.I.: An information retrieval approach to concept location in source code. In: 2004 Proceedings of 11th Working Conference on Reverse Engineering, pp. 214–223. IEEE (2004). https://doi.org/10.1109/WCRE.2004.10

19. Nebeling, M., Leone, S., Norrie, M.C.: Crowdsourced web engineering and design. In: Brambilla, M., Tokuda, T., Tolksdorf, R. (eds.) ICWE 2012. LNCS, vol. 7387, pp. 31–45. Springer, Heidelberg (2012). https://doi.org/10.1007/978-3-642-31753-8_3

20. Nebeling, M., Speicher, M., Norrie, M.: CrowdAdapt: enabling crowdsourced web page adaptation for individual viewing conditions and preferences. In: Proceedings of the 5th ACM SIGCHI Symposium on Engineering Interactive Computing System, pp. 23–32 (2013). https://doi.org/10.1145/2480296.2480304

21. Rose, J., Jones, M., Furneaux, B.: An integrated model of innovation drivers for smaller software firms. Inf. Manag. **53**(3), 307–323 (2016). https://doi.org/10.1016/j.im.2015.10.005

22. Satzger, B., et al.: Toward collaborative software engineering leveraging the crowd. In: Economics-Driven Software Architecture, pp. 159–182. Elsevier (2014). https://doi.org/10.1016/B978-0-12-410464-8.00008-8

23. Saxe, J., Turner, R., Blokhin, K.: CrowdSource: automated inference of high level malware functionality from low-level symbols using a crowd trained machine learning model. In: 2014 9th International Conference on Malicious and Unwanted Software: The Americas (MALWARE), pp. 68–75. IEEE, October 2014. https://doi.org/10.1109/MALWARE.2014.6999417

24. Shepherd, D., Fry, Z.P., Hill, E., Pollock, L., Vijay-Shanker, K.: Using natural language program analysis to locate and understand action-oriented concerns. In: Proceedings of the 6th International Conference on Aspect-Oriented Software Development - AOSD 2007, p. 212. ACM Press, New York (2007). https://doi.org/10.1145/1218563.1218587

25. Stol, K.J., Fitzgerald, B.: Two's company, three's a crowd: a case study of crowdsourcing software development. In: Proceedings of the 36th International Conference on Software Engineering - ICSE 2014, pp. 187–198. ACM Press, New York (2014). https://doi.org/10.1145/2568225.2568249

26. Wagner, C.: Model-Driven Software Migration: A Methodology. Springer, Wiesbaden (2014). https://doi.org/10.1007/978-3-658-05270-6

27. Warren, I.: The Renaissance of Legacy Systems: Method Support for Software-System Evolution. Springer, Heidelberg (2012). https://doi.org/10.1007/978-1-4471-0817-7

28. Weidema, E.R.Q., López, C., Nayebaziz, S., Spanghero, F., van der Hoek, A.: Toward microtask crowdsourcing software design work. In: Proceedings of the 3rd International Workshop on CrowdSourcing in Software Engineering - CSI-SE 2016, pp. 41–44. ACM Press, New York (2016). https://doi.org/10.1145/2897659.2897664

A Detailed Analysis of the Influence of Saudi Arabia Culture on the Requirement Engineering Process

Tawfeeq Alsanoosy, Maria Spichkova[✉], and James Harland

School of Science, RMIT University, Melbourne, Australia
{tawfeeq.alsanoosy,maria.spichkova,james.harland}@rmit.edu.au

Abstract. Requirements Engineering (RE) process involves intensive communication and collaboration among software stakeholder members. Therefore, cultural values might influence both the RE process and its outcomes. The purpose of this study is to explore the influence of culture on the RE process in a context of a conservative culture: Saudi Arabia. Our goal is to understand how the RE process can be adapted, taking into account cultural aspects. We explored and analyzed the influence of Saudi culture though Hofstede's cultural theory. The empirical data was collected through a pilot case study with Saudi requirements engineering practitioners and software engineering researchers. The results are discussed, with a particular focus on the cultural influences on RE activities and the high-level descriptive models of the RE process.

Keywords: Requirement engineering · Software engineering · Software development process · Cultural aspects

1 Introduction

Requirements Engineering (RE) is one of the key phases of the software development life cycle. RE refers to the process of identifying and documenting the stakeholder's requirements. It was initially introduced for use within Western culture before the expected benefits began attracting the RE practitioners in various other cultures, to adopt the RE process. The RE process has a critical impact on software quality. It requires intensive communication between the requirements engineers and software stakeholders, in order to elicit, validate, and refine the requirements. This requires comprehensive communication skills, and an understanding of the individuals' behavior and culture [1,2].

Culture has a great influence on how individuals and companies operate and how they adopt techniques, methods, and practices to achieve their goals. Culture shapes the way in which people think, communicate, understand, and select what is important [3]. Cultures have distinctive beliefs, customs, and approaches to communication. This diversity is influenced by the behavior practice within these cultures. Hanisch et al. [4] argued that the social and cultural aspects of

© Springer Nature Switzerland AG 2019
E. Damiani et al. (Eds.): ENASE 2018, CCIS 1023, pp. 240–260, 2019.
https://doi.org/10.1007/978-3-030-22559-9_11

RE affect the success of software development and it cannot be ignored. The objectives of our research are to identify the cultural influences on the RE processes and practices, and to analyze how the RE process can be adapted to take into account cultural aspects.

To analyze cultural aspects, many social psychologists propose theoretical frameworks that illustrate the key cultural factors that distinguish one culture from another, cf. e.g., Hofstede et al. [3], Trompenaars [5], and Hall [6]. However, Hofstede cultural theory is the most accepted cultural theory. To the best of our knowledge, our previous work was the first study adopted Hofstede cultural theory to explore the influence of Saudi culture on the RE process [7]. Our studies focus on individual and social aspect of software development, cf. [8,9], as well as requirements for global product development, focusing on diversity of regulations, laws, and cultural aspects cf. [10,11]. In this study, we went further and investigated cultural aspects in details, focusing on the Saudi Arabian culture.

Contributions: The RE process is originated from Western culture and hence most of the standard RE practices are driven by its culture. Successfully applying such process/practice within different cultural context should, therefore considering the cultural differences. This study investigates the impact of the Saudi national culture on the practice of RE process. We collected data through interviewing 6 requirement engineer practitioners and 2 software engineering researchers about the RE practices that were performed and adapted the Saudi Arabian culture. We then identified a model designed to illustrate the interplay between the core RE process and the Hofstede cultural theory, within the Saudi culture. Also, this study reveals 10 cultural factors and 5 high-level descriptions of the RE process model used in the Saudi context. The results demonstrate the feasibility of our hypothesis. This study will be useful for improving the RE process within the Saudi culture and any culture that has similar national cultural profiles, as per Hofstede [3].

Outline: This chapter is structured as follows. Section 2 introduces the background of our research, focusing on RE processes and Hofstede's cultural theory. Our conceptual Model and hypotheses are presented in Sect. 3. Section 4 describes the research methodology. The results of the case study are presented in Sect. 5. The related work is discussed in Sect. 6. Section 7 summarizes the paper.

2 Background

2.1 Requirements Engineering Process

Zave [12] defines RE as *"the branch of software engineering that is concerned with the real-world goals for, functions of, and constraints on software systems. It is also concerned with the relationship of these factors to precise specifications of software behavior, and to their evolution over time and across software families"*. As highlighted by Nuseibeh [13], the above definition features three important aspects of RE: (1) RE is concerned with real-world goals, (2) its aim is to provide precise specifications of the requirements, and (3) the definition emphasizes the reality of the rapid change of user's needs. Thus, requirements specification serves as a basis for the development of the system, its design and architecture, cf. [14]. In this paper, the term *requirements engineer* is used to refer to the practitioner who works on specifying, analyzing, and documenting users' requirements.

The RE process is usually described as the following five core (sub-)processes/ activities, cf. also [15–17]:

- **Requirements Elicitation:** The process of gathering and identifying stakeholders' functional and nonfunctional requirements;
- **Requirements Analysis:** The process of refining stakeholders' requirements to ensure that all stakeholders' requirements are clear, complete, and consistent;
- **Requirements Specification:** The process of creating a written description of stakeholders' requirements, needs and constraints in a consistent format;
- **Requirements Validation:** The activity to ensure that the requirements are correct, demonstrate the wanted quality and will satisfy stakeholders' need;
- **Requirements Management:** The process of tracing changes to the requirements over the time of system development.

The sequence of the above five activities (RE process model) is often preformed in different orders. Most of the RE process models fall into three structures: linear, linear with iterations between activities, and iterative cf. [18,19]. In practice, RE model is iterative, incremental, and interlace. Wiegers and Beatty [20] structure the RE model as a linear sequence with iterations between its activities because it allows for better management and implementation of the requirements. As an example of iterative/incremental approach is agile RE. In the past decade, agile RE approach have been widely adopted for eliciting users' requirements to overcome the challenges emerged from the traditional RE practice. Agile RE allows for iterative implementation of requirements and focuses on continuous releases and incorporating customer feedback with every iteration. However, the nature of the requirements, the behavior of stakeholders, the experiences of software teams, and national and organizational culture influence the RE process and its practises [21–23]. As a result, RE process model might be preformed differently from culture to another.

2.2 Hofstede's Cultural Theory

There are several definitions for *"culture"*. One of the most highly accepted definitions is introduced by Hofstede. Hofstede[1] defines *culture* as *"collective programming of the mind which distinguishes members of one human group from another"* [3,24]. We adopt this theory as background for our research not only because Hofstede conducted one of the most inclusive studies on the influence

---

[1] This work has been cited 82,496 times according to the Google Scholar, retrieved 20/08/2018.

of cultural values on the workplace, but also because Hofstede theory is widely accepted and adopted in software engineering cultural studies, cf. [25–27]. Hofstede conducted the research with employees working for IBM, covering more than 70 countries. The model describes the influences of a individuals' culture on the values of its members, and how these values correlate with behavior.

Hofstede [3] proposed to focus on the following six dimensions of a national culture:

- **Power Distance Index (PDI):** expresses the degree to which the less authority individual accepts that power and privilege are unequally distributed among the society members. The main concern of this dimension is about how a society handles inequalities among the society members such as power, status or wealth.
- **Individualism Versus Collectivism (IDV):** expresses the degree to which individual within a society collaborates with others. In the high individualism societies (individualist), the interests of an individual predominate over the interests of a group as well as it would encourage individual achievement. In contrast, the low individualism (collectivist) societies the interest of a group predominates over the interest of an individual as well as it would encourage group achievement.
- **Masculinity Versus Femininity (MAS):** expresses the degree to which the gender roles are allocated. A society is described as masculine *"when emotional gender roles are clearly distinct: men are supposed to be assertive, tough, and focused on material success, whereas women are supposed to be more modest, tender, and concerned with the quality of life"*. However, a society is described as feminine *"when emotional gender roles overlap: both men and women are supposed to be modest, tender, and concerned with the quality of life"*.
- **Uncertainty Avoidance Index (UAI):** expresses the degree to which individuals feel either uncomfortable or comfortable toward unfamiliar situations. Low uncertainty societies are more tolerant with unusual situations and new technology or process. Meanwhile, high uncertainty societies fear of unfamiliar situations and new technology or process.
- **Long- vs. Short-term Orientation (LTO):** expresses the degree to which people within a society are linked to past while dealing with the present and the future challenges. Long-term oriented society stands for *"the fostering of virtues oriented toward future rewards"*. This has been explained through comparison of attributes like respect for circumstances and having a sense of shame. Short-term orientation stands for *"the fostering of virtues related to the past and present"*. This has been explained through comparison of attributes respect traditions and preservation individuals' face.
- **Indulgence Versus Impulses (IND):** expresses the degree to which people within a society have fun and enjoy life without restrictions and regulations.

Figure 1 shows the Hofstede's scores for Saudi Arabia and the United States, for each cultural dimension. In Hofstede theory, each country is allocated a numerical score within the above dimensions to define the society of this country.

The score runs from 0–100 with 50 as a natural value. The Hofstede's rule for the score is that if a score is above 50, the culture relatively high on that dimension. For example, the United States score of the IDV dimension is (91) and it is considered high.

As our study argues that most of the RE standards are driven by the United States culture and the adaptation of the RE process requires considering the cultural differences, let us present a brief comparison between Saudi Arabia and the United States as per Hofstede [3].

The score of PDI is very high (95) in Saudi Arabia, which means that Saudi people accept authority's decisions without any justifications and expect to be told what to do. In the United States the score of PDI is 40, which means that a person is able to influence other people's ideas and behavior. With a score of 25, Saudi Arabia is considered as a collective society where people belong to group that takes care of them. In contrast, the United State's scores very high (90) on the IDV dimension, which indicates that it is more individualist than Saudi Arabia and thus people look after themselves and their immediate families only. Saudi Arabia scores 80 for UAI which means that Saudi people prefer avoiding uncertainty situations, which may express the difficulties of coping with unexpected situations. In the United State, there is fair degree of acceptance for new innovative or idea and a willing to do something new.

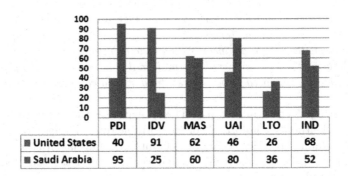

	PDI	IDV	MAS	UAI	LTO	IND
■ United States	40	91	62	46	26	68
■ Saudi Arabia	95	25	60	80	36	52

Fig. 1. Hofstede's culture scores for Saudi Arabia and the United States.

For the MAS dimension, a score of 62/60 for Saudi Arabia and the United States indicate that conflicts are resolved by letting the strong win and high authorities are supposed to be decisive. The low score of LTO for both cultures indicate that establishing trust is the main concern as well as respect for traditions. Lastly, Saudi Arabia with a score of 52 does not clearly show any preference of IND dimension. Whereas, a score of 68 in the United States indicates that people work hard and play hard.

3   Conceptual Model and Proposition

Table 1 presents our conceptual model that is adopted from our previous work, presented in [7]. Each "?" in the table means that the corresponding cultural dimension might have a major influence on the corresponding RE activity, whereas each "X" means that the corresponding cultural dimensions might have less/no influence on the corresponding RE activity.

Table 1. Influence of cultural dimensions on RE activities (adopted from [7]).

RE activity	Cultural dimensions					
	PDI	IDV	MAS	UAI	LTO	IND
Elicitation	?	?	?	?	?	X
Analysis	?	?	?	?	?	X
Specification	X	X	X	?	?	X
Validation	?	?	?	X	?	X
Management	?	?	X	X	X	X

Referring to the Hofstede's scores, we believe that three of Hofstede's dimensions have major impacts on the practice of RE process in Saudi Arabia, while the other dimensions might impact. Therefore, we formulated the following three propositions:

- **High Impact:** The high value/score of PDI/IDV/UAI in Saudi Arabia has a significant impact on the RE activities.
- **Low Impact:** The slightly low value/score of MAS/LTO in Saudi Arabia may have an impact on the RE activities.
- **No Impact:** The IND dimension has no impact on the RE activities in Saudi Arabia.

4   Research Methodology

In an effort to explore the influence of Saudi Arabia culture on the RE process, we conducted a qualitative study through a pilot case study. Qualitative research is used to investigate a social behavior from the view of the study participants to achieve a comprehensive understanding of the phenomena. We interviewed a number of Saudi software practitioners and academics in order to understand their view about the RE process in Saudi Arabia. Here, we used a pilot case study to understanding the Saudi cultural influence on the RE process. The study was conducted following the process suggested in [28], where the process contains the following steps: First, we defined the research questions and contracted the study design. Then, we developed the case study procedure and protocol for data collection. Next, we conducted in-depth interviews in Saudi Arabia. Finally, the data analysis procedure was applied to the data. The following research questions were formulated:

RQ1: What requirements engineering activities are adopted by the Saudi requirements engineers?

RQ2: What cultural aspects and traditions influence the requirements engineering practice in Saudi Arabia?

RQ3: How requirement engineering process is adapted for use in the context of the Saudi culture?

4.1 Data Collection

To collect the data, we interviewed eight participants: six software practitioners, one senior academic, and one lecturer in a Saudi university. The snowballing technique was used to recruit the participants. Participants were asked to propose other persons who could probably contribute to the study. Neuman [29] suggests that snowballing sampling is often used if the sample size is small or if there is a preference to select well-informed participants. In addition, the snowball recruiting technique was beneficial for this study because social networking, in a collectivist society, is the main source of information [3].

The practitioners interviewees were selected based the following criteria:

1. The participants had to be involved in the RE process during systems development;
2. Working in a Saudi software company;
3. Be employed in a small- to a medium-sized organization; and
4. Engaged in eliciting the requirements from Stakeholders.

The academics interviewees were selected based the following criteria:

1. The participants had to be involved in the RE process; and
2. Working in a Saudi university.

The social nature of this study leaded us to adopt semi-structured interviews. The questions were mixed of open-ended and close-ended types including 30 questions, focusing on the RE process adopted in Saudi Arabia and the cultural factors influence the RE process from Saudi Arabian context. When the participants accepted the invitation to participate, the following documents were sent to them one day before the face-to-face interview: the interview questions, the explanatory statement and the consent form. The average duration of the interviews was about 90 min. Some interviews held in Arabic where other in English, based on the interviewees' preferences.

4.2 Data Analysis

A thematic analysis method was used to analyze data from the interview transcripts, following the guidelines described by Braun and Clarke [30]. As per Marks and Yardley [31], the benefit of thematic analysis is that it allows to combine analysis of the frequency of codes with analysis of their meaning in context, to overcome the major criticisms of content analysis. The process of thematic data analysis goes through six phases as described in [7]. All recordings were transcribed and coded manually using coding and pattern matching techniques [32]. Codes that emerged in each interview were compared and analyzed. Finally, we grouped the emerged 16 themes into three main groups: the RE process, aspect, the cultural aspects, and the RE process model.

4.3   Validity and Reliability

Validity and reliability of research aim to ensure the trustworthiness of a study. We considered the three validity aspects of exploratory research recommended by Yin [33]: First, we constructed this study through in-depth reviewing of the literature. Second, we reviewed some of the participants' software documentation that was obtained during the interview as a second source of evidence. Finally, we established a chain of evidence from the beginning of the search through selecting the study interviewees, using the interview process and transcribing and interpreting the data. External validity achieved by using Braun's guidelines for coding and analyzing the data [34]. The reliability was achieved by documenting a rich description of the research method and the interview protocol as it is recommended by Neuman [29].

5   Results and Discussion

This section reports and discusses the results obtained through 8 interviews to answer our three research questions. First, we report the adopted RE activities by the Saudi study participants. Then, we present 10 cultural aspects influencing the RE process in the Saudi Arabian context. Finally, we present 5 RE process models adopted by the study practitioners, taking into account Saudi cultural aspects.

5.1   Requirement Engineering Process

To collect the responses to the first research question, the interviewees were asked to describe the RE processes performed in all software development projects they conducted. From the participants' responses, we identified core aspects that describe the state of RE practice in the Saudi context, related to the 5 RE activities (see Sect. 2.1).

Requirements Elicitation
Requirements elicitation was named by all participants as an important part of the process. The interviewees generally elicit requirements (1) either from software stakeholders directly, or (2) by searching about the problem domains, or (3) by asking stakeholders for examples of similar systems. Four requirement elicitation techniques were noted: interviews, focus groups, observations and prototypes.

The interviewees believed that it was important to understand the vision of the top managers or software owner before eliciting the requirements from the end users, especially for a new system. The goals, scope, objectives and main issues from high authority people were used as guidelines to develop software that meets the company's vision, where the end users' needs are less important.

Almost 80% of the interviewees agreed that a face-to-face interview was the best method used for eliciting customers' requirements. Adopting interview as an elicitation method assisted the study participants to

- acquire a comprehensive knowledge about users' requirements;
- verify the requirements during the session;
- help clients to express their needs freely;
- minimize the time to establish a trust; and
- build a good relationship with the customers.

One participant reported one serious problem in implementing software sponsored by the government: requirements were identified by representative stakeholders from the government and no end users participated the elicitation session.

Requirement Analysis

Another RE activity reported by almost all participants was requirements analysis. The main objective of this activity is to (1) detect and resolve conflicts and (2) to know how the requirements should be implemented.

The participants expressed that analyzing the requirements not only involve examining the software functionality, but also the technical, business and cultural aspects. As an example of the business aspect was that an end user may request to delete records in the business sheet, whereas according the international financial and accounting standard, such records cannot be removed. An example of technical aspects was that an end user might request a feature that threatens the company's security. For cultural aspects, an end user might ask for changing the interface language. To analyze the requirements, two interviewees used a scenario-based analysis method, which is a description of the steps needed to complete a given task.

Requirement Validation

As indicated by interviewees, requirements validation was not an independent phase, as validation activities are either embedded in the requirement analysis phase, or not conducted at all. One participant stated that *"we only analysis the requirement if we are confident that it should be implemented"*, whereas other participant stated that *"we do not have a validation phase"*. According to Hofstede et al. [3], high uncertainty avoidance culture such as Saudi Arabia (cf. Sect. 2.2) prefers a need for more short-term feedback. This might explain why the Saudi RE participants joined the requirement analysis and validation in one activity.

Requirement Specification

All participants from industry did not adopt any recommended requirements specification standard and did not follow any guidelines in constructing the documentation template. Instead, the requirements specification was structured based on the requirement engineer's experience or following a documentation template used for some previous projects. The participants gave the following three reasons for not adopting any requirements documentation standards:

- The requirement engineer and the client were satisfied with the current requirements specification;
- None of the existing specification standards has been released in an Arabic requirements documentation version; translating or using English documentation standards was not convenient.
- The software teams are highly qualified (by their own definition) and, therefore, there was no need for a high level description of the process.

However, from the point of view of academic participants, following the international specification standards (e.g., IEEE Standard 830-1998 [35], ISO/IEC/IEEE 29148:2011 [36]) with a customization to the company standard is seen as a more preferable solution than structuring the software specification based on the requirement engineer's experience.

Interestingly, a practitioner developed a document management system to store all projects' requirements and documentation. The software archived including, information about the company, all user requirements, UML diagram and flowchart, appendixes, and any document that obtained from the user. Thus, all departments and teams within the company were able to get access to the software and system documentation anytime.

Requirement Change Management

Interestingly, the participants did not perceive requirements change management as a part of the RE process. However, requirements changes were occurred often, and the study participants accepted changes. 2 out of 5 participants tracked changes to in the requirements over the time of system development. To manage the changes, the software team examined the effectiveness of this change on the software and then reported the implication of the proposed change to the client. While, other participants either did not accept any additional requirements after freezing the RE process because they followed a waterfall model or managing the requirements in ad-hoc manner.

This demonstrates that adaptation of the good practices and standards of the RE process is still in progress in Saudi Arabia. The findings of our study concur with Alnafjan's work [37].

5.2 Cultural Influences on the Requirement Engineering Process

Based on the result of the interviews, we identified 10 cultural aspects influencing the RE process: deference, autocratic decision-making, limited trust, belief in expertise, relationships, empathy with clients, letting the strongest win, gender segregation, dress code, and using English language. We grouped these aspects into 5 cultural dimensions. We covered 4 out of 6 Hofstede' s dimensions (PDI, UAI, IDV, MAS) and introduced a new dimension to present specific cultural factors that cannot fit the Hofstede's dimensions.

Table 2 illustrates the RE cultural model of Saudi Arabia culture, adopted from [7]. In this model, we exclude two of the Hofstede's cultural dimensions and added a new dimension. We exclude the LTO and IND dimensions because of our data does not explore any influences or dependencies of this dimension on the Saudi RE process. This support our hypothesis that IND does not have an influence on the RE process. Also, we add the specific cultural factors, as it emerges during analyzing the study participants' interviews. We name it specific because it is exclusively distinct to the Saudi culture.

Table 2. Influence of Saudi culture on RE activities, adopted from [7].

RE activity	Cultural dimensions				
	PDI	IDV	MAS	UAI	Specific
Elicitation	✓	✓		✓	✓
Analysis	✓		✓	✓	
Specification		✓			✓
Validation	✓		✓		
Management	✓	✓			

Power Distance Index

As mentioned in Sect. 2.2, the score of Power Distance Index (PDI) in Saudi Arabia is defined as 95 (very high). The following three points fit this dimension: deference to elderly people and to high authorities, autocratic decision-making, and lack of trust.

Deference: Deference to elderly people and to high authorities was identified as a Saudi cultural aspect effecting the RE process. As per Hofstede et al. [3], in the countries with a high PDI, showing respect for parents and older people is a basic and lifelong virtue. The data collection highlighted the fact that due to the Saudi Arabian culture, demonstrating respect was habitually practiced. A total of five participants reported that deference of customers, especially elderly and high authorities, is seen by them as a standard practice. One of the participants stated that *'most of the time, I cannot argue with elderly or high authority employees'*.

Autocratic Decision-Making: Hofstede et al. [3] stated that *"power distance will affect the degree of centralization of the control and decision-making structure and the importance of the status of the negotiators"*. In that context, the analysis of the collected data demonstrated that the decision-making was significantly consultative and autocratic rather than democratic. The reason for this is a centralized decision-making in Saudi Arabia, i.e., all decisions are taken by high authorities.

Three participants believed that *'the manager will agree on what he thinks it is beneficial to the business. All about business. If it is beneficial, he will accept it'.* and therefore the study participants accept and agree one what is decided by the top managers. However, one participant claimed a critical drawback to the centralized decision as *'If he [decision maker] is satisfied, we do not care about the end users' needs'.*

Limited Trust: According to Hofstede et al. [3], high PDI cultures suffer from lack of trust. A total of five participants mentioned that lack of trust in both Saudi and non-Saudi requirements engineer was a problematic issue. During the elicitation session, clients tended to not openly discuss the main core of the business issues, instead, clients may ask the requirements engineer about: the number of projects he was involved in, years of experience, race, the education and technique background, etc. Surprisingly, the level of trust is normally established based on the requirements engineering's nationality or based on the strength of the relationship that built during the RE phase. One participant commented that some nationalities were highly trusted just because Saudi people believe in them. Also, three participants agreed that establishing a good relationship with customers significantly increased the trust level. However, if the level of trust is not maintained on the early stage of the software development life cycle, the RE process might end up with an absolute failure to achieve its purposes.

Uncertainty Avoidance Index
The score of Uncertainty Avoidance Index (AUI) in Saudi Arabia is defined as 80 (very high), cf. Sect. 2.2. According to Hofstede et al. [3], in high uncertainty cultures, strong belief in expertise and their knowledge is common.

The participants assume that Saudi customers accept their recommendations and suggestions not because they are experts in the field, but because these recommendations are important and valuable. According to the interviewees, presenting facts about the best way to solve the problem can change software stakeholders' minds easily. However, this expresses only the view point and self-estimates of requirements engineers rather than provides a complete real picture, where the belief in expertise (including the belief in one's own expertise) plays a large role.

Individualism
Saudi Arabia is considered as a low Individualism (refer to collectivism, cf. Sect. 2.2) society, where the following points play an important role: building a relationship and empathy with users.

Building a Relationship: In a collectivism cultures, building a relationship in workplaces is very important, similar to family relationships. Interviews, as a face-to-face method to elicit the requirements, permit the software engineers to create an emotional relationship with the client, which was indicated as a positive culture aspect. Six participants highlighted that building a good relationship means having an in-depth understanding of users' problem domain as well as establishing a certain level of trust. For example, during the requirements elicitation building a relationship with the clients can be used as facilitator to overcome barriers (e.g, lack of user involvement) or challenges in general such as project over-budget.

Empathy with Users: Achieving user satisfaction was continually mentioned as the reason to accept new changes, which can be explained in terms of feeling empathy with the client to fulfill his needs. Four participants agreed that clients should be satisfied, as participant expressed *'He is a client. We cannot make him unhappy'.*

Masculinity

Solving conflicts by **letting the strongest win** was often mentioned in the transcript. As per Hofstede' theory, the resolution of conflicts in a masculine society (Saudi Arabia is considered a masculine society with score 60) is solved by letting the strongest win [3].

Autocratic behavior was indicated when the interviewee spoke about solving conflicts between end users and high authorities. The findings showed that most of the conflicts were resolved by agreeing with the top managers' preferences rather than giving end users an opportunity to justify this need. Moreover, we find that this cultural aspect is highly related to the PDI dimension.

Specific Cultural Factors

The study identified three points that are very for Saudi culture: gender segregation, dress code, and English language, where the first two can also be seen as a very special application of masculinity dimension.

Gender Segregation: A total of five participants asserted that communicating with Saudi women during the RE process, even during the elicitation activity, was not an issue. The study participants approached the female end users in their workplace, even though the workplace was separated into male and female sections. The practitioners elicited the requirements through either face-to-face meetings or using communication applications such skype or e-mail. However, only one participant reported that gathering the requirements from female was difficult due to shyness and self-respect of the Saudi women.

Dress Code: This theme identified when the participants mentioned how the clients perceive the dress code. One practitioner mentioned that *'So, somehow it is a cultural perspective: If you are wearing a suit, if you are speaking English, then you are doing the right thing'.*

English Language: Even though the official written language in Saudi Arabia is Arabic, all participants indicated that software documentation is usually written in English, especially for government businesses. Since Saudi people have diverse levels of the speaking and writing English language skills, adopting English language to communicate and document the requirements might introduce miscommunication and misunderstanding between the clients and requirements engineers and, therefore, it might affect the overall RE process.

Requirement Engineering Process Model

New: To collect the responses to the third research question, only the requirements engineer practitioners were requested to allocate each RE activity in sequence as it is performed. The data was used to represent the RE precess model for each study practitioners, except for one. We excluded the RE process model of one practitioners because no clear RE process model was identified. We used the names Alfa, Bate, Gamma, Delta and Epsilon to refer to the anonymised Saudi RE practitioners.

The RE process model adopted by Alfa consisted of three main activities: elicitation, analysis, and specification, as represented in Fig. 2. The requirements were elicited first from top managers and decision-makers then from end users. Next, the requirements were analyzed. Alfa analyzed by searching for the actual procedure/ requirements that used in the similar problem domain. The goal of search was to match and validate the procedure/requirements with international standards and principles. Alfa stated: *'we need to search in order to understand the process alignment with gathering the requirements. So, we then match users' need and procedure with the search outcomes.'* Then, the user requirements, without the proposed solutions, were documented. The requirements specification should be approved by the end users' manager in order to be implemented. Alfa followed a linear model with iteration.

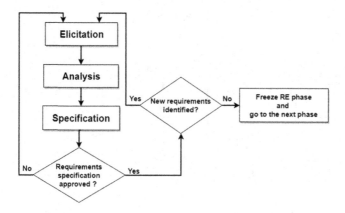

Fig. 2. The RE process model followed by Alfa.

The RE process model adopted by Beta consisted of two independent phases. The first phase started internally with involving only the software team members. The purpose of this phase, as stated by Beta was to *'capture the most common issues on the searched problem domain'* and use it to propose requirements/solutions to the clients. The team searched and analyzed using different resources (e.g. the Internet, previous software, similar software) to gain insight into the potential needs of the users and the domain problems. The discovered problems were analysed to find the best solutions, documented, implemented, and stored in the repository. The repository was created to store the identified critical problem and the proposed solutions, user requirements and information.

The second phase started with the clients. At this phase, the real requirements were elicited from end users, and then analysed by adapting the user' requirements with the predefined issues in the first phase. Then, Beta sought decision-makers approval of the requirements, which might take several meetings to match the vision of the manager and end users. Only if the requirements were approved by the decision-makers, Beta added it into the requirements specification. As it was explained by Beta, *'after we analyse the requirements, we seek approval and agreement. Then, we can document the requirement. [what about the validation? Interviewer asked] Validation, we have already validated the requirement in the analysis because we only analysis the requirement if we are confident that it should be implemented.'*

Figure 3 depicts the ER process model adopt by Beta. Beta's RE process model had a generally linear structure with some iterations among the RE activities. The time Beta's company allocated to the RE process was nearly 40% of the project time because of (1) the time spend at the first phase to analysis the problem domain and (2) the frequent acceptance of new requirements/changes at any stage of the software life cycle. Thus, the RE process performed several times across the software life cycle.

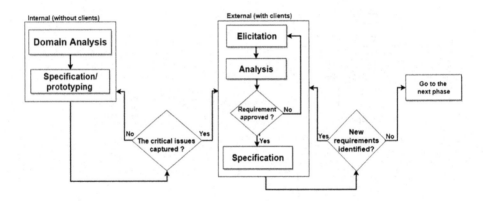

Fig. 3. The RE process model followed by Beta.

The RE process model Gamma's company used was primarily adapted from Enterprise Resources Planning (ERP) methodology (Fig. 4). According to Gamma, the methodology consisted of five phases: *'scope, blueprint, realisation, user acceptance test and go-live'*. Two phases dedicated to the RE process: scope and blueprint.

The purpose of the scope phase was to identify what requirements were in/out of the scope for the corresponded release or iteration. In the blueprint phase, the users' requirements and the proposed solutions were analyzed, documented and validated with the users. The main goal of the blueprint phase was to make sure that only the approved requirements, with the estimated cost and time, would be implemented during the current release. According to Gamma *'in the blue print, we document all the user requirements including our solution. This may take several meeting with the client till the document is signed off. Also, we estimate the time/cost needed to deliver during this phase.'* Gamma RE process model had generally linear sequence with iterations within each phases.

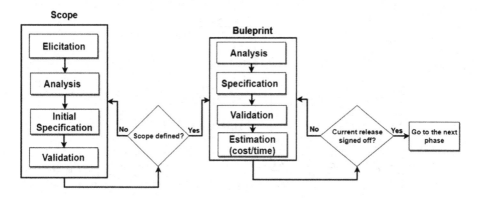

Fig. 4. The RE process model followed by Gamma: for one release.

The RE process model adopted by Delta software company consisted of two phases (Fig. 5). As mentioned by Delta, *'there are two phases: before signing the contract and after signing the contract'*. The goal of the first phase was to elicit high level requirements in order to estimate the approximate cost of the project and sign off the contract. After the of project was singed, the second RE method phase started. This phase consisted of four activities: requirement elicitation, analysis, specification, and sign off the requirement specification. The goal of the second phase was to deeply elicit and understated users' requirements. This involved having several meeting with the client and decision makers to obtain and approve the requirements. Most the time, Delta meet the decision makers and visionaries from the client side. The time Delta allocated to the RE process was nearly 25% of the project time and the RE process model had generally linear sequence with iterations within only the second phase.

The RE process model adopted by Epsilon generally included three activities: elicitation, specification and prototype (Fig. 6). These three activities were performed iteratively until the client satisfied with the prototype version. For Epsilon, providing prototype helped him to get a frequent feedback from clients and helped clients to make quick decisions.

Table 3 summaries the RE process models identified from the study participants. There is an assumption that the RE process has a universal standard process [15,18,20]. However, the empirical data illustrates that each study participant created his own RE process model, which appropriate for the client and organization culture. The study participants tended to follow a linear with iteration RE process model. Also, in the most cases RE was performed at the start of the project and each time requirements were added or changed.

RE activities tended to occur across two phases. Although each participant named the phases differently, the main purpose of each phase were nearly the same. For example, Gamma used the first phase (Scope) to define the boundary between what is in/out for specific release, whereas Delta dedicated the first phase to identify the high level requirements in order to estimate the project cost,

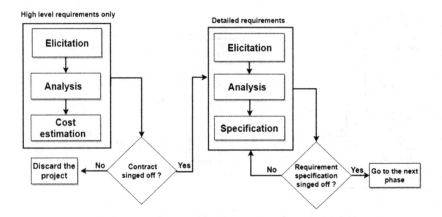

Fig. 5. The RE process model followed by Delta.

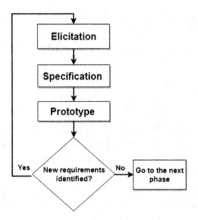

Fig. 6. The RE process model followed by Epsilon.

and therefore sign off the contract. Eventually, the outcome was to define the product vision and scope. The vision and scope document, for both practitioners, contained the software's business requirements and common understanding of the software's outcome. Moreover, we found that tow study participants used a incremental approach to identify the requirements.

As the culture has an influence on the RE process, it can be concluded that adapting the linear with iterative RE process model in the Saudi context emerged from 5 cultural aspects. These cultural aspects can be categorized into 3 of the Hofstede's dimensions: PDI, IDV, and UAI.

The high PDI in Saudi Arabia lead to (1) **the centralization of the decision-making** and (2) the **different vision and needs between the decision-makers and end users**. Because the practitioners cannot only rely on end users to approval the requirements or obtain his need, the RE practition-

Table 3. Requirements engineering process models.

Participant	RE in project lifecycle	Number of phases	Model
Alfa	Start of the project	1	Linear with iteration
Beta	Continuous	2	Linear with iteration
Gamma	Start of each iteration	2	Incremental
Delta	Start of the project	2	Linear with iteration
Epsilon	Continuous	1	Incremental
Zeta	Not clear	Not clear	Not clear

ers need to approve the requirements from the high authority and satisfy the visual of the decision-makers, if it conflicts with the end user need. As a result, the practitioners iteratively perform the RE process till satisfy the stakeholders.

The low IDV of the Saudi Arabia people lead to (1) **the high tolerance with requirement change** and (2) the **high concern to achieve user satisfaction**. These two cultural aspects contribute to adopting liner with iteration because most of the study participants want to fulfill stakeholders' needs. Thus, the frequent accept of requirements or changes force the practitioners to perform the RE process several times.

The high UAI in Saudi Arabia lead to **the absence of validating users' requirements**. Most of the study participants did not spend time with the client to validate each requirement. Thus, detecting defects at a later stage cause a high number of iteration of the RE phase and other software development phases to solve the issue.

6   Related Work

Several studies have investigated the impact of culture and cultural differences on RE processes. For example, Damian and Zowghi [38] analyzed the challenges faced by stakeholders during the RE process in distributed multi-site organizations. By conducting in-depth interviews, the study showed that culture and cultural differences have negative impacts on RE activities. However, the existing studies do not propose any solution that can be generalized and applied in the future. The goal of our work is to solve this problem.

Thanasankit [1] conducted a study on whether the specifics of Thai culture might have influences on the RE process, in particulate, the concept of power distance. According to the authors, the communication and decision-making process in Thailand is influenced by the unequal power distribution and the level of uncertainty. Based on Thai cultural aspects, the researchers suggested some strategies to improve RE practices. These strategies focus on Thai culture only. However, the results of the study concur with our hypothesis that the cultural influence on the RE process might be significant and it should be taken into account to improve the RE practices. In contrast to Thanasankit [1], our research adopted the six dimensions of the Hofstede's cultural theory on the RE process and the results of the pilot case study demonstrated the feasibility of our approach.

Isabirye and Flowerday [39] evaluated the existing requirements elicitation techniques and methodologies in the context of rural culture in South Africa, coming to the conclusion that the stakeholders' culture plays a significant role in undertaking the RE process, which concurs with our hypotheses. Borchers [25] analyzed the impact of culture on the software engineering techniques in Japan, India, and the United States. The study also demonstrated that cultural differences have a great influence on software engineering process. In our work, we go further and focusing on the development of the corresponding framework.

7   Conclusion

The RE process is crucial phase in any software development. It requires extensive communication skills to identify and document users' requirements. RE is social and human activity and thus, it is highly sensitive to cultural aspects. Several studies have recognized that a success RE process does not only depend on the technique or method used but also depends on understanding the individuals' behavior and culture. We explore the influence of culture on the process of the RE activities and model from a conservative culture, Saudi Arabia.

We conducted semi-structured interviews with Saudi requirements engineering practitioners and software engineering researchers. The empirical data were thematically analysed. This study reveals 10 cultural factors play a role in the RE practice and 5 high-level descriptions of the RE process model used in the Saudi context. We map the Hofstede's cultural theory to the core parts of the RE process to investigate the possible dependencies and influences.

Hofstede's culture theory allows us to find relevant correlation regarding the influence of culture on RE practices. The result of this study, therefore, would help RE practitioners in Saudi Arabia and other cultures, having the similar national cultural profile as per Hofstede [3], to identify the potential cultural implications and the preferable RE process model.

Future Work: As the next steps, we are going to expand the scope of the study (1) to cover other countries, (2) to gather the information on the software stakeholders' view points, as they are a very important actors within the RE process, (3) to cover not only small-to-medium companies but also a large ones, as this might provide additional aspects.

Acknowledgements. We would like to thank participants for kindly accepting to participate in this research project. We appreciate their cooperation and engagement. The first author is supported by a scholarship from Taibah University in Saudi Arabia.

References

1. Thanasankit, T.: Requirements engineering – exploring the influence of power and thai values. Eur. J. Inf. Syst. **11**, 128–141 (2002)

2. Hanisch, J., Corbitt, B.: Impediments to requirements engineering during global software development. Eur. J. Inf. Syst. **16**, 793–805 (2007)
3. Hofstede, G., Hofstede, G.J., Minkov, M.: Cultures and Organizations: Software of the Mind: Intercultural Cooperation and its Importance for Survival. McGraw-Hill, New York (2010)
4. Hanisch, J., Thanasankit, T., Corbitt, B.: Understanding the cultural and social impacts on requirements engineering processes-identifying some problems challenging virtual team interaction with clients. In: ECIS 2001 Proceedings, p. 43 (2001)
5. Trompenaars, F., Hampden-Turner, C.: Riding the Waves of Culture: Understanding Diversity in Global Business. Nicholas Brealey Publishing, Boston (2011)
6. Hall, E.T.: Beyond Culture. Anchor, Hamburg (1989)
7. Alsanoosy, T., Spichkova, M., Harland, J.: Cultural influences on requirements engineering process in the context of Saudi Arabia. In: Proceedings of the 13th International Conference on Evaluation of Novel Approaches to Software Engineering - Volume 1: ENASE. SciTePress, INSTICC, pp. 159–168 (2018). https://doi.org/10.5220/0006770701590168. https://www.scitepress.org/PublicationsDetail.aspx?ID=hgBYzaTdyLE=&t=1. ISBN 978-989-758-300-1
8. Alharthi, A., Spichkova, M.: Individual and social requirement aspects of sustainable elearning systems. In: International Conference on Engineering Education and Research, pp. 1–8. WSU (2016)
9. Alharthi, A., Spichkova, M., Hamilton, M.: Requirements engineering aspects of elearning systems. In: Proceedings of the ASWEC 2015 24th Australasian Software Engineering Conference, pp. 132–133. ACM (2015)
10. Spichkova, M., Schmidt, H.W., Nekvi, M.R.I., Madhavji, N.H.: Structuring diverse regulatory requirements for global product development. In: 2015 IEEE Eighth International Workshop on Requirements Engineering and Law, pp. 57–60. IEEE (2015)
11. Spichkova, M., Schmidt, H.: Requirements engineering aspects of a geographically distributed architecture. In: 10th International Conference on Evaluation of Novel Approaches to Software Engineering (2015)
12. Zave, P.: Classification of research efforts in requirements engineering. In: Proceedings of 1995 IEEE International Symposium on Requirements Engineering, vol. 29, pp. 315–321 (1997)
13. Nuseibeh, B., Easterbrook, S.: Requirements engineering: a roadmap. In: Conference on the Future of Software Engineering, pp. 35–46. ACM (2000)
14. Spichkova, M.: Architecture: requirements + decomposition + refinement. Softwaretechnik-Trends **31**, 1–4 (2011)
15. Sommerville, I., Lenarcic, J.: Software Engineering, 9th edn. Pearson/Addison-Wesley, Boston (2011)
16. Abran, A., Moore, J.W., Bourque, P., Dupuis, R., Tripp, L.L.: Guide to the software engineering body of knowledge: 2004 version SWEBOK. IEEE Computer Society (2004)
17. Pandey, D., Suman, U., Ramani, A.: An effective requirement engineering process model for software development and requirements management. In: Advances in Recent Technologies in Communication and Computing (ARTCom), pp. 287–291. IEEE (2010)
18. Loucopoulos, P., Karakostas, V.: System Requirements Engineering. McGraw-Hill Inc., New York (1995)
19. Kotonya, G., Sommerville, I.: Requirements Engineering: Processes and Techniques. Wiley, Hoboken (1998)

20. Wiegers, K., Beatty, J.: Software Requirements. Pearson Education, London (2013)
21. Passos, C., Mendonça, M., Cruzes, D.S.: The role of organizational culture in software development practices: a cross-case analysis of four software companies. In: 2014 Brazilian Symposium on Software Engineering (SBES), pp. 121–130. IEEE (2014)
22. Thanasankit, T., Corbitt, B.: Understanding thai culture and its impact on requirements engineering process management during information systems development. Asian Acad. Manag. J. **7**, 103–126 (2002)
23. Palvia, S.C., Hunter, M.G.: Information systems development: a conceptual model and a comparison of methods used in Singapore, USA and Europe. J. Glob. Inf. Manag. **4**, 5–17 (1996)
24. Hofstede, G.: Cultures and Organizations: Software of the Mind. McGraw-Hill, New York (1991)
25. Borchers, G.: The software engineering impacts of cultural factors on multi-cultural software development teams. In: 25th International Conference on Software Engineering (ICSE), pp. 540–547 (2003)
26. Lim, S.L., Bentley, P.J., Kanakam, N., Ishikawa, F., Honiden, S.: Investigating country differences in mobile app user behavior and challenges for software engineering. IEEE Trans. Softw. Eng. **41**, 40–64 (2015)
27. Ayed, H., Vanderose, B., Habra, N.: Agile cultural challenges in Europe and Asia: insights from practitioners. In: 39th International Conference on Software Engineering, pp. 153–162. IEEE (2017)
28. Runeson, P., Höst, M., Rainer, A., Regnell, B.: Case Study Research in Software Engineering: Guidelines and Examples. Wiley, Hoboken (2012)
29. Neuman, L.W.: Social Research Methods: Qualitative and Quantitative Approaches. Allyn and Bacon, Boston (2002)
30. Braun, V., Clarke, V.: Using thematic analysis in psychology. Qual. Res. Psychol. **3**, 77–101 (2006)
31. Marks, D.F., Yardley, L.: Research Methods for Clinical and Health Psychology. SAGE Publications, Thousand Oaks (2003)
32. Miles, M.B., Huberman, A.M., Saldana, J.: Qualitative data analysis: a sourcebook, Beverly Hills(1984)
33. Yin, R.K.: Case Study Research: Design and Methods. Sage publications, Thousand Oaks (2013)
34. Huberman, A.M., Miles, M.B.: Assessing local causality in qualitative research. In: The Self in Social Inquiry: Researching methods, pp. 351–381 (1985)
35. IEEE Std 830-1998: IEEE recommended practice for software requirements specifications, pp. 1–40. IEEE Std 830-1998 (1998)
36. ISO/IEC/IEEE International Standard: Systems and software engineering - life cycle processes - requirements engineering, pp. 1–94. ISO/IEC/IEEE 29148:2011(E) (2011)
37. Alnafjan, K.: An empirical investigation into the adoption of software engineering practice in Saudi Arabia. Int. J. Comput. Sci. Issues (IJCSI) **9**, 328–332 (2012)
38. Damian, D.E., Zowghi, D.: RE challenges in multi-site software development organisations. Require. Eng. **8**, 149–160 (2003)
39. Isabirye, N., Flowerday, S.: A model for eliciting user requirements specific to South African rural areas. In: Annual Conference of the South African Institute of Computer Scientists and Information Technologists, pp. 124–130. ACM (2008)

Formal Verification of Cyber-physical Feature Coordination with Minimalist Qualitative Models

Hermann Kaindl[✉], Ralph Hoch, Michael Rathmair,
and Christoph Luckeneder

Institute of Computer Technology, TU Wien, Vienna, Austria
{hermann.kaindl,ralph.hoch,michael.rathmair,
christoph.luckeneder}@tuwien.ac.at
https://www.ict.tuwien.ac.at/

Abstract. Undesired feature interaction may lead to safety-critical behavior in cyber-physical systems (CPSs). For specifying feature coordination of a cyber-physical software system (i.e., its cyber-part), an approach based on the Situation Calculus was previously published. However, no verification of the feature coordination in the physical environment was possible in spite of its formal specification. Verification of (safety-critical) feature coordination in CPSs is important, however, and requires additional models.

This paper shows that a specification of feature coordination can be formally verified against a safety-relevant property, when combined with an additional (simple) physical model and a model of an independent embodied entity in the environment. These models are qualitative and intended to be minimalist, in order to facilitate formal and tool-supported verification. We demonstrate formal verification of the combined model twice, through model-checking a representation in synchronized finite-state machines against the property formulated in time logic, and through a planner with an inverted goal condition, based on a systematically derived model in Fluent Calculus. The results of verification are consistent, and we contrast and discuss both approaches. In summary, we present formal verification of cyber-physical feature coordination with minimalist qualitative models.

Keywords: Verification · Cyber-physical · Feature coordination ·
Model checking · Fluent Calculus

1 Introduction

Formal verification of CPSs such as automotive systems is desirable, since they are safety-critical. In particular, it is important with regard to the functional safety standard for road vehicles ISO 26262 [8].

If such systems have many features to be selected, the so-called optional feature problem arises. It may lead to *feature interaction*, when the interplay

© Springer Nature Switzerland AG 2019
E. Damiani et al. (Eds.): ENASE 2018, CCIS 1023, pp. 261–287, 2019.
https://doi.org/10.1007/978-3-030-22559-9_12

of two or more features gives rise to an overall system behavior that is not easily deducible from the individual behaviors of the features involved, and often unexpected [1]. *Undesired* feature interaction can lead to safety-critical behavior, e.g., in automotive systems.

An approach for *detecting* feature interactions automatically through *model checking* can be found in [10]. A feature interaction may result directly from conflicting requests to a single variable in the software (as studied for the speed of a vehicle in [10]). This is sufficient for detecting that there is a feature interaction, but not for investigating its influence on the environment. This would require an additional physical model and, potentially, a model of independent embodied entities in the environment.

Once undesired feature interaction is known, the features involved need to be coordinated in order to avoid it. Especially the verification of *feature coordination* requires such additional models, since the effects of the coordination on the environment cannot be taken into account otherwise. Since the inclusion of such additional models increases the complexity and, therefore, the combinatorics of model checking, *minimalist* models have been developed in an incremental approach in [17]. Even for a small system, model checking faces combinatorial problems with quantitative models. Hence, these models are *qualitative* rather than quantitative in order to keep the runtimes for model-checking them short.

Bocovich and Atlee [4] addressed feature interaction resulting from a conflict of features accessing the same software variable(s) at the same point in time. Since the granularity of features may be relevant, resolution for each software variable under conflict was proposed for feature *coordination* (with examples in the automotive domain). They showed how such a resolution can be specified using the *Situation Calculus*. However, without a physical model or any independent embodied entity in the environment, no verification is possible of whether such a resolution as specified for the software actually achieves its purpose in the overall CPS.

Artificial Intelligence techniques like the Situation Calculus may be a good fit for modeling such a system qualitatively, since they have been proposed and used early on in the context of robot planning. Hence, they offer also planning capabilities, so that not only the specification of a feature coordinator is possible, but also some means for verifying whether it actually works.

We were interested in developing such a verification approach, and to contrast it with the widely studied verification approach based on model checking. We thus transfer the model of [17] systematically to the *Fluent Calculus*, a derivative of the Situation Calculus as used in [4] for specifying feature coordination within software, and use the resulting model for a new approach to the verification of cyber-physical feature coordination. This approach involves a tool supporting the Fluent Calculus and a simple planner that we implemented on top of it. When the planner can find a sequence of actions for achieving a goal that formulates a property to be avoided, then it actually presents an example of what is to be avoided. This corresponds to a counterexample in model checking. Note, that this approach uses a planner for verification, while the approach in [3] uses a model checker for planning.

Our running example is based on *Adaptive Cruise Control* (ACC), which is penetrating the automotive market [26]. It has already been studied as a Simulink model, but with a completely different focus [22]. While ACC is already well understood as a single feature from an engineering viewpoint, we study it from the perspective of a *composite feature*. It includes both *Cruise Control* (CC), as widely used in cars, and *Distance Control* (DC) of a vehicle A following another vehicle B. DC obviously has to take the influence of speed also on the distance to vehicle B into account, and vehicle B is an independent embodied entity in the environment. Since ACC per se and its inherent feature interactions are well understood already, we can focus in our work on automated verification of feature coordination.

The remainder of this paper is organized in the following manner. First, we provide some background material on formal approaches for making this paper self-contained, and relate it to previous work on feature coordination. Then we elaborate on our ACC model as an example of a minimalist qualitative model of cyber-physical feature coordination. We show both its representation as synchronized finite-state machines (FSMs) and its systematic transformation to a representation in the Fluent Calculus. Based on these different model representations, we show related verification approaches and how they automatically achieve consistent results with tool support. Finally, we provide a more general discussion, future work, and the conclusion.

2   Background and Related Work

We cover here some background on and related work to the Fluent Calculus, feature coordination, model checking, and the given model of ACC that we transform to the Fluent Calculus for verification with our new approach.

2.1   Background on Model Checking

Model checking (or property checking) is a formal verification technique based on models of system behavior and properties, specified unambiguously in formal languages (see, e.g., [2]). The behavioral model of the system under verification is often specified using an FSM, in our case using synchronized FSMs. Their expressiveness is sufficient for our case, but Petri nets, e.g., could be used as well, if needed (depending on the tool used). The properties to be checked on the behavioral model are formulated in a specific property specification language, usually based on a temporal logic. Several tools such as NuSMV [16] exist for performing these checks by systematically exploring the state-space of the system. When such a tool finds a property violation, it reports it in the form of a counterexample.

Many model checking approaches use *Computational Tree Logic* (CTL) for property specification, with the following CTL operators:

- AG (Always Globally): an expression p is true in the initial state s_0 and in each state of all transitions $s_0 \to s_1 \to s_2 \to \cdots \to s_n$.
- EF (Eventually in the Future): for an expression p and an initial state s_0, there exists a state sequence $s_0 \to s_1 \to s_2 \to \cdots \to s_n$ such that p is true in s_n.

2.2 Background on the Fluent Calculus

The original idea was introduced by McCarthy and Hayes [14] long time ago. Their Situation Calculus consists of three elements:

1. Situations
   represent the evolving states of the domain, where certain conditions hold in each state.
2. Actions
   represent the changes between situations. A special predicate *poss* determines whether a specific *action* can be performed or not.
3. Fluents
   represent the elements of the domain that can change over time. Typically, predicates are used for this representation, which take a situation as an argument. An example is the fluent *carrying(o,s)*, which states if an object o is carried, e.g., by a robot, in situation s.

Based on previous work on the Situation Calculus such as [18], Thielscher [23] developed the Fluent Calculus. It differs from the Situation Calculus in how situations are treated and how fluents are used. The Fluent Calculus defines that a new state after the execution of an action is equal to the previous state with exceptions to the effects of the action. In addition, fluents are treated as functional terms. The fluents from the Situation Calculus are stripped off the situation parameter, and special predicates, e.g., *holds*, are introduced. These special predicates take a functional term and a state as an argument. They are used to check whether specific conditions hold in a specific state or not. For example, the fluent *carrying(o,s)* from the Situation Calculus translates to a functional term *carrying(o)* in the Fluent Calculus. Hence, this term is not depended on the current state anymore. To check whether this term holds in a specific state s, the *holds* predicate is used, e.g., *holds(carrying(o), smedium)*.

Hence, the Fluent Calculus provides a formalism to model specific *actions* that lead from one situation to another. This is specified using the *poss* and *state_update* predicates. These predefined predicates model the preconditions (*poss* statement) and effects (*state_update*) of an action. Together, they provide a formal specification of an action.

An implementation of the Fluent Calculus called FLUX [24] is available for the constraint logic programming system ECLiPSe.[1] To illustrate how such an action in Fluent Calculus is applied in FLUX, we use a simple example. Let us assume that a vehicle B is currently driving with *medium speed* and wants to change to *high speed*. This simplistic example already utilizes the main parts of the Fluent Calculus. The driving speed of the vehicle changes over *time* and thus is a *fluent*. The change of the driving speed is performed by an *action*. For this example, we assume that the name of this action is *switchMediumSpeedToHigh-SpeedVehicleB*. What is missing, is the situation of the domain. In the current situation, the speed of vehicle B is medium speed. This information is only part

---

[1] ECLiPSe Constraint Programming System: http://www.eclipseclp.org.

```
poss(switchMediumSpeedToHighSpeedVehicleB(B), Z) :-
    % Input has to be of type VehicleB %
    knows_val([B], vehicleB(B), Z),
    % Precondition that the speed of B is set to mediumSpeed
            in State Z %
    holds(vehicleBIsSetTo(B, mediumSpeed), Z).
```

Listing 1.1. Preconditions of the medium-to-high-speed action in FLUX.

```
state_update(Z1, switchMediumSpeedToHighSpeedB(B), Z2, [])
    :-
    update(Z1, % original state %
        % Statements added to the State %
        [vehicleBIsSetTo(B, highSpeed)],
        % Statements removed from the State %
        [vehicleBIsSetTo(B, mediumSpeed)], Z2
        % new State is stored in Z2 %
    ).
```

Listing 1.2. Effects of the medium-to high-speed-action in FLUX.

of a more complex situation specification, but is sufficient for this example. In essence, the action *switchMediumSpeedToHighSpeedVehicleB* can only be executed if the current speed of vehicle B is medium speed. This is a precondition for the execution of the action. The *holds* predicate checks if a specific value *vehicleBIsSetTo(B, mediumSpeed)* holds in state Z. Listing 1.1 shows this precondition in FLUX.

When the action is executed, it has effects on the situation of the domain, e.g., the speed of vehicle B changes. In our example, vehicle B is set to *high speed*. However, this is not sufficient, since we also have to specify that vehicle B is not driving with medium speed anymore. This fact is removed from the state. Listing 1.2 shows the effects of the action in FLUX. Basically *vehicleBIsSetTo(B, highSpeed)* is added and *vehicleBIsSetTo(B, mediumSpeed)* removed from Z1 and results in Z2.

In fact, we previously proposed a verification approach based on the Fluent Calculus already in [7], which verifies sequences of semantically specified services against the specifications of its atomic services. In this paper, we propose a completely different verification approach, where all possible sequences are exhaustively tried out by a planner and checked against a goal condition that is actually to be avoided.

2.3   Related Work on Feature Coordination

Automatically detecting and analyzing feature interactions is outside the scope of this paper, which focuses on coordinating features with known interactions. Even if these are known, coordinating the features involved poses additional challenges, and to our best knowledge, there has not yet been much work published on coordinating interacting features. Jackson and Zave [9] presented early and seminal work on coordinating interacting features in the telecommunications domain. In essence, this approach avoids undesired feature interactions through central control, which implements serialization for disabling a feature in favor of another one. Ertl et al. [5] used the Mediator software pattern in order to reduce the coupling among feature implementations in automotive software. The coordinator uses given compiled knowledge on feature interaction to give one feature priority over others. Wagner et al. [25] included soft and hard constraints for optimization of desired feature interaction, and dynamic adjustment of influence in the utility function for handling feature interactions.

In particular, the challenge of coordinating features in a cyber-physical system has not yet attracted enough attention. The formulation of resolutions as proposed in [4] uses the Situation Calculus implemented in GOLOG [12]. This work did not investigate, however, the physical effects from a feature interaction of a software variable, and it did not include independent physical variables outside the control of the software. Hence, no verification was possible of whether such a resolution as specified actually achieves its purpose.

In fact, we can also use this approach for specifying a coordination of CC and DC as given in Formula 1.

$$Poss(setSpeedA(SPEED), Z) \equiv$$
$$\exists ValueCC.ccVehicleAIsSetTo(cc, ValueCC) \land$$
$$\exists ValueDC.dcVehicleAIsSetTo(dc, ValueDC) \land$$
$$minimum(ValueCC, ValueDC, SPEED). \qquad (1)$$

Our actual implementation in FLUX differs slightly from this equation, since we use a qualitative model. Several *Poss* statements have a set of non-overlapping conditions and the minimum is built by choosing the fitting *Poss* statement.

GOLOG differs from FLUX in the way it handles variable resolution. GOLOG uses (backward) regression as opposed to the forward progression of FLUX. More information on this and how GOLOG programs can be interpreted in FLUX is given in [19].

3   A Minimalist Qualitative Model of Cyber-Physical Feature Coordination

Now let us present our minimalist qualitative model of cyber-physical feature coordination, starting with the inclusion of a physical model with an independent embodied entity. This additional entity is vehicle B in front of vehicle A in the ACC example. Because its behavior is not under control of vehicle A and because of the physical dependency between these vehicles, vehicle A needs a controller to avoid a collision. We illustrate this in an overview first and then present the ACC model in FSMs, where one of these FSMs implements a closed-loop controller qualitatively. Based on this model, we present how to transform it to an ACC model in the Fluent Calculus.

3.1 Inclusion of a Physical Model with an Independent Embodied Entity

The physical model is very simple and minimalist, since it captures only what appears to be absolutely necessary for the purpose of verifying a qualitative ACC model. Of course, it only requires Newtonian physics as its basis. It does not even take into account the effect of masses. And every speed change involved at a state transition happens instantaneously, i.e., there are discrete states with defined transitions in this physical model. In the context of ACC, this simplification does not matter with respect to collisions, since it is the same for both vehicles. Finally, only longitudinal motion is relevant for ACC, cf. [20].

The basic physical chain of speed and distance is illustrated in Fig. 1. The speed of vehicle B, an independent embodied entity, is included as an independent variable, since it is out of control of vehicle A. The distance of vehicle A to vehicle B in front of it depends on the speed of vehicle B, of course, much as on its own speed. Vehicle A can change its speed, as determined by a coordinator C based on the speed requests from CC and DC, and these changes are reflected in the physical chain. Also this is a simplification, since actually torque requests are made in the cyber-part of a real car, which lead to acceleration changes and, in turn, to speed changes.

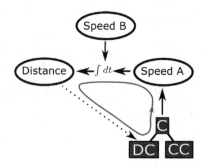

Fig. 1. Physical chain with interacting features CC and DC (adapted from [17, Fig. 1]). (Color figure online)

Since the models in our approach are qualitative, discrete values are defined for the real-valued physical variables speed and distance. Since these models are intended to be minimalist, three distinct speed values are defined: Low Speed, Medium Speed, and High Speed. A further simplification to two different speed values would not allow realistic control and the detection of undesired feature interaction in the scenario checked in [21]. Defining discrete distance values for this model is more intricate. In the course of incremental modeling in [17], it was shown through model checking that an analogous definition of three values was insufficient. Therefore, the FSM for distance classification in Fig. 5 below contains four states.

3.2   Overview of the Cyber-physical ACC Model

Figure 1 also depicts a simple model of the features involved, CC and DC. Both of them independently request certain speed values, and the coordinator C chooses one of them. Unless these speed values are the same, the coordinator has to resolve the conflict caused by this feature interaction of CC and DC. This is exactly the case of a conflicting request to a single variable studied before in [10]. In contrast to this previous work, the speed value determined by the coordinator feeds into a physical model (as simple as it may be). Therefore, we actually study a cyber-physical ACC model.

The high-level structure of this CPS model is illustrated in Fig. 2. It contains a model of vehicle A, which only includes the coordinator and the features CC and DC. DC measures the speed of vehicle B, which together with the speed of vehicle A influences the distance in the environment as represented by the minimalist physical model above. Since the distance between vehicles A and B is important with respect to a potential accident, DC measures it (in reality using a sensor).

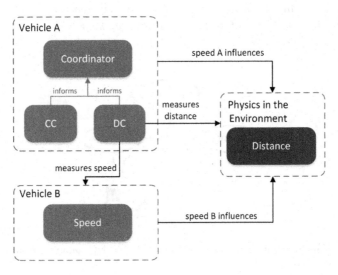

Fig. 2. High-level structure of the cyber-physical ACC model (adapted from [6, Fig. 1]).

This cyber-physical model includes a control loop, illustrated in Fig. 1 in red. The dotted arrow shows that the (measured) distance value is fed back to DC, so that it can keep control on a target distance. In fact, DC is a *closed-loop controller*.

3.3   The ACC Model Represented in FSMs

For the purpose of verification through model checking, a concrete ACC model with this structure has been developed and represented formally in FSMs [17]. It includes a single FSM for vehicle B given in Fig. 3, three FSMs for vehicle A given in Fig. 4, and a single FSM for the distance classification given in Fig. 5. The FSMs in these figures are isomorphic to the ones in [17].

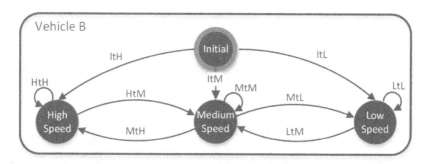

Fig. 3. FSM of vehicle B (adapted from [6, Fig. 2]).

However, for showing the correspondence to the actions in the Fluent Calculus more clearly, the FSMs in this paper have action names as labels on transitions. The name of each action is defined using the names of the root and target states of the corresponding transition and is constructed as *switch* {*FSM.transition.root.name*} *To* {*FSM.transition.target.name*} {*FSM.name*}. For example, the transition from *Medium Speed* to *Low Speed* (in the FSM defining the behavior of vehicle B in Fig. 3) has the action name *switchMediumSpeedToLowSpeedVehicleB*. In order to avoid cluttering the diagrams, we actually use abbreviations of these action names for labeling the transitions. For example, the action name *switchMediumSpeedToLowSpeedVehicleB* is abbreviated as *MtL* in the FSM of Fig. 3.

Figure 3 depicts the FSM that defines all possible driving behaviors of vehicle B. It is isomorphic to the FSM in [17, Fig. 6] but with the different transition labels. Table 1 lists for each transition its label and the action name abbreviated by it, as well as its transition condition. This model has to cover all possible behaviors, since vehicle B is an independent embodied entity, i.e., its speed is a variable *not* under control of ACC. It is in the environment of vehicle A, whose speed *is* being controlled by ACC.

The FSMs defining the behavior of vehicle A in Fig. 4 are isomorphic to the corresponding ones in [17, Fig. 6]. These FSMs qualitatively define the behavior of the features CC and DC as well as that of their coordinator. The FSM of CC is fairly simple. The initial value (set by the driver in a real car) determines the state of the given target speed. The FSM transitions to this state and stays there. In this way, CC keeps the given target speed, which can take one of the three values defined in the qualitative model. Table 2 lists the transition conditions of the CC FSM.

The FSM of DC is much more intricate than the FSM of CC, since it implements a closed-loop controller that tries to keep a given (constant) target distance in the context of our qualitative model. As explained below, this is not always possible, however. Still, DC has to make sure that no collision occurs, cf. the Collision state in Fig. 5 below. For its control task, this FSM uses (input) values of the distance (measured in reality by a sensor) and the estimated

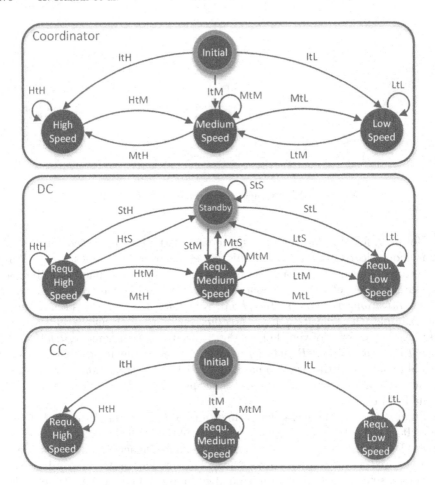

Fig. 4. FSM of vehicle A (adapted from [6, Fig. 3]).

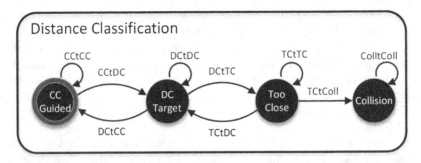

Fig. 5. FSM of the distance classification (adapted from [6, Fig. 4]).

Table 1. Transition labels, action names, and transition conditions of the vehicle B FSM.

Label	Action name	Transition condition
ItL	switchInitialToLowSpeedVehicleB	$initSpeed == LowSpeed$
LtL	switchLowSpeedToLowSpeedVehicleB	$hold \lor decelerate$
LtM	switchLowSpeedToMediumSpeedVehicleB	$accelerate$
ItM	switchInitialToMediumSpeedVehicleB	$initSpeed == MediumSpeed$
MtL	switchMediumSpeedToLowSpeedVehicleB	$decelerate$
MtM	switchMediumSpeedToMediumSpeedVehicleB	$hold$
MtH	switchMediumSpeedToHighSpeedVehicleB	$accelerate$
ItH	switchInitialToHighSpeedVehicleB	$initSpeed == HighSpeed$
HtH	switchHighSpeedToHighSpeedVehicleB	$hold \lor accelerate$
HtM	switchHighSpeedToMediumSpeedVehicleB	$decelerate$

Table 2. Transition labels, action names, and transition conditions of the CC FSM.

Label	Action name	Transition condition
ItL	switchInitialToRequLowSpeedCC	$initSpeedCC == Low\_Speed$
ItM	switchInitialToRequMediumSpeedCC	$initSpeedCC == Medium\_Speed$
ItH	switchInitialToRequHighSpeedCC	$initSpeedCC == High\_Speed$
LtL	switchRequLowSpeedToRequLowSpeedCC	$True$
MtM	switchRequMediumSpeedToRequMediumSpeedCC	$True$
HtH	switchRequHighSpeedToRequHighSpeedCC	$True$

Table 3. Transition labels, action names, and transition conditions of the DC FSM.

Label	Action name	Transition condition
StS	switchStandbyToStandbyDC	$DIST$
StL	switchStandbyToRequLowSpeedDC	$(DC\_Low \land !DIST)$
StM	switchStandbyToRequMediumSpeedDC	$(DC\_Med \land !DIST)$
StH	switchStandbyToRequHighSpeedDC	$(DC\_High \land !DIST)$
LtS	switchRequLowSpeedToStandbyDC	$DIST$
LtL	switchRequLowSpeedToRequLowSpeedDC	DC_Low
LtM	switchRequLowSpeedToRequMediumSpeedDC	$DC\_Med \lor DC\_High$
MtS	switchRequMediumSpeedToStandbyDC	$DIST$
MtL	switchRequMediumSpeedToRequLowSpeedDC	DC_Low
MtM	switchRequMediumSpeedToRequMediumSpeedDC	DC_Med
MtH	switchRequMediumSpeedToRequHighSpeedDC	DC_High
HtS	switchRequHighSpeedToStandbyDC	$DIST$
HtH	switchRequHighSpeedToRequHighSpeedDC	DC_High
HtM	switchRequHighSpeedToRequMediumSpeedDC	$DC\_Low \lor DC\_Med$

Table 4. Transition matrix for the DC FSM.

Distance\Speed B	Low	Medium	High
DC target	DC_Low	DC_Med	DC_High
Too close	DC_Low	DC_Low	DC_Med

speed of vehicle B. Since estimating this speed may take its time in reality, our model includes a time delay of one cycle for the state changes of the distance classification.

The Standby state is the initial state of DC. This FSM stays in or transfers to this state, whenever the distance is greater than the target distance. Under this condition, DC as modeled here does not control the distance and, therefore, not request a speed value. The other three states correspond to the three speed values as requested by DC. The closed-loop controller is actually implemented by the transitions between these three states, more precisely their transition conditions listed in Table 3, where DIST denotes that the distance to Vehicle B is greater than the target distance. Since this detailed specification may be hard to understand, Table 4 provides an overview of the DC behavior.

The FSM of the *coordinator* implements the approach of [26], where the minimum of the CC and DC values is taken. As indicated above, we take the minimum of speed instead of acceleration values, however. This corresponds to the specification using the resolution formalism of [4] given in Formula 1 above. The FSM implements taking the minimum of two qualitative values. The structure of this FSM is similar to the FSM of DC, but it has different transition conditions referring to the requested values from CC and DC, respectively, see Table 5. Table 6 provides an overview of the coordinator behavior.

Table 5. Transition labels, action names, and transition conditions of the coordinator FSM.

Label	Action name	Transition condition
ItL	switchInitialToLowSpeedCoordinator	Co_Low
LtL	switchLowSpeedToLowSpeedCoordinator	Co_Low
LtM	switchLowSpeedToMediumSpeedCoordinator	$Co\_Med \lor Co\_High$
ItM	switchInitialToMediumSpeedCoordinator	Co_Med
MtL	switchMediumSpeedToLowSpeedCoordinator	Co_Low
MtM	switchMediumSpeedToMediumSpeedCoordinator	Co_Med
MtH	switchMediumSpeedToHighSpeedCoordinator	Co_High
ItH	switchInitialToHighSpeedCoordinator	Co_High
HtH	switchHighSpeedToHighSpeedCoordinator	Co_High
HtM	switchHighSpeedToMediumSpeedCoordinator	$Co\_Low \lor Co\_Med$

Table 6. Transition matrix for the coordinator FSM.

Speed DC\CC	Low	Medium	High
Low	Co_Low	Co_Low	Co_Low
Medium	Co_Low	Co_Med	Co_Med
High	Co_Low	Co_Med	Co_High

The FSM defining the *distance classification* in Fig. 5 is isomorphic to the one in [17, Fig. 6], which has been the result of the incremental modeling approach. It is a logical model of the relevant distance categories based on the physical variable *distance*, but does not even assign qualitative values. Table 7 lists the transition conditions for the distance classification FSM, with auxiliary specifications in Table 8. Together with the FSM defining the behavior of vehicle B, this FSM defines the behavior of the environment of vehicle A.

These FSMs are synchronized for their interplay through events raised by their transitions. All these FSMs together specify the qualitative ACC model.

Table 7. Transition labels, action names, and transition conditions of the distance classification FSM.

Label	Action name	Transition condition
CCtCC	switchCCGuidedToCCGuidedDistance	$Dist\_H \lor Dist\_I \lor Dist\_D$
CCtDC	switchCCGuidedToDCTargetDistance	$Dist\_D$
DCtCC	switchDCTargetToCCGuidedDistance	$Dist\_I$
DCtDC	switchDCTargetToDCTargetDistance	$Dist\_H$
DCtTC	switchDCtargetToTooCloseDistance	$Dist\_D$
TCtDC	switchTooCloseToDCTargetDistance	$Dist\_I$
TCtTC	switchTooCloseToTooCloseDistance	$Dist\_H$
TCtColl	switchTooCloseToCollisionDistance	$Dist\_D$
ColltColl	swtichCollisionToCollisionDistance	$True$

Table 8. Auxiliary condition specifications.

Name	Condition
$Dist\_H$	$(LowSpeedA \land LowSpeedB)\lor$ $(MediumSpeedA \land MediumSpeedB)\lor$ $(HighSpeedA \land HighSpeedB)$
$Dist\_D$	$(MediumSpeedA \land LowSpeedB)\lor$ $(HighSpeedA \land LowSpeedB)\lor$ $(HighSpeedA \land MediumSpeedB)$
$Dist\_I$	$(LowSpeedA \land MediumSpeedB)\lor$ $(LowSpeedA \land HighSpeedB)\lor$ $(MediumSpeedA \land HighSpeedB)$

3.4   The ACC Model Represented in the Fluent Calculus

We also represent this ACC model in the Fluent Calculus. For making sure that both models capture the same overall behavior of ACC, we transform the model represented in synchronized FSMs to a model represented in the Fluent Calculus. In fact, we specify a systematic transformation approach that could, in principle, also be automated. We explain it in two major steps, where the first one defines the counterparts of FSM elements in Fluent Calculus, and the second step defines the semantics of the elements created.

First of all, we specify how the following terms in the Fluent Calculus are derived:

- terms identifying the state machines,
- terms for each state in each state machine,
- terms for each state transition.

Based on these terms, we define the preconditions and effects of all actions as derived from the conditions of state transitions, the state from where a transition is going out (its root), and the state where the transition leads to (its target).

The systematic transformation approach to this derivation is as follows:

- Each FSM is a term *{FSM.name}{FSM.context}* with an argument. The argument *{FSM.name}* is a constant used during the verification process to ensure that actions are only performed when appropriate. The suffix *{FSM.context}* is not necessary, but makes the term more human readable. Example: FSM of CC is *ccVehicleA(cc)*. *FSM.context* is *VehicleA* since CC is executed for Vehicle A.
- Each FSM is also a compound term *{FSM.name}{FSM.context}IsSetTo (object, value)* with two arguments. This term may change over time and, thus, is a *fluent*. The first argument is the object on which the term operates and the second argument is the value. Example: FSM of CC results in *ccVehicleAIsSetTo(object, value)*, where object and value are to be reset for concrete values, e.g., *ccVehicleAIsSetTo(cc, requLowSpeed)*.
- Each state of an FSM is a value that the term of this FSM can hold. The value is represented as a constant and is the name of the state *{FSM.state.name}{FSM.name}*. Example: The state *Requ Low Speed* of the CC FSM in Vehicle A results in the value *requLowSpeedCC*. This value is used with the corresponding term *ccVehicleAIsSetTo* of the FSM. The result is *ccVehicleAIsSetTo(cc, requLowSpeedCC)*.
- Each transition in an FSM is transformed to an *action* in the Fluent Calculus. The name of the action is defined through the root and target state of the transition and is *switch{FSM.transition.root.name}To{FSM.transition.target.name}{FSM.name}*. Example: The transition in the CC FSM from *Requ Medium Speed* to *Requ Low Speed* results in the action *switchRequMediumSpeedToRequLowSpeedCC*.

(

    $(requMediumSpeedCC \wedge \neg requLowSpeedDC)$ $\vee$
    $(\neg requLowSpeedDC \wedge requMediumSpeedDC)$

) $\vee$
(

    $(requHighSpeedCC \wedge \neg requLowSpeedDC \wedge \neg requMediumSpeedDC)$ $\vee$
    $(\neg requLowSpeedDC \wedge \neg requMediumSpeedDC \wedge requHighSpeedDC)$

)

Listing 1.3. Example condition on a transition.

The FSM in Fig. 3 contains the action *switchMediumSpeedToHighSpeedVehicleB* as a transition, which corresponds to the example of an action specified in the Fluent Calculus above (in the Background section). Still, we have to explain how the action specifications in the Fluent Calculus can be systematically transformed from the FSMs (based on the terms derived above):

- Transitions between states are transformed to actions. Actions consist of *state_update* and *poss* statements.
- Conditions of the actions are given as propositional logic formulas in disjunctive normal form.
- The arguments of an action are *all* distinct elements of the propositional logic formula.
- The root of the state transition in the FSM is a precondition in the corresponding *poss* statement of the action in the Fluent Calculus.
- For each disjunctive part of the condition of a transition, one *poss* statement is created.
- The effects of an action are modeled via a *state_update* predicate.
- The positive effect of an action is the target node.
- The negative effect of an action is the root node.

To demonstrate this systematic transformation, let us consider the transition from low speed to medium speed in the coordinator FSM. It consists of two separate *or*-connected conditions *condCo_M* and *condCo_H* given as propositional formulas in [17]. These conditions consist of several logical expressions related to states in the FSMs. The disjunctive normal form of this condition is shown in Listing 1.3.

Hence, there are *or*-connected blocks of *and*-connected atoms. Each *or*-block, e.g., *(requMediumSpeedCC ∧ ¬requLowSpeedDC)*, is treated as one set of preconditions for an action, in this case the *switchLowSpeedToMediumSpeedCoordinator* action. That is, the action can only be executed if (at least) one set of preconditions is fulfilled. E.g., the precondition set *(requMediumSpeedCC ∧ ¬requLowSpeedDC)* states, that the corresponding action can only be executed if the cruise control requests medium speed and, at the same time, the distance control does not request low speed.

In the coordinator FSM, the condition on the transition specifies that the CC FSM has to be in state *requMediumSpeed* and the DC FSM cannot be in state *requLowSpeed* to trigger the transition. In the Fluent Calculus, these states are terms ({*FSM.state.name*} {*FSM.name*}) related to the terms of the FSM ({*FSM.name*}{*FSM.context*}*IsSetTo(object, value)*) and, thus, we can systematically derive a representation. For example, the atomic element *requMediumSpeedCC* in the condition is a value of *ccVehicleAIsSetTo* and only holds if *ccVehicleAIsSetTo(cc, requMediumSpeedCC)* is true. That is, this part of the condition only evaluates to true if cruise control requests medium speed. This is one part of the precondition set. The second part is ¬*requLowSpeedDC* and is transformed to *dcVehicleAIsSetTo(DC, requLowSpeedDC)*. Together, they are one precondition set for the corresponding *switchLowSpeedToMediumSpeedCoordinator* action.

While the FSM models have a condition on each transition, which defines whether a transition can be triggered or not, this condition defines in the Fluent Calculus, whether the corresponding action is executable or not. That is, the condition of a transition in an FSM becomes the precondition of the corresponding action in the Fluent Calculus. Preconditions are checked via the *poss* predicate in the Fluent Calculus. In fact, there can be many *poss* statements with different conditions for one action. We utilize this and generate one *poss* statement per precondition set. Each *poss* statement also contains the root state of the transition in the FSM as an additional precondition. Hence, the switch from low speed to medium speed has the additional precondition that the coordinator has currently set the speed to low speed. Corresponding *poss* statements in FLUX for the first two *or*-connected sets in Listing 1.3 are shown in Listing 1.4.

The arguments of the action are given through the elements it depends upon. In Listing 1.4, the arguments are A, DC and CC, or the vehicle, the distance control and the cruise control, respectively. It has to be noted that this is not necessarily required, the arguments could also be omitted, but we include them for better readability.

Still missing are the effects of an action. The effects are the fluents that are added and removed when an action is performed. In our example, the effect of switching from low speed to medium speed is that the vehicle is driving with medium speed after execution of the action. Additionally, the fact that the vehicle is driving low speed has to be removed. Hence, the positive effect is the addition of the target state as a value, and the negative effect is the removal of the root state as a value. The effects are specified via the *state_update* predicate and shown in Listing 1.5.

Using the systematic transformation defined above, a very verbose model results. Often, many state transitions in the FSM have the same conditions but different root states, or they have repeating conditions on different state transitions. For example, the *condCo_M* condition shown above is used in a transition from low speed to medium speed, medium speed to medium speed and high speed to medium speed.

```
% requMediumSpeedCC and not requLowSpeedDC %
poss(switchLowSpeedToMediumSpeedCoordinator(A, DC, CC), Z)
    :-
    % object that the action operates on %
    knows_val([A], vehicleA(A), Z),
    % root state in FSM as a precondition %
    holds(coordinatorVehilceAIsSetTo(A, lowSpeed), Z),
    % requMediumSpeedCC precondition %
    holds(ccVehicleAIsSetTo(CC, requMediumSpeedCC), Z),
    % not requLowSpeedDC precondition %
    knows_not(dcVehicleAIsSetTo(DC, requLowSpeedDC), Z).

% requMediumSpeedDC and not RequLowSpeedCC %
poss(switchLowSpeedToMediumSpeedCoordinator(A, DC, CC), Z)
    :-
    % object that the action operates on %
    knows_val([A], vehicleA(A), Z),
    % root state in FSM as a precondition %
    holds(coordinatorVehilceAIsSetTo(A, lowSpeed), Z),
    % requMediumSpeedDC precondition %
    holds(dcVehicleAIsSetTo(DC, requMediumSpeedDC), Z),
    % not requLowSpeedCC precondition %
    knows_not(ccVehicleAIsSetTo(CC, requLowSpeedCC), Z).
```

Listing 1.4. Example poss statements for actions.

```
state_update(Z1, switchLowSpeedToMediumSpeedCoordinator(A,
 _, _), Z2, []) :-
    update(Z1,
        % positive effect: adding medium speed %
        [coordinatorVehilceAIsSetTo(A, mediumSpeed)],
        % negative effect: removing low speed %
        [coordinatorVehilceAIsSetTo(A, lowSpeed)],
        Z2
    ).
```

Listing 1.5. Example state_update statement of an action.

With this in mind, the transformation can be optimized. All conditions that are repeated on different state transitions leading to the same state can be written as a single *poss* statement. In this case, the root nodes are *or*-connected preconditions. Hence, *condCo_M* can also be written as shown in Listing 1.6. Note, that also the name of the action has changed, since it does not depend on the root state anymore.

The effects of this action have to be adapted as well. The result is shown in Listing 1.7.

```
% requMediumSpeedDC and not requLowSpeedDC %
poss(switchToMediumSpeedVehicleA(A, DC, CC), Z) :-
    % object that the action operates on %
    knows_val([A], vehicleA(A), Z),
    (
        % root state low speed as a precondition %
        holds(coordinatorVehilceAIsSetTo(A, lowSpeed), Z);
        % root state medium speed as a precondition %
        holds(coordinatorVehilceAIsSetTo(A, mediumSpeed), Z);
        % root state high speed as a precondition %
        holds(coordinatorVehilceAIsSetTo(A, highSpeed), Z)
    ),
    % requMediumSpeedCC precondition %
    holds(ccVehicleAIsSetTo(CC, requMediumSpeedCC), Z),
    % not requLowSpeedDC precondition %
    knows_not(dcVehicleAIsSetTo(DC, requLowSpeedDC), Z).

% not requLowSpeedCC and requMediumSpeedDC %
poss(switchToMediumSpeedVehicleA(A, DC, CC), Z) :-
    % object that the action operates on %
    knows_val([A], vehicleA(A), Z),
    (
        % root state low speed as a precondition %
        holds(coordinatorVehilceAIsSetTo(A, lowSpeed), Z);
        % root state medium speed as a precondition %
        holds(coordinatorVehilceAIsSetTo(A, mediumSpeed), Z);
        % root state high speed as a precondition %
        holds(coordinatorVehilceAIsSetTo(A, highSpeed), Z)
    ),
    % requMediumSpeedDC precondition %
    holds(dcVehicleAIsSetTo(DC, requMediumSpeedDC), Z),
    % not requLowSpeedCC precondition %
    knows_not(ccVehicleAIsSetTo(CC, requLowSpeedCC), Z).
```

Listing 1.6. Example of optimized poss statements for actions.

```
state_update(Z1, switchToMediumSpeedVehicleA(A, _, _), Z2, []) :-
    update(Z1,
        % positive effect: adding medium speed %
        [coordinatorVehilceAIsSetTo(A, mediumSpeed)],
        % negative effect: removing low speed AND high speed %
        [
            coordinatorVehilceAIsSetTo(A, lowSpeed),
            coordinatorVehilceAIsSetTo(A, highSpeed)],
        Z2
    ).
```

Listing 1.7. Example of optimized state_update statement of an action.

Certain self-transitions can be omitted as well. For example, it is not necessary to set the speed in cruise control to high speed if it is already at high speed. However, for the sake of verification, the approach described above is sufficient and further optimizations are omitted here.

With the approach defined above, the environment part is transformed accordingly. After the transformation, the coordinator shown in Fig. 4 already contains the means to resolve conflicts of features. This approach is similar to the one introduced by Bocovich et al. [4] (and sketched above), since actions may influence the same variable. In contrast, in our case the variable is not a single statement, but a value of different terms. The conflict between the values of these terms are resolved in the coordinator according to the definition in [17]. Although we do not use the same variable, the approach of Bocovich et al. could be implemented as well. Currently, our model uses *requMedium-SpeedDC* and *requMediumSpeedCC* to define values of terms related to DC and CC. However, there could also be one general term *requestSpeedIsSetTo(speed, Value)* that states a request on the speed variable. In this case, the variable resolution of Bocovich et al. can be used directly.

4   Tool-Supported Formal Verification of Qualitative Models

Based on the two different representations of the qualitative ACC model, two different approaches can be used for tool-supported formal verification. First, we briefly explain the more common approach of model checking. Then we elaborate on our verification approach based on the Fluent Calculus and a (simple) planner. Finally, we contrast these two approaches.

4.1   Verification Using Model Checking

The ACC model represented in the (synchronized) FSMs can be verified against defined properties using model checking. The property that this model has been checked against in [17] formalizes an accident, more precisely a rear-end collision accident that DC has to avoid, and hence also ACC. Formula 2 defines this property in CTL in the sense that it is always (globally) true that the physical distance is different from a collision:

$$AG(state\_phy\_dist \neq COLLISION) \tag{2}$$

This formula was actually used when running the NuSMV tool for model checking, which performed reachability analyses in the following sense. Starting from initialization, there exists no computation path where the Collision state of the Distance Classification FSM is reached. If it is, however, then the tool outputs a counterexample.

Note that there is a logically equivalent property according to the CTL theorem $AG(\neg\phi) = \neg EF(\phi)$ [11], see Formula 3:

$$\neg EF(state\_phy\_dist = COLLISION) \tag{3}$$

It specifies the alternative view that it is *not* the case (eventually) in the future that the physical distance is equal to a collision. Also this formula could have been used for model checking.

In the course of the incremental approach to modeling, a distance classification model with three states, e.g., led to a counterexample in [17]. This counterexample indicated a case where a collision occurs. Having learned from this case that an additional state (named Too Close) was necessary, an FSM with four states resulted, isomorphic to the one in Fig. 5.

In contrast, the model-checking run of the model isomorphic to the set of synchronized FSMs given above did not find any violation of the accident property in Formula 2. Since this was an unbounded and, therefore, complete model-checking run, this amounts to a proof that no rear-end collision accident can occur according to this qualitative ACC model.

4.2   Verification Based on the Fluent Calculus Using a Planner

Much as verification through (unbounded) model checking provides a proof (or disproof) of given properties (such as strict avoidance of a collision situation), we strive for such a verification based on the Fluent Calculus. A key question is how to handle such a property in this context, and how to check it. The Situation Calculus and the Fluent Calculus have been used traditionally, e.g., for robot planning, where a formula specifies a *goal* condition. In such a setting, the planner tries to find a sequence of actions (called a *plan*) that leads to a situation where this condition is fulfilled. Our key idea for *verification* using a planner is to formulate a property to be avoided (e.g., a collision) as a goal condition. If the planner finds a related plan for achieving such an *inverted* goal condition, then it actually presents an example of what is to be avoided. This corresponds to a counterexample in model checking. Otherwise, however, the planner needs to perform an exhaustive search that does not find any such goal for proving that no property violation can occur.

Under such an exhaustive search regime, each and every combination of actions is visited, so that the search space is fully explored. Any search approach could be used, in principle, for implementing such an exhaustive planner. We chose *depth-first search* because of its linear-space requirements, and since it is already provided in the PROLOG-based tool environment. In essence, all possible sequences of actions are tried recursively until a situation with the given goal condition is found, or all possibilities are exhausted. Starting from the given root node, the first child node is generated. From this newly generated node, again the first child node is generated. In this way, the depth-first search follows one path in the tree until it cannot be extended any further (having reached a leaf node), from where it backtracks to the previous node and continues with the next node, etc. This is illustrated in Fig. 6(a). This search continues until a situation satisfying the goal condition is found, or there is no further action to be tried.

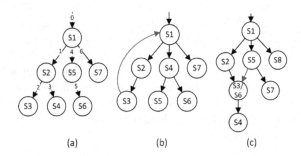

Fig. 6. Search space of planner (copied from [6, Fig. 5]).

It is well known, however, that depth-first search can, in general, result in infinite cycles. This happens if and when an action leads from one situation to an already visited situation on the same path. Figure 6(b) illustrates an example of such a cycle. To prevent this, usually the already visited nodes are stored for guaranteeing that only new situations are explored in each path. When the already visited situations are stored, the search can look them up and recognize that a newly generated situation, e.g., node *S3* in the figure, is the same as an already visited one, e.g., node *S1*. This path is terminated and the planner backtracks to continue with the next situation, e.g., node *S2*. With this cycle detection and avoidance, a termination of the search is guaranteed for a finite state space.

Storing only the visited nodes for the path from the root to the currently visited situation has linear-space requirements. However, this may lead to visiting situations more than once, if they can be reached from the root via several different paths. This is called a directed acyclic graph (DAG). An example of such a graph is illustrated in Fig. 6(c). We chose to store all visited states for detecting DAGs as well and for terminating corresponding branches. For example, in Fig. 6, node *S3/S6* can be reached through two different paths. However, the child nodes of *S3/S6* only have to be expanded once. When arriving again from node *S5*, the path can be terminated. In general, this approach has exponential space requirements, but it can still be used when enough storage is available (like in our example). For implementing such an approach to storing nodes, many PROLOG engines provide a *tabling* technique. The engine in ECLiPSe, however, has no built-in support for tabling, which made a custom implementation necessary.

So far, this planning approach looks straight-forward, but there is an intricacy involved. As described in the previous section, each FSM has a predicate with corresponding actions. In the model-checking tool NuSMV (used in [17]), all state transitions of all the synchronous FSMs happen in one execution cycle. This is in contrast to our planner, where the actions are executed one after the other. To ensure that each part of the overall system has all information available for its execution, a linearization is required. Since some parts of the system depend on environment values, a specific order of execution can be derived. For example, the distance control depends on the value of the distance classification. The coordinator depends on the distance and cruise control. In contrast, the cruise control and vehicle B do not depend on the other parts of the model. Hence, a possible execution sequence for the planner is:

1. Vehicle B
2. CC (of vehicle A)
3. DC (of vehicle A)
4. Coordinator (of vehicle A)
5. Distance classification

However, this execution sequence does not take into account that sensor values can only be read with a delay, which is essential in the model in [17]. Since the distance control measures the speed of vehicle B and also the distance, there is such a delay involved. In the original model of [17], this is solved by using temporary variables that hold the values of the previous cycle. In our approach, this delay of sensors is implemented by rearranging the execution sequence of the actions. Since DC has to use the values of the previous cycle, the actions of vehicle B and the distance classification are the last steps in an execution cycle. By doing so, DC can only access the values of the previous cycle, since the new values are generated thereafter. Figure 7 illustrates this execution cycle actually used by our planner, whose implementation in FLUX is given in Listing 1.8.

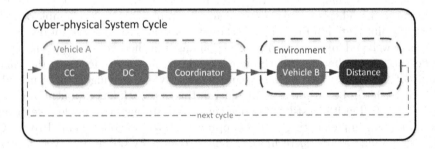

Fig. 7. Execution cycle (adapted from [6, Fig. 6]).

```
schedule_plan (Z,P,Zn):−
    (
        % first : execute CC %
        schedule_planCCA (Z,P,Z1) ,
        % second: execute DC, use result of CC as world state %
        schedule_planDCA (Z1,P,Z2) ,
        % third : execute Coordinator , use result of DC as
                world state %
        schedule_planCoodA (Z2,P,Z3) ,
        % fourth: execute Vehicle B, use result of Coordinator
                as world state %
        schedule_planVehB (Z3,P,Z4) ,
        % fifth : execute DistanceClassification , use result of
                Vehicle B as world state %
        schedule_planDistance (Z4,P,Z5)
    ) ,
    schedule_plan (Z5,P,Zn) . % continue with next cycle %
```

Listing 1.8. Planner in FLUX.

Each *schedule_planXX* statement calls a function that determines, which specific action of the FSM is executed. The possible actions are all actions that are generated for a specific FSM. Only one of the actions, based on their preconditions, is chosen and executed. Listing 1.9 shows the possible actions for Vehicle B.

```
schedule_planSpeedVehB (Z, [ VehB | P] , Zn):−
    (VehB=switchToLowSpeedVehicleB ( _ ) , poss (VehB,Z) ,
        state_update(Z,VehB,Z1 ,[] ) );
    (VehB=switchToMediumSpeedVehicleB ( _ ) , poss (VehB,Z) ,
        state_update(Z,VehB,Z1 ,[] ) );
    (VehB=switchToHighSpeedVehicleB ( _ ) , poss (VehB,Z) ,
        state_update(Z,VehB,Z1 ,[] ) );
    (VehB="VehB − Nothing" ,Z1=Z, true ) .
```

Listing 1.9. Vehicle B planner.

The sequence given in Listing 1.8 is executed until the goal state is reached or the exhaustive search is finished. In our case, the goal condition is a property to be avoided. It is fulfilled if and when the distance classification detects a collision. Listing 1.10 specifies this property in FLUX.

```
schedule_plan (Z,_,Z):−
    knows_val ([ Distance ] , distanceIsSetTo (Distance ,
        collision ) , Z ) .
```

Listing 1.10. Property to be avoided.

4.3   Contrasting these Approaches

Let us contrast these two approaches now in terms of verification results, execution time for verification of our example, and conceptually.

First of all, it is important that our new approach using the Fluent Calculus delivers the same verification results as model checking (as reported by Rathmair et al. [17]). Hence, we ran the planner as specified above, and it did not find a plan (a sequence of actions) leading to a goal specified through the collision property. This verified the model, and this verification result is consistent with the verification result reported in [17] for the model that we transformed ours from systematically (as specified above). Rathmair et al. model-checked a slightly simpler model as well (one without the *Too Close* state in the distance classification). This led to a counterexample of a collision. We modified our derived model in the same way and, in fact, our planner found a sequence of actions leading to a goal state with the collision condition. Therefore, also our approach based on the Fluent Calculus did not verify this simpler model. Again, this result is consistent with the one reported in [17].

According to [17], a verification run against the collision property using the model checking tool NuSMV takes a fraction of a second on a usual PC. We measured the execution times needed for verification by our planner, and they are also within a fraction of a second.

Hence, for this minimalist model, the execution times for verification are negligible for both approaches. As our planner is not really optimized for speed, it is conceivable that model checking will run faster for larger search spaces than our planner. Still, such a comparison for scaling is left for future work. Anyway, in theory the complexity is the same for both approaches (without bounds).

We use the Fluent Calculus as a means for verification in this paper, but such a model may be used for other purposes as well. Since the model primarily specifies *actions*, these specifications may also be used for planning or plan execution. After all, related approaches have been proposed long time ago in the context of robot planning and execution, see, e.g., [15]. This is in contrast to model checking, where only verification is possible.

5   Discussion and Future Work

In general, models abstract and, therefore, simplify. In particular, our minimalist qualitative models involve many simplifications. Physical dependencies of relative speed between the considered vehicles and changes in their distance are represented in a coarse way, since we attempted to model the logical essence in a minimalist way. Starting from such a qualitative model, systematically deriving a *quantitative* model with the same properties is important [13].

How realistic is it actually to have a Too Close state? While this may be surprising first, both human driving and ACC in reality typically lead to such situations. After all, both keep a distance (in meters or, more realistically, in seconds) exactly for the reason that there is a reaction time required for the critical case that the vehicle in front suddenly reduces its speed. This will inevitably lead to getting closer than a given target distance, which would be too close for following but still not an accident. Hence, the usual follow-up action will be to reduce the speed for increasing the distance again. In this respect, an interesting case happens in our qualitative model, where it gets stuck in the Too Close state when vehicle B does not accelerate and vehicle A cannot be slower. While this is an artefact of having a strict lower speed for both vehicles, this case is actually more realistic when considering it up to the point when both vehicles stop with a distance still greater than 0.

In fact, keeping a distance is, in reality, not just a matter of reaction time (as often tacitly assumed). Even when both vehicles had the same speed and have the same negative acceleration, the one in front starts breaking earlier. Therefore, it is always slower than the one behind, so that they will get closer and closer even when both are already breaking.

For formal verification of such models, model checking and its tool support are fairly mature. Our verification approach based on the Fluent Calculus and a planner, however, is new and its implementation more or less ad hoc. For instance, there are other search regimes that could be tried, but depth-first search was sufficient in our case. Optimizations are possible, for instance, by letting the planner identify states that cannot lead to a goal. For example, if vehicle B is driving at high speed and cruise control of vehicle A is at low speed (with distance control on standby), a collision cannot occur. If a sequence of actions is found that leads to such a state, then this path can be terminated. This approach could be used to narrow the search space actually explored.

In our running example, we only used one property to verify against, but there is also a possibility to use more than one property at the same time. For example, the negative goal could combine both reaching a collision and driving with high speed. In this case, the properties are *and*-connected and both of them have to be fulfilled for satisfying the goal. If properties are *or*-connected, only one of them has to be fulfilled, of course. A combination of both, *and*- and *or*-connected properties, is also possible.

6   Conclusion

In this paper, we study two different approaches to formal and tool-supported verification of cyber-physical feature coordination with minimalist qualitative models. Model-checking is based on a representation in synchronized FSMs, while a new planner-based approach uses a representation in the Fluent Calculus. For model-checking, the condition to be checked against is given in time logic (as usual), while it is defined for the planner-based approach as an inverted goal condition (a new contribution).

Both approaches are fully implemented for the model taken from [17], from which our representation in the Fluent Calculus is systematically transformed from. This transformation is new and could be more generally used for deriving representations in the Fluent Calculus.

Since actually a model of a cyber-physical system is verified here, it includes a (very simple) physical model. In addition, it includes a model of an independent embodied entity. This allows for formal verification of the effects of a feature coordinator, while previously only the specification of a software coordinator was published in [4].

Although such models are high-level abstractions, in our case even a minimalist model, key aspects (like avoiding a collision) can be covered. In this sense, our verification approaches offer means for studying the essence of certain safety aspects.

Our study does not, however, indicate a clear preference for either verification approach. In particular, it is hard to judge, in general, which formal verification approach is easier to use. For someone having specified a feature coordinator according to [4] through such a calculus, using it for verification purposes as well seems more appropriate than using FSMs and model checking. Still, model checking is the more widely used approach to verification and better understood.

Acknowledgments. The FeatureOpt project (No. 849928) has been partially funded by the Austrian Federal Ministry of Transport, Innovation and Technology (BMVIT) under the program "ICT of the Future" between June 2015 and May 2018. More information can be found at https://iktderzukunft.at/en/.

References

1. Apel, S., Batory, D., Kästner, C., Saake, G.: Feature-Oriented Software Product Lines: Concepts and Implementation. Springer, Heidelberg (2013). https://doi.org/10.1007/978-3-642-37521-7

2. Baier, C., Katoen, J.P.: Principles of Model Checking. MIT Press, Cambridge (2008)

3. Bensalem, S., Havelund, K., Orlandini, A.: Verification and validation meetplanning and scheduling. Int. J. Softw. Tools Technol. Transf. **16**(1), 1–12 (2014). https://doi.org/10.1007/s10009-013-0294-x

4. Bocovich, C., Atlee, J.M.: Verification and validation meetplanning and scheduling. In: Proceedings of the 22nd ACM SIGSOFT International Symposium on Foundations of Software Engineering, FSE 2014, pp. 553–563. ACM, New York (2014). https://doi.org/10.1145/2635868.2635927

5. Ertl, D., Dominka, S., Kaindl, H.: Using a mediator to handle undesired feature interaction of automated driving. In: 2013 IEEE International Conference on Systems, Man, and Cybernetics, pp. 4555–4560, October 2013. https://doi.org/10.1109/SMC.2013.775

6. Hoch, R., Kaindl, H.: Verification of feature coordination using the fluent calculus. In: Damiani, E., Spanoudakis, G., Maciaszek, L.A. (eds.) Proceedings of the 13th International Conference on Evaluation of Novel Approaches to Software Engineering, ENASE 2018, Funchal, Madeira, Portugal, 23–24 March 2018, pp. 169–179. SciTePress (2018). https://doi.org/10.5220/0006771401690179

7. Hoch, R., Kaindl, H., Popp, R., Ertl, D., Horacek, H.: Semantic service specification for V&V of service composition and business processes. In: Proceedings of the 48th Annual Hawaii International Conference on System Sciences (HICSS-48). IEEE Computer Society Press, Piscataway (2015)

8. ISO 26262: ISO 26262, road vehicles - functional safety, November 2011

9. Jackson, M., Zave, P.: Distributed feature composition: a virtual architecture for telecommunications services. IEEE Trans. Softw. Eng. (TSE) **24**(10), 831–847 (1998)

10. Juarez-Dominguez, A.L., Day, N.A., Joyce, J.J.: Modelling feature interactions in the automotive domain. In: Proceedings of the International Workshop on Models in Software Engineering, MiSE 2008, pp. 45–50. ACM, New York (2008). https://doi.org/10.1145/1370731.1370743

11. Kropf, T.: Introduction to Formal Hardware Verification. Springer, Heidelberg (1999). https://doi.org/10.1007/978-3-662-03809-3

12. Levesque, H.J., Reiter, R., Lespèrance, Y., Lin, F., Scherl, R.B.: GOLOG: a logic programming language for dynamic domains. J. Log. Program. **31**(1), 59–83 (1997). https://doi.org/10.1016/S0743-1066(96)00121-5. http://www.sciencedirect.com/science/article/pii/S0743106696001215

13. Luckeneder, C., Kaindl, H.: Systematic top-down design of cyber-physical models with integrated validation and formal verification. In: 40th International Conference on Software Engineering Companion, ICSE 2018 Companion. ACM (2018)

14. McCarthy, J., Hayes, P.J.: Some philosophical problems from the standpoint of artificial intelligence. In: Meltzer, B., Michie, D. (eds.) Machine Intelligence, vol. 4, pp. 463–502. Edinburgh University Press, Edinburgh (1969)

15. Nilsson, N.J.: Principles of Artificial Intelligence. Springer, Heidelberg (1982)

16. NuSMV: NuSMV: a new symbolic model checker, October 2018. http://nusmv.fbk.eu/

17. Rathmair, M., Luckeneder, C., Kaindl, H.: Minimalist qualitative models for model checking cyber-physical feature coordination. In: Proceedings of the 23rd Asia-Pacific Software Engineering Conference (APSEC). IEEE, December 2016

18. Reiter, R.: The frame problem in situation the calculus: a simple solution (sometimes) and a completeness result for goal regression. In: Lifschitz, V. (ed.) Artificial Intelligence and Mathematical Theory of Computation, pp. 359–380. Academic Press Professional Inc., San Diego (1991). http://dl.acm.org/citation.cfm?id=132218.132239

19. Schiffel, S., Thielscher, M.: Interpreting golog programs in flux. In: 7th International Symposium On Logical Formalizations of Commonsense Reasoning. The AAAI Press (2005)

20. Schramm, D., Bardini, R., Hiller, M.: Vehicle Dynamics. Springer, Heidelberg (2014). https://doi.org/10.1007/978-3-540-36045-2

21. Simko, G., Jackson, E.K.: A bounded model checking tool for periodic sample-hold systems. In: Proceedings of the 17th International Conference on Hybrid Systems: Computation and Control, pp. 157–162. ACM (2014)

22. Sivaji, V., Sailaja, M.: Adaptive cruise control systems for vehicle modeling using stop and go manoeuvres. Int. J. Eng. Res. Appl. (IJERA) **3**, 2248–9622 (2013). ISSN

23. Thielscher, M.: Introduction to the fluent calculus. Electron. Trans. Artif. Intell. **2**, 179–192 (1998)

24. Thielscher, M.: FLUX: a logic programming method for reasoning agents. Theory Pract. Log. Program. **5**(4–5), 533–565 (2005)

25. Wagner, D., Kaindl, H., Dominka, S., Dübner, M.: Optimization of feature interactions for automotive combustion engines. In: Proceedings of the 31st Annual ACM Symposium on Applied Computing, pp. 1401–1406. ACM (2016)

26. Winner, H., Schopper, M.: Adaptive cruise control. In: Winner, H., Hakuli, S., Lotz, F., Singer, C. (eds.) Handbuch Fahrerassistenzsysteme. A, pp. 851–891. Springer, Wiesbaden (2015). https://doi.org/10.1007/978-3-658-05734-3_46

AHM: Handling Heterogeneous Models Matching and Consistency via MDE

Mahmoud El Hamlaoui[1(✉)], Saloua Bennani[1,2(✉)], Sophie Ebersold[2(✉)], Mahmoud Nassar[1(✉)], and Bernard Coulette[2(✉)]

[1] IMS Team, ADMIR Laboratory, ENSIAS, Rabat IT Center, Mohammed V University, Rabat, Morocco
{Mahmoud.El-Hamlaoui,Saloua.Bennani,Mahmoud.Nassar}@um5.ac.ma
[2] SM@RT Team, IRIT Laboratory, University of Toulouse-Jean Jaurès, Toulouse, France
{Saloua.Bennani,Sophie.Ebersold,Bernard.Coulette}@irit.fr

Abstract. To understand and manipulate a complex system, it is necessary to apply the separation of concerns and produce distinct parts called partial models. These partial models are manipulated by different designers, and are thus generally heterogeneous, that is conform to different metamodels. Global model creation requires identifying existing correspondences between the elements of the partial models. However, in practice these correspondences are either incompletely identified or not sufficiently formalized to be maintained when the partial models evolve. This restricts their use and does not allow to fully exploit them for building the global model.

In order to have a complete view of the application domain, without combining the partial models in a single one, we have proposed AHM (Alignment of Heterogeneous Models), an approach to organize partial models as a network of models through a virtual global model called M1C (Model of correspondences between models) that conforms to a Meta-Model of Correspondences (MMC). As models evolve, we should consider the impact of changing an element involved in a correspondence on other models to keep the coherence of the global view. So, we have defined a process that automatically identify changes, classify them and treat their potential repercussions on elements of the other partial models in order to maintain the global model consistency. The approach is illustrated by the example of a Conference Management System and applied on a case study of an Hospital Emergency Department using HMCS (Heterogeneous Matching and Consistency management Suite) a developed support tool.

Keywords: Process · Metamodel · Heterogeneous models · Matching · Consistency · Correspondences · Impacts

1 Introduction

Complex systems design involve a varied set of modeling experts from different business areas. These designers can be located in distant geographical areas,

© Springer Nature Switzerland AG 2019
E. Damiani et al. (Eds.): ENASE 2018, CCIS 1023, pp. 288–313, 2019.
https://doi.org/10.1007/978-3-030-22559-9_13

as it is the case in distributed collaborative development in big software companies. Several approaches have been developed to face complex systems' modeling. The most used one is the multi-modeling approach [1]. It consists in elaborating separate partial models that correspond to different business views on the system [2]. This approach helps designers focus in isolation on different parts (partial models) of the system. However, at some point, it is mandatory to construct a global model to understand and effectively exploit the whole system. Our approach sets a matching process as presented in [7]. It allows the creation of a global view of the system through a composition based on aligning partial models. Our matching process first identifies correspondences between elements of metamodels (meta-elements). We call those correspondences HLC - High Level Correspondences- then, the process generates semi-automatically correspondences between models' elements (LLC - Low Level Correspondences). HLCs and LLCs are stored respectively in M2C (Model of correspondences between metamodels) and M1C (Model of correspondences between models). Thus, the global model is the network of partial models elements, linked thanks to the established correspondences.

Partial models may evolve during the system life cycle. As their design was made separately by different designers, their evolution within a system may occur in an uncoordinated manner. Changing one or several elements, involved in a correspondence, may cause the inconsistency of the global model. Our current objective is to ensure the consistency of M1C by re-evaluating LLCs after the evolution of each partial model. One possible approach would be to relaunch the matching process after each evolution. This solution is not optimal as it reproduces the model of correspondence "from scratch" ignoring the previously created matches. Furthermore, no trace of the changes will be kept. Our proposition takes part in the GEMOC initiative [11]. In this paper, we present an overview of the matching approach (detailed in [7]) and present thereafter the consistency management which is the added value and the core of this current work. Its role is to automatically detect changes from many heterogeneous models and treat their impacts automatically (in some cases semi-automatically) in order to ensure the coherence of the system. The process of maintaining consistency is automatically activated when the matching process produces M1C. It takes as input all the partial models of the application domain and the model of correspondence M1C as presented in Fig. 1. Our approach does not concern intramodel changes (elements changes that impacts other elements of the same partial model); it is up to the designers of partial models to manage the internal repercussions of changes made on their models and to ensure their validity. Thus, apart from the added elements, only changes (modification and deletion) that have an effect on the elements of the M1C are treated.

The rest of this paper is organized as follows: Sect. 2 introduces the Conference Management System that was chosen to apply our approach. Section 3 presents a general view of the matching approach whereas Sect. 4 describes in detail the consistency management approach. Section 5 details the validation of our approach on a Emergency Department (ED) case study. Section 6 presents the related work. We conclude this paper by some perspectives and a conclusion in Sect. 7.

2   Running Example: CMS (Conference Management System)

Production and reviewing of documents are widely used in various contexts such as project management, software development, conference management, etc. A Conference Management System (CMS) is a system designed to automate the main functions needed for the management of a scientific conference, namely: call for papers, papers submission, papers assignment for evaluation, notification of the final decision, registration, etc. Although, this system is not very complex, we had chosen it for two reasons; firstly, it is well known by almost every researcher; secondly and most importantly, it involves different designers, working with different points of view.

We represent this system by three models: a software design model, a business process model and a persistence model. Due to space limit, we refer to [6] where we provide and present in detail the three models and their respective metamodels.

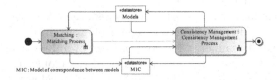

Fig. 1. Overall process of our approach [9].

3   Matching Approach

Our matching approach consists in analyzing input models (and their respective metamodels) in order to identify correspondences that exist among them. Correspondences are stored into a model of correspondences (M1C) conforming to a metamodel of correspondences (MMC). As mentioned earlier, we only consider intermodels correspondences. So, correspondences between elements of the same partial model are out of the scope of our research study. We present below the elaboration of M1C as well as the proposed iterative matching process.

3.1   Metamodel of Correspondences

MMC represented in Fig. 2 identifies the different concepts through which M1C is created. *CorrespondenceModel* contains correspondences established between at least two (meta)-elements (*RefElement*) from different (meta)models through their *references*. We store references as String to encapsulate information about both their source model and metamodel. The *Correspondence* meta-class has two attributes that works for the consistency management process: the *mandatory* attribute specifies whether a correspondence is obligatory to the studied system or not. The *weight* attribute represents the weighting coefficient associated to each correspondence. These two attributes will be explained in Sect. 4.

The *correspondence* meta-class is composed of at least two referenced elements and the *Relationship* that connects them. The *bidirectional* attribute specifies whether the relationship is bidirectional or not. If the relationship is bidirectional, the concerned (meta)elements are all source ones and there is no (meta)element of type target, as specified by the OCL rule: *self.bidirectional implies self.target →isEmpty ()*. The priority attribute, which is also used in the consistency management process, granted a priority value to each type of relationship.

Relationship is an abstract generalization of *DIR* (Domain Independent Relationship) and *DSR* (Domain Specific Relationship) meta-classes. The specialization of the first one allows representing generic relationships that are generic and independent from the domain of application. However, these relationships may be insufficient for a given domain. In this case, it is possible to add specific relationships by a specialization of the DSR meta-class.

The abstract meta-class *Level* is associated to a relationship to describe whether it represents a *High Level Relationship* (HLR) or a *Low Level Relationship* (LLR) or both. *HLR* allows representing relationships that are used in correspondences at metamodel level, whereas *LLR* represents relationships that are used in correspondences at model level. The OCL rule: *self.refined →forAll (r — r.adaptedTo → forAll (lv — lv.oclIsTypeOf (LLR) implies self.abstract.adaptedTo → forAll (lv — lv.oclIsTypeOf (HLR))))* specifies that any type of relationship usable at the HLR level is also usable at the LLR level. The opposite is not true. Other annotations are associated to relationships. They are created during the matching process and they contain their semantics expressions which will be used during the selection operation (Sect. 3.4). For example for the Similarity relationship, the semantic explains that this relationship is used in a correspondence involving two elements (recovered by the importSourceElts() operation) with indifferent types (Any, Any). It is described by an expression in Java. The condition explicitly states, using the sameAs function, that the related elements are similar.

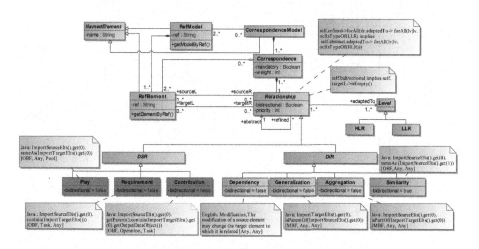

Fig. 2. MMC with semantic expressions [9].

3.2   Matching Process

The model of correspondences cannot be constructed in a monolithic manner. It follows a process that we call matching process. Figure 3 shows one iteration of the proposed process. The process involves two stakeholders, namely, an integrator expert who is the supervisor of the application domain, and a tool that assists the supervisor and enacts the automatic parts of the process.

Firstly, the process takes as input the various metamodels and the kernel of the metamodel of correspondences. Subsequently, the supervisor verifies if the MMC contains all needed relationships to set up correspondences between partial (meta)models. If he/she assumes that the proposed relationships are not sufficient to describe the given domain of application, the DSR meta-class of MMC is specialized. For the CMS, we had to add the following three DSRs to describe the whole system: *Play*, *Requirement* and *Contribution*. The first one highlights the role played by each conference attendee. The second allows us to know the required input for a task. The third identifies the operations that contribute to the success of a task.

The third activity of the matching process enriches the MMC with a Semantic Expression (SE) for each relationship. For this purpose, we proposed a Semantic

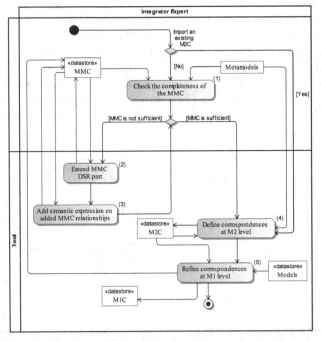

MMC : Metamodel of correspondence
DSR: Domain Specific Relationship
M2C : Model of correspondences between metamodels
M1C : Model of correspondences between models

Fig. 3. M2C Model for the CMS system [9].

Expression DSL [8] that is woven with the MMC as annotations. The advantage of using this DSL is primarily to have a structured common definition of each relationship. Secondly, it helps build M2C in an assisted way using information on the connected elements types. Thirdly, it helps filter out the correspondences in the selection step in order to keep only correspondences that match the semantics of their relationship.

Once the MMC is specialized, the matching operation begins, the supervisor identifies correspondences between meta-elements in order to produce the model of correspondences called M2C. M2C (Model of correspondences between metamodels) stores High Level Correspondences that contain meta-elements linked by High Level Relationships.

Fig. 4. Matching sub-process [9].

Figure 4 summarizes the twelve HLCs defined for CMS. We cite two examples: A *Contribution* correspondence links the meta-element *Task* from the *Business Process* metamodel to the meta-element *Operation* from the *Software Design* metamodel, since an operation can potentially contribute to the achievement of a task. A *Similarity* correspondence is established between the meta-elements *Table* and *Entity* in one side and between the meta-elements *Property* and *Column* on the other side.

HLCs are then refined in order to produce LLCs. Our developed tool produces them semi-automatically by performing a reproduction operation on the M2C followed by an operation of selection.

3.3   Reproduction

This operation is a homomorphism (structural preservation from one algebraic structure to another one) between correspondences in M2C and M1C. It duplicates all correspondences defined at the metamodel level into the model level. So, there will be as many potential LLCs for a given HLC as Cartesian product of instances of meta-elements involved in the HLC. This operation limits the generation of correspondences to elements whose type participates in a HLC.

Even if the contextual information helps avoiding the creation of correspondences between elements of types that do not match (e.g., an Operation and a Field) it does not guarantee that all generated correspondences are semantically correct.

3.4   Selection

This operation consists in filtering out correspondences produced by the reproduction operation in order to keep only those that are valid, with respect to
the semantic expression associated to their relationship, and filter out the incorrect ones. For relationships with informal expression (in natural language), the
supervisor decides whether or not to keep the correspondences depending on the
expression associated to their relationships. Considering the relationships with a
formal expression, their expressions (represented as a note in Fig. 2) have to be
executed. Execution of body's expressions requires an interpreter of the language
in which the expression is written (a Java Virtual Machine in our case).

Figure 5, illustrates the M1C model of CMS obtained when the expert manually does the selection phase. In parallel, the expert has performed the matching
process through the tool and compared the M1C that he has produced manually to the one generated by the tool. This comparison concerns only three
relationships (i.e. similarity, aggregation and contribution) as they are the only
ones currently implemented on the tool (by using some ontology-based techniques as shown in [10]). For example, executing the following sameAs method:
"Author".sameAs ("AuthorTable") returns true. Thus, the tool keeps the correspondence involving the two elements. Similarly, the execution of these two code
snippets: "firstName".isPartOf ("fullName") and "lastName".isPartOf ("full-
Name") return true. This leads to keeping the correspondence with the aggregation relationship between the two source elements (firstName, lastName) and the

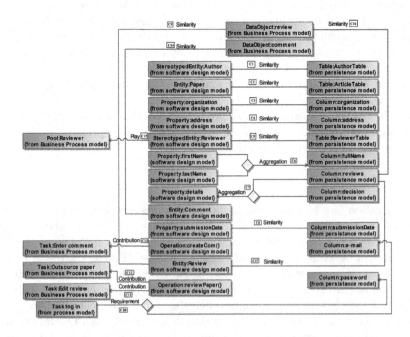

Fig. 5. M1C Model for the CMS system [9].

target element (fullName). Once the tool generates M1C, the expert evaluates the accuracy of produced LLCs. Considering precision and recall metrics, we have obtained a precision of 86% for the similarity relationship, 50% for the aggregation and 70% for the contribution. While the value of recall is respectively 75%, 75% and 100% for the similarity, aggregation and contribution relationships.

The following section will discuss the consistency management based on the manually produced model of correspondences presented in Fig. 5. The seventeen LLCs produced were numerated to facilitate their exploitation on the next section.

4   Consistency Management Approach

Since models evolution is generally not coordinated between partial models designers, each model may evolve independently. So, it is very tedious to rerun the matching process after each change due to the human effort required in the matching activity and the lack of changes tracking.

Our approach provides a consistency management process. This process is automatically activated using the Observer pattern [14] at the end of the matching process. It takes as input the system's partial models and the model of correspondences between them (M1C) and it follows six steps as shown in Fig. 6 (change detection, change analysis, cycle management, change scheduling strategy, change prioritization and change processing). The first step requires continuous monitoring while the others are triggered successively on the expert's demand. This process is carried out by a developed tool and imply the expert's intervention in phases that require a human expertise or configuration. Throughout this section, we are going to detail these six steps.

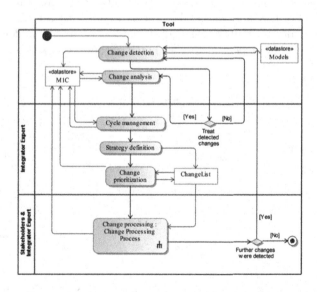

Fig. 6. Consistency management sub-process [9].

4.1   Changes Detection

Changes are detected when they occur through the Observer pattern model instead of differencing techniques as done in EMFCompare [3] that provides a generic algorithm for calculating differences between two versions of a model. The problem with these techniques is threefold. Firstly, the whole model must be parsed in order to check if an element has changed between two versions of a model, based on distance computing techniques. Secondly, there is a restriction on the number of models because comparison can be done with only two models of a given business domain. Thirdly, there is a waste of memory since they require keeping in memory the previous version of the input model as well as the current one.

Changes detected by the implementation of the Observer pattern are subsequently added to M1C using the MMC meta-classes *History, DiffElt, AddedElt, DeletedElt, ModifiedElt* (part 1 of Fig. 7). *History* is used to keep track of applied changes. *DiffElt* allows to record the trace of evolved elements. It has two attributes. The first attribute contains the change classification type. The second attribute contains the reference of the element constructed from the element's name, its meta-element and the model's name. *DeletedElt* represents an element that no longer exists in the original model but that is maintained for tracing purpose. *AddedElt* and *ModifiedElt* respectively represent newly added element and model element that has undergone a modification.

The extended MMC defines moreover a concept that represents the core of the observer pattern (part 2 of Fig. 7). The *Observer* meta-class specifies the model's element to be observed. It is a generalization of the subject meta-class which has three methods. Two of them (*attach* and *detach*) allow to fix or detach an observer object from a model element. The third method (*notify*) makes it possible to notify the M1C of the changes that have taken place. The *update* method of the meta-class Observer is used during the phase of changes processing in order to maintain the consistency of domain's models. The third part of Fig. 7 (i.e. the *impact* meta-class) defines the *impact kind* of each change

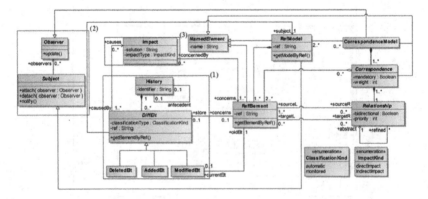

Fig. 7. Extension of the correspondence metamodel (MMC) to handle consistency management [9].

and the *solution* for each change. A change on an element may affect directly or indirectly elements that are linked to this element by a correspondence as we will see in Sect. 4.2.

The column change type of Table 1 summarizes the evolutions performed on the CMS models. These changes are automatically detected via the tool (with a continuous monitoring) and added to the M1C. Two roles (i. "chairman" and "author") have been added to the business process model. Moreover, the following elements have been removed: *Property:phoneNumber* and *Entity:Comment* from the software design model and *Task:outsource paper* from the business process model. We also consider that the software architect has renamed the operation *createCom()* and replaced the *Entity:Review* element with *Entity:Note* element.

Table 1. Steps of the consistency management process on the CMS system [9].

Model's Element	Type	Change Analysis		Change Priorization		Change Processing
		Classif.	Influenced Elts.	Weight	Order	
Pool:Chairman	A	Auto.	-	0	4	Matching process
Pool:Author	A	Auto.	-	0	3	Matching process
Task:Outsource paper	D	Auto.	Operation:reviewPaper()(Directly) Task:Edit review(Indirectly)	8	1	Restoring the deleted element
Property:phoneNumber	D	Auto.	-	-	-	-
Entity:Comment	D	Auto.	DataObject:Comment(Directly)	1	2	Deleting the correspondence
Old Operation:createCom() New Operation:createComments()	M	Moni.	Task:Enter comment(Directly)	4	6	Maintaining the correspondence
Old Entity:Review New Entity:Note	M	Moni.	DataObject:Review(Directly), DataObject:Review(Indirectly) Column:review(Directly), Property:details(Indirectly)	6	5	Modifying the correspondence's end element (C9) deleting the correspondence (C16)

A: Addition, D: Deletion, M: Modification, Classif: Classification, Auto: Automatic, Moni: Monitored

4.2 Changes Analysis

This analysis includes defining the type of change and the M1C elements that may be affected by this change. This is possible thanks to the extension of the MMC, which makes it possible to find for a modified element the correspondence(s) to which it belongs and thus to find the element(s) that may be affected. Directly impacted elements are elements directly related to a modified element, whereas indirectly impacted elements are elements that may be affected via a cascading effect.

Suppose we have two correspondences (Fig. 8), the first one linking an element A to an element B by the relationship Rx and the second one relating the element B to an element C by the relationship Ry. If element A is modified, element B can be influenced directly by this change, whereas element C may be affected indirectly via the cascading effect.

In this phase, we also classify changes in two categories: the automatic mode for added and deleted elements and the monitored mode for the modified elements.

Column *change analysis* of Table 1 shows the information that are automatically added to the M1C during this phase. The added elements are classified in the automatic mode since adding them does not affect the consistency of the M1C. Deleted items are also classified in the automatic mode. Deleting the

Fig. 8. Example of cascading effect [9].

Property:phoneNumber element has no effect on M1C since it does not participate in any correspondence. Deleting the *Entity:Comment* element has a direct
impact on the *DataObject:comment* (linked via correspondence C14 as shown in
Fig. 5) while deleting the *Task:Outsource paper* element has a direct influence
on the *Operation:reviewPaper()* element (correspondence C12) and an indirect
influence on the *Task:Edit review* element (correspondence C11). Modified elements are classified in guided mode. The modification of *Operation:createCom()*
element has a direct influence on the *Task:Enter comment* element (via correspondence C13), whereas the change on the *Entity:Review* has a direct influence
on the *DataObject:review* (correspondence C9) and *Column:reviews* (correspondence C16) and an indirect influence on the *DataObject:review* (correspondence
C17) and *Property:details* (correspondence C7).

4.3   Cycle Management

Once changes and their direct or indirect impacts are detected, the tool catches
automatically the cycles of cascading effects. Then the expert chooses to delete
one of the correspondences in order to break the cycle. Let's take the example
presented in Fig. 9, we have three correspondences. The first one relates an element A to an element B, the second one connects element B to an element C and
the third one relates C to A. If the element A is modified, the element B can be
directly influenced by this change, which indirectly influences the element C. In
the case where the element C is the one that causes the modification of the Element A, we will have a cascading cyclical effect. The various cascading cyclical
effects are reported to the expert to decide to delete one of these correspondences
in order to break the cycle.

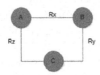

Fig. 9. An example of the cascading cyclical effect [9].

4.4   Change Scheduling Strategy

This step aims at producing an ordered list of changes. We propose two strategies for change ordering: classification-based strategy and impact-based strategy.

The classification-based strategy consists of creating a list of changes that contains, in order, changes that are classified in automatic mode followed by those in monitored mode. For example, by choosing this strategy, the list of changes produced in the CMS is as follows: *Pool:Chairman*, *Pool:Author*, *Task:Outsource paper*, *Property:phoneNumber*, *Entity:Comment*; *Operation:createComments()* and *Entity:Note*.

The second strategy that we propose creates an ordered list depending on the type of impact of each change. For example, the expert may start by processing the changes that have both direct and indirect impacts on other elements and leave changes that have only direct impacts on other elements to the end. By choosing this strategy, the list of produced changes for the CMS will be ordered as follows: *Entity:Note*, *Task:Outsource paper*, *Pool:Chairman*, *Pool:Author*, *Property:phoneNumber*, *Entity:Comment*, *Operation:createComments()*.

These two scheduling strategies work for changes that have different modes of change or different types of impact. In the next section, we will see how to classify changes that have the same type of impact or the same mode of classification.

4.5   Change Prioritization

Changes processing order has an impact on the system and its consistency. That's why we attribute a weighting coefficient to each correspondence so we can determinate a prioritized processing order. Taking the example of Fig. 9, assuming that elements A and C have been modified, the question to be raised is which change to treat first, knowing that both have an influence on the same element B? and will the two changes be treated?. Prioritization allows to answer these two questions. We first deal with the change that has the highest weighting coefficient, next change must then take into account the impact of the previous changes. In other words, if the change of the element A requires the modification of the element B, the element C can modify the element B only if the correspondence linking the element A and B has not been changed semantically. The order of processing is defined by calculating the weighting coefficient of the correspondence. This coefficient is calculated by the following formula:

$$weight = \sum_{k=0}^{n}(DirectlyAffectedElement_k * priority)$$

$$+ \sum_{k=0}^{n}(IndirectlyAffectedElement_k * priority)$$

Where the term priority is the level of priority given to each type of relationship. We consider that the supervisor gives level 1 to the relationship *Similarity*, level

2 to the *Aggregation*, level 3 to the *Play* relationship, level 4 to the *Contribution* and level 5 to the relationship of *requirement*.

Sub column *order* of column *change prioritization* of Table 1 illustrates the result of the change prioritization phase according to the strategy chosen in the previous step (in our case, automatic mode first) and to the calculated coefficients.

When several changes have the same weighting coefficient, it is up to the expert to decide on the processing order, except for the addition type changes for which there is no order preference given that all added elements are processed at the end of the change processing by using the matching process. Let's detail the weighing coefficient calculation for the highest change (deletion of *Task:OutsourcePaper*): This element is directly linked to *Operation:ReviewPaper()* via a *Contribution* link (priority 4) and indirectly linked to *Task:Edit Review* via a *Contribution* link also. The weighting coefficient is thus $4*1+4*1=8$.

4.6   Change Processing

In this step, M1C and the partial models may be modified to take account of the changes that have been detected. Figure 10 presents the change processing process. Changes categorized in automatic mode are processed automatically.

In case where an element has been added, the matching process is restarted at the end of the change process to handle the added elements all at once. In case an element has been deleted, all correspondences involving this element become orphaned. An orphaned correspondence is a correspondence for which one of its ends - a model element - is missing. When a correspondence becomes orphaned, the expert checks if it is mandatory for the concerned system (true in the mandatory attribute). In positive case, the deleted item is restored, otherwise the correspondence is deleted from the model of correspondences.

Concerning the second type of changes, namely changes occurring in a monitored mode, they are managed semi-automatically. The correspondence is maintained if, after the change of one of its ends, it remains correct regarding the semantic associated to its type of relationship. Otherwise, when an element is modified, it is necessary to modify each of the elements tied to it since this modification is possible. When it is impossible to modify an element, the correspondence is deleted if it is not mandatory (mandatory = false). Otherwise, a group decision making, involving the expert with partial model designers, takes place to decide whether to modify the concerned element or the element at the other end of the correspondence.

For the CMS example, we proceed following the column *order* of Table 1, the first removed element is restored because it is used in the correspondence C12 (see Fig. 5) and it is a compulsory correspondence (mandatory = true). Correspondence C14 involving the second element is deleted, since it is an orphan correspondence and it is not mandatory for the system consistency. The matching is invoked at the end of the process to search for possible correspondences

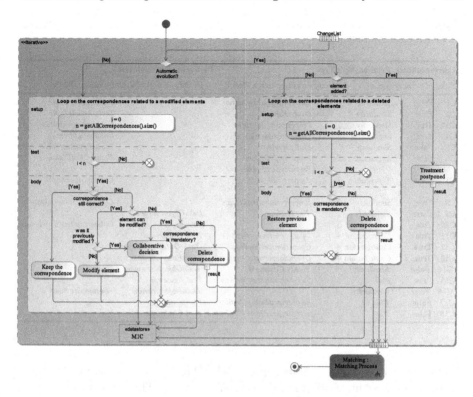

Fig. 10. Change processing steps [9].

for the third and the fourth element. Two correspondences using the *play* relationship are thus created (C17 and C18). The fifth element is involved in two correspondences C9 and C16. The first one links it to the *DataObject:review* element and the second to the *Column:reviews* element. The element of the opposite end of the first correspondence is modified since the correspondence is no longer correct. Concerning the second correspondence, since the opposite element cannot be modified (because of the choice to prohibit the modification or the deletion of any element of the persistence model) and the correspondence is not obligatory, it is then deleted.

Table 2 summarizes the change processing on the CMS and their impacts on the correspondences. Lines in bold indicate changes that have been made to M1C of Fig. 5. The underline lines concern added elements (i.e. new correspondences: C17 and C18), those in dotted lines concern modified elements (impacted correspondences: C12 and C13). Deleted elements are barred (C14 and C16).

5   Tool Support and Validation of the Approach

So far, we have validated our approach through the development of a HMCS prototype and different case studies. This section presents the Emergency

Table 2. CMS system's M1C model after models evolution and Consistency Management Process conduct [9].

Correspondence		Relationship's Type		Partial Models' Elements		
Name	Mandatory	Name	Priority	Software Design Model	Business Process Model	Persistence Model
C1	False	*Similarity*	1	*StereotypedEntity:Author*		*Table:AuthorTable*
C2	False	*Similarity*	1	*Entity:Paper*		*Table:ArticleTable*
C3	True	*Similarity*	1	*Property:organization*		*Column:organization*
C4	True	*Similarity*	1	*Property:address*		*Column:address*
C5	False	*Similarity*	1	*Entity:Reviewer*		*Table:ReviewerTable*
C6	False	*Aggregation*	2	*Property:firstName* *Property:lastName*		*Column:FullName*
C7	False	*Aggregation*	2	*Property:details*		*Column:reviews* *Column:decision*
C8	True	*Similarity*	1	*Property:submissionDate*		*Column:admissionDate*
C9	False	*Similarity*	1	*Entity:Note*	*DataObject:notice*	
C10	True	*Requirement*	5		*Task:logIn*	*Columns:password, e-mail*
C11	True	*Contribution*	4	*Operation:reviewPaper()*	*Task:Edit review*	
C12	**True**	**Contribution**	**4**	**Operation:reviewPaper()**	**Task:Outsource paper**	
C13	**True**	**Contribution**	**4**	**Operation:createComments()**	**Task:Enter comment**	
~~C14~~	~~False~~	~~*Similarity*~~	~~1~~	~~*Entity:Comment*~~	~~*DataObject:comment*~~	
C15	False	*Play*	3	*StereotypedEntity:Reviewer*	*Pool:Reviewer*	
~~C16~~	~~False~~	~~*Similarity*~~	~~1~~		~~*DataObject:review*~~	~~*Column:reviews*~~
C17	**False**	**Play**	**3**	**StereotypedEntity:Author**	**Pool:Author**	
C18	**False**	**Play**	**3**	**StereotypedEntity:Chairman**	**Pool:Chairman**	

Department case study, implemented with HMCS. The case study is related to the management of a Hospital Emergency Service. This work was led in collaboration with medical staff of the hospital of Montpellier (France) who helped us to define requirements for distribute designers teams. We think this case study is a real application example of complex systems that concern our research.

In this section, we first present the ED design viewpoints, then we conduct our approach using the HMCS Tool.

5.1   ED Case Study

Emergency Departments (EDs) represent a critical branch of any country's health system. Such departments are usually faced with emergency situations (accidents, natural disasters, terrorist attacks, wars, epidemics, etc.) that need special skills provided by a multidisciplinary approach where viewpoints are complementary. Thus a need of coordination between stakeholders must be taken into account in the design phase of such a system, so that the different models developed in this phase can be synchronized. Non optimal management of EDs - which can be noticed quite often - comes partly from an insufficient consideration of these factors at design time. In addition, models can evolve because laws, regulations, business rules, operating procedures, security constraints and personal data protection, etc., may change. In this study, we place ourselves specifically in the context of the ED of Montpellier public hospital.

Many actors are involved in the proper functioning of an ED, from nurse's aides to emergency physicians (i.e. surgeons). For the sake of simplicity, we have limited our case study to three business domains managed separately by the following actors:

- Medical report designer: responsible for building digital mockups that define an Emergency Examination Report (EER). He creates a model conform to a form metamodel,
- Software designer: responsible for the representation of organizational data of the information system through an object-oriented metamodel,
- Process designer: He defines medical protocols to be applied by ED staffs. He creates a model expressed through a process-based metamodel.

In the following, we present the requirements identified for the elaboration of models and their respective metamodels. We do not consider the concrete syntax of DSLs, so, in the context of this study, a DSL can be seen as a metamodel defining an abstract syntax.

Organizational Model. The organizational model (an extract is presented on Fig. 11) should represent the organization of an ED. An ED is described by its name, address and staff (administrative staff, technical staff, nurse, emergency physician and surgeon), patients and examination rooms. For each staff member, it is possible to know his certifications and skills, spoken languages, his hire date and his schedule. Technical staff maintain and order machines. Administrative Staff book rooms, collect payments, etc. An emergency physician gives advice and treats his patients.

The organizational model must conform to the metamodel shown in Fig. 12. This latter represents a simplified version of a design metamodel in an object-oriented form. The basic concept is the Package, which contains classes and interfaces. Each of them may have attributes and methods.

Medical Protocols Model. Model of medical protocols (extract on Fig. 13) intends to describe the different protocols to be applied by each category of staff. First, a sorting nurse receives each patient and directs him towards a medical service (medical or surgical). Then, a healthcare assistant installs the patient in a room. After that, a protocol interview is performed by a nurse in order to collect administrative data as well as medical ones. An emergency physician achieves a consultation and makes a prescription. The nurse goes back to the patient and executes the doctor's prescription.

The metamodel represented in Fig. 14 allows to construct the medical protocols model. It defines a concept called "ProcessModel" that includes products, roles and activities, as well as relations between them. Activities are related to each other through the abstract concept ActivityEdge. An activity is also related to the abstract concept ActivityNode.

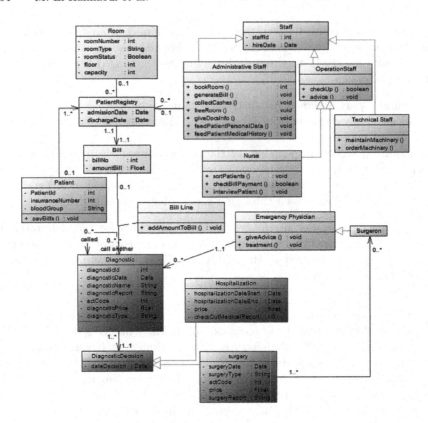

Fig. 11. Organizational model.

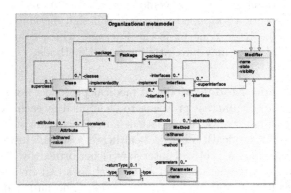

Fig. 12. Organizational metamodel.

Emergency Examination Report (EER) Model. An EER model (Fig. 15) represents information that will be produced by an emergency physician for a given patient. In a general way, it contains the identifier of the physician, information about the patient (social security number, first name, last name

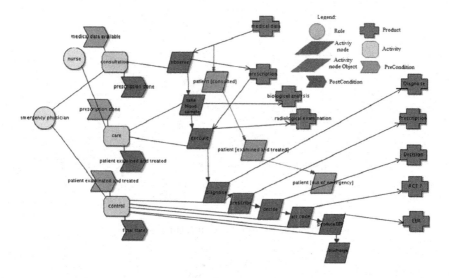

Fig. 13. Process model.

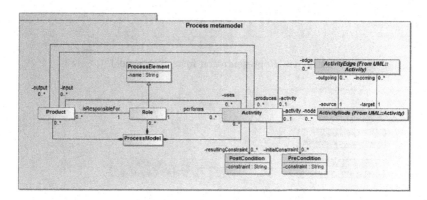

Fig. 14. Process metamodel.

and age), the patient's arrival date and his clinical observation. This latter is made using codified abbreviations and associated explanations. It identifies the pathology in order to direct the patient towards the appropriate service within the same institution or in another one.

The metamodel proposed in Fig. 16 allows the representation of an EER as a form with a set of optionally composite fields.

5.2 Application to the ED Case Study

Matching Process for ED System

Before starting the creation of the model of correspondences, MMC may need

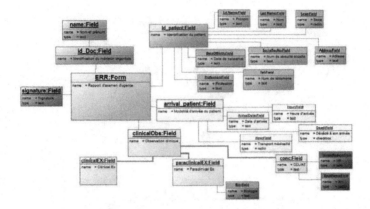

Fig. 15. Representation form model.

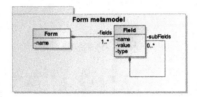

Fig. 16. Representation form metamodel.

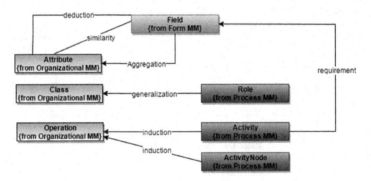

Fig. 17. ED HLCS.

to be specialized in order to add some relationships specific to the ED domain. Within this context, the three following relationships have been added to MMC's kernel: *Requirement, Deduction* and *Induction*. The first one allows to know the fields that an activity needs for its smooth running. The second one allows to deduce, through a function, the value of another element. The third one is used to represent the operations that an activity invokes for its execution.

The produced M2C model (Fig. 17) is composed of 7 HLCs created using the HMCS tool. As examples of created HLCs, we have three ones relating the meta-element *Attribute* from the organizational metamodel, to the meta-element *Field* from the Form metamodel through the following relationships: *Similarity*, *Deduction* and *Aggregation*.

Once M2C is built, the expert assigns each relationship type with a priority value. The priority values: 1, 1, 2, 2, 3, 3, 4 are assigned respectively to the types Similarity, Dependency, Aggregation, Generalization, Deduction, Induction and Requirement. The priority values will be used in the consistency management process. In the ED case study, 16 LLCs have been produced semi-automatically (automatically for the reproduction step and in assisted way for the selection step) as shown in Fig. 18.

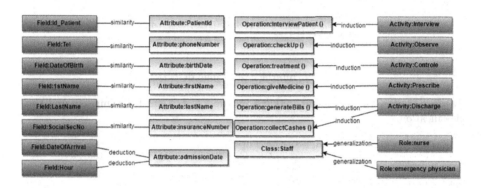

Fig. 18. ED LLCS.

Consistency Management Process for ED System

We present in this section the enactment of the consistency management process.

We consider that the ED viewpoints' models have undergo a set of changes. These changes are automatically detected via the HMCS tool and added to the M1C. Figure 19 presents some of the changes detected on the Representation Form model. Field *DateOfbirth* was deleted, likewise, Fields *SocialSecNo* and *Conc* were modified and become respectively *PatientRecordNo* and *Description*. The set of all changes performed on the ED viewpoints' models are described in the first two columns of Table 3: A role secretary has been added to the business process model. This role manages a patient's departure, and performs a number of tasks: he/she prints the orders as well as the emergency report, then edits the invoice and receives the payment.

Column "Change Analysis" of Table 3 defines, for each change, both the classification mode (automatic or monitored) and the elements that the change affect either directly or indirectly. This information is automatically integrated into the M1C by HMCS. For example, removing the *Field:DateOfBirth* has a direct influence on the *Atttribute:birthdate*, while removing the *Field:DateOfArrival* has no influence on the other models elements. These two changes are classified in automatic mode. The added elements (e.g. *Activity:Print Prescription*, *Activity:Print Emergency Report*) are also categorized in automatic mode and

Fig. 19. Interface of change detection.

Table 3. Overview of changes undergo by the ED system, their impacts and their classification.

Type	Model's element	Change analysis		Change prioritization	
		Classif.	Influenced Elts.	Weight	Order
A	*Role:Secretary*	Auto	-	0	4
A	*Activity:Print Prescription*	Auto	-	0	5
A	*Activity:Print Emergency Report*	Auto	-	0	6
A	*Activity:Edit Invoice*	Auto	-	0	7
A	*Activity:Receive Payment*	Auto	-	0	8
D	*Field:DateOfBirth*	Auto	*Attribute:birthdate (Directly)*	1	3
D	*Field:DateOfArrival*	Auto	-	0	
M	<u>Old</u>: *Field:SocialSecNo* <u>New</u>: *Field:PatientRecordNo*	Moni	*Attribute:insuranceNumber(Directly)*	1	2
M	<u>Old</u>: *Field:Conc* <u>New</u>: *Field:Description*	Moni	*Attribute:description(Directly)* *Activity:Diagnose(Directly)*	5	1

A: Addition, D: Deletion, M: Modification
Classif: Classification, Auto: Automatic, Moni: Monitored

adding them does not affect the consistency of the existing M1C. Modifying the *Field:SocialSecNo* has a direct influence on the *Attribute:insuranceNumber*. At the same time, changing the *Field:Conc* has a direct influence on the *Activity:Diagnose* and *Attribute:description*.

For the change prioritization step, the expert has to choose between two strategies: Classification based Strategy or Impact Based Strategy. In the ED case study, he chose the classification based strategy. Thus, change processing will start by the monitored one before dealing with those on automatic mode. Since we treat the evolution of one change at a time, changes from the same mode need to be classified between them. For that, we automatically calculate a weighting coefficient for each change. The weight equals the number of impacted elements multiplied by the priority of the relationship that linked them. Thus, for *Field:DateOfBirth*, the weight equals one (*Attribute:birthdate*) multiplied by the priority of the Similarity relationship (prioritySimilarity = 1). Likewise, for the *Field:Conc*, the weight equals Attribute:description * prioritySimilarity + Activity:Diagnose * priorityRequirement = 1*1 + 1*4 = 5.

The result of the prioritization is an ordered list of changes as presented by the sub column order of Table 3 (i.e. 1st *Field:Conc*, 2nd *Field:SocialSecNo*, 3rd *Field:DateOfBirth*, 4th *Role:Secretary*, 5th *Activity:Print Prescription*, 6th *Activity:Print Emergency Report*, 7th *Activity:Edit Invoice*, 8th *Activity:Receive Payment*.

Notice that changes of type addition were ordered randomly since they are treated at the end of change processing by recalling the matching process.

Once changes have been classified, their processing starts. For the first two changes (Field:Conc and Field:SocialSecNo), the correspondences concerned are maintained because they remain valid after their modification. This validity is verified by executing the body of the condition associated with the type of relationship involved in the correspondence. The removal of the third element (Field:DateOfBirth), causes the suppression of the correspondence since it became orphan and is not obligatory (mandatory = false). For the rest of changes (i.e. additions), the matching operation is invoked at the end of the process to check for potential correspondences.

Figure 20 illustrates the functionality provided by HMCS to manage change processing. For each history (box 1), the list of changes (box 2) ordered using the calculated weights is displayed. For the second change (SocialSecNo), the list of elements linked to it is shown in Box 3. As the implementation of relationships semantics is not yet complete, we added Box 4 which allows to the expert to decide for each change what to do in regard to the relationship condition. The restore action retrieves the previous version of the item, the modify action modifies the item at the end of the match. If the match is no longer valid, the delete action removes it from the model of correspondences.

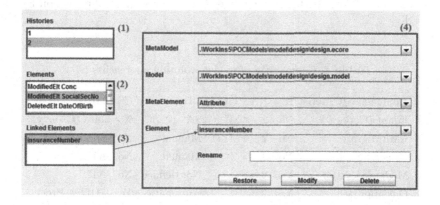

Fig. 20. Interface of models consistency management.

6   Related Work

A number of approaches described in the literature deal with view-based complex systems' design through models matching. As this paper mainly addresses the consistency management due to an evolution, in this section, we put the focus on the subset of these approaches that support one or several aspects of model evolution issue. To do that, we have studied a set of representative approaches, namely Edapt [15], previously called COPE [13], EMFMigrate [5], Model federation [12] and the one developed by Cicchetti et al. [4]. To lead this study we have defined and used the following criteria that we consider relevant in a multi-modeling environment: heterogeneity, number of input artifacts and their types, mechanism of change detection, adopted support of changes' classification, and migration rules. These criteria are defined as follows:

- Heterogeneity: expresses if the considered approach takes into account heterogeneous artifacts. We consider that two artifacts are heterogeneous if their modeling languages are themselves different,
- Number of input Artifacts: indicates the maximum number of input artifacts allowed by the approach,
- Types of Artifacts: identifies the shape of representing artifacts. The latters are not necessarily models, they might be rules of transformation or other types of artifacts,
- Change Detection: assesses how an approach proceeds to detect the elements of artifacts that have undergone an alteration,
- Classification Support: indicates whether the approach supports a classification of changes in order to assign to each kind of change a particular action. It is interesting to take this criterion into account, because the classification of changes allows the automation of the whole evolution management process or at least a part of it,
- Migration Rules: describes the language in which the migration rules are implemented. It is with this language that the treatment of evolution is realized.

Table 4. Comparison of model evolution approaches [9].

Approaches/Criteria	H	NA	TA	CD	CS	MR
Edapt (Cope)	No	2	M[a]	SA[c]	No	Java (Groovy)
EMFMigrate	No	2	M/T[b]	Manual	No	Specific DSL
Cichetti et al.	No	2	M	Manual	No	ATL[d]
Model federation	Yes	2..n	M	Not defined	No	ATL[4]
Our approach	Yes	2..n	M	Automatic	Yes	M1C + Process

[a] Model [b] Transformation rules [c] Semi-automatic [d] ATLAS Transformation Language

Table 4 presents a synopsis of the studied approaches, based on the established criteria. By analyzing it, we can deduce that the consistency management process has not reached a sufficient maturity yet. Firstly, the studied approaches do not define any classification support, a factor that we consider mandatory to automatically manage changes and their impacts on models, through predefined actions. Secondly, for a complex change which affects several elements at the same time, multiple rules are likely to be produced. Choosing the appropriate adjustment to run requires rules' customization and also some technical background knowledge. Thirdly, most of the approaches discussed above, except Model Federation and Cicchetti and al., focus on model evolution as a result of adaptation of their corresponding metamodels (co-evolution) to preserve the conformity relationship. That is to say that these approaches emphasize the vertical level (co-evolution) without considering horizontal evolution (between models). It is within the scope of this latter that models synchronization is based. Fourthly, EMFMigrate and Cicchetti and al. require a specific difference metamodel and it is up to the stakeholder to detect the changes and represent them in a difference model. Fifthly, the model federation approach responds to our problem by exploiting correspondences established for the consistency management. However, it does not propose a mechanism for managing traceability of changes. Moreover, the approach is based essentially on the modification change of type. Therefore, it does not manage impacts due to the addition or deletion of model elements. For the modification, the synchronization cannot be applied without defining a master and a slave model.

To sum up, the approaches presented above do not consider or respect all of the criteria described above and thus do not fully address some important aspects of model evolution. This is because they do not exploit previously established correspondences to provide a mechanism that ensures the consistency of the overall model.

7   Conclusion and Perspectives

Our general research work concerns design of complex information systems in a multi-views context. During the modeling cycle, partial models may evolve frequently due to the definition of new requirements or constraints. Thus, several changes can occur on different models of the system. To manage the consistency between these models, we provide an approach that (1) semi automatically establishes a model of correspondences among these models. Then (2) it uses this model of correspondences to treat the automatically identified changes. Indeed, the consistency management process handles changes performed on the partial models and their respectives impacts on the other interconnected models to maintain the global consistency.

As a proof of concept of our approach we are developing a support tool (HMCS for Heterogeneous Matching and Consistency management Suite). Its role is to provide assistance to the expert in the creation of the model of correspondences and the management of the consistency of the partial models when they evolve. HMCS is operational for the matching process but not complete for the consistency management one. This tool, once completed, will allow us to validate our approach and to conduct experiments to verify thereafter its scalability.

As a perspective for our work. We are considering the adaptation of the approach to support collaboration in both model matching and model of correspondences consistency management. Indeed, in real complex systems, designers should closely work together to complement each other since each one of them deals with a distinct point of view, and an expert role - that grasps all concerns of viewpoints - can hardly be defined for such systems.

References

1. Boronat, A., Knapp, A., Meseguer, J., Wirsing, M.: What Is a multi-modeling language? In: Corradini, A., Montanari, U. (eds.) WADT 2008. LNCS, vol. 5486, pp. 71–87. Springer, Heidelberg (2009). https://doi.org/10.1007/978-3-642-03429-9_6

2. Boulanger, F., Jacquet, C., Hardebolle, C., Rouis, E.: Modeling heterogeneous points of view with ModHel'X. In: Ghosh, S. (ed.) MODELS 2009. LNCS, vol. 6002, pp. 310–324. Springer, Heidelberg (2010). https://doi.org/10.1007/978-3-642-12261-3_29

3. Brun, C., Pierantonio, A.: Model differences in the eclipse modeling framework. UPGRADE Eur. J. Inf. Prof. **9**(2), 29–34 (2008)

4. Cicchetti, A., Di Ruscio, D., Eramo, R., Pierantonio, A.: Automating co-evolution in model-driven engineering. In: 12th International IEEE Enterprise Distributed Object Computing Conference EDOC 2008, pp. 222–231. IEEE (2008)

5. Di Ruscio, D., Iovino, L., Pierantonio, A.: What is needed for managing co-evolution in mde? In: Proceedings of the 2nd International Workshop on Model Comparison in Practice, pp. 30–38. ACM (2011)

6. El Hamlaoui, M.: Conference management system example, June 2017. https://cloud.irit.fr/index.php/s/6tSteLq1H1wLnDz

7. El Hamlaoui, M., et al.: Alignment of viewpoint heterogeneous design models: Emergency department case study. In: International Workshop On the Globalization of Modeling Languages (GEMOC) co-located with MODELS 2016. CEUR Workshop Proceedings (2016)

8. El Hamlaoui, M., Ebersold, S., Coulette, B., Anwar, A., Nassar, M.: Maintien de la cohérence de modèles de conception hétérogènes. Tech. et Sci. Informatiques **34**(6), 667–702 (2015)

9. El Hamlaoui, M., Bennani, S., Nassar, M., Ebersold, S., Coulette, B.: A MDE approach for heterogeneous models consistency. In: Proceedings of the 13th International Conference on Evaluation of Novel Approaches to Software Engineering, ENASE 2018, Funchal, Madeira, Portugal, 23–24 March 2018, pp. 180–191 (2018). https://doi.org/10.5220/0006774101800191

10. El Hamlaoui, M., Trojahn, C., Ebersold, S., Coulette, B.: Towards an ontology-based approach for heterogeneous model matching. In: 2nd International Workshop On the Globalization of Modeling Languages (GEMOC 2014) co-located with ACM/IEEE International Conference on Model Driven Engineering Languages and Systems (MODELS). CEUR Workshop Proceedings (2014)

11. GEMOC: Initiative on the globalization of modeling languages, April 2017. http://gemoc.org/ins/
12. Guychard, C., Guerin, S., Koudri, A., Beugnard, A., Dagnat, F.: Conceptual interoperability through models federation. In: Semantic Information Federation Community Workshop (2013)
13. Herrmannsdoerfer, M., Benz, S., Juergens, E.: COPE: a language for the coupled evolution of metamodels and models. In: International Workshop on Model Co-Evolution and Consistency Management (2008)
14. Vlissides, J., Helm, R., Johnson, R., Gamma, E.: Design Patterns: Elements of Reusable Object-Oriented Software. Addison-Wesley, Reading (1995)
15. Williams, J., Paige, R., Polack, F.: Searching for model migration strategies. In: Proceedings of the 6th International Workshop on Models and Evolution, pp. 39–44. ACM (2012)

GenesLove.Me 2.0: Improving
the Prioritization of Genetic Variations

José Fabián Reyes Román[1,2(✉)], Alberto García[1], Urko Rueda[1],
and Óscar Pastor[1]

[1] PROS Research Center, Universitat Politècnica de València,
Camino Vera S/N. 46022, Valencia, Spain
{jreyes, algarsi3, urueda, opastor}@pros.upv.es
[2] Department of Engineering Sciences, Universidad Central del Este (UCE),
Ave. Francisco Alberto Caamaño Deñó, 21000 San Pedro de Macorís,
Dominican Republic

Abstract. The objective of this research work is to present the advances obtained
in the development of the prototype called "*VarSearch*" (now called "*GenesLove.
Me 2.0*"), which aims to manage large amounts of genomic information for further
exploitation through of genomic reports that allow enhancing the highly
acclaimed "*Personalized Medicine*". This software project is considered from the
perspective of *Information Systems Engineering* (ISE) applied to the genomic
domain, this with the goal of eradicating or reducing the problems and challenges
present in the so-called "*genomic data chaos*". GenesLove.Me 2.0 (GLM 2.0) is
based on the *Conceptual Model of the Human Genome* (CMHG), which allows to
improve the understanding and reduce the complexity of the domain. Currently, it
has new phenotypes studied, which integrate within the methodology used a data
quality criteria that contribute to the management of curated data. Therefore,
providing a software tool based on conceptual models for the generation of
genomic reports is a breakthrough that improves the working methods and
techniques of all stakeholders (e.g., *geneticists*, *researchers*, *clinical laboratories*)
in the genomic and clinical context.

Keywords: GLM 2.0 · GeIS · Variation · Conceptual modeling · PM

1 Introduction

Understanding the human genome is a good example of such an extremely complex
problem. But it is important to highlight that thanks to the advances in NGS (*Next
Generation Sequencing*) [1], there has been considerable growth in the generation of
genomic and molecular information. All the interactions that have emerged from this
genomic knowledge have had a high and direct impact on the medical environment and
Precision Medicine (PM) [2].

Applying the Conceptual Modeling (CM) [3] techniques to the genomic domain
provides solutions and optimizes some of the processes carried out by experts (i.e.,
genetic laboratories, biologists, researchers or geneticists), and helps to solve the
problems that arise in handling the large amounts of information from different

E. Damiani et al. (Eds.): ENASE 2018, CCIS 1023, pp. 314–333, 2019.
https://doi.org/10.1007/978-3-030-22559-9_14

sequencing methods. The use of advanced *Information Systems Engineering* (ISE) approaches can be useful in this domain due to the huge amount of biological information to be captured, understood and effectively managed. The existence of a large set of diverse data sources containing large amounts of data in continuous evolution makes it difficult to find convincing solutions [4]. When we addressed this problem from the ISE perspective, we understood that precise CMs were required to understand the relevant information in the domain and to clearly fix and represent it to obtain an effective data management strategy.

Research and genetic diagnoses are typical examples of the work done by experts every day. However, some information is required to perform these tasks. Where are these data? Currently, this information is dispersed in genomic repositories (including *web sites, databanks, public files*, etc.) which are completely redundant, heterogeneous and inconsistent. In addition, most of these just focus on storing specific information to solve a specific problem (e.g. REACTOME, designed to provide molecular details of signal translation, transport, DNA replication, metabolism and other cellular processes, www.reactome.org).

Due to these characteristics, we are able to estimate the difficulty of experts in finding and manipulating certain genomic information, making this goal almost impossible to achieve. Another relevant factor in the domain is the constant growth and updating of the data (i.e., biological terms). The use of standard definitions of concepts is not mandatory, so that sometimes the same term can have different definitions, in which case the meaning of the concept depends on the interpretation given to it by the expert. After studying this situation, we decided to develop a Genomic Information System (GeIS) in the form of the VarSearch tool [5] for data treatment and management. This system contrasts a set of genomic variations with the information contained in a database that follows the *Conceptual Model of the Human Genome* (CMHG) [6]. Applying GeIS to the bioinformatics domain is an essential requirement, since it allows us to structure the Human Genome Database (HGDB) with "curated" and "validated" data. The application of CM helps us to better understand and manage the knowledge of the human genome.

In this context, the goal of the present work, which is based on our previous work [7], is to explain the current status of the prototype called "*VarSearch*", in the previous works [8, 9] explained the operation of the genomic tools "*GenesLove.Me*" and "*VarSearch*", which together aim to facilitate the genetic diagnosis. Currently, a software tool is being developed that integrates all the work done in the prototypes mentioned above so that in this way we foresee the creation of a new GeIS based on the holistic CMHG.

The advances over our previous work [7] are:

- The definition of a new design and implementation perspective for the tool "*GenesLove.Me 2.0*", with the aim of providing a comprehensive package that includes all tasks and/or processes related to the generation of genomic diagnosis, and
- The study of new diseases of genetic origin. For the study of this set of phenotypes we have used the SILE methodology, which integrates quality criteria that allow guaranteeing the use of curated and reliable data.

In the genomic domain we find large amounts of data, all this data is a palpable example of the Big Data problem [10], which is why the creation of this GeIS is intended to achieve a better understanding of all existing knowledge, since this is fundamental for the generation of software of quality, in this way the problem of "*Big Data*" really becomes a problem of selecting "*Right Data*" or "*Smart Data*" [11]. The *Smart Data* contains the famous 5 "V" of the Big Data, but also includes a sixth "V" that refers to the value of that information. In this work, we seek to enhance the value of genomic data in order to facilitate the acclaimed "*Precision Medicine*".

This paper is divided as follows: Sect. 2 describes the background in the bioinformatics domain. Section 3 presents the definition of a new perspective of design for the tool (including the application of CM in the genomic domain and the previous steps to prepare the *GenesLove.Me 2.0* tool). Section 4 describes the GLM 2.0 tool. Finally, Sect. 5 contains our conclusions and outlines future work.

2 Background

Bioinformatics is born from the interaction of molecular biology and computer science, with the objective of allowing biological data to be processed. This data is characterized by its large size and continuous growth, which is why it is necessary to develop tools to manage the information in an agile and efficient way, as well as new algorithms and statistical solutions oriented to the analysis of the DNA sequences and their variations [12].

Table 1. Most popular databases [12].

Name	DB type	Source	Start	Website
SNPedia	Polymorphisms	USA	2006	https://www.snpedia.com/
BioCyc	Metabolic pathways	USA	2005	https://biocyc.org/
Reactome	Metabolic pathways	EU	2004	https://reactome.org/
Ensembl	Genomics	EU	2000	https://www.ensembl.org/
UCSC	Genomics	USA	2000	https://genome.ucsc.edu/
dbSNP	Polymorphisms	USA	1998	https://www.ncbi.nlm.nih.gov/projects/SNP/
PubMed	Bibliographical	USA	1996	https://www.ncbi.nlm.nih.gov/pubmed/
KEGG	Metabolic pathways	Japan	1995	https://www.genome.jp/kegg/
OMIM	Genetic diseases	USA	1995	https://www.omim.org/
EMBL	Nucleotides	EU	1992	https://www.embl.de/
DDBJ	Nucleotides	Japan	1986	https://www.ddbj.nig.ac.jp/
Uniprot	Proteins	EU	1986	https://www.uniprot.org/
GenBank	Nucleotides	USA	1982	https://www.ncbi.nlm.nih.gov/genbank/
PDB	Proteins	USA	1971	https://www.rcsb.org/

In this sense, there are several standards and formats for the representation of nucleotide and protein sequences, programs of comparison of variations and frameworks for the exploration of genetic diseases, as well as databases with all genome sequences, nucleotides, proteins, proteins structures, human genetic diseases, and bibliography available for public study and research.

The Table 1 shows the main biological databases including the sequence data were created in the USA, EU and Japan from their beginnings date from 1971 to the present day.

On the other hand, all this biological information must be perfectly structured and bounded in an *Information System* (IS) that allows its treatment and exploitation in an efficient way. Understanding the genome is a complex task and generating a correct conceptual definition [3] that addresses all current genomic knowledge is essential to understand the - genomic - domain. In addition, this conceptual model must be subject to constant evolutions product of new discoveries in the context.

3 Defining a New Perspective of Design and Implementation

A *Genomic Information System* (GeIS) can be defined as a system that *collects*, *stores*, *manages* and *distributes* information related to the behavior of the human genome.

As mentioned above, the GeIS described here is based on the CMHG. This section deals with the considerations and steps prior to the design of the new framework (before called "*VarSearch*").

3.1 Conceptual Modeling in the Genomic Domain

In the field of genomic bioinformatics, the first works of conceptual modeling were given by Paton [13]. His essays were supported by previous work on modeling of protein structures [14], being a pioneer in the conceptual design of the eukaryotic cell, its genomic organization, transcriptome, proteome and metabolome modeling, among others; using the Unified Modeling Language (UML, http://www.uml.org/).

In addition, Ram et al. presents a conceptual modeling approach applied to the protein context, this paper states that the use of conceptual modeling facilitates the representation without semantic loss and comparison and search operations in complex structures, such as in the modeling of the three-dimensional structure of proteins, characterized by the large volume of data [15].

With these bases, the Genome Group of the *PROS Research Center*[1], of the *Universitat Politècnica de València* started in 2008 a line of research focused on the modeling of the human genome for analysis and study the most basic expression, genes, and their mutations within a chromosomal segment [16]. However, this model does not consider the existence of processes such as the regulation or coding of a single protein by two different genes, as well as the combined action of multiple genes. As detailed in the work of 2010 [17], this version of the conceptual model of the human genome is called the "essential" model and is composed of three views: (i) *Genome View*: model's human genomes, (ii) *Gene-Mutation View*: models the entities "*Gene*"

---

[1] http://www.pros.webs.upv.es/.

and *"Allele"*, and the knowledge of their structures, and (iii) *Transcription View*:
models transcription processes [12].

After this, the model is extended with a fourth view called *"Phenotype View"* that
allows for the phenotypic representation, that is, the concrete/visible manifestation of a
genotype in a given context. Subsequently, the CMHG migrated from modeling oriented to the study of genes to another centered on the concept of the chromosome, this
new approach was called CMHG v2 [4, 18].

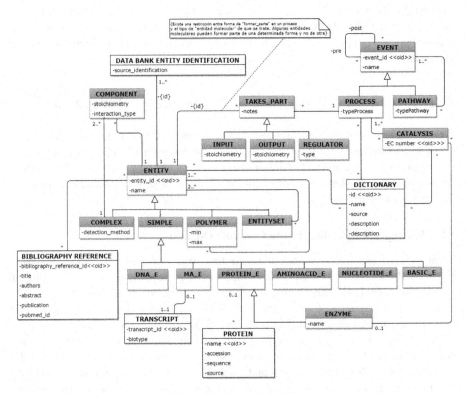

Fig. 1. Pathway view [6].

The Conceptual Model of the Human Genome (CMHG) version 2, is composed of
six independent but related views [19]. These views are *structural, transcription,
variations, phenotype, pathways* and *bibliography references*. Their function and
information are described below [18]:

- *Structural*: details the structure, organization and composition of the chromosomes,
  the transcribed elements, the genes involved, as well as the information of the
  organism to which it belongs, among others.
- *Transcription*: details the information of the exons, the transcribed elements that
  form it, and the proteins encoded by the different transcripts.

- *Variations*: details the variations that can a DNA sequence have, genetic polymorphisms, as well as precise and imprecise genetic mutations.
- *Phenotype*: shows the manifestation of a genotype in a given context and the relation with the variations that cause it.
- *Pathways*: shows the enzymatic and biochemical relationships involving the studied gene (see Fig. 1).
- *Bibliography references*: describes the sources of information, publications and authors involved in the research from which all genomic information has been extracted.

Once the CMHG has been defined, it is necessary to have an entity that allows the storage and access to this information in a fast and structured way. These operations are guaranteed by a relational database schema called *"Human Genome Database"* (HGDB), which currently models the structural view, variations, bibliography references, and validations through tables. For more information, see the full view and description in Reyes et al. [19].

This model remains in constant study, so it is necessary for the CMGH to continue evolving according to new discoveries and non-contemplated genetic structures, as well as the study of quality metrics to ensure the best definition of the domain [20].

3.1.1 SILE Methodology

The CMHG is the essential axis to manage genomic information. The SILE (*Search-Identification-Load-Exploitation*) method supports the search of relevant repositories as well as the identification, load and exploitation of high quality data through its four levels [11, 21]:

- Search: selection of the most suitable data sources by using the CMHG as a guide to determine the information required,
- Identification: selection of the most relevant data from each data source,
- Load: the identified data is loaded into a database, based on the structure provided by the CSHG, and
- Exploitation: the data stored in the database is efficiently analyzed and managed by a set of tools developed to be applied in the clinical practice.

All the process is supported by certain tasks specifically design to assure the quality on each level of the SILE method. The need to assure quality of genomic data is key due to two main aspects: (i) to achieve competitive advantages through its analysis by an IS and (ii) because decision making based on low genomic data quality may involve serious mistakes with important consequences when applied with clinical purposes.

Previous studies [21] in this regard have allowed us to classify the most common types of errors into six data quality dimensions: *Accuracy*, *Completeness*, *Consistency*, *Uniqueness*, *Currency* and *Reliability*. In order to minimize the impact of the detected errors, the measurement of the data quality dimensions identified has been incorporated to SILE (see Fig. 2), allowing to provide a higher level of granularity which helps to achieve more accurate results [11].

It is important to emphasize that before carrying out the loading in the HGDB, these quality criteria are executed for the data to guarantee its reliability in the generation of the genetic diagnosis.

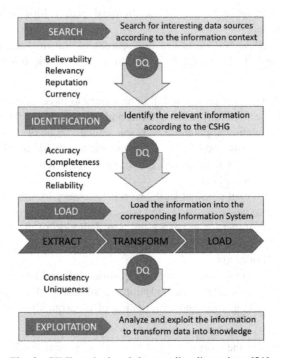

Fig. 2. SILE method and data quality dimensions [21].

3.2 Previous Steps

After the decision to start a new *Software Development Project* that would allow integrating all the knowledge gained over the years on the *treatment* and *management* of *genomic data*, the first step to take into account was the analysis of the previous works [7–9]. This allowed us to define a work methodology that would be efficient and that would prevent any design and implementation errors committed in the past.

For the implementation of this new tool, a series of previous steps were carried out, which would allow us to ensure the proper functioning of the software product. Next, the three fundamental elements (*previous*) that must be defined and raised before starting the tool (called "*GenesLove.Me 2.0*") are explained:

1. **Selection of the Different Data Sources:** *Genomic Databases*
   The medical and information community has carried out a large number of studies with the aim of finding convincing solutions to the management problems for genomic databases. These drawbacks lie in the need to manage large data sources, which requires greater investment in time, storage, and research, among other aspects that require continuous improvement.

Rouse defines the term database as *"a collection of information organized in such a way that it is easily accessible, managed and updated"* [22, 23].

As previously mentioned, the genomic domain is an environment that represents a great challenge with its final goal of *"understanding and manipulating the genome"*. Today there are a large number of biological databases. According to the work published on the database catalog of NAR (*Nucleic Acids Research*), in 2018 they updated their catalog and 88 new repositories (resources) were added, eliminating a total of 47 obsolete websites and finally leaving a list of up to 1,737 biological databases [24].

The HGVS6 (*Human Genome Variation Society*) also offers a catalog of genomic databases (for example, variations/mutations), for the year 2015 they had a total of 1,755 repositories listed [25].

Of this large number of repositories, the clear majority are focused on the solution of a specific aspect of the entire genome. In this domain, there are multiple cases that make the treatment of data difficult, giving rise to problems of *dispersion, heterogeneity, redundancy, inconsistency,* ... At the time of managing such data, this situation is generically denoted as *"chaos of genomic data"*. With the tools and current search engines can solve certain problems, but it is essential to define a holistic ontological framework that allows delimiting the relevant knowledge and that allows creating a clear and simple structure for the effective and efficient management of genomic data. The development of databases with delimited and revised information (*"curated"*) should be promoted, in order to achieve an optimization of the performance to report diagnoses of greater precision and quality.

To solve this problem, in this research work the development of the Human Genome Database (HGDB) is presented, which is based on the CMHG that is described in Sect. 3.1.

For this tool we have selected a set of genomic databases, most of which belong to the NCBI[2]. Within the list are: *ClinVar* [26], *RefSeq* [27], *Gene* [28], *PubMed* [29], *Ensembl* [30], *dbSNP* [31] and *Alzforum* [32].

2. **Human Genome Database (HGDB)**

The HGDB has been developed with the objective of integrating all existing knowledge in the genomic domain based on a holistic conceptual representation of the domain. To load the data, a series of studies and analyzes are carried out to filter/select the relevant data.

In this way, a repository with *"selective"* data is generated, which facilitates obtaining genomic diagnoses with *recent, credible* and *relevant scientific* support. To understand the need to have this universal conceptual repository of genomic data, it is necessary to understand the complexity introduced by the existing diversity in current genomic data sources.

The transformation of the model defined for the database schema (*logical model*) was almost automatic [7]; in this task, we found two different levels of abstraction in the model. The conceptual model represents the domain from the point of view of scientific knowledge, while the database schema focuses on the

---

[2] https://www.ncbi.nlm.nih.gov/.

efficient storage and retrieval of data. For this reason, the details of the physical representation must be considered to improve the final implementation.

To load the HGDB the SILE methodology [33] was used, which was developed to improve the loading processes and guarantee the treatment of "*curated data*". SILE was used to perform the "*search*" and "*identification*" of variations associated with a specific disease (a task validated by experts in the genetic domain).

When the identified and curated data have been obtained the "*selective loading*" is performed (through the loading module) in the HGDB (see Table 2). The data loaded are then "*exploited*" by *GenesLove.Me 2.0* (before called "*VarSearch*"). Some of the new diseases (of genetic origin) studied and loaded were *Epilepsy, Breast cancer (male), Early Onset Alzheimer, Cataracts* and others.

3. Genetic Loading Module

For the loading process of the HGDB, a load module was implemented to store the data from the previously mentioned repositories. This loading module was developed using an ETL strategy [34], with three different levels: Extraction-Transformation-Load (see Fig. 3). Each level is completely independent from each other, facilitating and clarifying the design of the system (improving its *flexibility* and *scalability*).

In the first layer (1), the extraction of all necessary information from the source data repositories was performed. This information is not structured, so all these data (*raw*) pass to the second layer (2), where several transformations are carried out with the aim of formatting the data according to the structure of the basic schema of defined data (HGDB). These transformed data are sent to the third layer (3), which communicates directly with the HGDB. Within the genome group of the PROS Center, loading mechanisms have been implemented, which were defined depending on the structure and way of obtaining the data from the source repository (for example, XML files or via an FTP server).

In the bioinformatic domain it is frequent to find software developments based on Python[3] technologies, this due to its greater use in the training of experts in the bioinformatics area [6].

As initial load mechanisms in the PROS Center, "*scripts*" were developed in Python with the aim of generating XML files whose structure is defined based on the CMHG, thus obtaining all the genes stored in the database of NCBI.

For this work, the generation of another 5 files was required (*gene_RefSeqGene.txt, output.xml, refseqgene1_genomic.gbff, ref-seqgene2_genomic.gbff* and *refseqgene3_ genomic.gbff,* these last three having the same format). With the exception of all the files, the generation of the file "*output.xml*" consisted in the download of the data through the following FTP site: *ftp://ftp.ncbi.nih.gov/refseq/H_sapiens/RefSeqGene/.* In the same way, scripts were implemented to extract information from the BIC database. Figure 4 shows a fragment of the code developed for the BIC parser. In this context, several studies have been studied and proposed, which sought to facilitate the loading process, taking into account the complexity (and great challenge) to integrate the various data structures provided by the genomic repositories.

---

[3] https://www.python.org/.

Table 2. Selection of partially annotated variations stored in the HGDB. For each phenotype, rs identifier (variation identifier), assembly, NC identifier, gene (ID symbol), position, the reference and alternative allele, specialization type and clinical significance are shown.

PHENOTYPE	DB_VARIATION_ID	ASSEMBLY	NC_IDENTIF.	ID_SYMBOL (Gene)	POSITION	REF	ALT	SPECIALIZATION_TYPE	CLINICAL_SIGNIFICANCE
Epilepsy	rs12744221	GRCh38	NC_000001.11	RNF115	145789475	C	T	SNP	Association
Epilepsy	rs535066	GRCh38	NC_000004.12	GABRA2	46238270	G	T	SNP	Association
Crohn's disease	rs1000113	GRCh38	NC_000005.10	IRGM	150860514	C	T	SNP	Risk
Breast cancer (male)	rs3803662	GRCh38	NC_000016.9	TOX3	52552429	A	G	SNP	Increased risk
Alzheimer's	rs63750004	GRCh37	NC_000014.8	PSEN1	73640363	T	C	SNP	Pathogenic
Cataracts	rs864309680	GRCh38	NC_000023.11	BCOR	40062174: 40062177	-	GAGA	DIV: deletion/insertion	Pathogenic

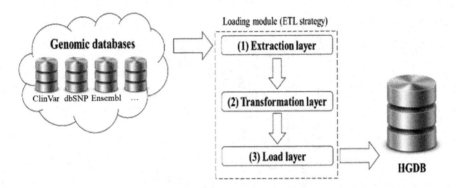

Fig. 3. Load module [7].

```
1    #!/usr/bin/env python
2
3    import sys, argparse, logging
4    from datetime import datetime
5
6    ######################### MAIN #########################
7
8    if __name__ == '__main__':
9        logging.basicConfig(filename=(sys.argv[0]).rstrip('py').rstrip('.')+'.log',format='[%(asctime)s] %(levelname)s: %(message)s',\
10                           filemode='w',level=logging.DEBUG)
11
12       # define options
13       parser = argparse.ArgumentParser()
14       parser.add_argument('-i','--input', nargs='+', required=True, help='BIC data files, first BRCA1, second BRCA2')
15       parser.add_argument('-o','--output', nargs=1, required=True, help='Output tabular data file')
16
17       # parse args
18       args = parser.parse_args()
19
20       # retrieve options
21       input = args.input
22       output = args.output[0]
23
24       var_index = {} # Variant Index
25
26       # Interesting columns in BIC data files:
27       #   0 - Accession number
28       #   7 - HGVS cDNA
29       #   13 - Clinically Important
30       #   26 - Reference
31
32       ng_identifiers = ["NG_005905.2", "NG_012772.3"]
33       ng_point = 0
34       for infile in input:
35           with open(infile) as bic_file:
36               # Leer primera linea (Cabecera)
37               bic_file.readline()
38               for line in bic_file:
39                   values = line.split('\t')
40                   # Eliminar posibles espacios en HGVS cDNA
41                   values[7] = values[7].replace(' ', '')
42
43                   # Check if the variation already exists in the variant index
44                   if var_index.has_key(values[7]) and (values[26].lower() not in ('-','unpublished')):
45                       var_values = var_index.get(values[7])
46                       var_values[3].append(values[26]) # Add a new reference for the variation
47                       var_index[values[7]] = var_values # Update variant data
48                   else:
```

Fig. 4. Chunk Python code: BIC's parser [6].

Another approach proposed was the development of a load module de-nominated "*Genome Data Loader*", implemented with Java technologies. This application integrated the three layers of the ETL (*extraction-transformation-load*) and focused basically on the databases of HGMD and BIC [35].

In the framework of this work a prototype of ETL was developed for the automatic loading of the data (see Fig. 5), this as a part of the investigation and embodied as a master's thesis (*to consult more information access to*: [36]). The application starts with the establishment of the connection to the database. For this, the prototype has a small connection management with which direct communication with the server is checked. Once established and validated, the application reports the status of the connection and allows the process of extracting and uploading information from the genomic repositories: *Clinvar, dbSNP, Gene, Nucleotide* and *PudMeb*. User management is done from the *"Users View"*. This load prototype consists of the following views: *detail view of variations, detail of the extraction of information,* and *detail of the data source view.* For more information about this loading module and the data loaded in the HGDB, see the work published in [36].

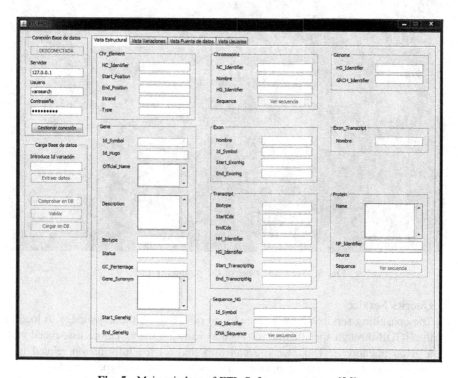

Fig. 5. Main window of ETL Software prototype [36].

4   GenesLove.Me 2.0

GenesLove.Me 2.0 (GLM 2.0) is the natural evolution of the prototype called *"Var-Search"*, this tool aims to integrate all previous genomic knowledge to improve and enhance the treatment of data, and thus facilitate genetic reports that help *prevent* and *treat* diseases of genetic origin (Fig. 6).

GLM 2.0 is a web application that allows the analysis of variations obtained from the DNA sequenciation of biological samples and which is stored in FASTA or VCF file formats [37]. In this new proposal, the design of the user interface has been completely changed in order to improve the ease of navigation within the application (independently of the type of user that uses it), as well as providing a more intuitive and simpler interface. Currently, GLM 2.0 functionality has been grouped into two main packages:

Fig. 6. Welcome page of the product (GLM 2.0).

1. **Queries Service**

The consulting services have as an explicit objective all the knowledge to load in the HGDB through specific queries, such as knowing the variations associated with a given phenotype. Thus, as you can also find all the information related to a specific variation. Access to queries services can be of two types (see Fig. 7):

- *Queries on data of variations*: this service allows access to all the "curated" data on variations, which allows for studies and analysis on their repercussions and interactions between different phenotypes. In addition, all the information loaded in the HGDB is provided by two types of "*SQL*" and "*NoSQL*" (or graph) technologies.

  The first one is implemented in MySQL, and the graph-based alternative is implemented in Neo4j [38]. One of the great benefits of these proposals is that it allows us to propose comparative analyzes between SQL and NoSQL technologies (being a practical case the treatment of the participating data in the human genome).

- *Queries about sample data*: this functionality aims to provide data related to samples uploaded to the platform through VCF or Sanger files. However, in order to access these services, special privileges (*administrator*) are required, so the information can only be consulted by a restricted group of users.

2 Diagnostics Service

This service allows the generation of genomic reports from the samples uploaded to the application (VCF or Sanger). The application performs the analysis from the data loaded in the HGDB, where it finally presents the list of variations found and their respective details.

All the information presented can be exported to different formats (*.csv, *.pdf, *.xls, etc.) for later download, and it is up to the user to generate the final genomic report from the results obtained.

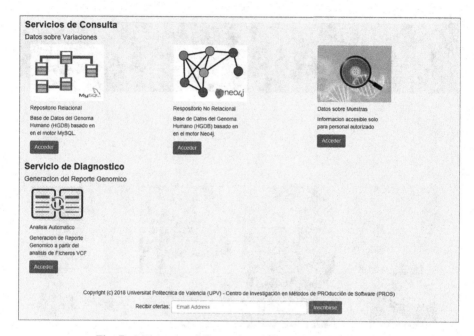

Fig. 7. Main page of the services offered in the application.

The development of this platform aims to cover the needs of a group of users of the genomic domain, among which we can find:

(i) *Researchers*: are those that are dedicated to the search and identification of genetic variations for one or several phenotypes, as well as the impact on human health from the existing data in various genomic repositories,

(ii) *Geneticists*: they are in charge of studying the genetic sequences, and that from specialized studies carried out with the latest generation technologies they try to detect new genetic variations in the human genome,

(iii) *Clinical laboratories*: are those that perform genetic studies and perform comparisons between the sequence obtained and the reference sequence, in order to find relevant variations that are associated with the disease under study. An example that we can mention is the case of the Pediatric Oncology group at the

Hospital Universitari i Politècnic La Fe[4] that dedicates one of its lines of
research to the clinical and genomic study of Neuroblastoma [39], and finally,

(iv) *Customers or end-users*: are those users who are facilitated through GLM 2.0 the
acquisition of direct-to-consumer genetic tests (DCGT) [8] for one or several
diseases offered in the platform (see Fig. 8), in this way they can obtain for a
cost affordable and in a short time a genomic report that allows you to improve
and prevent your personal health.

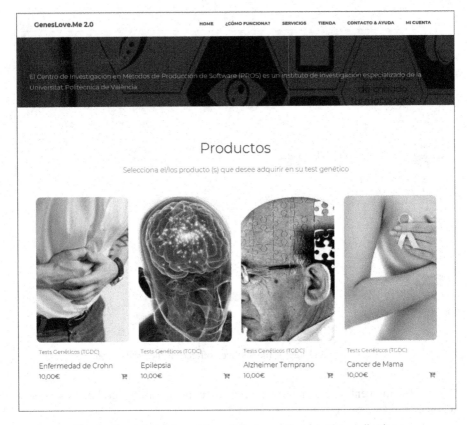

Fig. 8. Example of the catalog of diseases offered in the application.

GLM 2.0 includes an exhaustive study and analysis of the defined requirements
(initial and current), so the functionalities considered in the previous prototype [7] are
"integrated or in the process of being included" in the new application.

Next, in Figs. 9 and 10 the list of phenotypes loaded in the HGDB is presented for
the realization of the consultations and/or genomic report, the user selects the desired
phenotype and will automatically obtain a list with all the related genetic variations to

---

[4] www.hospital-lafe.com/.

said phenotype, as well as all the relevant information (i.e., data shown in Table 2) of the indicated variation. Among the data that can be found are a brief summary of the phenotype, list of related variations, and for each of them its identifier "*rs*" (variation_id), the initial position of the variation, its clinical significance, among others. You can also check all the information loaded in the database (which is based on the MCGH), for this, it is only necessary to click on the tab "*MySQL Tables*" or "*Neo4j Tables*" (Fig. 10) as the case may be.

It is important to emphasize that the proposed design consists of a preliminary proposal and that it remains in a process of continuous improvement.

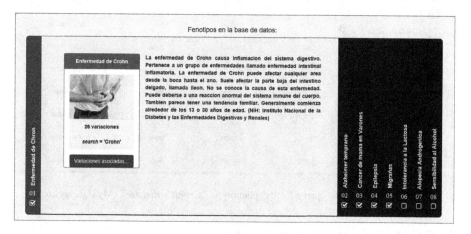

Fig. 9. List of phenotypes loaded in the HGDB.

4.1   Confidentiality of the Information

The management of genomic data requires the application of security mechanisms that can guarantee the *availability, integrity, confidentiality* (probably the most important), *traceability* and *authenticity of the information*, as well as taking into consideration all the legal aspects that have an impact on these data (*sensitive*). Only in this area should be highlighted the complexity derived from the need to legislate a matter so novel and in constant evolution. By way of example, the following legal norms are directly involved in this problem:

- *Law 14/2007, of July 3, on Biomedical Research.*
- *Law 14/1986, of April 25, General of Health.*

In addition, in the design and implementation of this new project, the application of the *New European Data Protection Law* (RGDP, https://protecciondatos-lopd.com/empresas/nueva-ley-proteccion-datos-2018/) was considered, thus avoiding any future inconvenience regarding the privacy of clinical and genomic data.

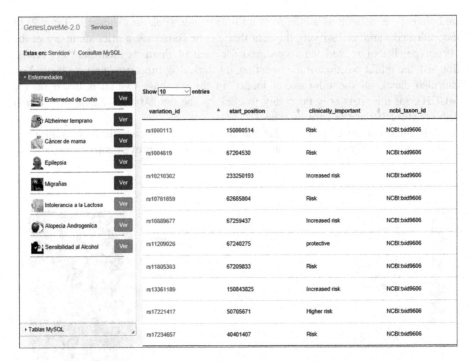

Fig. 10. Result of the query for the phenotype *"Crohn's disease"* (MySQL section).

5   Conclusions and Future Work

Thanks to advances in NGS, such as easier sequencing and reduced cost, in recent years they have generated large amounts of information that must be managed efficiently. And, on the other hand, there is the problem that there are not many people using the modeling techniques in this domain.

In this paper, we present the development of a software tool (GLM 2.0) based on the CMHG for the management of genomic data, with the aim of facilitating a genomic diagnosis -*precocious*- generated from the HGDB. This research process included the application of a methodology (*systematic*) for the obtention of the data so that it went from a *"massive load"* to a *"selective load"* of data. In this way, the use of cured data in the process of analysis of the application was guaranteed. Through this product software, users can manage their data, and keep track of the variations found and not found in the samples analyzed.

GenesLove.Me 2.0 is a flexible web application that provides a powerful resource for exploring both *"coding"* and *"non-coding"* genetic variations. To do this, GLM 2.0 integrates VCF format input/output with an expanding set of genome information. As the main users are now oriented to facilitating genetic procedures, web access, usability and feasibility, the definition of different profiles are therefore important goals. All this allows the user to configure the tool according to his specific needs. GLM 2.0 is in the development and testing period, and that is why it remains in a state of continuous improvement.

Future research work will also be aimed at: (i) Implementation of data management mechanisms to enhance the quality of personalized medicine, (ii) Development of verification mechanisms for information in source (*data source*), and (iii) Improving the current version of *GenesLove.Me 2.0* for genetic diagnosis (including the application of new views of the CMHG).

Acknowledgements. This work was supported by the Generalitat Valenciana through the Spanish Ministry of Science and Innovation through Project DataME (ref: TIN2016-80811-P) and the Generalitat Valenciana through the GISPRO project (PROMETEO / 2018/176).

The authors are grateful to Ana León Palacio, Carlos Iñiguez-Jarrín, Sipan Arevshatyan and Manuel Navarrete Hidalgo for their valuable assistance.

References

1. Mardis, E.R.: The $1,000 genome, the $100,000 analysis? Genome Med. **2**(11), 84 (2010)
2. Grosso, L.A.: Precision medicine and cardiovascular diseases. Rev. Colomb. Cardiol. **23**(2), 73–76 (2016). https://doi.org/10.1016/j.rccar.2016.01.026
3. Olivé, A.: Conceptual Modeling of Information Systems. Springer, Heidelberg (2007). https://doi.org/10.1007/978-3-540-39390-0
4. Reyes Román, J.F., Pastor, Ó., Casamayor, J.C., Valverde, F.: Applying conceptual modeling to better understand the human genome. In: Comyn-Wattiau, I., Tanaka, K., Song, I.Y., Yamamoto, S., Saeki, M. (eds.) ER 2016. LNCS, vol. 9974, pp. 404–412. Springer, Cham (2016). https://doi.org/10.1007/978-3-319-46397-1_31
5. Pastor López, Ó., Palacio, A.L., Reyes Román, J.F., Casamayor, J.C.: Modeling life: a conceptual schema-centric approach to understand the genome. In: Cabot, J., Gómez, C., Pastor, O., Sancho, M., Teniente, E. (eds.) Conceptual Modeling Perspectives, pp. 25–40. Springer, Cham (2017). https://doi.org/10.1007/978-3-319-67271-7_3
6. Reyes Román, J.F.: Diseño y Desarrollo de un Sistema de Información Genómica basado en un Modelo Conceptual holístico del Genoma Humano. Universitat Politècnica de València (2018). https://doi.org/10.4995/thesis/10251/99565
7. Reyes Román, J.F., Roldán Martínez, D., García Simón, A., Rueda, U., Pastor, Ó.: VarSearch: annotating variations using an e-genomics framework. In: Proceedings of the 13th International Conference on Evaluation of Novel Approaches to Software Engineering - Volume 1: ENASE, pp. 328–334 (2018). https://doi.org/10.5220/0006781103280334. ISBN 978-989-758-300-1
8. Reyes Román, J.F., Iñiguez-Jarrín, C., Pastor López, Ó.: GenesLove.Me: a model-based web-application for direct-to-consumer genetic tests. In: Proceedings of the 12th International Conference on Evaluation of Novel Approaches to Software Engineering - Volume 1: ENASE, pp. 133–143 (2017). https://doi.org/10.5220/0006340201330143. ISBN 978-989-758-250-9
9. Reyes Román, J.F., Iñiguez-Jarrín, C., Pastor, Ó.: Genomic tools*: web-applications based on conceptual models for the genomic diagnosis. In: Damiani, E., Spanoudakis, G., Maciaszek, L. (eds.) ENASE 2017. CCIS, vol. 866, pp. 48–69. Springer, Cham (2018). https://doi.org/10.1007/978-3-319-94135-6_3
10. Stephens, Z.D., et al.: Big data: astronomical or genomical? PLOS Biol. **13**(7), e1002195 (2015). https://doi.org/10.1371/journal.pbio.1002195

11. León Palacio, A., Pastor López, Ó.: From big data to smart data: a genomic information systems perspective. In: 2018 12th International Conference on Research Challenges in Information Science (RCIS), pp. 1–11 (2018). https://doi.org/10.1109/rcis.2018.8406658

12. Navarrete-Hidalgo, M., Reyes Román, J.F., Pastor López, Ó.: Design and implementation of a GeIS for the genomic diagnosis using the SILE methodology. Case Study: Congenital Cataract. In Proceedings of the 13th International Conference on Evaluation of Novel Approaches to Software Engineering – Vol. 1: ENASE, pp. 267–274 (2018). https://doi.org/10.5220/0006705802670274. ISBN 978-989-758-300-1

13. Bornberg-Bauer, E., Paton, N.W.: Conceptual data modelling for bioinformatics. Briefings Bioinform. 3(2), 166–180 (2002). https://doi.org/10.1093/bib/3.2.166

14. Gray, R.E., Grasso, D.G., Maxwell, R.J., Finnegan, P.M., Nagley, P., Devenish, R.J.: Identification of a 66 KDa protein associated with yeast mitochondrial ATP synthase as heat shock protein hsp60. FEBS Lett. 268(1), 265–268 (1990)

15. Ram, S., Wei, W.: Modeling the semantics of 3D protein structures. In: Atzeni, P., Chu, W., Lu, H., Zhou, S., Ling, T.-W. (eds.) ER 2004. LNCS, vol. 3288, pp. 696–708. Springer, Heidelberg (2004). https://doi.org/10.1007/978-3-540-30464-7_52

16. Pastor, O.: Conceptual modeling meets the human genome. In: Li, Q., Spaccapietra, S., Yu, E., Olivé, A. (eds.) ER 2008. LNCS, vol. 5231, pp. 1–11. Springer, Heidelberg (2008). https://doi.org/10.1007/978-3-540-87877-3_1

17. Pastor, M.Á., Burriel, V., Pastor, O.: Conceptual modeling of human genome mutations - a dichotomy between what we have and what we should have. In: Bioinformatics, pp. 160–166 (2010)

18. Reyes Román, J.F., León Palacio, A., Pastor López, Ó.: Software engineering and genomics: the two sides of the same coin? In: Proceedings of the 12th International Conference on Evaluation of Novel Approaches to Software Engineering - Volume 1: ENASE, pp. 301–307 (2017). https://doi.org/10.5220/0006368203010307. ISBN 978-989-758-250-9

19. Pastor, O., Reyes Román, J.F., Valverde, F.: Conceptual Schema of the Human Genome (CSHG). Technical report (2016). http://hdl.handle.net/10251/67297

20. León, A., Reyes, J., Burriel, V., Valverde, F.: Data quality problems when integrating genomic information. In: Link, S., Trujillo, J. (eds.) ER 2016. LNCS, vol. 9975, pp. 173–182. Springer, Cham (2016). https://doi.org/10.1007/978-3-319-47717-6_15

21. León Palacio, A., Pastor López, Ó.: Towards an effective medicine of precision by using conceptual modelling of the genome: short paper. In: Proceedings of the International Workshop on Software Engineering in Healthcare Systems, pp. 14–17. ACM (2018)

22. Rouse, M.: A data lake is a large object-based storage repository that holds data in its native format until it is needed (2014)

23. Breul, J.D.: Cyber Society, Big Data, and Evaluation: Comparative Policy Evaluation. Transaction Publishers, Piscataway (2017)

24. Rigden, D.J., Fernández, X.M.: The 2018 nucleic acids research database issue and the online molecular biology database collection. Nucleic Acids Res. 46(D1), D1–D7 (2017)

25. Alexov, E.: Navigating through genomics data to deliver testable predictions. Hum. Mutat. 36(2), v (2015)

26. Landrum, M.J.: ClinVar: public archive of interpretations of clinically relevant variants. Nucleic Acids Res. 44(D1), D862–D868 (2015)

27. Nasko, D.J., Koren, S., Phillippy, A.M., Treangen, T.J.: RefSeq database growth influences the accuracy of k-mer-based species identification. bioRxiv, p. 304972 (2018)

28. NCBI Resource Coordinators: Database resources of the National Center for Biotechnology Information. Nucleic Acids Res. 44(Database issue), D7 (2016)

29. NCBI Resource Coordinators: Database resources of the National Center for Biotechnology Information. Nucleic Acids Res. 45(Database issue), D12 (2017)

30. Zerbino, D.R., et al.: Ensembl 2018. Nucleic Acids Res. **46**(D1), D754–D761 (2017)
31. Bhagwat, M.: Searching NCBI's dbSNP database. Current Protoc. Bioinform. **32**(1), 1–19 (2010)
32. Kinoshita, J., Clark, T.: Alzforum. Neuroinformatics, pp. 365–381. Humana Press, New York (2007)
33. Reyes Román, J.F., Pastor López, Ó.: Use of GeIS for early diagnosis of alcohol sensitivity. In Proceedings of the 9th International Joint Conference on Biomedical Engineering Systems and Technologies - Volume 3: Bioinformatics (BIOSTEC 2016), pp. 284–289 (2016). https://doi.org/10.5220/0005822902840289. ISBN 978-989-758-170-0
34. Zhou, H., Yang, D., Xu, Y.: An ETL strategy for real-time data warehouse. In: Wang, Y., Li, T. (eds.) Practical Applications of Intelligent Systems Advances in Intelligent and Soft Computing, vol. 124. Springer, Heidelberg (2011). https://doi.org/10.1007/978-3-642-25658-5_41
35. Van Der Kroon, M.: Conceptual Modeling Applied to Genomics: Challenges Faced in Data Loading. Universitat Politècnica de València (2012). http://hdl.handle.net/10251/16993
36. Navarrete Hidalgo, M., Pastor, Ó., Reyes Román, J.F.: Diseño e Implementación de un Sistema de Información Genómico para el Diagnóstico de la Catarata Congénita utilizando la Metodología SILE. Universitat Politècnica de València (2017). http://hdl.handle.net/10251/90234
37. Claverie, J.M., Notredame, C.: Bioinformatics for Dummies. Wiley, New York (2011)
38. Miller, J.J.: Graph database applications and concepts with Neo4j. In: Proceedings of the Southern Association for Information Systems Conference, Atlanta, GA, USA, vol. 2324, p. 36 (2013)
39. Burriel, V., Reyes Román, J.F., Casanoves, A.H., Iñiguez-Jarrín, C., León Palacio, A.: GeIS based on conceptual models for the risk assessment of neuroblastoma. In: 2017 11th International Conference on Research Challenges in Information Science (RCIS), pp. 451–452. IEEE (2017). https://doi.org/10.1109/rcis.2017.7956581

Automated Multi-objective Refactoring Based on Quality and Code Element Recentness

Michael Mohan and Des Greer[✉]

Department of Electronics, Electrical Engineering and Computer Science,
Queen's University Belfast, Belfast BT7 1NN, UK
{mmohan03,des.greer}@qub.ac.uk

Abstract. Search-Based Software Engineering (SBSE) has been used to automate various aspects of the software development cycle. One particular case is refactoring, especially to improve software quality. However, often there are other factors that influence the refactoring process. One such factor, the recentness of the code elements, is identified in this paper as important. The paper describes the use of a multi-objective genetic algorithm to automate software refactoring based on a metric function for software quality and a second objective to measure the recentness of the code elements being refactored. The recentness measure is calculated from data on previous versions of the software. The multi-objective setup refactors the input program to improve its quality using the quality objective, while also focusing on the recentness of the code elements inspected. The approach is implemented in a tool, MultiRefactor and validated using a set of six open source Java programs. An experiment is described that compares the multi-objective approach against an alternative mono-objective approach that uses only the quality function. The results show that the multi-objective approach gives significantly better recentness scores without greatly degrading improvements in the quality score.

Keywords: Search based software engineering · Maintenance · Refactoring · Software history · Multi-objective optimization · Genetic algorithms

1 Introduction

Search-Based Software Maintenance (SBSM) uses refactorings, software metrics and search-based optimisation algorithms to automate aspects of the software maintenance process. Refactorings are used to improve the structure of software without affecting its functionality. Search-based optimisation algorithms can be adapted to use refactorings to modify software, relying on metrics to deduce how successful the refactorings have been along the way. Thus SBSM attempts to minimize the effort of maintaining a software product. The aim of refactoring (automated or not) is usually to increase the quality of the software. Given that quality metrics exist that can be calculated statically, the possibility of automated refactoring becomes a reality as demonstrated in previous work [15].

An increasing proportion of SBSM research is making use of multi-objective optimization techniques. Many multi-objective search algorithms are built using

© Springer Nature Switzerland AG 2019
E. Damiani et al. (Eds.): ENASE 2018, CCIS 1023, pp. 334–351, 2019.
https://doi.org/10.1007/978-3-030-22559-9_15

genetic algorithms (GAs), due to their ability to generate multiple possible solutions. Instead of focusing on only one property, the multi-objective algorithm is concerned with a number of different objectives. This is handled through a fitness calculation and sorting of the solutions after they have been modified or added to. The main approach used to organize solutions in a multi-objective approach is Pareto. Pareto dominance organizes the possible solutions into different nondomination levels and further discerns between them by finding the objective distances between them in Euclidean space.

In this paper, extended from [16], a multi-objective approach is created to improve software that combines a quality objective with one that incorporates the use of numerous previous versions of the software code. It is fairly common for a programming team to develop successive releases of a product in order to add new features over time. It is likely that the team will have a repository with various compilable versions of the code leading up to the current release. Therefore, it is possible to use these previous versions to gather information of the program and to allow that to aid in a maintenance approach of the current version. This idea forms the basis of the element recentness objective, by incorporating the use of multiple versions of the code as artifacts. The justification for including a recentness aspect is that, whereas older elements have been given the chance to be tested more and have likely already been updated, newer elements will not have been considered. Additionally, newer elements may be more likely to cause issues, especially if a software project has been established and the new functionality has had to be fitted into the current design (as is usually the case). Generally, a programmer may be more interested in testing the code that they have added to a project to ensure there are no unexpected issues caused by its presence. Thus, it can be argued that the more recent aspects of the code are more suitable candidates for refactoring than older aspects.

The element recentness uses previous versions of the target software to help discern between old and new areas of code. In order to calculate the objective, the program will be supplied with the directories of all the previous versions of the code to use, in successive order. To calculate the element recentness value for a refactoring solution, each element that has been involved in the refactorings (be it a class, method or field) will be inspected individually. For each previous version of the code, the element will be searched for using its name. If it is not present, the search will terminate, and the element will be given a value related to how far back it can be found. An element that can be found all the way back through every previous version of code will be given a value of zero. An element that is only found in the current version of the code will be given the maximum element recentness value, which will be equal to the number of versions of code present. For each version the element is present in after the current version, the element recentness value will be decremented by one. Once this value is calculated for one element in the refactoring solution, the objective will move onto the next element until a value is derived for all of them. The overall element recentness value for a refactoring solution will be an accumulation of all the individual element values.

To test the effectiveness of the element recentness objective, an experiment has been constructed to test a GA that uses it against one that does not. It may be argued that it is more relevant to refactor the older elements of the code (for instance, if the code has been around longer, it has had a better chance to build up technical debt and become incompatible with its surroundings). However, it is important to note that the purpose of this experiment is not to support either stance. The more important aspects of the code may be different depending on the circumstances and the developer's opinion. The choice has been made in this paper to focus on more recent elements instead of older elements in order to test the effectiveness of the objective itself in doing what it aims, and the objective can be tweaked to focus one way or the other depending on the developer's needs. In order to judge the outcome of the experiment, the following research questions have been derived:

RQ1: Does a multi-objective solution using an element recentness objective and a quality objective give an improvement in quality?
RQ2: Does a multi-objective solution using an element recentness objective and a quality objective refactor more recent code elements than a solution that does not use the element recentness objective.

In order to address the research questions, the experiment will run a set of tasks to compare a default mono-objective set up to refactor a solution towards quality with a multi-objective approach that uses a quality objective and the newly proposed element recentness objective. The following hypotheses have been constructed to measure success in the experiment.

H1: The multi-objective solution gives an improvement in the quality objective value.
H1$_0$: The multi-objective solution does not give an improvement in the quality objective value.
H2: The multi-objective solution gives significantly higher element recentness objective values than the corresponding mono-objective solution.
H2$_0$: There is no significant difference between the recentness objective value for the multi-objective and mono-objective approaches.

The remainder of this paper is organized as follows. Section 2 discusses related work and gives an overview of the previous studies in SBSM that have incorporated the use of software history. Section 3 describes the MultiRefactor tool used to conduct the experiment along with the searches, refactorings and metrics available in it. Section 4 explains the set up of the experiment used to test the element recentness objective. Section 5 analyses the results of the experiment, looking at the objective values and the times taken to run the tasks. Section 6 concludes the paper and discusses the significance of the findings.

2   Related Work

The use of multi-objective techniques has become more prominent in SBSM as algorithms are developed for this purpose. In employing multi objective approaches a large range of objectives have been used, studies identifying different aspects to explore. White et al. [31] used a multi-objective approach to find a tradeoff between the functionality of a pseudorandom number generator and the power consumption necessary to use it. De Souza et al. [27] investigated the human competitiveness of SBSE techniques in 4 areas of software engineering, and used mono-objective and multi-objective GAs in the study. Ouni et al. [18] created an approach to measure semantics preservation in a software program when searching for refactoring options to improve the structure, by using the NSGA-II search. Code smells are quite often targeted for automated refactoring and Ouni et al. [19] also expanded upon the code smells correction approach of Kessentini et al. [6] by replacing the GA used with NSGA-II. Wang et al. [30] also expanded on the approach of Kessentini et al. by combining the detection and removal of software defects with an estimation of the number of future code smells generated in the software by the refactorings. Ouni et al. [22] investigated the use of a chemical reaction optimization algorithm to explore the benefits of this approach for SBSM. They compared the algorithm against three other search algorithms including a GA. Mkaouer et al. [10, 12] experimented with combining quality measurement with robustness using NSGA-II to create solutions that could withstand volatile software environments. Mkaouer et al. [9, 11, 13] also used NSGA-III to experiment with automated maintenance.

More related to this paper, a few studies have used version history of the target software to aid in refactoring. Pérez et al. [25] proposed an approach that involved reusing complex refactorings that had previously been used. They aimed to mine the change history of the software project to find the refactorings used to fix design smells. The position paper introduced a plan to gather and compile the reusable refactorings in a structured way, in order to reapply them in the future. In order to do this, they introduced two approaches. One is a state-based approach that finds the differences between two versions of a system. They noted that, while a state-based approach is more commonly used, there are drawbacks. Finding refactorings by noting the differences between two versions of code loses the temporal order of the refactorings within that snapshot and it may also cause masking problems. For this reason they proposed to go with the other approach, to measure the changes made in real time using a logger that silently records the developer options. For this, they aimed to extend the ChEOPSJ system [26] and build a refactoring and design smell detector on top of it. ChEOPSJ supports change-centric software development by tracking the changes with a meta-model. The aimed to extend this system to find design smells that have been resolved, trace them back to the refactorings performed and reconstruct the refactoring order.

Ouni et al. [20, 23] used the state-based approach to find a set of refactorings applied in previous versions of the code. They implemented an objective as part of a multi-objective solution to encourage refactorings that are similar to those already applied to similar code fragments in the past. They used the Ref-Finder tool [7] to find refactorings between versions of code. Ref-Finder is able to detect complex refactorings comprising of atomic refactorings using logic-based rules. These refactoring operations can be detected with an average recall of 95% and an average precision of 79%. They also analyzed "co-change", an attribute that identifies how often two objects in a project are refactored together at the same time, as well as the number of refactorings applied in the past to the code elements [19]. They updated their objective function to provide a value relating to a set of elements as an average of these three measures using refactoring history. An extended study from 2015 [21] investigated the use of past refactorings from other projects to calculate the objective value when the change history for the applicable project is not available. Similarly, Tsantalis and Chatzigeorgiou [29] have also used previous versions of software code to aid in the removal of design smells in the current code. They used the previous versions of the code to rank refactoring suggestions according to the number, proximity and extent of changes related with the corresponding code smells.

3   MultiRefactor

The MultiRefactor approach used in this paper is publically available[1] and has been built in order to explore the possibilities in automated refactoring using mono, multi and many-objective approaches. In common with many other refactoring tools MultiRefactor uses the RECODER framework[2] to modify source code in Java programs. RECODER extracts a model of the code that can be used to analyze and modify the code before the changes are applied. MultiRefactor makes available various different approaches to automated software maintenance in Java programs. It takes Java source code as input and will output the modified source code to a specified folder. The input must be fully compilable and must be accompanied by any necessary library files as compressed jar files. The numerous searches available in the tool have various input configurations that can affect the execution of the search. The refactorings and metrics used can also be specified. As such, the tool can be configured in a number of different ways to specify the particular task that you want to run. If desired, multiple tasks can be set to run one after the other.

An earlier study [17] targeted technical debt reduction via refactoring and used the A-CMA [8] tool to experiment with different metric functions, but that work was not extended to produce source code as an output. The same is true for TrueRefactor [5] which only modifies UML and the approach in Ouni et al. [19] which generates proposed lists of refactorings, to be implemented later. MultiRefactor [15] was developed in order to be a fully-automated search-based refactoring tool that produces compilable, usable source code. As well as the Java code artifacts, the tool will produce an output file that gives information on the execution of the task including data about the parameters of the search executed, the metric values at the beginning and end of the search, and details about each refactoring applied. The metric configurations can be modified to include different weights and the direction of improvement of the metrics can be changed depending on the desired outcome.

MultiRefactor contains seven different search options for automated maintenance, with three distinct metaheuristic search techniques available. For each search type there is a selection of configurable properties to determine how the search will run. The refactorings used in the tool are mostly based on Fowler's list [4], consisting of 26 field-level, method-level and class-level refactorings, and are listed below.

---

[1] https://github.com/mmohan01/MultiRefactor.

[2] http://sourceforge.net/projects/recoder.

Field Level Refactorings: Increase/Decrease Field Visibility, Make Field Final/Non Final, Make Field Static/Non Static, Move Field Down/Up, Remove Field.

Method Level Refactorings: Increase/Decrease Method Visibility, Make Method Final/Non Final, Make Method Static/Non Static, Remove Method.

Class Level Refactorings: Make Class Final/Non Final, Make Class Abstract/Concrete, Extract Subclass/Collapse Hierarchy, Remove Class/Interface.

The refactorings used will be checked for semantic coherence as part of the search, and will be applied automatically, ensuring the process is fully automated. A number of the metrics available in the tool are adapted from the list of metrics in the QMOOD [1] and CK/MOOSE [2] metrics suites. The 23 metrics currently available in the tool are listed below.

QMOOD Based: Class Design Size, Number Of Hierarchies, Average Number Of Ancestors, Data Access Metric, Direct Class Coupling, Cohesion Among Methods, Aggregation, Functional Abstraction, Number Of Polymorphic Methods, Class Interface Size, Number Of Methods.

CK Based: Weighted Methods Per Class, Number Of Children.

Others: Abstractness, Abstract Ratio, Static Ratio, Final Ratio, Constant Ratio, Inner Class Ratio, Referenced Methods Ratio, Visibility Ratio, Lines Of Code, Number Of Files.

In order to implement the element recentness objective, extra information about the refactorings is stored in the refactoring sequence object used to represent a refactoring solution. For each solution, a hash table is used to store a list of affected elements in the solution and to attach to each a value that represents the number of times that particular element is refactored in the solution. During each refactoring, an element, considered to be most relevant to that refactoring, is chosen and the element name is stored. After the refactoring has executed, the hash table is inspected. If the element name already exists as a key in the hash table, the value corresponding to that key is incremented to represent another refactoring being applied to that element in the solution. Otherwise, the element name is added to the table and the corresponding value is set to 1. After the solution has been created, the hash table will have a list of all the elements affected and the number of times for each. This information is used to construct the element recentness score for the related solution.

To improve the performance of the tool, the recentness scores are stored for each element as the search progresses in another hash table. This allows the tool to avoid the need to calculate the element recentness scores for each applicable element in the current solution at the beginning of the search task. Instead, the scores are calculated as the objective is calculated, for each element it comes across. If the element hasn't previously been encountered in the search, its element recentness value will be calculated and stored in the hash table. Otherwise, the value will be found by looking for it in the table. This eliminates the need to calculate redundant element recentness values for elements that are not refactored in the search and spreads the calculations throughout the search in place of finding all the values in the beginning.

The objective has some weaknesses in the precision of its measurements. One condition that isn't accommodated is the case where a code element exists in one version of the software, is removed and then is added back again. The element recentness objective will look back from the most recent version of the code and see that the element is not present. It will not continue to look through the older versions to see if the element had been removed and added back in. Instead it will count that as a sign that the element was not present before the applicable version. Also, as the element names are used to check their presence in previous versions, the objective will not be able to accommodate for elements that were present but had different names. As far as the objective is concerned, an element with a different name is a different element and it will not count. For elements that have the same name in different classes, or classes that have the same name but are in different packages or are nested, the objective will not be able to tell the difference. It will look for that name and, if it is present in that version of the code, it will be counted. This introduces the possibility that code elements are noted as being older than they are, because another element with the same name was present when the relevant element wasn't. The issue with providing the class or package that the element is in to discern it from a possible duplicate is that the element may have been moved between classes from version to version. This would introduce the more likely possibility that an element that is older is not found with the element recentness objective. If the element is in a different class or the class is in a different package than it is located in the current version of the code read in, it will be thought of as a distinct element with the same name and the element will be noted as being more recent than it is. For this reason, the extra information isn't included when calculating the element recentness.

4   Experimental Design

The effectiveness and efficacy of MultiRefactor in respect of the element recentness objective was tested using a controlled experiment. In this experiment a set of tasks were developed that used the priority objective to be compared against a set of tasks that didn't. The control group is used a mono-objective approach that uses a function to represent quality in the software. The corresponding tasks use the multi-objective algorithm and have two objectives. The first objective is the same function for software quality used for the mono-objective tasks. The second objective is the element recentness objective. The metrics used to construct the quality function and the configuration parameters used in the GAs are taken from previous experimentation on software quality. Each metric available in the tool was tested separately in a GA to deduce which were more successful, and the most successful were chosen for the quality function. The metrics used in the quality function are given in Table 1. No weighting is applied for any of the metrics. The configuration parameters used for the mono-objective and multi-objective tasks were derived through trial and error and are outlined in Table 2. The hardware used to run the experiment is outlined in Table 3.

For the tasks, six different open source programs are used as inputs to ensure a variety of different domains are tested. The programs range in size from relatively small to medium sized. These programs were chosen as they have all been used in previous

Table 1. Metrics used in the software quality objective [16].

Metrics	Direction
Data access metric	+
Direct class coupling	−
Cohesion among methods	+
Aggregation	+
Functional abstraction	+
Number of polymorphic methods	+
Class interface size	+
Number of methods	−
Weighted methods per class	−
Abstractness	+
Abstract ratio	+
Static ratio	+
Final ratio	+
Constant ratio	+
Inner class ratio	+
Referenced methods ratio	+
Visibility ratio	−
Lines of code	−

Table 2. GA configuration settings [16].

Configuration parameter	Value
Crossover probability	0.2
Mutation probability	0.8
Generations	100
Refactoring range	50
Population size	50

Table 3. Hardware details for the experimentation [16].

Operating system	Microsoft windows 7 enterprise service pack 1
System type	64-bit
RAM	8.00 GB
Processor	Intel Core i7-3770 CPU @ 3.40 GHz

SBSM studies and so comparison of results is possible. Beaver is a parser generator. Apache XML-RPC is a Java implementation of XML-RPC that uses XML to implement remote procedure calls. JRDF is a Java library for parsing, storing and manipulating RDF (Resource Description Framework). GanttProject is a tool for project scheduling and management. JHotDraw is a two-dimensional graphics framework for structured drawing editors. Finally, XOM is a tree based API for processing XML. The source code and necessary libraries for all of the programs are available to download in the GitHub repository for the MultiRefactor tool. Each one is run five times for the mono-objective approach and five times for the multi-objective approach, resulting in 60 tasks overall. The inputs used in the experiment as well as the number of classes and lines of code they contain are given in Table 4. Table 5 gives the previous versions of code used for each input, in order from the earliest version to the latest version used (up to the current version being read in for maintenance). For each input, five different versions of code were used overall. Not all sets of previous versions contain all the releases between the first and last version.

Table 4. Java programs used in the experimentation [16].

Name	LOC	Classes
Beaver 0.9.11	6,493	70
Apache XML-RPC 3.1.1	14,241	185
JRDF 0.3.4.3	18,786	116
GanttProject 1.11.1	39,527	437
JHotDraw 6.0b1	41,278	349
XOM 1.2.1	45,136	224

Table 5. Previous versions of Java programs used in experiment [16].

Beaver	0.9.8	0.9.9	0.9.10	pre1.0 demo
Apache XML-RPC	2.0	2.0.1	3.0	3.1
JRDF	0.3.3	0.3.4	0.3.4.1	0.3.4.2
Gantt project	1.7	1.8	1.9	1.10
JHotDraw	5.2	5.3	5.4b1	5.4b2
XOM	1.1	1.2b1	1.2b2	1.2

In order to find the element recentness score for the mono-objective approach to compare against the multi-objective approach, the mono-objective GA has been modified to output the element recentness score after the task finishes. At the end of the search, after the results have been output and the refactored population has been written to Java code files, the recentness score for the top solution in the final population is calculated. Then, before the search terminates, this score is output at the end of the results file for that solution. This way the scores don't need to be calculated manually and the element recentness scores for the mono-objective solutions can be compared against their multi-objective counterparts.

For the quality function the metric changes are calculated using a normalization function. This function causes any greater influence of an individual metric in the objective to be minimized, as the impact of a change in the metric is influenced by how far it is from its initial value. The function finds the amount that a particular metric has changed in relation to its initial value at the beginning of the task. These values can then be accumulated depending on the direction of improvement of the metric (i.e. whether an increase or a decrease denotes an improvement in that metric) and the weights given to provide an overall value for the metric function or objective. A negative change in the metric will be reflected by a decrease in the overall function/objective value. In the case that an increase in the metric denotes a negative change, the overall value will still decrease, ensuring that a larger value represents a better metric value regardless of the direction of improvement. The directions of improvement used for the metrics in the experiment are given in Table 4. In the case that the initial value of a metric is 0, the initial value used is changed to 0.01 in order to avoid issues with dividing by 0. This way, the normalization function can still be used on the metric and its value still starts off low. Equation 1 defines the normalization function, where m represents the selected metric, C_m is the current metric value and I_m is the initial metric value. W_m is the applied weighting for the metric (where 1 represents no weighting) and D is a binary constant (-1 or 1) that represents the direction of improvement of the metric. n represents the number of metrics used in the function. For the element recentness objective, this normalization function is not needed. The objective score depends on the relative age of the code elements refactored in a solution and will reflect that.

$$\sum_{m=1}^{n} D.W_m \left(\frac{C_m}{I_m} - 1 \right)$$ (1)

The tool has been updated in order to use a heuristic to choose a suitable solution out of the final population with the multi-objective algorithm to inspect. The heuristic used is similar to the method used by Deb and Jain [3] to construct a linear hyper-plane in the NSGA-III algorithm. Firstly, the solutions in the population from the top rank are isolated and written to a separate sub folder. It is from this subset that the best solution will be chosen from when the task is finished. Among these solutions, the tool inspects the individual objective values, and for each, the best objective value across the solutions is stored. This set of objective values is the ideal point $\bar{z} = (z_1^{max})$, $(z_2^{max}), \ldots, (z_M^{max})$, where (z_i^{max}) represents the maximum value for an objective, and an objective $i = 1, 2, \ldots, M$. This is the best possible state that a solution in the top rank could have. After this is calculated, each objective score is compared with its corresponding ideal score. The distance of the objective score from its ideal value is found, i.e. $(z_i^{max}) - f_i(x)$, where $f_i(x)$ represents the score for a single objective. For each solution, the largest objective distance (i.e. the distance for the objective that is furthest from its ideal point) is stored, i.e. $fmax(x) = max_{i=1}^{M}[(z_i^{max}) - f_i(x)]$. At this point each solution in the top rank has a value, $fmax(x)$, to represent the furthest distance among its objectives from the ideal point. The smallest among these values, $min_{j=0}^{N-1} fmax(x)$ (where N represents the number of solutions in the top rank), signifies the solution that is closest to that ideal point, taking all of the objectives into consideration. This solution is then considered to be the most suitable solution and is marked as such when the population is written to file. On top of this, the results file for the corresponding solution is also updated to mark it as the most suitable. This is how solutions are chosen among the final population for the multi-objective tasks to compare against the top mono-objective solution.

For the element recentness objective, the recentness value of each element refactoring is calculated and then added together to get an overall score. Accumulating the score instead of getting an average recentness value avoids the solution applying a minimal number of refactorings in order to keep a low average and thus possibly yielding inferior quality improvements. Accumulating the individual values will encourage the solution to refactor as many recent elements as possible, and it will prioritize these elements, but it will also allow for older elements to be used if they improve the quality of the solution. Equation 2 gives the formula used to calculate the element recentness score in a refactoring solution using the hash table structure. m represents the current element, A_m represents the number of times the element has been refactored in the solution and R_m represents the recentness value for the element. n represents the number of elements refactored in the refactoring solution.

$$\sum_{m=1}^{n} = A_m . R_m \qquad (2)$$

5 Results

In all of the inputs, the mono-objective approach gives a better quality improvement than the multi-objective approach as can be seen from the average quality gain values for each input program (Fig. 1) used in the experiment with the mono-objective and multi-objective approaches. For the multi-objective approach all the runs of each input were able to give an improvement for the quality objective as well as look at the element recentness objective. For the mono-objective approach, the smallest improvement was given with GanttProject, and for the multi-objective approach, it was Apache XML-RPC. For both approaches, XOM was the input with the largest improvement. The mono-objective Beaver results were noticeable for having the most disparate range in comparison to the rest.

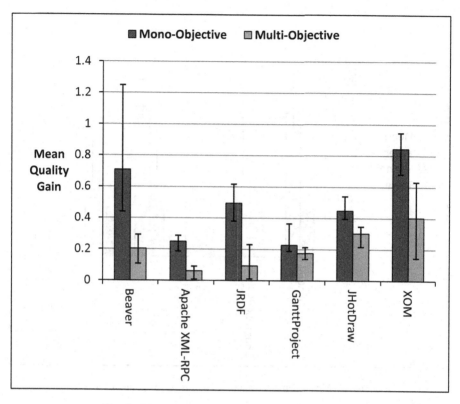

Fig. 1. Mean quality gain values for each input [16].

Figure 2 shows the average element recentness scores for each input with the mono-objective and multi-objective approaches. For all of the inputs, the multi-objective approach was able to yield better scores coupled with the recentness objective. The values were compared for significance using a one-tailed Wilcoxon rank-sum test (for unpaired data sets) with a 95% confidence level ($\alpha = 5\%$). The element recentness scores for the multi-objective approach were found to be significantly higher than the mono-objective approach. The scores tended to vary with both the mono-objective and multi-objective approaches. The exception to this in the XOM input which had a more refined set of results for both approaches. Also, for this input, in comparison to the others, the multi-objective approach didn't give as much of an improvement in the element recentness score in relation to its mono-objective counterpart. For the mono-objective GanttProject scores, one of the tasks gave an anomalous result of 784 (the other values were between 212 and 400) that was greater even than the average multi-objective score for the input, at 764.8.

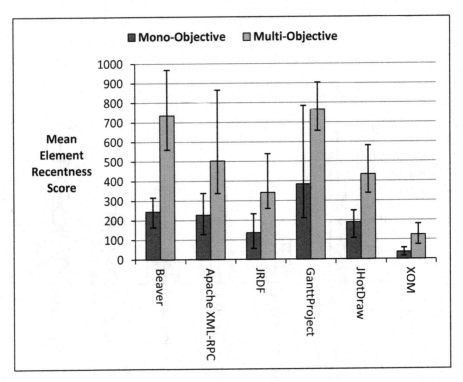

Fig. 2. Mean element recentness scores for each input [16].

Figure 3 gives the average execution times for each input with the mono-objective and multi-objective searches. The times for the mono-objective and multi-objective tasks mostly mirrored each other. For most input programs, the mono-objective approach was faster on average, with the exception being Beaver which takes slightly longer. The Wilcoxon rank-sum test (two-tailed) was used again and the values were found to not be significantly different. The times seemed to increase in relation to the number of classes in the project, although the mono-objective GanttProject time was slightly smaller than JHotDraw, an input with fewer classes. The multi-objective GanttProject times stand out as taking the longest, with the longest task taking almost 71 min to run. The average time for the multi-objective GanttProject tasks was just under 64 min, whereas the average time for the next largest input, JHotDraw, was only 41 min. Whereas the inputs had similar times for the mono-objective and multi-objective approaches, for GanttProject the multi-objective tasks took quite a bit longer (over 28 min longer on average).

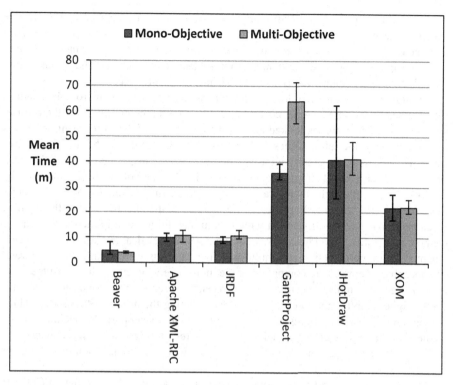

Fig. 3. Mean times taken for each input [16].

6 Conclusion

In this paper, an experiment was conducted to test a new fitness objective in the MultiRefactor tool. The element recentness objective measures the how recent each code element in a refactoring solution has been added to the project in relation to a set of previous versions of the input. It gives an ordinal score accumulating the individual recentness values of each element, with more recent elements being given higher scores. The element recentness objective was tested in conjunction with a quality objective (derived from previous experimentation) in a multi-objective setup. To measure the effectiveness of the recentness objective, the multi-objective approach is compared with a mono-objective approach using just the quality objective. The quality objective values are inspected to deduce whether improvements in quality can still be derived in this multi-objective approach. Then, the element recentness scores are compared to measure whether the developed function can be successful in focusing refactorings on more recently added elements in a software program.

The average quality improvement scores were compared across six different open source inputs and, for all input programs, the mono-objective approach gave better improvements. The multi-objective approach gave improvements in quality across all the inputs. The average element recentness scores were compared across the six inputs.

The scores for the multi-objective approach were better in each case. Finally, the average execution times for each input were inspected and compared for each approach. The times for each approach were similar but, for most inputs, the mono-objective approach was quicker than the multi-objective counterpart. The average times ranged from four minutes for Beaver, to 64 min for GanttProject.

In order to test the aims of the experiment and derive conclusions from the results a set of research questions were constructed. Each research question and their corresponding set of hypotheses looked at one of two aspects of the experiment. RQ1 was concerned with the effectiveness of the quality objective in the multi-objective setup. To address it, the quality improvement results were inspected to ensure that each run of the search yielded an improvement in quality. In all 30 of the different runs of the multi-objective approach, there was an improvement in the quality objective score, therefore rejecting the null hypothesis. RQ2 looked at the effectiveness of the element recentness objective in comparison with a setup that did not use a function to measure element recentness. To address this, a non-parametric statistical test was used to decide whether the mono-objective and multi-objective data sets were significantly different. The recentness scores were compared for the multi-objective approach against the basic approach and the multi-objective element recentness scores were found to be significantly higher than the mono-objective scores, rejecting the null hypothesis $H2_0$. Thus, the research questions addressed in this paper help to support the validity of the element recentness objective in helping to focus refactorings on recent elements in a software program with the MultiRefactor tool, while in conjunction with another objective.

Of the tools proposed in previous research, there are two that use the RECODER framework to modify source code in Java programs. The CODe-Imp platform, developed by Moghadam and Cinnéide [14], uses Abstract Syntax Trees to apply refactorings to a previously designed solution. It is outfitted with a selection of refactorings and metrics, and a number of search options, although there are no multi-objective search techniques available. Likewise, Trifu et al. [28] proposed an approach that uses RECODER to generate Abstract Syntax Trees. Their approach incorporates a number of tools to handle each stage. Their Inject/J tool is used to modify Java programs, with the help of RECODER. The MultiRefactor also uses RECODER in order to modify the Java code during the search. MultiRefactor, however, has a greater number of options than the other tools and a large amount of configurability. It has the ability to use both mono-objective and multi-objective approaches, and even has a many-objective genetic algorithm available. It also generates actual refactored, compiled code, in contrast to the majority of the refactoring approaches previously used. Many of these approaches only suggest refactoring sequences to be applied, and do not check the applicability of the refactorings. For a number of studies, methods were used to investigate using software history to aid with maintenance. These studies are concerned with the refactorings applied in the past. The difference with these studies and the objective proposed in this paper is that the element recentness objective investigates the presence of the code elements that have been refactored in the current solution and not the refactorings that have been applied in the past. The MultiRefactor tool also implements the element recentness objective as a fully automated solution, whereas the studies of Ouni et al. [24] (and likely of Pérez et al. [25] also if their approach was implemented) do not actually apply the proposed refactorings as part of the solution, rather they return a list of refactorings to be attempted. Likewise, Tsantalis and Chatzigeorgiou [29] investigate and prioritize previously suggested refactorings.

For future work, further experimentation could be conducted to test the effectiveness of the recentness objective. Further studies may help to investigate how well the recentness objective can perform along with other properties, using the multi-objective NSGA-III search available in the tool. The outcome of such studies may be helpful in order to create a better supported framework to allow developers to maintain software based on multiple preferences. It would also be useful to gauge the opinion of developers in industry and find out their opinion of the effectiveness of the MultiRefactor approach, and of the recentness objective in an industrial setting.

Acknowledgements. The research for this paper contributes to a PhD project funded by the EPSRC grant EP/M506400/1.

References

1. Bansiya, J., Davis, C.G.: A hierarchical model for object-oriented design quality assessment. IEEE Trans. Softw. Eng. **28**(1), 4–17 (2002)
2. Chidamber, S.R., Kemerer, C.F.: A metrics suite for object oriented design. IEEE Trans. Softw. Eng. **20**(6), 476–493 (1994)
3. Deb, K., Jain, H.: An evolutionary many-objective optimization algorithm using reference-point based non-dominated sorting approach, part I: solving problems with box constraints. IEEE Trans. Evol. Comput. **18**(4), 1–23 (2013)
4. Fowler, M.: Refactoring: Improving the Design of Existing Code. Addison Wesley, Boston (1999)
5. Griffith, I., Wahl, S., Izurieta, C.: TrueRefactor: an automated refactoring tool to improve legacy system and application comprehensibility. In: 24th International Conference on Computer Applications in Industry and Engineering (ISCA), pp. 35–42 (2011)
6. Kessentini, M., Kessentini, W., Erradi, A.: Example-based design defects detection and correction. In: Proceedings of 19th International Conference on Program Comprehension, ICPC 2011, pp. 1–32 (2011)
7. Kim, M., Gee, M., Loh, A., Rachatasumrit, N.: Ref-finder: a refactoring reconstruction tool based on logic query templates. In: Proceedings International Symposium on Foundations of Software Engineering, FSE 2010, pp. 371–372 (2010)
8. Koc, E., Ersoy, N., Andac, A., Camlidere, Z.S., Cereci, I., Kilic, H.: An empirical study about search-based refactoring using alternative multiple and population-based search techniques. In: Gelenbe, E., Lent, R., Sakellari, G. (eds.) Computer and Information Sciences II, pp. 59–66. Springer, London (2011). https://doi.org/10.1007/978-1-4471-2155-8_7
9. Mkaouer, M.W., Kessentini, M., Bechikh, S., Cinnéide, M.Ó., Deb, K.: On the use of many quality attributes for software. Empir. Softw. Eng. **21**, 2503–2545 (2015)
10. Mkaouer, M.W., Kessentini, M., Cinnéide, M.Ó., Hayashi, S., Deb, K.: A robust multi-objective approach to balance severity and importance of refactoring opportunities. Empir. Softw. Eng. **22**(2), 894–927 (2016)

11. Mkaouer, M.W., Kessentini, M., Bechikh, S., Deb, K., Cinnéide, M.Ó.: High dimensional search-based software engineering: finding tradeoffs among 15 objectives for automating software refactoring using NSGA-III. In: Genetic and Evolutionary Computation Conference (GECCO), pp. 1263–1270 (2014)

12. Mkaouer, M.W., Kessentini, M., Bechikh, S., Cinnéide, M.Ó., Deb, K.: Software refactoring under uncertainty: a robust multi-objective approach. In: Proceeding of Genetic and Evolutionary Computation Conference, GECCO 2014, pp. 168–183 (2014)

13. Mkaouer, M.W., et al.: Many-objective software remodularization using NSGA-III. ACM Trans. Softw. Eng. Methodol. **24**(3), 17:1–17:45 (2015)

14. Moghadam, I.H., Cinnéide, M.Ó.: Code-Imp: a tool for automated search-based refactoring. In: Proceedings of 4th Workshop on Refactoring Tools, WRT 2011, pp. 41–44 (2011)

15. Mohan, M., Greer, D.: MultiRefactor: automated refactoring to improve software quality. In: Felderer, M., Méndez Fernández, D., Turhan, B., Kalinowski, M., Sarro, F., Winkler, D. (eds.) PROFES 2017. LNCS, vol. 10611, pp. 556–572. Springer, Cham (2017). https://doi.org/10.1007/978-3-319-69926-4_46

16. Mohan, M., Greer, D.: Automated refactoring of software using version history and a code element recentness measure. In: Proceedings of 13th International Conference on Evaluation of Novel Approaches to Software Engineering (ENASE 2018), pp. 455–462 (2018)

17. Mohan, M., Greer, D., McMullan, P.: Technical debt reduction using search based automated refactoring. J. Syst. Softw. **120**, 183–194 (2016)

18. Ouni, A., Kessentini, M., Sahraoui, H., Hamdi, M.S.: Search-based refactoring: towards semantics preservation. In: Proceedings of 28th IEEE International Conference on Software Maintenance, ICSM 2012, pp. 347–356 (2012)

19. Ouni, A., Kessentini, M., Sahraoui, H., Boukadoum, M.: Maintainability defects detection and correction: a multi-objective approach. Autom. Softw. Eng. **20**(1), 47–79 (2013)

20. Ouni, A., Kessentini, M., Sahraoui, H., Inoue, K., Hamdi, M.S.: The use of development history in software refactoring using a multi-objective evolutionary algorithm. In: Genetic and Evolutionary Computation Conference (GECCO), pp. 1461–1468 (2013)

21. Ouni, A., Kessentini, M., Sahraoui, H., Hamdi, M.S.: Improving multi-objective code-smells correction using development history. J. Syst. Softw. **105**, 18–39 (2015)

22. Ouni, A., Kessentini, M., Bechikh, S., Sahraoui, H.: Prioritizing code-smells correction tasks using chemical reaction optimization. Softw. Qual. J. **23**(2), 323–361 (2015)

23. Ouni, A., Kessentini, M., Sahraoui, H., Inoue, K., Deb, K.: Multi-criteria code refactoring using search-based software engineering: an industrial case study. ACM Trans. Softw. Eng. Methodol. **25**(3) (2016)

24. Ouni, A., Kessentini, M., Sahraoui, H.: Search-based refactoring using recorded code changes. In: Proceedings of European Conference on Software Maintenance and Reengineering (CSMR), pp. 221–230 (2013)

25. Pérez, J., Murgia, A., Demeyer, S.: A proposal for fixing design smells using software refactoring history. In: Proceedings of International Workshop on Refactoring and Testing, RefTest, pp. 1–4 (2013)

26. Soetens, Q.D., Demeyer, S.: ChEOPSJ: change-based test optimization. In: Proceedings of European Conference on Software Maintenance and Reengineering (CSMR), pp. 535–538 (2012)

27. De Souza, J.T., Maia, C.L., de Freitas, F.G., Coutinho, D.P.: The human competitiveness of search based software engineering. In: Proceedings of 2nd International Symposium on Search-Based Software Engineering (SSBSE), pp. 143–152 (2010)

28. Trifu, A., Seng, O., Genssler, T.: Automated design flaw correction in object-oriented systems. In: Proceedings of 8th European Conference on Software Maintenance and Reengineering (CSMR), pp. 174–183 (2004)

29. Tsantalis, N., Chatzigeorgiou, A.: Ranking refactoring suggestions based on historical volatility. In: Proceedings of 15th European Conference on Software Maintenance and Reengineering (CSMR), pp. 25–34 (2011)
30. Wang, R., Purshouse, R.C., Fleming, P.J.: Preference-inspired coevolutionary algorithms for many-objective optimization. IEEE Trans. Evol. Comput. **17**(4), 474–494 (2013)
31. White, D.R., Clarke, J., Jacob, J., Poulding, S.M.: Searching for resource-efficient programs: low-power pseudorandom number generators. In: Proceedings of Genetic and Evolutionary Computation Conference (GECCO), pp. 1775–1782 (2008)

The Formal Reference Model for Software Requirements

Erika Nazaruka[✉] and Jānis Osis

Department of Applied Computer Science, Riga Technical University,
Sētas iela 1, Riga 1048, Latvia
{erika.nazaruka, janis.osis}@rtu.lv

Abstract. The formal reference model for software requirements must be useful for specification of mappings from both functional and non-functional requirements. The topological functioning model (TFM) can serve as such reference model for specifying mappings from software requirements to functional characteristics and structure of the modeled system. Different types of mapping of functional requirements and their aspects such as completeness and overlapping have mathematical background and can be described using mathematical constructs (the inclusion predicate, disjoint predicate, covering predicate, projection, and separation family of functions), as well as meta-classes in the metamodel. This paper continues the previous work and illustrates the way how specification of the TFM functional characteristics and causal relationships can be extended and can represent mappings from the requirements as tuples of TFM functional features extended with requirements sets and mapping characteristics, namely, completeness and overlapping for functional requirements, and, additionally, scope and dynamic characteristics for non-functional ones. This allows formal tracing from the whole set of requirements to software implementing constructs via TFM elements and vice versa, that could be useful for further architectural decisions and development of test cases.

Keywords: Topological functioning model · Functional requirements · Non-functional requirements · Requirements modelling · Reference model

1 Introduction

Software is everywhere, but software development projects fail very often [1]. Inadequate, incomplete, constantly changing software requirements remain one of the main risks in software development.

Software requirements specify the required functionality of the planned product as well as quality attributes, constraints and external interface requirements [2]. The last three are called non-functional requirements (NFRs). NFRs show how well the required functionality must be implemented. The quality attributes or "-ilities" constitute a large part of NFRs. NFRs sometimes are called also extra-functional requirements. According to [2], external quality attributes are availability, installability, integrity, interoperability, performance, reliability, robustness, safety, security, and usability.

© Springer Nature Switzerland AG 2019
E. Damiani et al. (Eds.): ENASE 2018, CCIS 1023, pp. 352–372, 2019.
https://doi.org/10.1007/978-3-030-22559-9_16

Functional requirements (FRs) are implemented as functional entities, while implementation of NFRs may differ corresponding to their nature [3] – they can contain technical information that relates to functional requirements, system architecture, design constraints, as well as implementation constraints [2].

A Topological Functioning Model (TFM) elaborated at the Riga Technical University, Latvia, in 1969 by Janis Osis specifies a system from three viewpoints – functional, behavioral and structural [4].

The functional viewpoint shows functional units of the system and their cause-and-effect relations. The behavioral viewpoint shows signal from the external environment and reaction of the system on them and to the external environment. The paths from the input signal to the output reaction is formed by cause-and-effect relations between the functional units that take part in the concrete behavioral scenario. The structural viewpoint shows domain objects that are presented and are used in the functional units that take part in the system's operation.

This model can serve as a root model for further analysis of the system and software domains and as a reference model for system/software requirements.

The term "root model" means that this model contains primary (core) knowledge about the modelled domain and the system. And this knowledge must be propagated into further analysis and design models as well as must be implemented in the code.

In its turn, the term "reference model" has several meanings. We use the following one [5]: "An abstract representation of the entities and relations within a problem space; it forms the conceptual basis to derive more concrete models from which an implementation can be developed."

The main distinction of the TFM from other models is formalism based on the algebraic topology and system theory. The formalism does not worsen holistic representation of the system in comparison with semi-formal modeling languages used nowadays, such as UML (Unified Modelling Language) or BPMN (Business Process Model and Notation). The modeled facts and knowledge about the system can be hold in different forms, e.g. as tuples of elements or a knowledge base, thus allowing controlled transformations from one view to another. Besides that, it is possible to create a model of the sub-system, e.g. a model of the supporting information system or a software system, and to keep consistency between models of the system and its subsystems in the mathematically formal way as well as to verify completeness and consistency of the gathered knowledge.

FRs can be mapped directly onto the TFM, thus leading to discovering incompliances between determined FRs and functional characteristics of the domain. Similarly, all NFRs can be mapped into the TFM, indicating the scope and dynamical characteristics of the requirements.

This work extends the summarized results of research on system/software requirements specification and verification by means of the TFM presented in the conference paper [6]. All mapping cases are explained using mathematical constructs, metamodel elements and small examples.

The paper is organized as follows. Section 2 describes main features of the TFM and its application in the field of functional requirements and summarizes the mentioned results on referencing NFRs to this model. Section 3 provides the illustrating example. Related work (Sect. 4) and conclusions (Sect. 5) end the paper.

2   TFM as a Reference Model

2.1   Mappings from Functional Requirements

The TFM is a formal mathematical model that allows modelling and analyzing functionality of the system [4]. It could be a business, software, biological system, mechanical system, etc. The TFM represents the modeled functionality as a digraph (X, Θ), where X is a set of inner functional characteristics (called functional features) of the system, and Θ is a topology set on these characteristics in a form of a set of cause-and-effect relations. TFM models can be compared for similarities using a continuous mapping mechanism [7]. Since 1990s the TFM is being elaborated for the software development [8] starting from principles of the object-oriented system analysis and design and ending with principles of Model Driven Architecture developed by Object Management Group.

The TFM is characterized by the topological and functioning properties [9]. The topological properties take their origin in topological algebra. They are connectedness, neighborhood, closure and continuous mapping.

Connectedness ensures that all functional characteristics of the system dependent from each other work in a direct or indirect way. Neighborhoods are sets, where each set is a functional characteristic of the system and its all direct predecessors and followers. Mathematical operation of union all neighborhoods of system inner functional characteristics is called "closure". The closure is used to mathematically define the border of the system to be modeled. Since any TFM is a topological space, they may be compared for similarity or refined/simplified. This is possible thanks to continuous mapping between topological spaces that preserves the initial structure of the topological models during their modifications.

The functioning properties take their origin in system theory. They are cause-and-effect relations, cycle structure, inputs and outputs. Cause-and-effect relations are those dependencies between functional characteristics of the system that allow system to function. The end of performing one functional characteristic triggers initiation of other depending functional characteristics. Since we talk about functioning system, these dependencies form a cycle (or cycles) of functionality. Behavior of the system depends on inputs from the external environment as well as of reactions of the system (output) to the external environment.

The composition of the TFM is presented in [4]. Rules of composition and derivation of the TFM from the textual system description within TFM4MDA (TFM for Model Driven Architecture) are provided by examples and described in detail in several publications [10–12]. The TFM can be manually created in the TFM Editor or can also be generated automatically from the business use case descriptions in the IDM toolset [13].

The main TFM concept is a functional feature that represents system's functional characteristic, e.g., a business process, a task, an action, or an activity [9]. It can be specified by a unique tuple (1).

$$< A, \textbf{R}, \textbf{O}, \textbf{PrCond}, \textbf{PostCond}, \textbf{Pr}, \textbf{Ex} > \qquad (1)$$

Where [4]:

- A is object's action,
- **R** is a set of results of the object's action (it is an optional element),
- **O** is an object that gets the result of the action or a set of objects that are used in this action,
- **PrCond** is a set of preconditions or atomic business rules,
- **PostCond** is a set of post-conditions or atomic business rules,
- **Pr** is a set of providers of the feature, i.e. entities (systems or sub-systems) which provide or suggest an action with a set of certain objects,
- **Ex** is a set of executors (direct performers) of the functional feature, i.e. a set of entities (systems or sub-systems) which enact a concrete action.

The second TFM concept is a cause-and-effect relation between functional features. It defines the cause from which the triggering of the effect occurs. The formal definition of the cause-and-effect relations and their combinations is given in [14]. It states that a cause-and-effect relation is a binary relationship that links a cause functional feature to an effect functional feature. In fact, this relation indicates control flow transition in the system. The cause-and-effect relations (and their combinations) may be joined by the logical operators, namely, *conjunction (AND), disjunction (OR), or exclusive disjunction (XOR)*. The logic of the combination of cause-and-effect relations denotes system behavior and execution (e.g., decision making, parallel or sequential actions).

The TFM can be manually (but according to the precise rules) transformed into most used UML diagram types (Fig. 1): class diagrams, activity diagrams, use cases and their textual specifications [15] and Topological UML [16] diagrams such as Topological Class diagrams, Topological Use Case diagrams, Activity diagrams, State Chart diagrams, Sequence and Communication diagrams [17].

Since the TFM specifies functioning of the system, it can be used for verification of FRs. The FRs can be mapped onto the TFM functional features (Fig. 1) as described in detail in [18–20]. As a result, mappings give the opportunity to find incomplete, additional, conflicting, unnecessary, as well as redundant requirements to the system functionality.

Types of FRs mappings onto the TFM can be *one-to-one, one-to-many, many-to-many, many-to-one*, as well as *zero-to-one* and *one-to-zero*. In terms of mathematics, mapping *one-to-one* is the *inclusion* predicate (Fig. 2a), *many-to-one* can be either the *disjoint (component)* predicate (Fig. 2c) or *covering* predicate (Fig. 2b), *one-to-many* is the *separating family of function* predicate (Fig. 2e), and *many-to-many* is a set of *projection* predicates (Fig. 2d). Let us explain each of the mappings on the examples.

A **one-to-one** mapping is when one functional requirement completely maps onto one functional feature; this means that the functional requirement completely specifies one functional characteristic of the domain. Let us have the business requirement FR1 "System shall provide authorization of a registered user" or, for example, a user story US1 "As a registered user I want to authorize in the library system so that I can use library online services". In the TFM, the functional feature that specifies this functional characteristic of the system is FF1 "Authorization of a registered user (Fig. 3).

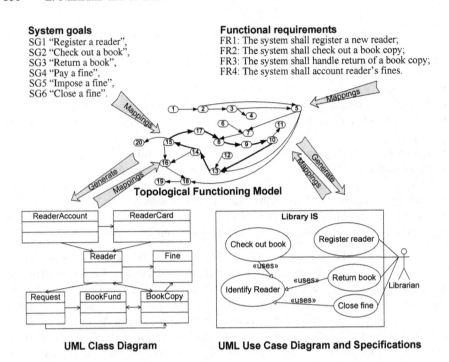

System goals
SG1 "Register a reader",
SG2 "Check out a book",
SG3 "Return a book",
SG4 "Pay a fine",
SG5 "Impose a fine",
SG6 "Close a fine".

Functional requirements
FR1: The system shall register a new reader;
FR2: The system shall check out a book copy;
FR3: The system shall handle return of a book copy;
FR4: The system shall account reader's fines.

Topological Functioning Model

UML Class Diagram   **UML Use Case Diagram and Specifications**

Fig. 1. Mappings from analysis artefacts to the TFM; some artefacts can be generated from the TFM [6].

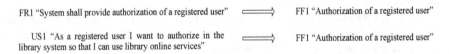

a) inclusion   b) covering   c) disjoint (component)   d)projection   e)separating family of functions

Fig. 2. Mappings from functional requirements to TFM functional features [18].

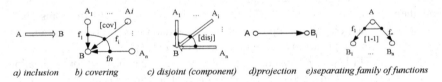

FR1 "System shall provide authorization of a registered user" ⟹ FF1 "Authorization of a registered user"

US1 "As a registered user I want to authorize in the library system so that I can use library online services" ⟹ FF1 "Authorization of a registered user"

Fig. 3. Examples of mapping *one-to-one*.

One-to-many, **many-to-many** and **many-to-one** mappings relate to situations when specifications of functional requirements and functional characteristics are at the different level of granularity. One-to-many and many-to-one are special cases of the relation type "many-to-many". These cases can be caused by the difference in levels of details between functional requirements and TFM functional features. Such cases indicate and help in discovering decomposed, overlapping or incomplete requirements.

Let us consider several examples. Imagine that we have two business requirements: FR1 "System shall provide authorization of a registered user using login name and password" and FR2 "System shall provide authorization of a registered user using a 5-digit code sent to a user mobile phone via SMS". But after analysis of the system, only one functional characteristic is defined, FF1 "Authorization of a registered user". In this case, two functional requirements will be mapped onto one functional characteristic in the model (Fig. 4a). Besides that, they both completely specify this concrete functional characteristic of the system and does not cover each other (the disjoint predicate).

Sometimes, analysis of the system may be more in detail than specification of requirements is. For example, imagine that we have defined two functional characteristics of the system: FF1 "Authorization of a user via login data" and FF2 "Authorization of a user via Google+ account". In its turn, functional requirement FR1 "The system shall provide authorization of a user via login or Google+ account" is defined in the specification. In this case, one functional requirement will be mapped onto two functional characteristics of the system (Fig. 4b).

Case "many-to-many" can occur when requirements to functionality of the system is unreasonably distributed in requirements, but the level of abstraction in the model is too low.

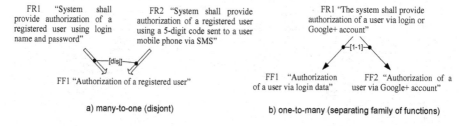

FR1 "System shall provide authorization of a registered user using login name and password"

FR2 "System shall provide authorization of a registered user using a 5-digit code sent to a user mobile phone via SMS"

FF1 "Authorization of a registered user"

a) many-to-one (disjont)

FR1 "The system shall provide authorization of a user via login or Google+ account"

[1-1]

FF1 "Authorization of a user via login data"

FF2 "Authorization of a user via Google+ account"

b) one-to-many (separating family of functions)

Fig. 4. Examples of mappings many-to-one (a) and one-to-many (b).

One-to-zero and **zero-to-one**. The former occurs when one functional requirement describes new (or undefined) functionality of the system that can cause modification of the system in its current configuration and its TFM (i.e., the required functionality is new and, thus, it may require changes in the existing processes of the system). For example, functional requirement FR "The system shall provide user authorization using Facebook account" for the system, which model contains only functional feature FF "Logging in of the user using login data". The functional characteristic in the model does not reckon for the ability to login using user's Facebook account. The latter occurs when the requirements specification does not contain any functional requirement corresponding to the already defined functional characteristics. This case indicates the functionality that either will not be implemented in the "target" system, or is missed (i.e., either it is not mentioned in the requirements specification, or it will be changed but it is not explicitly expressed). For example, when the model contains a functional characteristic of user logging in, but the requirement specification does not have the corresponding requirement.

The TFM itself can be defined in the metamodel which fragment is shown in Fig. 5. Mappings from FRs to the TFM are specified in instances of the meta-class Correspondence [4]. Instances of meta-class Correspondence are created for each case of mappings between functional requirements and functional features. In case of disjoint predicates or coverage predicates this knowledge is stored in Boolean variables *isComplete* and *isOverlapping*. The following cases are possible:

- If both *isComplete = true* and *isOverlapping = true*, this is mapping many-to-one (covering) from the collection *fRequirement::FunctionalRequirement[0..*]* to *feature::FunctionalFeature[0..*]*, where feature contains one element;

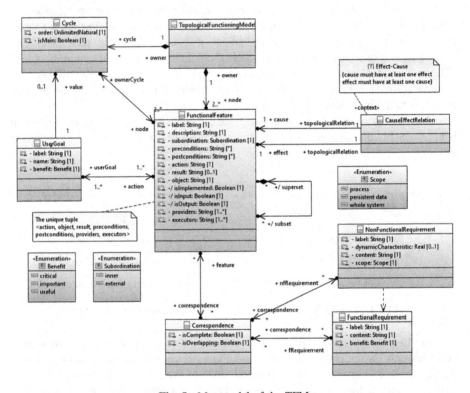

Fig. 5. Metamodel of the TFM.

- If *isComplete = true* and *isOverlapping = false*, this is mapping (1) many-to-one (decomposition) between those collections if *feature* contains one element, (2) one-to-one (inclusion) if both collections has only one element, or (3) one-to-many if *fRequirement* has only one element and *feature* has more than one element (separating family of functions);
- If *isComplete = false* and *isOverlapping = true*, this is mapping many-to-one (covering, incomplete) if *feature* contains one element and many-to-many (covering, incomplete) in case of more than one element in *feature* collection. This means that not all requirements are defined, or the functional feature will be implemented partially. If the latter, the TFM must be refined to correctly indicate functional characteristics to be implemented;
- If both *isComplete = false* and *isOverlapping = false*, this may indicate different cases of projections.

2.2 Mappings from Non-functional Requirements

Specified as tuples, the mappings between requirements and TFM functional features can be reversed and specified as references from the TFM to **FRs**. They can be added to the specification tuple (1) of the functional feature as shown in (2).

$$< A, R, O, PrCond, PostCond, Pr, Ex, FRs > \tag{2}$$

Where **FRs** is a set of references to functional requirements specified separately from the TFM.

NFRs similarly to FRs can be mapped onto the TFM functional feature or a set of features by providing referencing in a way similar to the specification of the corresponding FRs.

The possible types of NFRs mappings onto the TFM are the same as in case of FRs, i.e. one-to-zero, one-to-one, one-to-many, many-to-many, many-to-one, and zero-to-one, but the meaning differs:

- *One-to-one* is when one non-functional requirement is related to the concrete functional feature and must be implemented in the corresponding entities. For example, a functional feature specifies retrieving of all loans for some period from the database and a non-functional feature specifies that the accomplishment of the request must not exceed 3 ms (Fig. **6**).

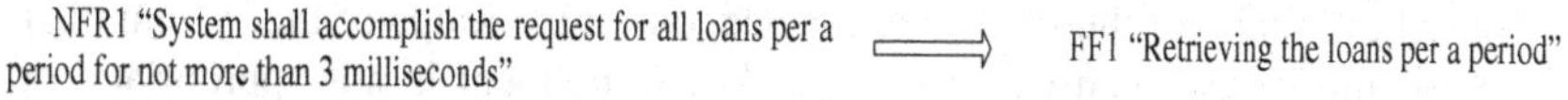

NFR1 "System shall accomplish the request for all loans per a period for not more than 3 milliseconds" ⟹ FF1 "Retrieving the loans per a period"

Fig. 6. Mapping one-to-one for non-functional requirements.

- *One-to-many* is when one non-functional requirement is related to all noted functional features and must be implemented in all the corresponding entities. For example, there are several functional features that specify retrieving data from the database and some successive calculations, and a non-functional requirement that specifies that accomplishment of the requests to the database must not exceed 3 ms (Fig. 7a). In such a general case it is a projection from the non-functional requirement to a set of functional features. In case, if this requirement relates to a sequence of functional features, the mapping is specified by predicate "separating family of functions" (Fig. 7c).
- *Many-to-one* is when more than one non-functional requirement is related to one noted functional feature and must be implemented in the corresponding entities. It could be considered as a special case of the *many-to-many* relationship. For example, there are two non-functional requirements that specify the needed language of the user interface and the requirement to the provided software interface. Both must be implemented in the input functional feature that specifies interaction with the users of software (Fig. 7b). Both requirements complement each other, and this fact can be specified by disjoint predicate. Another case may be when two non-functional requirements partially covers each other, e.g. when one states that processing of requests to the database must not exceed 3 ms, while another,

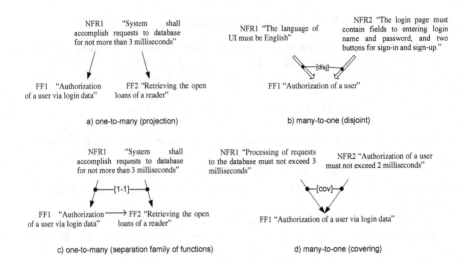

Fig. 7. Mappings one-to-many (a, c) and many-to-one (b, d) for non-functional requirements.

authorization of a user (that also includes the request to the database), states that it must not exceed 2 ms (Fig. 7d).

- *One to zero.* One non-functional requirement is not related to any functional feature and is not traceable in the model and in the code. This indicates that this requirement is out of the scope of the model and, hence, out of the scope of the system planned. There could be two causes, i.e., either the requirement is not appropriate, or the model lacks the required functionality. The latter may indicate incomplete analysis of the required functions that are new for the system where software will run.
- *Zero to one.* A functional feature is not related to any non-functional requirement. It is a reason to recheck the non-functional requirements.

The mappings between NFRs and the TFM functional features can also be specified in the tuple as element **NRFs** that is a set of references from a functional feature to NFRs (3).

$$< A, R, O, PrCond, PostCond, Pr, Ex, FRs, NFRs > \qquad (3)$$

Besides that, NFRs may be referenced only from those functional features that have references to FRs, since as FRs relate to functionality that will be implemented as NRFs relate to the same one.

Quantitative characteristics of NFRs can also be added to the specification of a functional feature in the TFM. All that is needed is to extend an element of set NFRs that will describe the needed characteristics value or limit D (4).

$$\mathbf{NFRs} = \{NFR_1, \ldots, NRF_n\}, \text{ where } NFR_i = < REF_{NFRi}, D_{NFRi}, SC_{NFRi} > \qquad (4)$$

For example, if non-functional requirement NFR1 has a dynamic characteristics D that can be expressed as a value or as a function (e.g. $D = f(p)$, where p is a parameter set of some function f). Thus, it could be added to the tuple of the functional feature specification in a form **NFRs** = {NFR1}, where NFR1 = $<REF_{NFR1}, D_{NFR1}>$ and REF_{NFR1} is a reference to the NFR1.

Scope of non-functional requirements may be a process, a persistent data, or a whole system. This list may be extended by values specific to the project. In the element specification (4), this value can be indicated as a value of variable SC_{NFRi} that corresponds to the enumeration {"process", "persistent data", "whole system"}.

Indeed, this specification is not as compact as instances of meta-class Correspondence (since most of NFRs refers to the whole system), but it is still formal and accurate.

However, to provide compactness, another specification that would hold knowledge of meta-class Correspondence may be introduced for both FRs and NFRs. Let us assume that we have a functional feature tuple FF (5) with additional element "id" that denotes an identifier of a FF.

$$FF = <\text{id}, A, \mathbf{R}, \mathbf{O}, \mathbf{PrCond}, \mathbf{PostCond}, \mathbf{Pr}, \mathbf{Ex}> \tag{5}$$

Then it is possible to specify mappings FR2FF (6) from FRs to functional features FFs like in meta-class Correspondence, where **FR** is a set of functional requirements, **FF** is a set of functional features, and *isComplete* and *isOverlapping* are Boolean variables for indicating complete or overlapping mappings.

$$\text{FR2FF} = <\mathbf{FR}, \mathbf{FF}, \text{isComplete}, \text{isOverlapping}> \tag{6}$$

In case of NFRs mappings can be specified as a tuple (7), where **NFR** is a set of non-functional requirements in the form indicated in (4), and **FF** is a set of functional features. The same as in case of functional requirements, the TFM can use instances of meta-class Correspondence to define mappings from a set of non-functional requirements *nfRequirement::NonFunctionalRequirement[0..*]* to a set of functional features *features::FunctionalFeatures[0..*]* (Fig. 5).

$$\text{NFR2FF} = <\mathbf{NFR}, \mathbf{FF}, \text{isComplete}, \text{isOverlapping}> \tag{7}$$

In general, the TFM and mappings from requirements onto it can be described as it is illustrated in (8).

$$\text{R2TFM} = \{\mathbf{FF}, \mathbf{NFR}, \mathbf{FR}, \mathbf{FR2FF}, \mathbf{NFR2FF}\} \tag{8}$$

2.3 Tracing Requirements to and from Design Constructs via TFM Elements

Certainly, specification of mappings is useless without using them further. Summary of traceability of requirements to TFM elements to elements of software architecture expressed in terms of modelling constructs of Unified Modelling Language [21] is given in Table 1.

Table 1. Tracing TFM elements into elements of software architecture [6].

Requirements	Elements in TFM	Implementing constructs in UML
FRs and NFRs	Action	Activities, operations, messages, events, entry and exit effects
FRs and NFRs	Object	Classes, objects
FRs and NFRs	Result	Classes, objects, states, associations between certain classes
FRs	Precondition	Guards in behavioural diagrams, states
FRs	Postcondition	States
FRs	Providers	Actors, subject, classes
FRs	Executors	Actors, classes, objects
FRs	Subordination	None
Dependencies among FRs, and NFRs	Cause-and-effect relation	Topological relationships, structural relationships, control flows, transitions
Dependencies among FRs, and NFRs	Functioning cycle	Topological relationships, structural relationships, control flows
FRs and NFRs	TFM itself	Subsystems or subjects; use cases, actors and relationships between them; objects, messages and their sequences; workflows; topological class diagrams, topological use case diagram, communication diagrams, and object diagrams; state diagrams; component and deployment diagrams

In general, requirements traceable to TFM functional features and cause-and-effect relations are traceable to the corresponding behavioral (e.g., an activity, a control flow) and structural constructs (e.g., a class) in UML diagrams that may be verified at different modularization levels starting from units and finishing by sub-systems or large modules.

Thus, FRs and NFRs can be designed and verified in the corresponding structural and behavioral constructs of UML diagrams such as classes, objects, activities, processes, events, sub-systems, components and so on and in the constructs of source code such as persistent (serializable) classes, methods and functions, processes, modules and assemblies, components and subsystems, etc.

Besides that, it is possible to trace backward from the design constructs to see what requirements can be affected by changes. Backward tracing of changes is possible thanks to explicit dependencies among requirements based on cause-and-effect relations among affected functional features in the TFM.

3   Illustrative Example

Let us consider the example of the TFM for a library system. The presented fragment is just a part of the library functionality.

Functional features of the TFM can be obtained from any verbal specifications, instructions, business documentation etc. Let us assume that in the result of gathering knowledge about the domain, we have defined the main functionality, provided by the library: registering persons as readers, and giving out and taking back the books as well as imposing a fine in case of damages of the book or the exceeded loan time. Besides that, the domain vocabulary has been defined and it includes the following domain objects:

- a person (name, surname, age),
- a request form for a reader card (person's data, request date),
- a reader card (date of issue),
- registration (date of registration),
- a reader account (account id),
- a request for a book (bibliographical description),
- a book (bibliographical description, condition, damage),
- book loan (bibliographical description, loan start date, loan end date),
- a fine (amount, last date for payment, date of payment).

The TFM (Fig. 8) specifies the main functionality provided by the library, i.e. registering persons as readers, and giving out and taking back the books as well as imposing a fine in case of damages of the book or the exceeded loan time. The specification of functional features is given in Figs. 9 and 10.

3.1   Mappings from Requirements to the TFM

Let us assume that the task is to create new software that should support librarians' work. Software functional requirements to the new system in the short form are stated as follows:

- FR1: The system shall provide registration of a new reader by creating a reader account and issuing a reader card to the registered person.
- FR2: The system shall provide giving out a book to the reader.
- FR3: The system shall provide the return of a loaned book to the library.
- FR4: The system shall show information of the reader's registration to the librarian.
- FR5: The system shall provide generation of a report on lost books for the indicated time period.
- FR6: The system shall provide generation of a report on damaged books for the indicated time period.

Software non-functional requirements are the following:

- NFR1: The user interface language must be English.
- NFR2: The search for a reader account must not exceed 2 s.
- NFR3: The system must be available from 8 to 20 o'clock from Monday to Friday.
- NFR4: All activities of the software user must be logged.

- NFR5: The system must create a backup for all data once in a day.
- NFR6: The software must support simultaneous work of 10 users.

References from TFM functional features to the FRs and NFRs are shown in Fig. 11.

Summarizing, in the example we have one-to-many, zero-to-one, and one-to-zero relationships among functional requirements and functional features:

- The *one-to-many* relationships are FR1 to functional features 2, 3, 4, 5, 6, 7, and 8; FR2 to 3, 11, 12, 13, and 14; FR3 to 3, 18, 19, 20, 21, 22, 23, 24, and 25; FR4 to 3 and 5.
- The *zero-to-one* relationships relate to functional features 1, 9, 10, 15, 16, 17, 26, and 27.
- The *one-to-zero* relates to FR5 and FR6.

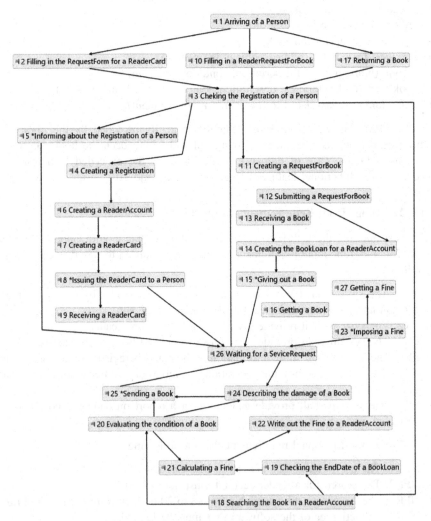

Fig. 8. The topological functioning model (simplified) of the library operation [6].

The last case indicates new functionality that must be introduced into software to be built and is not represented in the TFM of the current functioning of the library. This means that the TFM must be extended with several functional features that represents the required functional characteristics and revalidated. Then, FR5 and FR6 should be mapped to the new functionality.

In their turn, NFRs relate to functional features (that are related to FRs) with *one-to-many* and *one-to-one* relationships. So, NFR1, NFR3, NFR4 and NFR6 relate to the whole system (as to processes, as to data), NFR2 relates to functional feature 3, and NFR5 also relates to the whole system, but only to the persistent data.

id	Description	Action	Result	Object	S	Ex
1	Arriving of a Person	arrive	Person	Person	E	P
2	Filling in the RequestForm for a ReaderCard	request	RequestForm	ReaderCard	I	P
3	Cheking the Registration of a Person	check	Registration	Person	I	L
4	Creating a Registration	create	Registration	Registration	I	L
5	*Informing about the Registration of a Person	inform	Registration	Person	I	L
6	Creating a ReaderAccount	create	ReaderAccount	ReaderAccount	I	L
7	Creating a ReaderCard	create	ReaderCard	ReaderCard	I	L
8	*Issuing the ReaderCard to a Person	issue	ReaderCard	ReaderCard	I	L
9	Receiving a ReaderCard	receive	ReaderCard	ReaderCard	E	R
10	Filling in a ReaderRequestForBook	fillIn	ReaderRequestForBook	ReaderRequestForBook	I	L
11	Creating a RequestForBook	create	RequestForBook	RequestForBook	I	R
12	Submitting a RequestForBook	submit	RequestForBook	RequestForBook	I	L
13	Receiving a Book	receive	Book	Book	I	L
14	Creating the BookLoan for a ReaderAccount	checkOut	BookLoan	Book	I	L
15	*Giving out a Book	giveOut	Book	Book	I	L
16	Getting a Book	get	Book	Book	E	R
17	Returning a Book	return	Book	Book	E	R
18	Searching the Book in a ReaderAccount	search	Book	ReaderAccount	I	L
19	Checking the EndDate of a BookLoan	check	EndDate	BookLoan	I	L
20	Evaluating the condition of a Book	evaluate	condition	Book	I	L
21	Calculating a Fine	calculate	Fine	Fine	I	L
22	Write out the Fine to a ReaderAccount	writeOut	Fine	ReaderAccount	I	L
23	*Imposing a Fine	impose	Fine	Fine	I	L
24	Describing the damage of a Book	describe	damage	Book	I	L
25	*Sending a Book	send	Book	Book	I	L
26	Waiting for a SeviceRequest	wait	ServiceRequest	ServiceRequest	I	L
27	Getting a Fine	get	Fine	Fine	E	R

Fig. 9. The specification of TFM functional features, where S – subordination, I – inner of the system, E – external to the system, Ex – the executor, R – the reader, L – the librarian, P – the person [6].

In other words, FR1 is a requirement of implementation of the process of the registration of a new reader, where a user interface must be in English (NFR1), time required for searching a reader account must not exceed 2 s (functional feature 3, NFR2), this process must be available from 8 to 20 o'clock from Monday to Friday (NFR3), all user activities must be logged (NFR4), it must process at least 10 simultaneous requests (NFR6), and backups of data of persistent classes ReaderCard, RequestForm, Registration, Person, and ReaderAccount must be created (NFR5).

FR2 is a requirement of implementation of the process of loaning books, where a user interface must be in English (NFR1), time required for searching a reader account must not exceed 2 s (functional feature 3, NFR2), this process must be available from 8 to 20 o'clock from Monday to Friday (NFR3), all user activities must be logged (NFR4), this process must support 10 simultaneous requests (NFR6), and create a

id	Description	Preconditions	Postconditions
1	Arriving of a Person		A person is arrived
2	Filling in the RequestForm for a ReaderCard	A person is arrived	RequestForm is filled in
3	Cheking the Registration of a Person	((RequestForm is filled in) OR (ReaderRequestForBook is filled in) OR (Book is returned)) AND (Librarian is free)	(Person has Registration) OR (Person has no Registration)
4	Creating a Registration	Person has no Registration	Person has Registration
5	*Informing about the Registration of a Person	Person has Registration	Information of Registration is given
6	Creating a ReaderAccount	(Person has Registration) AND (ReaderAccount is not created)	ReaderAccount is created
7	Creating a ReaderCard	(ReaderAccount is created) AND (ReaderCard is not created)	ReaderCard is created
8	*Issuing the ReaderCard to a Person	ReaderCard is created	ReaderCard is issued
9	Receiving a ReaderCard	ReaderCard is issued	
10	Filling in a ReaderRequestForBook	A person is arrived	RaderRequestForBook is filled in
11	Creating a RequestForBook	ReaderRequestForBook is filled in	RequestForBook is created
12	Submitting a RequestForBook	RequestForBook is created	RequestForBook is submitted
13	Receiving a Book		Book is received
14	Creating the BookLoan for a ReaderAccount	(Book is received) AND (RequestForBook is submitted)	Book is checkedOut
15	*Giving out a Book	Book is checkedOut	Book is loaned
16	Getting a Book	Book is loaned	
17	Returning a Book	A person is arrived	Book is returned
18	Searching the Book in a ReaderAccount	Person has Registration	(Book is not found) OR (Book is checkedOut)
19	Checking the EndDate of a BookLoan	Book is checkedOut	(EndDate is exceeded) OR (EndDate is not exceeded)
20	Evaluating the condition of a Book	Book is checkedOut	(condition is good) OR (condition is damaged)
21	Calculating a Fine	(EndDate is exceeded) OR (condition is damaged)	Fine is calculated
22	Write out the Fine to a ReaderAccount	Fine is calculated	Fine is written out
23	*Imposing a Fine	Fine is written out	Fine is imposed
24	Describing the damage of a Book	(condition is damaged) AND (Librarian is free)	damage is described
25	*Sending a Book	(condition is good) OR (damage is described)	Book is sent
26	Waiting for a SeviceRequest	(Book is sent) OR (Book is loaned) OR (ReaderCard is issued) OR (Information of Registration is given) OR (Fine is imposed)	Librarian is free
27	Getting a Fine	Fine is imposed	Fine is delivered

Fig. 10. The specification of TFM functional feature preconditions and post-conditions [6].

backup data of persistent classes Registration, Person, RequestForBook, Book, and BookLoan (NFR5).

FR3 is a requirement of implementation of the process of returning loaned books, where a user interface must be in English (NFR1), time required for searching a reader account must not exceed 2 s (functional feature 3, NFR2), this process must be available from 8 to 20 o'clock from Monday to Friday (NFR3), all user activities must be logged (NFR4), this process must support 10 simultaneous requests (NFR6), and create a backup data of persistent classes Registration, Person, Book, ReaderAccount, BookLoan and Fine (NFR5).

FR4 is a requirement of implementation of the process of informing registration data, where a user interface must be in English (NFR1), time required for searching a reader account must not exceed 2 s (functional feature 3, NFR2), this process must be available from 8 to 20 o'clock from Monday to Friday (NFR3), all user activities must be logged (NFR4), this process must support 10 simultaneous requests (NFR6), and create a backup data of persistent classes Registration and Person (NFR5).

FR5 and FR6 specify new functionality that must be first added to the TFM, then the TFM must be revalidated, and the necessary NFRs must be referenced to the introduced functional features.

id	Description	FRs	NFRs
1	Arriving of a Person		
2	Filling in the RequestForm for a ReaderCard	FR1	NFR1, NFR3, NFR4, NFR5 (persistent data), NFR6
3	Checking the Registration of a Person	FR1, FR2, FR3, FR4	NFR2, NFR1, NFR3, NFR4, NFR5 (persistent data), NFR6
4	Creating a Registration	FR1	NFR1, NFR3, NFR4, NFR5 (persistent data), NFR6
5	*Informing about the Registration of a Person	FR1, FR4	NFR1, NFR3, NFR4, NFR5 (persistent data), NFR6
6	Creating a ReaderAccount	FR1	NFR1, NFR3, NFR4, NFR5 (persistent data), NFR6
7	Creating a ReaderCard	FR1	NFR1, NFR3, NFR4, NFR5 (persistent data), NFR6
8	*Issuing the ReaderCard to a Person	FR1	NFR1, NFR3, NFR4, NFR5 (persistent data), NFR6
9	Receiving a ReaderCard		
10	Filling in a ReaderRequestForBook		
11	Creating a RequestForBook	FR2	NFR1, NFR3, NFR4, NFR5 (persistent data), NFR6
12	Submitting a RequestForBook	FR2	NFR1, NFR3, NFR4, NFR5 (persistent data), NFR6
13	Receiving a Book	FR2	NFR1, NFR3, NFR4, NFR5 (persistent data), NFR6
14	Creating the BookLoan for a ReaderAccount	FR2	NFR1, NFR3, NFR4, NFR5 (persistent data), NFR6
15	*Giving out a Book		
16	Getting a Book		
17	Returning a Book		
18	Searching the Book in a ReaderAccount	FR3	NFR1, NFR3, NFR4, NFR5 (persistent data), NFR6
19	Checking the EndDate of a BookLoan	FR3	NFR1, NFR3, NFR4, NFR5 (persistent data), NFR6
20	Evaluating the condition of a Book	FR3	NFR1, NFR3, NFR4, NFR5 (persistent data), NFR6
21	Calculating a Fine	FR3	NFR1, NFR3, NFR4, NFR5 (persistent data), NFR6
22	Write out the Fine to a ReaderAccount	FR3	NFR1, NFR3, NFR4, NFR5 (persistent data), NFR6
23	*Imposing a Fine	FR3	NFR1, NFR3, NFR4, NFR5 (persistent data), NFR6
24	Describing the damage of a Book	FR3	NFR1, NFR3, NFR4, NFR5 (persistent data), NFR6
25	*Sending a Book	FR3	NFR1, NFR3, NFR4, NFR5 (persistent data), NFR6
26	Waiting for a SeviceRequest		
27	Getting a Fine		

Fig. 11. The specification of mappings between TFM functional features and both functional (FRs) and non-functional requirements (NFRs) [6].

Concluding, TFM as a reference model allows showing required functionality and its extra-functional characteristics already at the stage of problem/solution domain modeling and analysis.

3.2 Tracing Requirements to and from Design Constructs

Let us consider tracing of the requirements to several constructs of the design model, in our case, topological UML class diagram. This diagram keeps cause-and-effect relations between classes in addition to standard elements of UML class diagrams. In our case, cause-and-effect relations are presented using unidirectional and bidirectional associations among classes.

According to the defined TFM, the following classes (that implement the domain objects) are obtained after transformation of the TFM (Fig. 12): RequestForm, ReaderCard, Person, Registration, RequestForBook, ReaderAccount, Book, BookLoan and Fine. Cause-and-effect relations among them indicate transition of the control flow when objects of those classes interact. Operations in the classes are actions of the corresponding TFM functional features.

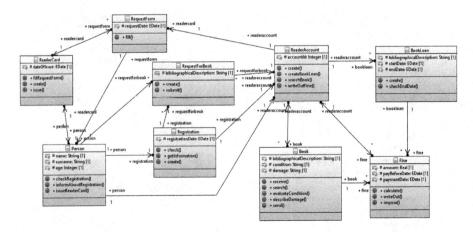

Fig. 12. Cause-and-effect relations between domain objects to be implemented.

Mappings from the software requirements to the TFM functional features and from the functional features to the classes allow establishing trace links among these elements (Fig. 13). For example, trace links shows us that functional characteristics modeled by functional feature 3 is the most actively used, it is affected by all the requirements, and is implemented in classes Registration and Person. So, in case of changes in these classes, all implemented functional requirements will require verification.

Trace links show also difference in levels of details and number of functions required for implementation of functional requirements, e.g., implementation of FR1 and FR3 could be more time consuming than implementation of FR2 and FR4. A class that has more diverse behavior is Book, since it has more trace links from functional features than other classes.

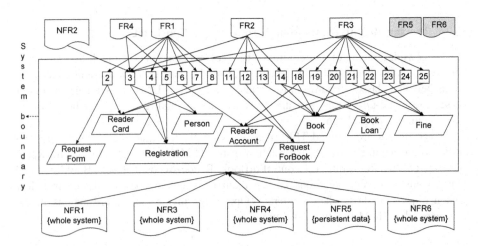

Fig. 13. Trace links among requirements, TFM elements and topological UML classes.

Functional requirements FR5 and FR6 does not have mappings to functional features, since they represent functionality that is not modelled in the TFM (new to the existing system).

Functional features 1, 9, 10, 15, 16, 17 and 27 are not presented in figure, since they correspond to not computerized activities in the system.

Concluding, TFM as a reference model allows establishing trace links for functional and non-functional requirements to and from design elements. It gives the following benefits: explicit dependencies between requirements and their implementing constructs, analysis of influence of changes either in requirements or in design constructs to other functionality of the system.

4 Related Work

Modeling and further analysis of NFRs in the context of Requirements Engineering and early stages of Model Driven Software Development (MDSD) is quite actual at the present.

Liu *et al.* [3] provide their own solution based on analysis of FRs implementation in use case, class and sequence diagrams. Analysis of these diagrams allows authors to annotate corresponding constructs in the diagrams and to use them as root nodes for creation of a soft goal graph with NFRs. Then the soft goal graph is refined to sub-NFRs. Operationalizations for these sub-requirements are identified in the corresponding sequence and class diagrams. Potential conflicts and synergy are identified during this process, too. At the result, two models are created, namely, functional and non-functional. These models are integrated using JointPoint elements. However, as the authors mention, the suggested approach is suitable mainly for NFRs that are closely related to the functionality. Besides that, a quantitative part of NFRs is not modelled.

The same conception of soft goal graphs is applied in [22–24], etc. The first authors introduce their own ontology-based language for NFRs specification. The reason is to model NFRs and analyze possible conflicts among them as early as possible at the development. The authors illustrate that a use of ontology in NFRs modeling is one of current trends in requirements modeling and analysis. Similarly to our approach, specifications of NFRs and FRs relate to each other. The difference is in a referencing model, the authors use the soft goal interdependency graph, while in our approach we make a use of the TFM. Ahmad *et al.* [23, 25] use the KAOS based approach with domain specific language that extends special requirements specification language Relax. In their turn, the latter authors apply Pareto Efficiency to optimize NFRs satisfaction and as a reference model they use the $i*$ (i-star) [soft goal] model.

Extended NFRs framework based on the soft goal model [26] suggest an approach, where weights are added on edges between parent and child goals, thus allowing dynamic analysis of the possible design alternatives for soft goal satisfaction by agents.

Phalnikar and Jinwala [27] provide a simple framework for Service-Oriented Requirements Engineering that uses the semi-formal approach of graph transformation and transformation of WSDL (Web Service Definition Language) specifications in XML into GGX (Graph Grammar Language) format. As a result, analysis of critical pairs of requirements is conducted. This approach applies the similar idea that NFRs must be specified as addition to behavioral and structural diagrams of the system model.

In MDSD, dealing with NFRs remains a challenge [28]. In practice, NFRs can be specified separately or in-place with the main model as stereotyped classes. For example, the separate specification can be done by creating a standalone metamodel or an extension to the metamodel of the main model, e.g., a "quality viewpoint" based on a metamodel that defines such elements as constraints in OCL (Object Constraint Language) and in natural language, references to quality attributes and "entity classes" as well as measurements and decision criteria [29]. Another variant is a use of the previously considered soft goal models [30] that are referenced to architectural knowledge, thus allowing propagation of NFRs to platform independent and platform specific models.

5 Conclusions

Frequent changes in software requirements may raise conflicts, contradictions and incompleteness among them. Verification of requirements and analysis of their conformance to the existing design or implementation constructs is a challenge for software developers. It is a common-known fact that discovering any inconsistency at the early stages of software development improves the quality of the final product and reduces costs of re-work.

In this paper we have presented our vision on referencing functional and non-functional requirements to the formal reference model, namely, the topological functioning model. This model provides the formal analytical means for functional requirements verification. However, this means can also be used for specification and further analysis of non-functional requirements in the quite similar way – only meaning of the several constructs changes, and a few additional aspects are added.

Formal mappings from software requirements to the TFM functional features allow, first, tracing them to implementing design and code constructs and vice versa, and, second, discovering possible incompleteness and conflicts in software requirements at the stage of problem or change analysis and decision making on design or architectural solutions. Additionally, the TFM can be used to discover those requirements and corresponding implementation constructs in the design or code that could be affected by changes. Following cause-and-effect relations among the functional features of the TFM, it is possible to find out all dependent elements.

Implementation of the presented approach and integration of it with the domain knowledge base is one of the future research directions in this field.

References

1. Charette, R.N.: Why software fails. IEEE Spectrum (2005). https://spectrum.ieee.org/computing/software/why-software-fails. Accessed 19 Aug 2018
2. Wiegers, K., Beatty, J.: Software Requirements, 3rd edn. Microsoft Press, Redmond (2013)

3. Liu, Y., Ma, Z., Shao, W.: Integrating non-functional requirement modeling into model driven development method. In: 2010 Asia Pacific Software Engineering Conference, Sydney, pp. 98–107. IEEE (2010)
4. Osis, J., Asnina, E.: Topological modeling for model-driven domain analysis and software development : functions and architectures. In: Model-Driven Domain Analysis and Software Development: Architectures and Functions, pp. 15–39. IGI Global, Hershey (2011)
5. IGI Global: What is reference model. https://www.igi-global.com/dictionary/reference-model/24810. Accessed 19 Aug 2018
6. Nazaruka, E., Osis, J.: The topological functioning model as a reference model for software functional and non-functional requirements. In: Proceedings of the 13th International Conference on Evaluation of Novel Approaches to Software Engineering, {ENASE} 2018, Funchal, Madeira, pp. 467–477. SciTePress, Portugal (2018)
7. Asnina, E., Osis, J.: Computation independent models: bridging problem and solution domains. In: Proceedings of the 2nd International Workshop on Model-Driven Architecture and Modeling Theory-Driven Development, Lisbon, pp. 23–32. SciTePress - Science and Technology Publications (2010)
8. Osis, J., Asnina, E., Grave, A.: Computation independent representation of the problem domain in MDA. e-Informatica Softw. Eng. J. 2(1), 29–46 (2008). http://www.e-informatyka.pl/index.php/einformatica/volumes/volume-2008/issue-1/article-2/. Accessed 04 Jan 2018
9. Osis, J., Asnina, E.: Is modeling a treatment for the weakness of software engineering? In: Model-Driven Domain Analysis and Software Development, pp. 1–14. IGI Global, Hershey (2011)
10. Asnina, E.: The computation independent viewpoint: a formal method of topological functioning model constructing. Appl. Comput. Syst. 26, 21–32 (2006)
11. Osis, J., Asnina, E., Grave, A.: MDA oriented computation independent modeling of the problem domain. In: Proceedings of the 2nd International Conference on Evaluation of Novel Approaches to Software Engineering - ENASE 2007, Barcelona, pp. 66–71. INSTICC Press (2007)
12. Osis, J., Asnina, E., Grave, A.: Formal problem domain modeling within MDA. In: Filipe, J., et al. (eds.) ICSOFT/ENASE 2007, pp. 387–398. Springer, Heidelberg (2008). https://doi.org/10.1007/978-3-540-88655-6_29
13. Šlihte, A., Osis, J.: The integrated domain modeling: a case study in databases and information systems. In: Proceedings of the 11th International Baltic Conference (DB&IS 2014), pp. 465–470. Technology Press of Tallinn University, Tallinn (2014)
14. Asnina, E., Ovchinnikova, V.: Specification of decision-making and control flow branching in topological functioning models of systems. In: ENASE 2015 - Proceedings of the 10th International Conference on Evaluation of Novel Approaches to Software Engineering, Lisbon, pp. 364–373. SciTePress - Science and and Technology Publications (2015)
15. Osis, J., Asnina, E.: Derivation of use cases from the topological computation independent business model. In: Model-Driven Domain Analysis and Software Development, pp. 65–89. IGI Global, Hershey (2011)
16. Donins, U., Osis, J., Slihte, A., Asnina, E., Gulbis, B.: Towards the refinement of topological class diagram as a platform independent model. In: Proceedings of the 3rd International Workshop on Model-Driven Architecture and Modeling-Driven Software Development, MDA and MDSD 2011, in Conjunction with ENASE 2011, Lisbon, pp. 79–88. SciTePress (2011)
17. Osis, J., Donins, U.: Formalization of the UML class diagrams. In: ENASE 2009, vol. 69, pp. 180–192. Springer, Heidelberg (2010). https://doi.org/10.1007/978-3-642-14819-4_13

18. Osis, J., Asnina, E.: Enterprise modeling for information system development within MDA. In: Proceedings of the 41st Annual Hawaii International Conference on System Sciences (HICSS 2008), Waikoloa, USA, p. 490. IEEE (2008)

19. Osis, J., Asnina, E.: A business model to make software development less intuitive. In: 2008 International Conference on Computational Intelligence for Modelling Control and Automation, pp. 1240–1245. IEEE (2008)

20. Asnina, E., Gulbis, B., Osis, J., Alksnis, G., Donins, U., Slihte, A.: Backward requirements traceability within the topology-based model driven software development. In: Proceedings of the 3rd International Workshop on Model-Driven Architecture and Modeling-Driven Software Development, MDA and MDSD 2011, in Conjunction with ENASE 2011, pp. 36–45. SciTePress (2011)

21. Donins, U.: Topological unified modeling language: development and application. Ph.D. thesis. Riga Technical University, Latvia (2012)

22. Xiang, H., et al.: Semantic modelling and automated reasoning of non-functional requirement conflicts in the context of softgoal interdependencies. IET Softw. 9(6), 145–156 (2015)

23. Ahmad, M., Bruel, J.-M., Laleau, R., Gnaho, C.: Using RELAX, SysML and KAOS for ambient systems requirements modeling. Procedia Comput. Sci. 10, 474–481 (2012)

24. Zubcoff, J.J., Garrigos, I., Casteleyn, S., Mazon, J.N., Aguilar, J.A.: Evaluating the use of pareto efficiency to optimize non-functional requirements satisfaction in i* modeling. IEEE Latin Am. Trans. 14(1), 331–338 (2016)

25. Ahmad, M., Belloir, N., Bruel, J.-M.: Modeling and verification of functional and non-functional requirements of ambient self-adaptive systems. J. Syst. Softw. 107, 50–70 (2015)

26. Goncalves, J., Krishna, A.: Dynamic non-functional requirements based model-driven agent development. In: 2015 24th Australasian Software Engineering Conference, pp. 128–137. IEEE (2015)

27. Phalnikar, R., Jinwala, D.: Analysis of conflicting user requirements in web applications using graph transformation. ACM SIGSOFT Softw. Eng. Notes 40(2), 1–7 (2015)

28. Ameller, D., et al.: Handling non-functional requirements in Model-Driven Development: an ongoing industrial survey. In: 2015 IEEE 23rd International Requirements Engineering Conference (RE), pp. 208–213. IEEE (2015)

29. González-Huerta, J., Insfran, E., Abrahão, S., McGregor, J.D.: Non-functional requirements in model-driven software product line engineering. In: Proceedings of the Fourth International Workshop on Nonfunctional System Properties in Domain Specific Modeling Languages - NFPinDSML 2012, New York, USA, pp. 1–6. ACM Press, New York (2012)

30. Ameller, D., Franch, X., Cabot, J.: Dealing with non-functional requirements in model-driven development. In: 2010 18th IEEE International Requirements Engineering Conference, pp. 189–198. IEEE (2010)

Effective Decision Making in Self-adaptive Systems Using Cost-Benefit Analysis at Runtime and Online Learning of Adaptation Spaces

Jeroen Van Der Donckt[1], Danny Weyns[1,2](✉)(iD), M. Usman Iftikhar[1,2](iD), and Sarpreet Singh Buttar[2]

[1] Department of Computer Science, KU Leuven, Leuven, Belgium
`danny.weyns@kuleuven.be`
[2] Department of Computer Science, Linnaeus University, Växjö, Sweden

Abstract. Self-adaptation is an established approach to deal with uncertainties that are difficult to predict before a system is deployed. A self-adaptative system employs a feedback loop that tracks changes and adapts the system accordingly to ensure its quality goals. However, making effective adaptation decisions at runtime is challenging. In this chapter we tackle two problems of effective decision making in self-adaptive systems. First, current research typically focusses on the benefits adaptaton can bring but ignores the cost of adaptation, which may invalidate the expected benefits. To tackle this problem, we introduce CB@R (Cost-Benefit analysis @ Runtime), a novel model-based approach for runtime decision-making in self-adaptive systems that handles both the benefits and costs of adaptation as first-class citizens in decision making. Second, we look into the adaptation space of self-adaptive systems, i.e. the set of adaption options to select from. For systems with a large number of adaptation options, analyzing the entire adaptation space is often not feasible given the time and resources constraints at hand. To tackle this problem, we present a machine learning approach that integrates learning with the feedback loop to select a subset of the adaption options that are valid in the current situation. We evaluate CB@R and the learning approach for a real world deployed Internet of Things (IoT) application.

Keywords: Self-adaptation · MAPE · Models at runtime ·
Statistical model checking · Cost-Benefit Analysis Method · CBAM ·
Machine learning · Adaptation space · Internet-of-Things · IoT

1 Introduction

Modern software systems often operate in highly dynamic environments, exposing them to various types of uncertainties. Examples are large-scale supply chain

© Springer Nature Switzerland AG 2019
E. Damiani et al. (Eds.): ENASE 2018, CCIS 1023, pp. 373–403, 2019.
https://doi.org/10.1007/978-3-030-22559-9_17

systems that ensure sufficient, safe, and nutritious food to the global population [3], and unmanned underwater vehicles (UUVs) that operate in oceanic areas to monitor pollution levels [19]. Dynamics in the environments where these systems operate are often difficult or even impossible to anticipate before deployment. Hence, these systems require a manner to resolve the uncertainties during operation. A common technique to deal with uncertainties in software systems is self-adaptation [32,33,39,44] that equips a system with a feedback loop system. The aim of self-adaptation is to let the system collect additional knowledge about itself and its environment, and adapt itself to satisfy its goals under the changing conditions, or if necessary degrade gracefully. Various types of self-adaptation exist [12], this research focuses on architecture-based self-adaptation [17,30,46]. In this approach, the self-adaptive system consists of a managed system that contains the domain logic and a managing system that contains the adaption logic. To managing system manages the managed system through sensors and actuators using four basic functions: monitor, analyze, plan, and execute.

This chapter tackles two problems of effective decision making in self-adaptive systems. First, current self-adaptation approaches tend to look only at the benefits that can be gained by adaptation [45]. These benefits are generally improvements in terms of system qualities (self-optimization, self-healing, etc. [30]). However, realizing adaptation may also incur costs. These costs are domain specific and may be expressed in terms of the extra use of resources or the time or energy that it takes to apply the adaptation actions. For example, in a networked IoT system with battery-powered motes, the cost may be expressed as the energy required to communicate adaptation actions to the motes that need to adapt their network settings. Examples of initial work in this direction are [4] that uses an adaptation cost model for quantifying the overhead introduced by autonomic behavior in an adaptive parallel application, and [8] that performs a tradeoff analysis for runtime adaptation to increase the satisfaction rate of system goals. However, to the best of our knowledge, there exists no systematic approach today that considers both the benefits and costs for adaptation as first-class citizens in the decision-making for self-adaptation. Hence, to make effective adaptation decisions, the first research problem we tackle is:

How to enable decision-making in self-adaptive systems that considers both the benefits of adaptation and the costs for realizing adaptation as first-class concerns?

To underpin the relevance of this research question, we start with demonstrating that the costs for adaptation can be significant. To that end, we apply a state-of-the-art approach for self-adaptation [23] to DeltaIoT, an Internet of Things (IoT) application. DeltaIoT has been proposed as an exemplar for research in the field of self-adaptive systems [24]. To tackle the first research problem, we introduce CB@R (Cost-Benefit analysis @ Runtime), a new effective method for decision-making in self-adaptive systems that exploits models at runtime [5]. CB@R leverages on the principles of the Cost-Benefit Analysis Method (CBAM), which is an established approach for analysing costs and benefits of decisions in architectural design [42]. CB@R considers both the expected benefits produced by adaptation and the expected cost implied to realise adaptation as first class concerns when selecting an adaptation option. We evaluate CB@R with the DeltaIoT application and compare it both with a conservative approach that is applied in practice and a state-of-the-art adaptation approach. The answer to the first research question leverage on the work presented in [43].

Second, we look into the decision making problem of selecting an adaptation option from the set of all available options, we refer to this set as the adaptation space. Existing approaches in self-adaptive systems such as Active FORmal Models for Self-Adaptation (ActivFORMS) [23] and Runtime Quantitative Verification (RQV) [9] use model checking techniques to analyze the adaptation options and select an option to adapt the managed system. This runtime verification requires substantial resources, e.g. time and memory. Consequently, these approaches are limited to systems with relatively small adaptation spaces. However, in practical systems, the adaptation space may consist of thousands or even more adaptation options [10,48]. In such situations it is infeasible to analyze all the adaptation options. Hence, our second research question is:

How to effectively reduce the adaptation space in self-adaptive systems using machine learning?

To tackle this research problem, we present a machine learning approach that integrates learning with the feedback loop to select a subset of the adaption options that are valid in the current situation. This subset will be further analyzed by the feedback loop to select the best adaptation option. The machine learning approach learns on the fly which adaptation options should be selected [35]. We evaluate the machine learning approach also for DeltaIoT and compare is with a standard state-of-the-art self-adaptation approach.

The remainder of this chapter is structured as follows. Section 2 provides some basics of CBAM, machine learning, self-adaptation, and DeltaIoT. In Sect. 3, we show the relevance of costs for adaptation by applying an existing adaptation approach to DeltaIoT. Section 4 introduces CB@R, the novel cost benefit analysis approach for decision-making at runtime in self-adaptive systems. In Sect. 5, we evaluate CB@R and compare it with two other approaches. Section 6 introduces the learning approach to reduce the adaptation space and presents evaluation results. In Sect. 7 we discuss related work. Finally, Sect. 8 draws conclusions and outlines plans for future work.

2   Background

2.1   CBAM

The Cost Benefit Analysis Method (CBAM) is an established method for analysing the costs and benefits of architectural designs of software systems [42]. CBAM takes the uncertainty factors regarding costs and benefits into account. This provides a basis for informed decision-making about architectural design or upgrades. The concepts of CBAM are used as inspiration for CB@R.

Given that the resources for building and maintaining a software-intensive system are finite, there must be a rational process that helps to choose among architectural options. An *architectural option* refers to a candidate design of a software-intensive system that is based on applying a particular architectural approach (for example a peer-to-peer style or a client-server style). Different architectural options will have different technical and economic implications. The technical implications are the various implemented features and the qualities associated with them, each of which brings some benefit to the organization. A direct economic implication is the cost of implementing the system.

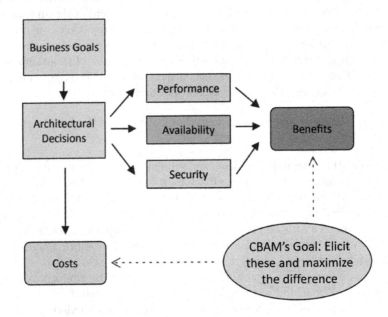

Fig. 1. Context for CBAM process (based on [2]).

CBAM models the benefits and costs of architectural design decisions providing a mean for optimizing such decisions. Figure 1 illustrates CBAM. In the example, the relevant qualities may be performance, availability and security, each with a particular importance. Each architectural design (resulting from a set of architectural decisions) yields different values for these qualities, resulting in some benefit for the system stakeholders. Each architectural design will also incur a cost. For example, using redundant hardware to achieve a desired level of availability has a cost, while check-pointing to a disk file has a different cost. As shown in the figure, the goal of CBAM is to maximize the difference between the benefit derived by the system design and the cost of implementing the design.

Using the benefit and cost of each architectural design, CBAM allows the stakeholders to choose among different architectural designs based on their Value For Cost (VFC), i.e., the ratio of utility to cost:

$$VFC = \frac{TotalBenefit}{Cost} \qquad (1)$$

TotalBenefit represents the overall utility of an architectural design. This total benefit is defined as the weighted sum of the utility values for the examined quality attributes. The VFC values are used to rank the architectural designs (and thus design decisions), from which the stakeholders can choose.

2.2 Machine Learning

Machine learning is part of artificial intelligence that defines algorithms to make predictions based on experience obtained in the past. Typically, the experience consists of collected data, such as a set of labeled examples, where the quality and the number of examples are essential. Machine learning offers a large variety of approaches, for example supervised learning, unsupervised learning, semi-supervised learning, reinforcement learning, etc. [35]. In our research, we focus on supervised learning, which involves two sequential phases. First, the training phase in which the learning algorithm learns from a set of labeled examples, also known as the training dataset. Second, the testing phases in which the learning algorithm receives a testing dataset and predicts the output [34].

Classification, regression, ranking, etc. are common approaches used in supervised learning. We limit the scope of this research to classification and regression. In classification, the targets in the training dataset are classes, whereas in regression they are real values. Supervised learning can be done either during design time (offline learning) or runtime (online learning). We applied online learning in this research. In online learning, the training and testing phases are interwoven, enabling the learning algorithm to interact with them multiple times. For instance, the learning algorithm predicts in the testing phase the targets of the items. Then it moves to the training phase and receives the same items with their actual targets. These interactions enable the learning algorithm to continuously adapt itself to the constant flow of data. Therefore, online learning fits in various application scenarios such as learning in an uncertain environment, life-long learning, etc. These scenarios are often present whenever a system behaves autonomously, for example automated driving or robotics [18].

2.3 Self-adaptation

As noted earlier, we apply architecture-based self-adaptation (see Fig. 2). A self-adaptive system consists of a Managed System that operates in an Environment and provides the domain functionality to users. The Managing System monitors the Managed System and its Environment and uses this knowledge to adapt the system to realize the Adaptation Goals [1,17,31,36,47].

At a given time, the Managed System has a particular configuration that is determined by the arrangement and settings of its running components. We refer to the different options for adaptation from a given configuration as the *adaptation options*. Adapting the managed system means selecting an adaptation option and changing the current configuration accordingly. The Environment in which the system operates can be the physical world or computing elements that are not under control of the system. The Environment and the Managed System may expose stochastic behavior.

A common approach to realize the Managing System is by means of a MAPE-K feedback loop [14,30,39,46] that comprises four elements: Monitor, Analyze, Plan, and Execute that share common Knowledge. Knowledge comprises models of the managed system referring to its structure, behavior, goals, and other relevant aspects of the system or its adaptation [47]. The Monitor collects runtime data from the Environment and the Managed system to resolve uncertainties keeping the models up to date. The Analyzer analyzes the qualities of the different adaptation options and compares these with the qualities of the current configuration to determine whether adaptation is required or not. If so, the Planner selects the best adaptation option based on the adaptation goals and composes a plan to adapt the system. Finally, the Executer executes the plan.

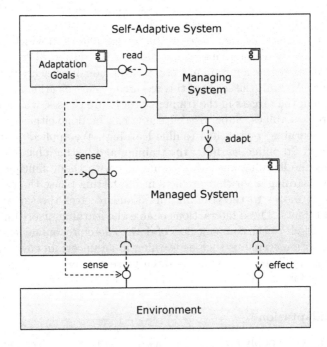

Fig. 2. Basic conceptual model of self-adaptive system [44].

ActivFORMS (Active FORmal Models for Self-adaptation) is a model-based approach that provides guarantees for the adaptation goals of self-adaptive systems with some degree of confidence [22,23]. In ActivFORMS, formally specified feedback loop models are verified for correctness before deployment and then deployed on top of a virtual machine that directly executes the models to realize adaptation. ActivFORMS extends the MAPE-K loop with a statistical model checker that connects with the Analyzer. The statistical model checker supports the Analyzer with estimating the quality properties that are subject to adaptation for each adaptation option. The statistical model checker uses simulation and statistical techniques to estimate the quality requirements. The confidence of the estimated values is dependent on the number of simulations.

2.4 DeltaIoT

DeltaIoT is a reference Internet of Things application (IoT) that has been developed by KU Leuven and VersaSense[1] to evaluate new self-adaptation approaches and compare their effectiveness with other solutions [24]. DeltaIoT comprises both a simulator for offline experimentation as well as real physical setup.

DeltaIoT consists of 15 Long-Range IoT motes (LoRa) that are deployed at the KU Leuven campus as shown in Fig. 3. The motes are strategically placed to provide access control to labs (via RFID), monitor the movements and occupancy status (via passive infrared) and sense the temperature (via heat sensors). Each mote in the network relays its sensor data to the gateway using wireless multihop communication. Communication in the network is time-synchronized and organized in cycles. Each cycle comprises a fixed number of communication slots. Each slot defines a sender mote and a receiver mote that can communicate with one another. The communication slots are fairly divided among the motes. For example, the system can be configured with a cycle time of 570 s (9.5 min), each cycle comprising 285 slots, each of 2 s. For each link, 40 slots are allocated for communication between the motes.

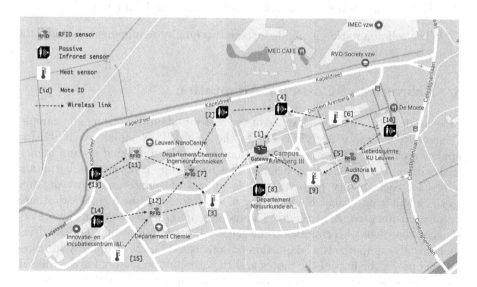

Fig. 3. DeltaIoT deployment at KU Leuven Campus [43].

[1] www.versasense.com.

Two key qualities of DeltaIoT are energy consumption and reliability. Since motes are battery powered and sending messages is dominates the energy cost, it is crucial for the system to optimize communication. Two factors determine the critical quality properties: the transmission power settings used by the motes for communication (ranging from 1 for min power to 15 for max power) and the distribution of the messages sent by each mote over the links to its parents (e.g., for motes with two parents: 0% to one parent and 100% to the other, 20/80, 40/60, 60/40, 80/20 and 100/0). DeltaIoT offers a user interface for operators to set both the power settings of the motes and the distribution of messages in the network. This interface shows the status of user defined properties.

The DeltaIoT network is subject to various uncertainties. We consider network interference (e.g. due to activities of neighboring computing systems, or due to changing whether conditions) and fluctuating load of messages (messages generated by motes may depend on various factors, such as the presence of people). These uncertainties make it hard to guarantee the required system qualities. To deal with these uncertainties, current practice typically applies a conservative approach, where the transmission power is set to maximum and all messages are forwarded to all parents. Operators may then tune some of these settings based on observations and experiences. This approach guarantees high reliability, but implies high energy consumption and thus reduced lifetime of the network.

For the evaluation with DeltaIoT, we define two concrete quality requirements that need to be realized regardless of possible network interference and fluctuating load of messages generated in the network:

R1: The average packet loss over 15 h should not exceed 10%.
R2: The average energy consumption over 15 h should be minimized.

When self-adaptation is applied, these two quality requirements become the adaptation goals.

3   Relevance of Costs for Adaptation

First we demonstrate the relevance of the cost for adaptation using an example. Concretely, we apply ActivFORMS to the DeltaIoT exemplar. ActivFORMS applies architecture-based self-adaptation, where the managing system is realized with a MAPE-K feedback loop. The Knowledge compromises a runtime model for each quality property that is subject of adaptation (corresponding to the adaptation goals). Each quality model is specified as a stochastic timed automaton (or network of these). The monitor updates variables in these models that represent uncertainties using data collected at runtime. The Analyzer dynamically computes the adaptation options based on the variability in transmission power settings of the motes and the distribution factors for the links in the network (see Sect. 2.4). For each adaptation option, the Analyzer estimates the expected qualities by running a number of simulations on the quality models. The results for the qualities of the adaptation options are used as selection criteria in the Planner. In particular, the Planner selects the best option by applying rules that express the system quality requirements for DeltaIoT. For the best option a plan is composed. This plan defines the adaptation actions per mote (change power setting and/or distributed factor) that are required to adapt the current configuration to the configuration of the selected best adaptation option. The Executor then executes the actions of the plan.

When applied to DeltaIoT, the approach described above only considers the benefits of adaptation (i.e. the contribution of adaptation to the adaptation goals). To determine the importance of the cost for realizing adaptations, we start with defining this cost. In DeltaIoT, there is an upstream communication of messages with data from the motes to the gateway. The benefits are defined for this upstream communication. The adaptation actions are sent downstream, from the gateway to the motes. We define the cost as the energy that is consumed for sending and receiving the adaptation message downstream. Default, ActivFORMS does not take this cost into account when selecting adaptation options. We study the impact of the cost based on two definitions [43]:

$$CostV_1 = \sum_x pLenA(x) * R + (pLenA(x) - 1) * S \qquad (2)$$

$$CostV_2 = \sum_y pLenL(y) * R + (pLenL(y) - 1) * S \qquad (3)$$

With x referring to a distinct adaptation action (e.g. change the power setting of mote m_7 along the link to m_2 to 6), while y refers to all the adaptation actions of a link (e.g. change the power of mote m_7 along the link to mote m_2 to a setting of 6, and change the distribution factor of this link to 40%). R and S refer to the energy consumption of receiving or sending a message respectively. $pLenA()$ and $pLenL()$ return the length of the path from the gateway to the source mote of the link that is subject of adaptation. Since the gateway is directly connected to the electricity net, the cost of downstream communication of the first link is not relevant; this explains the minus symbol in both definitions. It is important to note that this is not the case for receiving, since the gateway only sends and does not receive any messages in the downstream. In the first version of the cost, the information for each adaptation is (naively) sent as a separate message; in the second definition, adaptations per link are sent in one message.

To determine the impact of the cost for adaptation, we compute the total energy cost as follows:

$$TotEnergyConsV_i = EnergyCons + CostV_i \qquad (4)$$

where i can be either 1 or 2 referring to one of the cost functions. $EnergyCons$ refers to the energy consumption for downstream messages, while $CostV_i$ refers to the energy required for transmitting the adaptation actions upstream. Hence, the total energy consumption is defined as the sum of both.

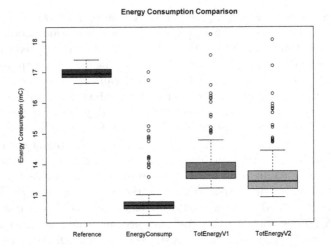

Fig. 4. Impact of cost for ActivFORMS on DeltaIoT [43].

To determine the impact of the cost for adaptation, we test the following hypothesis:

H_T : *The total energy cost for communication, including up- and downstream, is higher than the cost to transmit the message with data to the gateway.*

We used a setup with 15 motes (Fig. 4) with 256 adaptation options. The network was initialized using the reference configuration (max. power settings and duplicate messages sent to all parents), referred as the *Reference* approach. We performed four runs of 96 cycles on the simulator. Figure 4 shows the results.

When comparing the energy consumption using plain ActivFORMS (*EnergyCons*) with the approaches that take into account the cost for adaptation ($TotEnergyConsV_i$), we observed a statistically significance difference (p-values smaller than $2.2 * 10^{-16}$ using Wilcox rangsum test). For the first definition of cost the average reduction of energy consumption is 5.60% (mean 14.07 compared to 12.98 for plain ActivFORMS), while for the second definition the average reduction of energy consumption is 7.75% (mean 13.75). In practice, the increase of the lifetime of the network may be smaller as not all motes consume the same amount of energy over time, but of course this applies to all evaluated approaches. Since the total cost for V_2 is lower than for V_1, we use the V_2 definition for the evaluation in Sect. 5.

To conclude, we can accept hypothesis H_T. For ActivFORMS, a state-of-the-art adaptation approach, applied to the DeltaIoT exemplar, realizing adaptation has a significant cost and cannot be ignored.

4 Cost Benefit Analysis at Runtime

We now present CB@R (Cost-Benefit analysis @ Runtime) that enables effective decision-making in self-adaptive systems by explicitly considering benefits and costs. The approach is inspired by CBAM. However, in contrast to CBAM, CB@R is an automated approach that makes (architectural) reconfiguration decisions of the system at runtime to deal with uncertainties. Hence, CB@R can be considered as a runtime extension of CBAM, where reconfiguration of the system is necessary during operation to guarantee the best Value For Cost (VFC). Figure 5 shows how CB@R is integrated in a MAPE feedback loop.

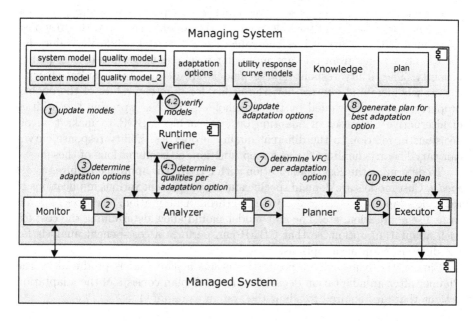

Fig. 5. MAPE feedback loop with runtime decision-making using CB@R [43].

4.1 Knowledge Runtime Models

Central to the realisation of CB@R are a set of runtime models maintained in the Knowledge repository of the MAPE feedback loop. The models include a *system model* that provides an abstraction of the managed system relevant to realize the adaptation goals, and a *context model* that provides an abstraction of the relevant parts of the environment in which the system operates.

Next, the Knowledge repository contains a *quality model* for each quality property that is subject to adaptation. These quality models (possibly combined with a system model and/or a context model) allow a runtime verifier to estimate the quality properties for a particular configuration of the managed system (i.e., an adaptation option as explained next).

To make an adaptation decision, CB@R requires a set of *adaptation options*. Each adaptation option defines a particular configuration of the system that can be reached through adaptation from the current configuration. The set of adaptation options defines all such possible configurations of the managed system. For now, we assume that the managed system has a limited number of adaptation options. This set may dynamically change over time. This implies that system parameters with a continuous domain that determine configurations need to be discretized. In Sect. 6 we present a learning approach that allows reducing a large adaptation space to a subset of relevant adaptation options.

To determine the benefits of adaptation with CB@R, a set of runtime *utility response curve models* are required, one for each quality property that is subject of adaptation. A utility response curve model [2] for a particular quality expresses the utility for the range of possible values of that quality property. In a response curve model, the utility values can range from 0 to 100, while the values for the qualities range from relevant minimum to maximum values of the quality property. The utility response curve models are defined in consultation with the stakeholders and express how the utility for different values of the quality property changes as valued by the stakeholders. Hence, capturing the utilities of alternative responses of adaption options enables CB@R to make tradeoff decisions in relation to the different quality properties. Utility response curves can vary linearly, nonlinearly, as a step function, or combinations of these.

To determine the cost of adaptation with CB@R, the approach requires a *cost model*. Cost models are domain specific and may represent various implications of realising adaptation, such as delay caused through adaptation, resources required to realise adaptation, etc. The cost model should allow determining the cost for each adaptation option, so that CB@R can perform a cost-benefit analysis for the different adaptation options.

Finally, the Knowledge repository contains a *plan* that is produced by the Planner after an adaptation decision is made. A plan consists of the adaptation actions that are required to adapt the system as required.

4.2   Realisation of CB@R

The MAPE elements exploit the runtime models to realise CB@R as follows. The *Monitor* tracks quality properties and uncertainty parameters of the managed system and the environment. The collected data is used to update the system model, the context model, and the different quality models ① When the *Analyzer* is triggered ② it determines the adaptation options ③, i.e., all relevant configurations of the managed system that can be reached through adaptation from the current configuration. For each adaptation option, the Analyzer determines the expected qualities that are relevant for adaptation using the *Runtime Verifier* ④.① To that end, the verifier uses the runtime models of the different qualities, possibly combined with the system and context models, and computes estimates for the different qualities of each adaptation option ④.②. The verification results, i.e., the expected values of the quality properties associated with the different adaption options, are then updated in the Knowledge repository ⑤.

Next ⑥, the *Planner* determines the Value For Cost (VFC) for each adaptation option ⑦. To calculate the total benefit of an adaptation option the Planner first computes the utility for each quality. To that end, the Planner uses the estimates for each quality as determined by the Analyzer. The Planner determines the utility for each estimated quality property using the utility response curves model for the quality. This is repeated for each quality that is subject to adaptation. As different quality attributes will have different importance to the stakeholders, each quality is assigned a weight (the weights express the relative importance of a qualities, so the sum of the weights should be equal to one). The Planner determines the expected overall benefit B_i for each adaptation option i by summing the utility associated with each quality weighted by the importance of that quality attribute as follows:

$$B_i = \sum_j (U_j(x_{(i,j)}) - U_j(c_j)) * W_j \tag{5}$$

Where the Planner takes the sum over each quality j, with $x_{i,j}$ the value for the jth quality of the ith adaptation option and $U_j(x_{(i,j)})$ the expected utility for this quality (determined by the utility response curve model). c_j is the value for the jth quality in the current configuration and $U_j(c_j)$ the corresponding utility. W_j is the weight for the quality. To determine the expected benefit for an adaptation option, the Planner takes the sum of the difference between the expected utility and the current utility for each quality taking into account the respective weights.

Next, the Planner uses the domain-specific cost model to determine the expected cost for each adaptation option. With the estimates for the benefits and the costs for each adaptation option, the Planner can finally calculate the VFC. As introduced in Sect. 2, for each adaptation option, VFC is defined as the ratio benefit B_i, to cost C_i:

$$VFC_i = \frac{B_i}{C_i} \tag{6}$$

The values for VFC are then used to rank the adaptation options under consideration. CB@R selects the adaptation option with the highest VFC value. For this option, the Planner generates a plan ⑧ and updates the Knowledge repository. Finally, when the *Executor* is triggered ⑨, it starts executing the plan produced by the Planner, adapting the managed system according to the selected adaptation option ⑩.

Example – We illustrate the principles of CB@R by applying them to the DeltaIoT exemplar. The two adaptation goals in DeltaIoT correspond with the two requirements: energy consumption and packet loss. Figure 6 shows the runtime model that the Analyzer uses to estimate energy consumption.

The verifier uses this model to estimate the energy consumption for the different adaptation options. In DeltaIoT the adaptation options are determined by the power settings used by the motes to communicate messages and the distribution of messages sent to parent motes (see Sect. 2.3). Hence, the parameters of

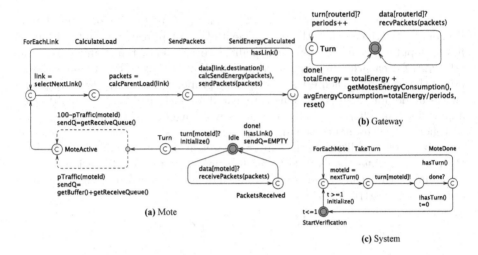

Fig. 6. Runtime model to estimate consumed energy by adaptation options [43].

the models are configured for each adaptation option accordingly. Furthermore, the values of the parameters that represent uncertainties tracked by the Monitor are set; e.g., the values of *pTraffic(moteID)* represents the traffic that a mote with a given *id* is expected to generate. Once the settings for an adaptation option are set, the estimated energy consumption is determined. To that end, the System automaton activates the motes one by one *moteId = nextTurn()*. Each Mote can then send messages to its parents in the time slots dedicated to it (*sendPackets(packets)*). The energy required to send the messages is then computed (*calcSendEnergy(packets)*). When the Gateway gets its turn, it computes the total energy consumed by the motes both to send and receive messages. This process is repeated for 30 times to compute and estimated average energy consumption with a required confidence. For each simulation run the verifier assigns uncertainty values for pTraffic(moteId) per mote.

The adaptation goals are defined with two utility-response curve models, one for each quality of interest as shown in Figs. 7 and 8. The utility response curve model for energy consumption was defined in consultation with engineers of VersaSense based on the results of the self-adaptive solution presented in the previous section. From the simulation runs on DeltaIoT we know that the mean value of the energy consumption is around 13 mC. This explains the first vertical drop on the graph. Values between 13 mC and 12 mC are progressively considered better, while any value below 12 mC is consider excellent. Values between 13 mC and 15 mC are acceptable, but poor. Any value above 15 mC is considered inferior. The utility response curve model for the packet loss was defined similarly. The utility slowly decreases between 0% and 5% packet loss. From 5% onwards, the utility decreases faster and values above 10% are considered inferior.

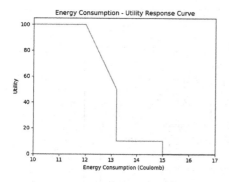

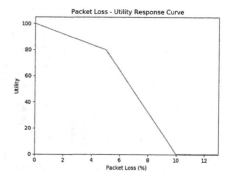

Fig. 7. Utility response curve for energy consumption [43].

Fig. 8. Utility response curve model for packet loss [43].

The cost model in DeltaIoT is determined by the energy that is required to send the adaptation messages from the gateway to the respective motes. We explained this in detail in Section 3.

To illustrate the computation of the VFC, consider that we have two adaptation options, one with 2% as estimated value for the packet loss and one with 9%, both satisfying the first quality requirement of DeltaIoT. Let us assume that the estimated energy consumption for both options are about the same. In CB@R, the expected utility induced by the 2% packet loss (around 90% see Fig. 8) will have a substantial influence on the total benefit of the adaptation option being considered (for packet loss 9% the expected utility will be around 10%). In case the adaptation costs for both options are similar, this will lead to a higher VFC value for the option with 2% packet loss, and consequently this configuration will be higher ranked than the 9% option. However, in case the cost for adaptation of the 2% option would be substantially higher, this option may not be selected. Compared to rule-based approaches this offers significant flexibility for decision-making.

Prototype Realization – Figure 9 shows the architecture of the self-adaptive DeltaIoT system realization. The *Managed System* that consists of the network of motes and the gateway is connected to a *Client* that provides an interface to the system. The client offers an interface to the IoT system to monitor various parameters and perform adaptations.

The *Managing System* is deployed on top of the client. For the realisation of CB@R we have used networks of timed automata (TA) for the specification of MAPE feedback loop. We used a set of model templates for the specification and the verification of the correctness of the MAPE feedback loop models [25]. We applied the approach presented in [23] that allows deploying and directly executing these models to realise self-adaptation at runtime using a virtual machine,

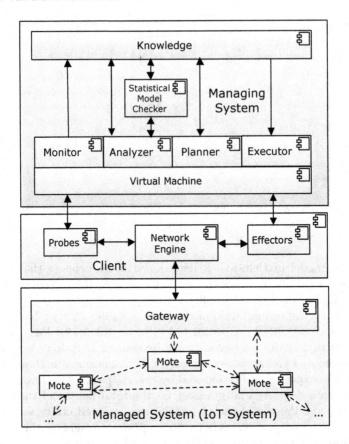

Fig. 9. CB@R applied to DeltaIoT [43].

as shown in Fig. 9. The Analyser in the DeltaIoT realisation uses a *Statistical Model Checker* as verifier to make estimates for the different qualities of the adaption options. Figure 10 shows the planner model used in the realisation. The planner waits in the Waiting state to be triggered by the analyser (*plan?*). It then selects the best adaptation option (*selectBestAdaptationOption()*). The pseudo code of this function, which is at the heart of the CB@R method, is shown in Algorithm 1. If a valid adaptation option is found a plan is created (per link of the DeltaIoT network a set of *ChangePower* and *ChangeDistribution* actions are composed). If no valid option is found a failsafe strategy is applied. When the plan is ready, the executer model is triggered to execute the plan (*execute!*). The complete evaluation packages with all models is available online.[2]

---

[2] https://people.cs.kuleuven.be/danny.weyns/software/ActivFORMS/.

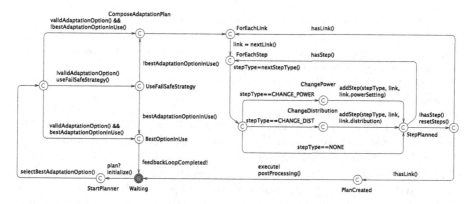

Fig. 10. Planner model for CB@R used in prototype realization [43].

Algorithm 1. Selection procedure of CB@R used in the planner model [43].

1: **procedure** SELECTBESTADAPTATIONOPTION
2:     $bestAdaptationOption \leftarrow EMPTY$
3:     $bestVFC \leftarrow -MAXVALUE$
4:     **for each** $x \in Knowledge.AdaptationOptions$ **do**
5:         $benefit \leftarrow calculateBenefit(x)$ ▷ Knowledge
6:         $cost \leftarrow calculateCost(x) + 1$ ▷ Knowledge
7:         $VFC \leftarrow benefit/cost$
8:         **if** $VFC > bestVFC$ **then**
9:             $bestVFC \leftarrow VFC$
10:            $bestAdaptationOption \leftarrow x$
11:        **end if**
12:    **end for**
13: **end procedure**

---

5   Evaluation of CB@R

For the evaluation of CB@R we used the physical setup of the DeltaIoT network deployed at the KU Leuven Campus, which is remotely accessible for use [24]. We used a standard setting with 15 motes as shown in Fig. 3 with communication cycles of 9.5 min. We compared three approaches: a conservative approach applied by VersaSense in similar domains (i.e., the reference approach), a rule based approach (that takes into account cost for adaptation similar to what we discussed in Sect. 3), and CB@R (we applied equal weights for the quality properties). Each approach ran for 15 h on the physical network, i.e., 90 communication cycles. In each cycle, the network can be adapted. As mentioned in the previous section, the two quality requirements are used as adaptation goals: (1) keep the average packet loss under 10% and (2) minimize the average energy consumption, both over 15 h. We test the following hypothesis:

H_1 *Both adaptation approaches outperform the reference approach for the energy consumption requirement;*

H_{21} *The rule-based approach achieves the packet loss requirement;*
H_{22} *CB@R achieves the packet loss requirement;*
H_{31} *CB@R has significantly better results than a rule-based approach for the average energy consumption;*
H_{32} *CB@R has significantly better results than a rule-based approach for average packet loss.*

First, we look at energy consumption. Figure 11 shows the test results. The mean value for average energy consumption of the reference approach is 17.07 mC; for the rule-based approach it is 13.10 mC and for CB@R 12.98 mC. Clearly, both adaptation approaches outperform the reference approach (p-value $2.2e^{-16}$ Wilcox rangsum test). Hence, we can accept hypothesis H_1.

The mean values for energy consumption of the rule based approach and CB@R are similar. The difference of the data distribution in favour of CB@R (p-value 0.044 with Wilcox rangsum test) is from a practical point of view not relevant (the relative gain in energy consumption of rule-based is versus CB@R is 0.8%). Hence, we have to reject hypothesis H_{31}.

Figure 12 shows the results for packet loss. The mean value for the average packet loss for the reference approach is 5.39%. The mean value for the rule-based approach is 15.32% and for CB@R it is 9.96%. Given that the average packet loss should be below 10%, we have to reject hypothesis H_{21} (the rule-based approach achieves the packet loss requirement) and we can accept hypothesis H_{22}. With a significant difference between the results for both approaches (p-value $6.258e^{-6}$ with Wilcox rangsum test), we can also accept hypothesis H_{32} (packet loss for CB@R is significantly better as for the rule-based approach).

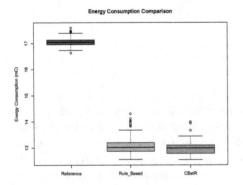 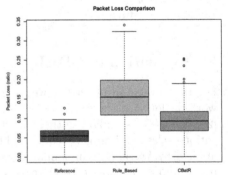

Fig. 11. Results: energy consumption [43].

Fig. 12. Results: packet loss [43].

Discussion. For energy consumption, both self-adaptive approaches are significantly better as the reference approach. On the other hand, the rule-based approach is not able to realise the packet-loss requirement, while CB@R achieves the requirement although only with a small surplus. These results show that substantial benefits can be gained by applying CB@R compared to the conservative approach. Note that differentiations to the weights for the quality properties and adjustments to the quality response curve models may help to further enhance CB@R and help improving the results for packet loss, possibly at a small extra cost of energy consumption.

Feedback from the VersaSense staff confirmed that the problem of finding and maintaining an optimal configuration of low-power wireless networks for a given problem domain is notoriously difficult and that a self-adaptive solution that automates the management of the network is a major benefit. On the other hand, the staff highlights the potential risks of automation in terms of ensuring stability during the adaptation process as well as handling outliers events. The staff also noticed the need for domain-specific models, including for different quality properties, that may not be easy to design. However, the staff acknowledges that building up experience over time can mitigate such risks.

6   Reduction of Adaptation Space

We now look into the adaptation space of self-adaptive systems, i.e. the set of adaption options to select from. For systems with a large number of adaptation options, which is typically the case for practical systems, analyzing the entire adaptation space is often not feasible given the time and resources constraints at hand. To tackle this problem, we present a machine learning approach that integrates with the MAPE-K work-flow, following the principles of architecture-based self-adaptation. Figure 13 shows the architecture of the approach concretely applied to ActivFORMS.

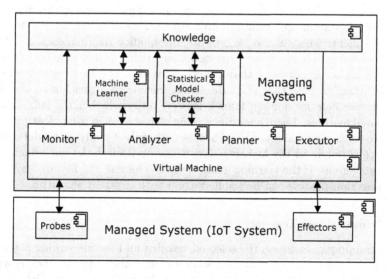

Fig. 13. Architecture with the learning approach applied to ActivFORMS.

The analyzer now connects with a machine learner and a model checker. The machine learner predicts the values of the relevant qualities for each adaptation option. These predicted values are used by the analyzer to select the adaptation options that are relevant under the current uncertainties. This subset of adaptation options are then further verified by the model checker. The analysis results of the selected adaptation options are used to determine whether and how the system should be adapted. Finally, the analyzer feeds the verification results of the relevant adaptation options to the machine learner. This enables the machine learner to adapt accordingly and make more accurate predictions in the future. Figure 13 shows a concrete instance of the learning approach for ActivFORMS. However, the approach is not limited to a particular type of adaptation approach. We now elaborate on the different stages of the learning approach.

6.1   Preprocessing

Preprocessing is a general phase in machine learning. It plays an important role in reducing redundancy in the data, increasing the accuracy of the learning algorithms, and decreasing the training time of the learning algorithms [20,37] This phase requires raw data from the self-adaptive system. Recall that in machine learning the quality of the data is very important. Therefore, we collect the raw data that contains examples of the adaptation decisions made by the MAPE elements of the self-adaptive system. An adaptation decision contains two key values: the current uncertainties of the managed system and its environment, and the value of the quality requirement with each adaptation option.

Once the raw data is collected, we can apply the preprocessing steps on it. First, the data preprocessing step removes redundant and unwanted values from the data, considering features and targets. The feature values in our case consist of adaptation options and uncertain values of the managed system and its environment, whereas the targets are the quality requirements of interest. Second, we iteratively use a feature selection algorithm to find a subset of features that have higher importance than others. This step is called feature selection. It is important to note that the subset may vary from algorithm to algorithm. Therefore, we can use domain knowledge tho verify whether the subset has all the required features. Then, a feature scaling step is applied where feature scaling is used to rescale the values of the features uniformly. Finally, in model selection we iterate through all the learning algorithms and select the one which fulfills the learning goals. If the learning goals are not achieved, the feature scaling and model selection process can be applied again with different algorithms.

6.2   Training and Testing

During training and testing, the selected learning and feature scaling algorithms are added to the MAPE-K feedback loop. In the training phase, the algorithms are trained, in the testing phase the learning algorithms make predictions.

During the initial training phase, we train the learning algorithm on a specific number of adaptation cycles that result from the model selection process. In

Fig. 13 the flow of the Monitor, Planner and Executor components is the same as in ActivFORMS, see Sect. 4. The Analyzer reads the adaptation options and the current uncertain values of the managed system and its environment. Then it sends this data to the Statistical Model Checker. The Model Checker reads a corresponding quality model and simulate it with each adaptation option for estimating the values of the quality requirements. Then it sends the estimated values back to the Analyzer. First, the Analyzer updates the placeholders of the adaptation options with the corresponding estimated values. Next, the Analyzer sends the verified adaptation options and current uncertain values to the Machine Learner in the form of a training dataset. The Machine Learner uses the feature scaling algorithm to rescale the features values in the training dataset and then train the learning algorithm on that dataset. Then, the Analyzer determines whether the current configuration is able to realize the adaptation goals. If this is not the case, the Analyzer triggers the Planner to realize adaptation.

During the testing phase, again the Analyzer reads the adaptation options and current uncertain values of the managed system and its environment. Then, it sends this data to the Machine Learner in the form of a testing dataset. The Machine Learner uses the feature scaling algorithm to rescale the features values in the testing dataset. Subsequently, it uses the learning algorithm to predict the values of the quality requirement(s) for each adaptation option. Then, it sends the predicted values back to the Analyzer. First, the analyzer uses the predicted values to select the relevant adaptation options which fulfill the quality requirement(s). Note that if there are no such adaption options, the Analyzer selects all available adaptation options. Next, it sends the selected adaptation options and the current uncertain values to the Model Checker. The Model Checker reads a corresponding quality model and simulate it with each selected adaptation option for estimating the values of the quality requirements. Then it sends the estimated values back to the Analyzer. First, the Analyzer updates the placeholders of the selected adaptation options with the corresponding estimated values. Here, the testing phase is interwoven with the training phase. Afterwards, the Analyzer sends the verified adaptation options and the current uncertain values to the Machine Learner in the form of a training dataset. The Machine Learner uses the feature scaling algorithm to rescale the features values in the training dataset and train the learning algorithm on that dataset. Then, as in the training phase the Analyzer determines whether the current configuration is able to accomplish the adaptation goals. If the current configuration is not able to realize the adaptation goals, the Analyzer triggers the Planner.

6.3   Applying the Learning Approach to DeltaIoT

In the preprocessing phase, all unwanted values from the raw data are removed and the data needs to be converted into sets that work with classification and regression. The datasets in our case contain the same features, i.e., SNR, packets distribution, and traffic load. For regression, the targets are real values of packet loss. In contrast, the classification has class 0 when packet loss is $\geq 10\%$ and class

1 when it is <10%. Each item in the datasets represents an adaptation option and has 48 features (17 SNR, 17 packet distribution, and 14 traffic load).

Both datasets used in preprocessing have a high number of features [7]. We used a tree-based feature selection algorithm to select the most useful features [20]. This algorithm selects the same subset for both approaches, but their importance score is different. We applied domain knowledge to verify both subsets.

The features that we selected have different value ranges, e.g. $SNR = -40...+20$, distribution $= 0...100$, and traffic $= 1..10$. To balance the features, these large differences required feature scaling. We used min-max, max-abs, and standardization feature scaling algorithms to rescale the features values [20,37]. In order to find the most suitable feature scaling algorithm, the feature scaling process is combined with the model selection process. We selected three learning algorithms: Stochastic Gradient Descent (SGD) [20], Perceptron [21], and Passive-Aggressive (PA) [13] for model selection. We defined two learning goals:

LG1: The error rate should be less than 5%.
LG2: The number of training cycles required to achieve this error rate should be minimized.

For the selection procedure, the datasets with rescaled features are divided into five different training and testing sizes, e.g. 15 cycles training and 65 cycles testing, 30/45, 45/30, 60/15, and 70/10. Each learning model is trained and tested for 20 times on each of the sizes in order to achieve reliable results.

For classification, Fig. 14 shows that SGD fulfilled the learning goals with the min-max and max-abs feature scaling algorithms. However, only one needs to be selected. Therefore, we selected SGD with min-max because the initial testing error rate of SGD was lower compared to max-abs. The figure also indicates that SGD requires at least 30 adaptation cycles to achieve the first adaption goal. Hence, we initially trained SGD on 30 cycles during the training phase.

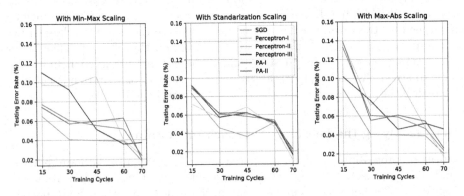

Fig. 14. Performance of the learning algorithms for classification approach.

Figure 15 shows that for regression SGD fulfilled the learning goals with the max-abs feature scaling algorithm. Just as for the classification approach, the first learning goal is achieved by applying 30 adaption cycles. Therefore, we initially trained SGD on 30 cycles during the training phase.

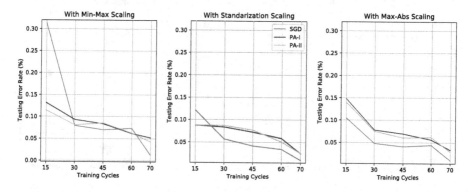

Fig. 15. Performance of the learning algorithms for regression approach.

The selected learning and feature scaling algorithms are placed in the MAPE-K feedback loop. SGD classifier and min-max are applied for classification, and SGD regressor and max-abs for regression. During the initial training phase, the learning algorithms are trained on 30 adaptation cycles. Packet loss and energy consumption models are the quality models. The rest of the knowledge repository contains similar models as mentioned in Sect. 4.1.

6.4   Evaluation

We evaluated the learning approach with two experiments. In the first experiment, we compared the adaptation results of plain ActivFORMS, ActivFORMS with classification, and ActivFORMS with regression. In the second experiment we compared the adaptation options selected by the different approaches. The experiments are conducted on the simulator provided by DeltaIoT.

Evaluation of Adaptation Results. In the first experiment, we independently ran ActivFORMS, classification, and regression. With each approach, we ran the simulator for 300 adaptation cycles. With classification and regression, we initially trained the learning algorithms for the first 30 adaptation cycles. Figure 16 shows the results for these approaches from 31–300 adaptation cycles.

All approaches achieved the quality requirements, i.e. packet loss <10%, while minimizing energy consumption. However, ActivFORMS constantly explored all the available adaptation options (216 here) to accomplish the adaptation goals. Classification only explored 40 adaptation options on average, reducing the adaptation space by on average 81.2% compared to ActivFORMS. Regression

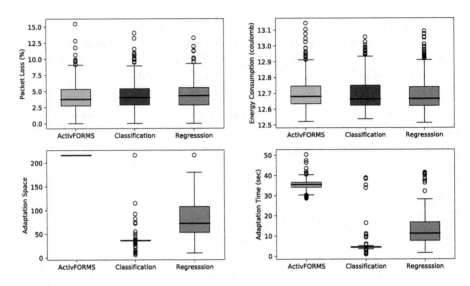

Fig. 16. Comparison of ActivFORMS, classification and regression approaches.

explored 90 adaptation options on average, reducing the adaptation space by on average 58.3% compared to ActivFORMS. The reduced adaptation space also helped classification and regression to decrease the adaptation time to on average 5.2 and 12.7 s respectively compared to ActivFORMS with 34.8 s. Note that the adaptation time with classification and regression includes the training and prediction time of the learning algorithms at each adaptation cycle. The average initial training time is 0.02 and 0.03 s for classification and regression respectively. Similarly, the average prediction time with classification is 0.006 s, whereas with regression it is 0.007 s. The average training time after making the prediction is 0.008 and 0.010 s with classification and regression respectively. These results show that by combining classification or regression with a model checker we can reduce the adaptation space in self-adaptive systems, while still achieving the same quality requirements as a state-of-the-art approach. Notably, the learning algorithms used in classification and regression are significantly fast in the training and testing phases. This shows that learning for the given setting produces almost no overhead on the adaptation time.

Evaluation of Selected Adaptation Options. During the second experiment, DeltaIoT was effectively managed by ActivFORMS. In each adaptation cycle, ActivFORMS first analyzed the complete adaptation space. Then it compared its relevant adaptation options (i.e., the adaptation options that comply with the packet loss requirement) with the adaptation options selected by classification and regression. Again, we trained the learning algorithms during the first 30 adaptation cycles before starting the testing.

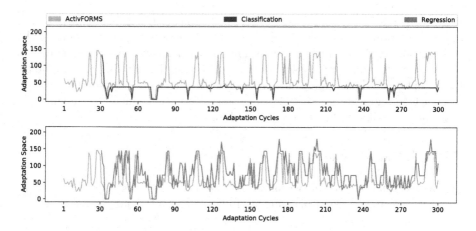

Fig. 17. Overview of selected adaptation options.

Figure 17 shows the results. It is clear that classification selected mostly a lower number of adaptation options than ActivFORMS throughout all the adaptation cycles. In contrast, regression selected mostly a slightly higher number of adaptation options. Note that there is also distinctly less variance in the number of selected adaptation options for classification compared to regression. This indicates that regression may be more adaptive than classification in terms of selecting relevant adaptation options under changing conditions. Figure 18 shows a more detailed view on the selected adaptation options for a particular cycle. The red line separates the relevant adaptation options (on the left) from the irrelevant options (on the right). We can see that ActivFORMS analyzed all

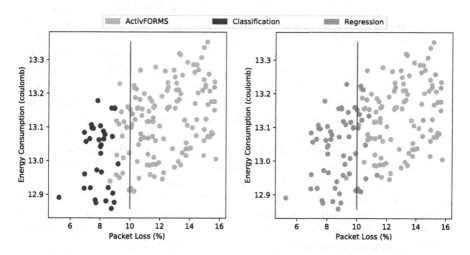

Fig. 18. Selected adaptation options: ActivFORMS, classification, regression.

the available adaptation options. Whereas, classification selected a subset of the relevant adaptation options. On the other hand, regression selected most of the relevant adaptation options as well as a number of irrelevant options in addition.

We can conclude that classification is superior in determining relevant adaptation options, while regression is more adaptive than classification. Still, this did not help regression to beat classification in terms of reducing the adaptation space and the time to make adaptation decisions.

7   Related Work

We discuss related work in two parts: first we focus on work related to CB@R, then we look at the use of machine learning to reduce the adaptation space.

Related Work on CB@R. Until recently, most research on self-adaptation has largely ignored the implications of adaptation as documented by surveys, see for example [45]. We start with providing brief descriptions of approaches related to CB@R. Then we position CB@R in the landscape of existing work.

Bertolli et al. define a cost model for quantifying the overhead introduced by autonomic behavior in an adaptive parallel application [4]. Different component versions are dynamically selected based on an adaptation strategy to achieve the required quality levels. The adaptation cost model is used to estimate the overhead for reconfiguring a component when switching between different versions.

Camara et al. propose a latency-aware adaptation approach focusing on the time between the adaptation is applied and the time when the effects of the adaptation are observed [11]. At design time, the approach uses model checking of Stochastic Multiplayer Games models to quantify the maximum improvement a latency-aware strategy is able to obtain. At runtime, a latency-aware adaptation algorithm is applied that uses simulation to support the adaptation decisions.

Cailliau and van Lamsweerde apply tradeoff analysis in an obstacle-driven runtime adaptation approach to increase the satisfaction rate of probabilistic system goals [8]. The approach uses obstacle/goal refinement trees. Leaf obstacles are monitored at runtime to determine the satisfaction rate of high-level goals. When the satisfaction rate is below a threshold, a tradeoff analysis guides the selection of alternatives to maximize satisfaction rates under cost constraints.

Poladian et al. propose so called anticipatory configuration to predict future resource availability to improve the utility of concurrent adaptive applications [38]. The results demonstrate that anticipatory configuration provides better utility to users compared to reactive re-configuration when there is a cost (e.g., reconfiguration cost) associated to certain adaptation operations.

There are a number of related approaches that use elastic controllers in cloud-based applications to adjust the allocation of resources with awareness of the cost of adaptation. Jamshidi et al. use an elastic controller to handle unpredictable workloads in cloud applications [26]. The elastic controller, based on fuzzy logic to specify elasticity rules, aims at reducing the cost of ownership of the service level agreements, while auto-scaling the dynamic resources. Gambi et al.

propose a framework that explicitly takes into account the time each control action takes to complete, called actuation delay [16]. The proposed framework estimates actuation delay using change point detection algorithms. Fokaefs et al. use a business ecosystem of cloud computing as an economy of scale [15]. The goal is to take into the account cost of infrastructure with revenue from service delivery and the profit of the service provider. Jung et al. present the Mistral framework that uses a utility-based model to predict power consumption, cost of adaptation, and workload to maximize overall utility in cloud applications [29].

In summary, a variety of approaches have been devised to deal with the implications and costs of self-adaptation. Contrary to existing approaches that do not clearly distinguish between costs and benefits, CB@R treats cost and benefits as first-class citizens in the decision-making of adaptation. Furthermore, most of the existing approaches focus on specific types of cost for self-adaptation, ranging from overhead, latency, required resources, time for adaptation, and cost of infrastructure. CB@R does not focus on any particular type of cost, but provides a reusable framework that considers the cost for adaptation as a first-class concern that can be instantiated for the domain and problem at hand.

Related Work on Machine Learning to Reduce Adaptation Spaces. To the best of our knowledge there is no previous work which combines machine learning with model checking to reduce the adaptation space to achieve the adaptation goals of self-adaptive systems more effectively. Hence, our work is exploratory. However, some studies use machine learning to support decision making in self-adaptive systems. These studies are only partially relevant here, but they give an insight into how machine learning has been applied in self-adaptation.

Most of the approaches that applied machine learning used a configurable system which consists of many features or configuration options. Each configuration option can affect the system's functional and non-functional requirements. The performance of these systems depends on parameter values of these features [40]. Machine learning is then used to find the optimal configuration based on learning and sampling. For example, [27] proposes BO4CO that uses Bayesian learning to find the optimal configuration in stream processing systems. [50] uses Fourier learning to predict software performance predictions with guaranteed accuracy and confidence levels. [49] explores machine learning based performance models to auto-tune the configuration parameters of Hadoop MapReduce. [41] combines machine learning and sampling heuristics to derive a performance-influence model for a given configurable system which describes all relevant influences of configuration options and their interactions. The approach reduces the solution space to a tractable size by integrating binary and numeric configuration options and incorporating the domain knowledge. [6] applies reinforcement learning for autonomic configuration and reconfiguration of multi-tier web systems. The approach adapts the web system based on performance and workload by changing virtual machine configurations. The learning time for online decisions is reduced using an efficient initialization policy. [28] proposes a cost-aware transfer learning method that learns accurate performance models for configurable software from other resources such as simulators, etc. The approach uses a regression model which learns the relationship between source and target using only a few samples taken from the real system, leading to faster learning period.

8   Conclusions and Future Work

This research targeted effective decision making in self-adaptation from two perspectives: on the one hand the need to take into account cost as fist-class concern in selecting adaptation options, on the other hand the need for reducing the adaptation space to relevant adaption options to scale well.

As a first contribution, we presented CB@R, Cost-Benefit analysis at Runtime, a reusable approach for decision-making in self-adaptive systems that considers both the benefits of adaptation and the cost to realise the adaptation as first-class citizens. The approach takes inspiration from CBAM, an established approach to deal with the economics of benefits and costs in architectural design. CB@R defines the benefits of adaptation options as the weighted utility of the qualities that the options can provide to the stakeholders. The approach defines cost as a domain-specific property that needs to be defined for the problem at hand. We applied CB@R to a real world deployment of an IoT application. The results show that CB@R outperforms a conservative approach that is often used in practice. The results also show that contrary to a rule-based approach, CB@R achieves the adaptation goals under various types of uncertainties.

As a second contribution, we presented an online learning approach that allows reducing the size of an adaptation space significantly, resulting in lower adaptation time. The approach integrates machine learning with a model checker with the analysis of the MAPE-K work flow. This integration enables machine learning to select a subset of the adaptation options which can be further verified by the model checker. Evaluation of the approach to a real world IoT application show that the learning approach significantly reduces the adaptation space without jeopardizing the adaptation goals of the IoT system. This paves the way to applying formal techniques at runtime in self-adaptive systems for systems with large adaptation spaces.

In future work, we plan to study different topics related to the work presented in this chapter. Regarding CB@R, we plan to study the influence of varying the utility response curve models and the weights assigned to the qualities on the Value For Cost. We plan to look into methods that allow fine tuning the curves and weights automatically using learning algorithms combined with direct or indirect feedback from stakeholders. We plan to perform a systematical study of the types of costs that apply to self-adaptation to define methods supporting different types of such costs. Regarding learning techniques to reduced adaptation spaces, we plan to evaluate the proposed approach to systems with larger adaptation spaces. We also aim to test the approach for multiple adaptation goals, and investigate different machine learning techniques. Last but not least, we aim to investigate how we can put bounds on the guarantees when combining formal analysis techniques with machine learning to reduce the adaptation space.

References

1. Andersson, J., de Lemos, R., Malek, S., Weyns, D.: Modeling dimensions of self-adaptive software systems. In: Cheng, B.H.C., de Lemos, R., Giese, H., Inverardi, P., Magee, J. (eds.) Software Engineering for Self-Adaptive Systems. LNCS, vol. 5525, pp. 27–47. Springer, Heidelberg (2009). https://doi.org/10.1007/978-3-642-02161-9_2

2. Bass, L., Clements, P., Kazman, R.: Software Architecture in Practice. Addison-Wesley, Boston (2013)

3. Bennaceur, A., et al.: Feed me, feed me: an exemplar for engineering adaptive software. In: Software Engineering for Adaptive and Self-Managing Systems (2016)

4. Bertolli, C., Mencagli, G., Vanneschi, M.: A cost model for autonomic reconfigurations in high-performance pervasive applications. In: Workshop on Context-Awareness for Self-Managing Systems. ACM (2010)

5. Blair, G., Bencomo, N., France, R.B.: Models@ run. time. Comput. **42**(10), 22–29 (2009)

6. Bu, X., Rao, J., Xu, C.Z.: A reinforcement learning approach to online web systems auto-configuration. In: 2009 29th IEEE International Conference on Distributed Computing Systems. IEEE (2009)

7. Buttar, S.S.: Applying machine learning to reduce the adaptation space in self-adaptive systems: an exploratory work. Linnaeus University (2018)

8. Cailliau, A., van Lamsweerde, A.: Runtime monitoring and resolution of probabilistic obstacles to system goals. In: In 2017 IEEE/ACM 12th International Symposium on Software Engineering for Adaptive and Self-Managing Systems (2017)

9. Calinescu, R., Ghezzi, C., Kwiatkowska, M., Mirandola, R.: Self-adaptive software needs quantitative verification at runtime. Commun. ACM **55**(9), 69–77 (2012)

10. Calinescu, R., Grunske, L., Kwiatkowska, M., Mirandola, R., Tamburrelli, G.: Dynamic QoS management and optimization in service-based systems. IEEE Trans. Softw. Eng. **37**(3), 387–409 (2011)

11. Cámara, J., Moreno, G.A., Garlan, D., Schmerl, B.: Analyzing latency-awareself-adaptation using stochastic games and simulations. ACM Trans. Auton. Adapt. Syst. **10**(4), 23 (2016)

12. Cheng, B.H.C., et al.: Software engineering for self-adaptive systems: a research roadmap. In: Cheng, B.H.C., de Lemos, R., Giese, H., Inverardi, P., Magee, J. (eds.) Software Engineering for Self-Adaptive Systems. LNCS, vol. 5525, pp. 1–26. Springer, Heidelberg (2009). https://doi.org/10.1007/978-3-642-02161-9_1

13. Crammer, K., Dekel, O., Keshet, J., Shalev-Shwartz, S., Singer, Y.: Online passive-aggressive algorithms. J. Mac. Learn. Res. **7**, 551–585 (2006)

14. Dobson, S., et al.: A survey of autonomic communications. ACM Trans. Auton. Adapt. Syst. **1**(2), 223–259 (2006)

15. Fokaefs, M., Barna, C., Litoiu, M.: Economics-driven resource scalability on the cloud. In: Proceedings of the 11th International Symposium on Software Engineering for Adaptive and Self-Managing Systems. ACM (2016)

16. Gambi, A., Moldovan, D., Copil, G., Truong, H.L., Dustdar, S.: On estimating actuation delays in elastic computing systems. In: Proceedings of the 8th International Symposium Software Engineering for Adaptive and Self-Managing Systems. IEEE (2013)

17. Garlan, D., Cheng, S., Huang, A., Schmerl, B., Steenkiste, P.: Rainbow: architecture-based self-adaptation with reusable infrastructure. Comput. **37**(10), 46–54 (2004)

18. Gepperth, A., Hammer, B.: Incremental learning algorithms and applications. In: European Symposium on Artificial Neural Networks (2016)
19. Gerasimou, S., Calinescu, R., Shevtsov, S., Weyns, D.: UNDERSEA: an exemplar for engineering self-adaptive unmanned underwater vehicles. In: 2017 IEEE/ACM 12th International Symposium on Software Engineering for Adaptive and Self-Managing Systems. IEEE (2017)
20. Géron, A.: Hands-on Machine Learning with Scikit-Learn and TensorFlow: Concepts, Tools, and Techniques to Build Intelligent Systems. O'Reilly Media Inc., Sebastopol (2017)
21. Hackeling, G.: Mastering Machine Learning with Scikit-Learn. Packt Publishing Ltd., Birmingham (2017)
22. Iftikhar, M.U.: A Model-Based Approach to Engineer Self-Adaptive Systems with Guarantees. KU Leuven and Linnaeus University (2017)
23. Iftikhar, M.U., Weyns, D.: ActivFORMS: active formal models for self-adaptation. In: Proceedings of the 9th International Symposium on Software Engineering for Adaptive and Self-Managing Systems. ACM (2014)
24. Iftikhar, M.U., et al.: DeltaIoT: a self-adaptive internet of things exemplar. In: Proceedings of the 12th International Symposium on Software Engineering for Adaptive and Self-Managing Systems. IEEE (2017)
25. de la Iglesia, D.G., Weyns, D.: Mape-k formal templates to rigorously design behaviors for self-adaptive systems. ACM Trans. Auton. Adapt. Syst. 10(3), 15 (2015)
26. Jamshidi, P., Ahmad, A., Pahl, C.: Autonomic resource provisioning for the cloud. In: Proceedings of the 9th international symposium on Software Engineering for Adaptive and Self-Managing Systems. ACM (2014)
27. Jamshidi, P., Casale, G.: An uncertainty-aware approach to optimal configuration of stream processing systems. In: 2016 IEEE 24th International Symposium on Modeling, Analysis and Simulation of Computer and Telecommunication Systems. IEEE (2016)
28. Jamshidi, P., Velez, M., Kästner, C., Siegmund, N., Kawthekar, P.: Transfer learning for improving model predictions in highly configurable software. In: 2016 IEEE 24th International Symposium on Software Engineering for Adaptive and Self-Managing Systems. IEEE (2017)
29. Jung, G., Hiltunen, M.A., Joshi, K.R., Schlichting, R.D., Pu, C.: Mistral: dynamically managing power, performance, and adaptation cost in cloud infrastructures. In: 2010 IEEE 30th International Conference on Distributed Computing Systems. IEEE (2010)
30. Kephart, J., Chess, D.: The vision of autonomic computing. Comput. 36(1), 41–50 (2003)
31. Kramer, J., Magee, J.: Self-managed systems: an architectural challenge. In: Future of Software Engineering. IEEE (2007)
32. de Lemos, R., et al.: Software engineering for self-adaptive systems: research challenges in the provision of assurances. In: de Lemos, R., Garlan, D., Ghezzi, C., Giese, H. (eds.) Software Engineering for Self-Adaptive Systems III. Assurances. LNCS, vol. 9640, pp. 3–30. Springer, Cham (2017). https://doi.org/10.1007/978-3-319-74183-3_1
33. de Lemos, R., et al.: Software engineering for self-adaptive systems: a second research roadmap. In: de Lemos, R., Giese, H., Müller, H.A., Shaw, M. (eds.) Software Engineering for Self-Adaptive Systems II. LNCS, vol. 7475, pp. 1–32. Springer, Heidelberg (2013). https://doi.org/10.1007/978-3-642-35813-5_1
34. Louridas, P., Ebert, C.: Machine learning. IEEE Softw. 33(5), 110–115 (2016)

35. Mohri, M., Rostamizadeh, A., Talwalkar, A.: Foundations of Machine Learning. MIT Press, Cambridge (2012)
36. Oreizy, P., Medvidovic, N., Taylor, R.: Architecture-based runtime software evolution. In: Proceedings of the 20th International Conference on Software Engineering. IEEE (1998)
37. Pedregosa, F., et al.: Scikit-learn: machine learning in python. J. Mac. Learn. Res. **12**, 2825–2830 (2011)
38. Poladian, V., Garlan, D., Shaw, M., Satyanarayanan, M., Schmerl, B., Sousa, J.: Leveraging resource prediction for anticipatory dynamic configuration. In: International Conference on Self-Adaptive and Self-Organizing Systems. IEEE (2007)
39. Salehie, M., Tahvildari, L.: Self-adaptive software: landscape and research challenges. ACM Trans. Auton. Adapt. Syst. **4**(2), 14 (2009)
40. Sarkar, A., Guo, J., Siegmund, N., Apel, S., Czarnecki, K.: Cost-efficient sampling for performance prediction of configurable systems (t). In: 2015 30th IEEE/ACM International Conference on Automated Software Engineering. IEEE (2015)
41. Siegmund, N., Grebhahn, A., Apel, S., Kästner, C.: Performance-influence models for highly configurable systems. In: Proceedings of the 2015 10th Joint Meeting on Foundations of Software Engineering (2015)
42. Software Engineering Institute, C.M.U.: Cost Benefit Analysis Method (2018). https://www.sei.cmu.edu/architecture/tools/evaluate/cbam.cfm
43. Van Der Donckt, J., Weyns, D., Iftikhar, M.U., Singh, R.K.: Cost-benefit analysis at runtime for self-adaptive systems applied to an Internet of Things application. In: 13th International Conference on Evaluation of Novel Approaches to Software Engineering (2018)
44. Weyns, D.: Software engineering of self-adaptive systems: an organised tour and future challenges. In: Software Engineering Handbook. Springer, Heidelberg (2018)
45. Weyns, D., Ahmad, T.: Claims and evidence for architecture-based self-adaptation: a systematic literature review. In: Drira, K. (ed.) ECSA 2013. LNCS, vol. 7957, pp. 249–265. Springer, Heidelberg (2013). https://doi.org/10.1007/978-3-642-39031-9_2
46. Weyns, D., Iftikhar, M.U., Söderlund, J.: Do external feedback loops improve the design of self-adaptive systems? A controlled experiment. In: Proceedings of the 8th International Symposium on Software Engineering for Adaptive and Self-Managing Systems (2013)
47. Weyns, D., Malek, S., Andersson, J.: FORMS: unifying reference model for formal specification of distributed self-adaptive systems. ACM Trans. Auton. Adapt. Syst. **7**(1), 8 (2012)
48. Weyns, D., et al.: Perpetual assurances for self-adaptive systems. In: de Lemos, R., Garlan, D., Ghezzi, C., Giese, H. (eds.) Software Engineering for Self-Adaptive Systems III. Assurances. LNCS, vol. 9640, pp. 31–63. Springer, Cham (2017). https://doi.org/10.1007/978-3-319-74183-3_2
49. Yigitbasi, N., Willke, T.L., Liao, G., Epema, D.: Towards machine learning-based auto-tuning of mapreduce. In: 2013 IEEE 21st International Symposium on Modelling, Analysis and Simulation of Computer and Telecommunication Systems. IEEE (2013)
50. Zhang, Y., Guo, J., Blais, E., Czarnecki, K.: Performance prediction of configurable software systems by fourier learning (t). In: 2015 30th IEEE/ACM International Conference on Automated Software Engineering. IEEE (2015)

Author Index

Alsanoosy, Tawfeeq 240
Assy, Nour 137

Bennani, Saloua 288
Bogner, Justus 45
Borchert, Angela 71
Bouziane, Hinde Lilia 186
Buchmann, Thomas 98
Buttar, Sarpreet Singh 373

Coulette, Bernard 288

da Silva Filho, Heleno Cardoso 3
de Figueiredo Carneiro, Glauco 3
Dony, Christophe 186

Ebersold, Sophie 288
El Hamlaoui, Mahmoud 288

Frey, Georg 165

Gaedke, Martin 215
García, Alberto 314
Greer, Des 334

Harland, James 240
Heil, Sebastian 215
Heisel, Maritta 71
Hoch, Ralph 261

Iftikhar, M. Usman 373

Jugel, Dierk 45

Kaindl, Hermann 261
Khalgui, Mohamed 165
Kotecka, Dagmara 119

Lakhdhar, Wafa 165
Liu, Cong 137
Luckeneder, Christoph 261

Meis, Rene 71
Mohan, Michael 334
Möhring, Michael 45
Mzid, Rania 165

Nassar, Mahmoud 288
Nazaruka, Erika 352
Ng, Yen Ying 119

Omerovic, Aida 71
Osis, Jānis 352

Pastor, Óscar 314
Przybyłek, Adam 119

Rathmair, Michael 261
Reyes Román, José Fabián 314
Roubtsova, Ella 24
Rueda, Urko 314

Sandkuhl, Kurt 45
Schmidt, Rainer 45
Selmadji, Anfel 186
Seriai, Abdelhak-Djamel 186
Siegert, Valentin 215
Spichkova, Maria 240
Stølen, Ketil 71

Van Der Donckt, Jeroen 373
van Dongen, Boudewijn F. 137
van der Aalst, Wil M. P. 137

Westfechtel, Bernhard 98
Weyns, Danny 373
Wiersma, Niels 24
Wirtz, Roman 71

Zakrzewski, Mateusz 119
Zimmermann, Alfred 45

Printed in the United States
By Bookmasters